THE BUSH PRESIDENCY

America is never wholly herself unless she is engaged in high moral principle. We as a people have such a purpose today. It is to make kinder the face of the nation and gentler the face of the world.
—George Bush, inaugural address, 1989

THE BUSH PRESIDENCY
FIRST APPRAISALS

Edited by

COLIN CAMPBELL, S.J.
Georgetown University

and

BERT A. ROCKMAN
University of Pittsburgh / Brookings Institution

CHATHAM HOUSE PUBLISHERS, INC.
Chatham, New Jersey

23768 785

THE BUSH PRESIDENCY
First Appraisals

CHATHAM HOUSE PUBLISHERS, INC.
Post Office Box One
Chatham, New Jersey 07929

PUBLISHER: Edward Artinian
PRODUCTION SUPERVISOR: Christopher Kelaher
JACKET AND COVER DESIGN: Lawrence Ratzkin
COMPOSITION: Bang, Motley, Olufsen
PRINTING AND BINDING: R.R. Donnelley & Sons Company

LIBRARY OF CONGRESS CATALOGING-IN-PUBLICATION DATA

The Bush presidency : first appraisals / edited by Colin Campbell and
   Bert A. Rockman.
      p.   cm.
   Includes bibliographical references and index.
   ISBN 0-934540-90-x. — ISBN 0-934540-91-8 (pbk.)
   1. United States—Politics and government—1989– 2. Bush, George,
1924– . I. Campbell, Colin, 1943– . II. Rockman, Bert A.
E881.B87   1991
973.928—dc20   91-18333
                                                         CIP

Manufactured in the United States of America
10   9   8   7   6   5   4   3   2   1

Contents

Preface

Edward I. Koch, the outspoken former mayor of New York, when meeting his constituents, often asked, "How am I doing?" The audiences to whom he addressed the question, usually his supporters, seldom found the answer to be in doubt. To sitting political officeholders, of course, the question "How am I doing?" translates into "How popular am I?" This book asks of George Bush, "How is he doing?" It is the first in a quadrennial series to pose the question "How is the president doing?"

Our concerns, however, are not simply a matter of polls and popular approval, though we are willing to concede that a sitting president who does badly in those categories is not likely to have the leverage to do well in others. Instead, our effort is to understand the president's situation roughly in the middle of his elected term—the political and policy context in which he is situated, the style of the president and the presidency that has evolved to deal with that context, and the implications that this interaction of style and context have for presidential political and policy behavior.

Our objectives are not simply to render a descriptive account of events that have transpired up to the midpoint of the presidential term. We assume our readers have at least a basic familiarity with these; in any event, they are better covered by journalists on the beat than by political scientists. Nor is our objective merely to render sweeping judgments of the incumbent president or the system he is trying to operate in. Such judgments are bountiful on editorial pages of daily newspapers. They are the stuff of punditry, if any stuff that be. The authors in this volume do describe events that have been relevant to various aspects of the Bush presidency, and they surely have not been reticent to cast judgment on the president's handling of them. Yet the comparative advantage that political scientists can bring to evaluating the officeholder is that they are apt to locate the incumbent president in a web of strategic constraints and opportunities. The authors are likely to see presidents as actors in a continuous game, one in which they can ill afford to throw all their chips away on a single roll of the dice. They also are likely to look at the constraints and opportunities that the political system requires all presidents to navigate through, and some, such as King and Alston in chapter 9, conclude that the American system provides daunting obstacles to effective policy leadership. Most authors, however, see varying constraints and opportunities within the context of a political system that is not often president friendly. So, what opportunities are offered by the situations presidents inherit or that ripen on their watch? How do individual presidents interact strategically with them? The overall effort of this book and of each specific chapter is to interpret the particular (presidential behavior) within the context of a theory about the general (structural and situational opportunities and constraints). Viewing our problem in this form is likely to lengthen the shelf life of our effort to assess the particular (George Bush) in the midst of the ephemeral (his presidential term).

Some presidents etch their political personalities in unmistakable terms. Lyndon Johnson was a politician with robust appetites for power and doing something with it. His was a restless presidency—for those who worked in it as well as perhaps for those governed by it. Alternatively, Ronald Reagan was as laid-back as LBJ was frenetic. Yet, if anything, Reagan was even more goal focused. Certainly, Reagan never backed away from an opportunity for confrontation when he believed there was a matter worth confronting. Most residents of the Oval Office, however, are less clearly definable in their presidential styles. The contrasts of the restless (Johnson) and the relaxed (Reagan) are stark; most presidents are more nondescript and less susceptible to personal stereotyping. George Bush is one of these, a more typical case than not. His leadership style therefore tends to blend into a set of political circumstances that offer him slim pickings. He is a pastel political personality serving in a mostly pastel time that offers him a limited range of shades from which to choose. The first two chapters of this book—that of Bert Rockman and that of Charles Jones—emphasize the interplay of Bush's style of leadership and the strategic political circumstances that he inherited and that have not appreciably changed. "Meeting low expectations" and "rounding hard edges" have set much of the tone of the Bush White House up to now.

The next two chapters, those by Paul Quirk and by Larry Berman and Bruce Jentleson, focus on Bush as a policy president. Quirk emphasizes domestic policy; Berman and Jentleson, foreign policy. Each chapter unveils some of the more mysterious characteristics of the Bush policy style, especially the combinations of flexibility and rigidity and that of focused attention in a reactive mode. Quirk sees a president more flexible about big things than small ones; Berman and Jentleson see Bush as an effective policy maker in the here and now but, for him, that which is out of sight seems also to be out of mind. If anything is clear from these views of Bush as a policy maker, it is that the Bush presidency is more inclined to react to events than to anticipate them.

Although it hardly could have been expected when George Bush was inaugurated, he has been the most popular president since approval ratings have been regularly taken. George Edwards examines the relations between George Bush and the public. These relations have been at least partially assisted by a strategy of inclusion, in contrast to the clear partisan tone of Bush's predecessor. Bush has done better with groups outside his natural party-based constituency than have other recent presidents.

Yet Bush came into the White House with substantial Democratic majorities in both chambers of Congress, and the Democrats still have those majorities even after the 1990 midterm elections. How does a Republican president deal with these hostile numbers? Barbara Sinclair suggests that one has to govern ugly—or "unheroically," to use her language. In Bush's case, he has had to govern virtually between parties, offering cooperation with the Democratic leadership without offending his own but still minority party base. It could be done otherwise, and was by Reagan, if the president were to choose the path of "principled" confrontation. Not choosing that as the dominant path means that dealing with Congress will have more than the usual zigs and zags. If it is obvious that Bush's dealings with Congress are not pretty, are they nonetheless effective?

The next two chapters, those by Colin Campbell and by Joel Aberbach, try to evaluate Bush's governance within the executive branch. Campbell focuses on the White House and cabinet, whereas Aberbach looks more broadly toward the cast of senior civil servants and political officials in the departments. The two authors tend to evaluate what they see differently. Aberbach contrasts the Bush administration's approach with that of the Reagan administration. The assertiveness of the latter has mellowed in the Bush administration. The bureaucracy is not, at least inherently, the enemy to the Bush administration. Campbell sees a less mellow White House in which arrogance, disorganization, and ham-handedness abound, personified by Chief of Staff John Sununu and the counselor to the president, Boyden Gray. Is the real George Bush the Tory insider president, then, or simply another prickly (and inept) White House aggrandizer? Does George Bush make use of the resources of government or ignore them? Will the real George Bush please stand up?

Finally, Anthony King and Giles Alston provide an external perspective on the Bush presidency. In their view, one has to begin with the nature of the American political system and its high-risk character. By making politicians more visible and, hence, accountable to more different kinds of constituencies, the high-risk system produces low-risk politicians who see few rewards and great costs in trying to deal with major problems. So why try? In their view, Bush is nearly at one with the system he presumably heads. He is a low-risk leader for a system that makes risk taking especially problematic.

The editors conclude by trying to integrate some of the different arguments that have been made throughout the book. Although the editors do not always agree with one another, they are in accord that how we see George Bush as president has much to do with our own conceptions of leadership and what it is possible to do in the American system.

THE BUSH PRESIDENCY

The Leadership Style of George Bush

BERT A. ROCKMAN

What can be more fascinating, yet more perplexing, than making sense of a political leader's style of leadership? The leadership style of an American president is especially intriguing in this regard because, unlike his peers in prime ministerships, he is typically a figure less predictably molded than they are. They, typically, have climbed up their party ladders, whereas he, to take two recent examples, could be a former movie actor or peanut farmer. So we know less about him to begin with, and in that there is inherent attraction. Observing a president's leadership style is compelling not because it fully (or even mostly) determines his fate, but because it could determine ours. It is perplexing, too, because what "leadership style" is, how important it is, what explains it, and how we can even observe and conceptualize it are immensely complicated.

Leadership Style: Inference and Consequence

Judgments about a president's leadership are almost inseparable from judgments about numerous other factors. Do we, for example, agree or disagree with the incumbent president, share or not share the directions and policies associated with him? How much can we actually know of a president's behavior and how he calculates, assuming that calculations are taking place? Can we know very much about a president's style of behavior in the midst of his presidency? How much is hidden from us? To what extent do the situations and contexts within which presidents operate limit their capacity to lead? Indeed, what precisely is leadership? One style of leadership, for example, may emphasize articulating direction. Another may emphasize the calculation of minimum loss. These are very different styles, to be sure. Are they both aspects of leadership? I suspect they are, but probably would not generally be viewed as such. Articulating direction seems to be obvious as a form of leadership, though it may lead to tilting at windmills. Calculating minimum losses, in contrast, seems almost the antithesis of romanticized forms of leadership behavior, but unless the world ends tomorrow, one has to be prepared to come to work on the day after. That, too, in its own way, may be an element of leadership. Nowhere is it ordained that rhetoric is necessarily a more important element of leadership than is an appreciation of political strategy and the judicious use of political resources.

Styles of leadership vary with the temperaments of presidents, their values, and the contexts in which they operate. And, of course, what constitutes leadership varies with the preferences and assumptions of commentators on the subject. Goal maximization, for example, has been celebrated by Richard Neustadt as a sign of presidential achievement, whereas public harmony and governmental legitimacy have been viewed by Fred Greenstein as key ingredients of a different style of presidential leadership.[1] Thus, from Neustadt's earlier and then contemporary perspective, Dwight Eisenhower was an underachieving president who, by cashing in few of his ample resources, failed to achieve his goals. But from Greenstein's later perspective, popularity and approval were themselves the principal goals of Eisenhower.

We see now why leadership style is so attractive a topic of political conversation—it is the manipulable factor in a sea of largely nonmanipulable forces—and why it is so difficult to make sense of. The difficulty is that frequently presidents are subjected to forces that pull them to act in similar ways, despite their variations in temperament. At the same time, the actual contexts that presidents operate in, the expectations they have to deal with, and the political and policy resources with which they have to work vary, and condition the ways in which presidents can exercise leadership. A further complicating consideration is that we have to live with large degrees of uncertainty about the motives and calculations of actors currently on the scene. History and archives help us later, but even these cannot assure certainty. What we have to go on when we try to assess a leader who is presently on stage are inferences from apparent consistencies of behavior to an underlying set of "principles" that govern that behavior. This is a task that in some rare instances, such as those of Ronald Reagan, Margaret Thatcher, and Harry Truman, seems to be relatively uncomplicated in proportion to their own relatively uncomplicated personalities. But in most cases, the evidence of stylistic regularity is not so clear. The inferential trail is not so distinctly or persistently marked. Both interpretations and appraisals, therefore, need to be more tentative. Early returns might well be reversible. George Bush, I believe, is among the more ambiguous cases—more like than unlike most political leaders—in this respect and, specifically, more like than unlike most modern American presidents.

If leadership style is not so easy as it may seem to determine, an even more important issue is exactly what we know once we are able to describe it. Are we spending an inordinate amount of effort on something that is entertaining but of little explanatory value? For while it is clear that presidents vary in their temperaments, it is less clear what difference this makes. The obvious way to think about the problem is to think counterfactually about the way different leadership styles would interact with the same problem set. The world, unfortunately, does not provide perfect laboratory conditions for social scientists, and so we cannot reach definitive conclusions about how different leaders would react to the same problems, since they are not always faced with the same problems. Indeed, antecedents are important to political leaders. For the problem set with which leaders deal derives significantly from the "solutions" bequeathed them by their predecessors. Thinking about leadership style, however, does require thinking about the consequences it has for interacting with the problems that face all incumbents of the role: setting a presidential agenda, building both electoral and governing coalitions, constructing a system of staffing and advice, and, inter alia, decision making.

In organizing this midterm assessment of George Bush's style of leadership, I find it useful to consider three general questions. First, what are a president's inheritances or legacies, and how do these constrain him, disadvantage him, or advantage him? Much of my attention in a chapter devoted to Bush's leadership is riveted on the legacies that condition his behavior and choices. Second, how does the president relate to the presidency as a corporate enterprise? Is he a chief but not an executive, as was Reagan, or an executive but not a chief, as was Carter? Answers to the first question help us situate the president. Answers to the second question describe how he handles the office. The third question asks how the president carries out his personal leadership role. Answering this third question also provides some of the glue that helps us to understand why Bush (or any president) responds to his context as he does and attends to his office in the way he has. Finally, in concluding, I want to assess what the Bush leadership style is likely to mean for the ultimate successes and failures of a Bush presidency.

The Legacies

George Bush was elected as a Republican essentially to continue the Reagan agenda in a somewhat more tempered way. While it is objectively impossible to discern a presidential mandate arising from an electoral outcome, it may be less difficult judging what a president was elected *not* to do. George Bush was *not* elected to be a Democratic president or to fulfill a Democratic party agenda. If little else is clear, that much is. Consequently, judgments rendered about the Bush presidency as though its major failing lay in not trying to reverse the eight years preceding it are untenable. We have to begin with the assumption that the political and policy status quo inherited by Bush fundamentally were favorable to him. Maintenance and incremental adjustment, therefore, would be the expected watchwords of the Bush presidency.

Four legacies are of special importance to the Bush presidency. The first of these is the *succession*. Every leader is partly defined by the preceding incumbent. A second legacy influencing the Bush presidency was the *election* of 1988, in regard both to the character of the campaign and the electoral results. A third legacy is the *budget* context bequeathed by the tax policies of the 1980s and the deficit-targeting (Gramm-Rudman-Hollings) response to it that came about in the middle part of the decade. A fourth legacy is the remarkable set of world *events,* and a less remarkable set of domestic ones, that came to pass toward the latter stages of the Reagan administration and through the first year of the Bush administration.

THE SUCCESSION

Despite occasional rhetorical flourishes that presidents give in ascending to office that suggest they have powers to re-create the world, the most obvious fact that defines their incumbency is both who and what preceded them. In this regard, presidents are not unlike other leaders in any other field of activity. How successful and well regarded or seemingly failed and ill regarded one's immediate predecessor is determines the extent to which the new incumbent will seek to adhere to, or depart from, the status quo. The predecessor also will define the mark from which the new incumbent will be judged. It is easy to tumble from the top, but hard to fall off the floor. The predecessor also leaves a bundle of assets and liabilities to the successor, although these may not be so neatly sorted out and perceived as such at the time of transition.

To draw a parallel with transitions of leadership in the world of professional (North American) football, one can ask the following analogic question: George Bush is to Ronald Reagan as (*a*) Phil Bengtson is to Vince Lombardi or (*b*) George Seifert is to Bill Walsh? A little background is necessary. Vince Lombardi was the enormously successful coach of the Green Bay Packers football team from 1959 to 1967. The team that Lombardi inherited in 1959 was woefully weak, but in the next eight years his team won five championships. He retired after the last one. The Packers have yet to win another. Phil Bengtson was a renowned football technician and was elevated to head coach of the Packers for the 1968 season. The team he inherited was aging and became physically brittle. The coach he followed was a legend. The expectations developed around Packer performances were astronomically high.

Bill Walsh also was an extremely successful coach, for the San Francisco 49ers football team throughout the 1980s, winning three Super Bowl championships in that time. He left the coaching ranks after winning his third championship and being hailed as a football genius. Another football technician, much like Phil Bengtson two decades earlier, arose from the ranks of the 49ers' coaching staff to assume the head post. His name was George Seifert. Seifert, like Bengtson, inherited a team at the top of its game. Bengtson's Packer team fell to mediocrity instantly; Seifert's 49ers team, if possible, rose to even higher levels of success in the year following Walsh's departure and came breathtakingly close to repeating that success in the subsequent season. Walsh's last Super Bowl championship was not the last for the 49ers, who lost but one game the following season and just missed returning again to the Super Bowl in the second post-Walsh year.

Why, if at all, is this instructive for learning about the succession from Reagan to Bush in regard to the bundle of assets and legacies left by the predecessor? One thing that Phil Bengtson, George Seifert, and George Bush had in common at the moment of their elevation was the need to *maintain* a desirable situation. Each came to his position on the heels of a successful administration as judged by the standards of their respective trades. In the Lombardi-Bengtson transition, the successor was dealt a bad hand, in spite of surface symptoms to the contrary. Alternatively, in the Walsh-Seifert transition, the successor inherited a well-stocked operation bolstered further by good fortune. Of course, I do not mean to imply that Bengtson and Seifert lacked responsibility for their fates. Seifert well may have been more adept than Bengtson at adjusting to his situation. That is obviously well beyond any competency I have to judge. But presidency watchers can learn by looking at leadership transitions in other forms of organizational life because both individuals, Bengtson and Seifert, came to their positions as experienced insiders, well groomed for their jobs. If they differed in their own capabilities, these differences seem unable to be systematically conceptualized or explained by the kinds of variables we employ to size up individual capabilities in the presidency. If experience and grooming count, they should count equally for both. If they do not count, we are left with random noise.

For most of his presidency heretofore, Bush shared George Seifert's happier fate more than Phil Bengtson's less pleasant one. Throughout most of his first twenty months in office, George Bush and George Seifert were leading inspired lives (if, in the case of the former George, failing to inspire others). After all, for much of this time, the economy continued to be robust in spite of sectoral difficulties (the thrift crisis). Confidence in the presidency, which had been regenerated under Reagan, continued under Bush. And the historical watershed of the fall of European communism and the end to the cold war provided an era of good feeling. Certainly, all these trends either continued or culminated ones that had occurred under the prior administration. For Bush, the good news was that he was a president for good times, and the times he inherited were mostly good.

The bad news would come later, but this too was a legacy from the prior administration. The budget-deficit issue would begin to pinch Bush's no-new-taxes pledge and put him at odds with sizable parts of his congressional party, as well as his party in the precincts. The Iraqi military buildup and aggression in the Persian Gulf, to some extent, also were fed by the American tilt toward Iraq during the Iraq-Iran war of 1980–88. Thus, if George Bush began looking like George Seifert, he may wind up looking more like Phil Bengtson with the progress of time. The key to political success in the White House, of course, is to manage this progression in precisely the reverse order, as Bush's predecessor did so well. Thus, for Bush, the bad news is that the problems that have ripened as his to handle can lead him into political difficulties even should he manage the policy problems well—a prospect that has overtones from the Carter era.

Policies and the economic and political environment are part of the legacy that presidents have to deal with. For football coaches, the only thing that counts is whether the team performs, and the equivalent—how well the country is doing or how well people think it is doing—counts for a lot with political leaders too. It is a dominant but not exclusive criterion in sizing up a president's fate. The presentation of self matters too, if ineffably. In the electronic media age, the presentation of self is a collective enterprise, not merely an individual one. Of course, the principals matter most, and George Bush is not Ronald Reagan or John F. Kennedy before the television cameras. He most resembles Gerald Ford; it is a style of presentation that emphasizes athleticism, human interest, and wooden expression. Bush does not stir hearts. Nor does he stir sentiment of virtually any sort. As an individual, he contrasts markedly with Reagan in presenting self. Reagan stirred partisan hearts, but opposition fears. Bush does neither. Reagan could express radical ideas in dulcet tones. By contrast, Bush sounds flat and, when excited, even a bit tinny. The late John Mitchell, attorney general at the outset of the Nixon administration, advised reporters at that time to watch what the administration did, rather than listen to what it said. Ironically, as matters turned out, his advice would have been better rendered on behalf of the Bush than the Nixon administration.

But if Bush lacks the ability to find the right words or mood, his family advantages him as Reagan's mostly disadvantaged Reagan. While Nancy Reagan, who was an actress by prior trade, seemed petty and vengeful (the astute quality of her political advice aside), Barbara Bush exudes warmth, charm, and the ability to strike the proper note. The presidential spouses seem to be almost reverse images of their husbands. The larger presidential families also contrast starkly. The Reagan children stepped out of a soap opera. They frequently made the news for their clashes with their parents or with one another. Aside from the embarrassment of Neil Bush's involvement on the board of directors with the failed Silverado Savings and Loan and his interest-free (and unreported) loan, President and Mrs. Bush's large family of children and children-in-law have provided good photo opportunities and little cause for embarrassment. Even comparison of the family dogs provides the Bushes with an advantage. Millie has achieved canine fame. One would be hard put to remember the Reagan dog(s). Spouses, families, and even presidential dogs obviously are not the prime factors in accounting for how presidents are perceived, much less how they perform. But presentation of self in both the formal presidential role and in the familial role have enhancing effects. While in his formal role Bush does not fare so well on this aspect of his presidency in contrast to Reagan, the collective portrait of the presidential family (human and canine) is far more advantageous to Bush. In accordance with a practice that apparently has not survived across administrations, President Bush could thank his lucky stars for this.

Familial trimmings aside, Bush's navigational problem was to maintain directions that at least seemed to be successful, yet round out the harsher edges of Reaganite doctrine. Two problems would result from this. One problem was that the Republicans' hearts, for the most part, still belonged to Reagan. No doubt Harry Truman, on succeeding Franklin Roosevelt, had similar difficulties. Bush needed to extol the merits of an administration he was a part of and from which there was no need to run. But he also needed some product differentiation from the prior administration. That, and possibly his own temperament, led him to his "kinder, gentler" pledge, which, of course, was interpreted as rounding off the sharp edges of Reaganism. If the kinder, gentler line gave Bush partisans some pause, it also gave Democrats a hook to criticize Bush for not supporting their preferred programs. One of the reasons, among others, for the emergence of the kinder, gentler theme was to soak up political support from the center during the 1988 election. The nature of that election, both the campaign and the outcome, was also one of the key legacies influencing the leadership style of George Bush.

THE ELECTION

When Ronald Reagan came into office in January 1981, he could realistically conclude that he had a mandate for change; he also could infer that he had latitude to move in the broad directions he wished to (lower taxes, easing of regulations, more defense spending), if not necessarily in all the specifics. Not only had Reagan won big (more accurately his opponent lost big), but he had defeated a sitting president. Moreover, the Republicans made great gains in the congressional vote, winning a party majority in the Senate for the first time since the 1952 elections and picking up sufficient seats in the House to give them real majorities on a number of issues. Beyond this, there were large dissatisfactions with the status quo. Stagflation, as it was then called, was rampant. The combination of high interest rates, recessionary economic conditions, and inflationary prices came on top of oil shortages in 1979 resulting from the revolution in Iran. The humiliation of the United States with the American embassy being taken and American diplomats being held hostage added powerfully to the view of a great power in decline. The military parity and arguably even superiority of the Soviet Union also were highlighted by the Soviet intervention in Afghanistan. Above all, though, a president with powerfully held if simple ideas about what he wanted to achieve came into office. And he came into office at a time when the trade in conservative policy ideas was bullish. Deep dissatisfaction, political majorities for change, the appearance of a political mandate, and the presence of a rich market in conservative policy ideas all set the tone for a highly goal-directed president by the name of Ronald Reagan. When the election of 1980 is seen as a composite of all these factors, it stands out as a rare and remarkable moment of political clarity on the landscape of American national politics.[2]

As clarity often does, it provoked confrontation. The 1980s produced an unusually high degree of partisan conflict, especially in the House of Representatives. If the Democrats were uncertain about what they stood for, they were certain that they did not stand for Reaganism. After 1982, when the Democrats regained a real instead of merely nominal foothold in the House of Representatives, divided government came to be accepted as the norm. The Reagan economic package of 1981, with its large tax cuts and accompanying structural budget deficits, cut down the field of play and maneuverability within it. Not so surprisingly, therefore, the Democratic nominee in 1988, Michael Dukakis, emphasized competence, rather than policy or program, as his lodestar.

The setting for the 1988 election, therefore, was inherently likely to be less about bold initiatives (such as Reagan's economic package) than about a referendum on the status quo. Of course, issues did lie underneath the surface and were played out by the symbols in the campaign. The symbols of patriotism (beckoned by Bush's Pledge of Allegiance passion) and crime and race (the Willie Horton ads) were used in the Bush campaign to cultivate the cultural divide, a division the Republican campaign managers believed would be to their advantage. On other matters, the Bush campaign sent out massively mixed signals: He would be an environmentalist, supportive of education, a stimulant for social good (a thousand points of light); but he would also resist the means to pay for any of these by opposing new taxes, and he would make a (halfhearted) play for the right-to-life constituency that Ronald Reagan successfully bagged for the Republican party. Alternatively, the Democrats, in a highly budget-constrained environment, were left with relatively few arrows in their campaign quiver. Fairness (the sense that prosperity was unevenly distributed) was one of them. But proposals for social insurance extensions (the Dukakis medical insurance plan) were at best muted in the 1988 campaign.

Political contests that are not turbocharged with big ideas are fertile territory for symbolic appeals and innuendoes. The 1988 campaign, precisely because it was so devoid of policy ideas (unlike 1980), fed on symbols and innuendoes. The perceptions on the part of Democrats that Bush's campaign played dirty pool produced a powerful desire among them to wreak vengeance on Bush when he became president. Unlike 1981, the Democrats were not cowed by the outcome. If they once again lost the White House, their inclination was to blame the loss on their candidate, rather than their ideas. They saw no mandate for a Bush program, if for no other reason than that the program largely consisted of Bush's hyperrhetoric on no new taxes, more flags, and no furloughs for (black) criminals. In brief, the Democrats saw an issueless but vile campaign, a president without a message or a mandate, and themselves having done well in the election except for the presidency. Thus the Democrats believed themselves to be well positioned to force Bush to come to them.

Even as the 1988 campaign was being conducted, the world was rapidly changing, and it would change even more in 1989. The cold war issues and political divisions were beginning to crumble as it became clear that the Soviet Union no longer could afford the costs of arms buildups and maintaining and subsidizing an East European empire. At the same time, the budgetary constraints operating on the federal government dampened demand for domestic expenditures that were not otherwise accompanied by earmarked revenues. Hence, the emergence of catastrophic health insurance legislation was accompanied by an earmarked but politically catastrophic tax that caused the program to be gutted in the next Congress. The political demand to extend the social insurance state, consequently, was weakened.

If ever there was a moment when little initiative taking was exactly the right political position to take, that moment was when Bush came into office. This, naturally, turned out to be politically fortuitous for Bush as well, since it played almost perfectly into his set of political circumstances. For if Bush needed Congress to enact White House-sponsored legislation, he would have been in deep trouble simply on the basis of the numbers arrayed against him. Bush came into office with few levers at his disposal and an angered Democratic congressional majority on Capitol Hill. It is useful also to keep in mind that the Democratic party leader in the House then was not the accommodating Tom Foley but the combative partisan Jim Wright. In the Senate, the new Democratic leader, George Mitchell, became the leader precisely because he was an articulate advocate for the Democrats. The man he replaced, Robert Byrd, was largely a political technician. Clearly, this was not the time to be putting forth an expansive legislative agenda from a Republican White House. More reactive than proactive in terms of a policy agenda, Bush came into office perfectly congruent with his historical and political moment.

Following the political demise of Richard Nixon, Gerald Ford gestured for reconciliation toward Congress—another way of saying that his Republican administration and the Democratic majorities on Capitol Hill were going to have to find some reasonable way to coexist. The gestures did not imply that the president and Congress would govern together but that they would find some way to stay out of one another's hair, and when they had to quarrel, to do so by more bounded methods. Although George Bush came into office after a relatively popular rather than disastrous presidency, he read his situation well. His situation, much like Ford's or Eisenhower's after the 1958 election or Reagan's after the 1986 election, was that Congress would be in the position of proposing and that the president would be in the position of disposing, a reversal of what many have taken to be the prevailing norm of interbranch relations. Not only was Bush's political situation weak, he followed Ronald Reagan, a powerfully polarizing president. Reagan galvanized Democrats' oppositional instincts. So Bush was now dealing with Democratic majorities used to giving little quarter to the White House. Alternatively, under Reagan, Congress was used to receiving the White House gauntlet. Like Ford before him, Bush tried to mollify the majority Democratic opposition in Congress by playing heavily on the kinder, gentler theme, by adopting compromise rather than confrontational stances, and by emphasizing harmony and conciliation.[3]

Adopting a conciliatory stance toward Congress may well have accorded with Bush's own personal instincts. But whether it did or not, it clearly accorded with Bush's political needs. He did not, after all, require Congress to act on a big political agenda; nor did he even need to throw down the gauntlet toward Congress. All he basically needed was to keep Congress out of his hair, and when he could not do that, to govern with one-third plus one—the minority necessary to sustain his vetoes.

The 1988 election meant that Bush was enmeshed in a political mode increasingly normal for latter-day American politics: divided government and unclear directional signals. The 1990 election largely reinforced 1988. Government remains divided. Directions remain unclear. These conditions, however, are not inhospitable to a presidency such as Bush's. The element that has changed significantly has been a governing legacy left by the Reagan administration, namely, the weight of the structural budget deficits engendered by a government that, like the citizens it governs, prefers to purchase goods on credit.

THE BUDGET

Until the summer of 1990 when President Bush reversed Candidate Bush's pledge never to raise taxes, the monumental budget deficits that the Bush administration inherited from the Reagan presidency were a double-edged sword. On one side, the budget deficits heavily constrained what the next presidential administration could do by narrowing the range of feasible options. On the other side, these constraints could provide the perfect cover for a president who did not mind being fiscally constrained. Indeed, the budget constraint could allow the Bush presidency to indulge in the symbols of ameliorative social policies without having to take direct responsibility for proposing any. In one sense, therefore, Ronald Reagan's legacy was George Bush's meal ticket. Bush could not afford to put his money where his mouth was, and insofar as his interests were concerned, that was not an unreasonable spot for him to be situated in. It would have been far more difficult for him, of course, were he a Democrat.

The stream of world events until the Iraqi invasion of Kuwait also put further downward pressure on the defense budget. By accepting a more modest set of cuts in the defense budget relatively early in 1990, Bush also positioned himself to look neither excessively dovish nor hawkish.

The budget constraint on the domestic policy board, however, could still allow Bush to look kinder and gentler (if not kind and gentle enough for liberal editorial writers or liberal Democrats in Congress). Kinder and gentler are in the comparative form, and the comparison inevitably was with the Reagan administration. The key here was to engage in the politics of low-cost social harmony. Symbols are important to this politics. One of these symbols is people. Personnel appointments send symbolic messages at the least, and they are an important element to the kind of politics an administration wants to pursue. If, for the Reagan administration, personnel appointments symbolized a politics of confrontation and ideology, for Bush these appointments in the main seemed to be an important ingredient to the politics of social harmony. Overall, Bush tended to appoint firefighters rather than flamethrowers. The appointment of William Reilly as Environmental Protection Agency administrator was intended to make a statement, whatever

Reilly's influence or lack thereof in the Bush administration.[4] Appointments to the judiciary, while remaining partisan, were not put through the intense vetting process to uncover deviationism that was part of the Reagan presidency's effort to place its stamp on and ensure commitment to its dogmas within the judiciary. In addition, bureaucracy bashing has been noticeably absent from Bush administration practices.

The politics of social harmony is not driven by strong ideas; indeed, it is a politics that is virtually antithetical to powerful ideas. Thus the antiregulatory passions of the Reagan administration were cooled somewhat during the Bush administration, but certainly not fundamentally reversed.

Further, while the Reagan administration, like Mrs. Thatcher in Britain, seemed more radical than conservative—driven by the goal of individual accumulation as the engine of economic growth in a low-tax, low-profile state—the Bush administration regarded social policy initiatives acceptable as long as the funding for them did not have to come from the federal government. While early drafts of the Reagan tax-reform proposal that initially surfaced in 1985 were designed to punish residents of high-tax states, therefore placing pressure on those states to cut taxes and, inevitably, social expenditures, Bush did not discourage social policy. He merely discouraged the expectation that it would be forthcoming at the federal level.

The situation of tight budget constraint also allowed Bush to emphasize even more the role that he clearly enjoys most, that of foreign-policymaker-in-chief. This also was where he showed to best advantage in contrast to Ronald Reagan. As with Richard Nixon, foreign policy was Bush's meat. Most else was small potatoes. Unlike Richard Nixon, Bush's perspective as foreign-policymaker-in-chief was not shaped by a grand design or concept but by caution and temperamental conservatism. Like a well-honed bureaucrat, Bush has a high regard for the virtues of "not doing." In the midst of a historic transition in the Soviet Union, and under considerable criticism for failing to respond adequately to these changes, Bush proclaimed that he could best help move things along by "avoid[ing] doing dumb things."[5] This is the response, not of a strategist, but of a foreign policy bureaucrat—the elevation of antiaction to a modus operandi. If Bush is a man of few ideas, correspondingly few are disastrously bad. Bush reacts. And both the international atmosphere he inherited and the domestic budget-constrained one he was bequeathed provided a soothing setting for a reactive, but by no means uninvolved, president.

These conditions changed radically. The forecast slackening of an economy that had set records for consecutive quarters of growth during the 1980s brought concerns of what a recession would do to an already expansive structural budget deficit by adding to it the costs in reduced revenues and automatic expenditure increases that accompany business downturns. An increased deficit undoubtedly would push up interest rates as the Federal Reserve likely would seek to protect the dollar and lure foreign investment in American securities to pay the costs of the budget deficits. Immediately lurking around the corner was the Gramm-Rudman-Hollings law's automatic sequestration provisions that, if put into effect, would reduce dramatically whatever discretionary room was left in the federal budget. For Bush, the budget deficit was moving from a justification to a problem, and the problem was monumental from a political as well as policy standpoint. Bush's coach was beginning to turn into a pumpkin.

How the Bush presidency would wrestle with the budget-deficit issue through the summer and autumn of 1990 arguably has been simultaneously the highlight and lowlight of the Bush administration. Certainly the agreement that eventually came about in the autumn of a midterm election year was itself overshadowed by the political fallout that accompanied it. A European prime minister who orchestrated an unpopular but perhaps necessary outcome and left no conclusive evidence as to "who done it" would no doubt be regarded as a remarkably shrewd tactical politician. An American president doing much the same, but in the open with little cover for tactical retreats and regroupings, would, as Bush did, suffer his first substantial loss of popular approval. He took a beating from his own political party, at least in the House of Representatives. He suffered humiliation in the press and among the political intelligentsia for his seeming lack of a gyroscope. The budget crisis forced Bush into his first unpopular set of decisions. Whether he was up to the task or not may hinge on whether one emphasizes his making of the deal or his political gyrations accompanying the deal making. Certainly the making of the budget deal of 1990 showed Bush at his worst and at his best, though the worst aspects are the more visible, if not necessarily the more important ones.

What the budget deal revealed was that Bush has a difficult time mobilizing others. (All presidents do, of course—this being a stunningly overstressed capacity.) He has difficulty articulating a bold vision and staying with it. Bush is not Winston Churchill. He is not even Ronald Reagan. Yet, Reagan accepted new taxes without saying so. Bush knew he had to say so, because he proclaimed he would not. Stitching a deal together, working with other elites, syndicating responsibility, and recognizing the need to compromise are Bush's strengths, and these were in evidence during the budget negotiations. But perhaps most powerfully, Bush understood that there would have to be negotiations and that to make those negotiations succeed, he would have to put his "no new taxes" pledge on the table.

Divided government forces unpopular decisions to be syndicated, if they are to be made at all. A Harold Wilson, rather than a Winston Churchill, is the more likely leader for this situation. Indeed, as Wilson had, Bush was faced with holding down rebellion within his own party. To syndicate deals, of course, means to traffic with the opposition, and to traffic with the opposition lessens one's zealotry on behalf of party orthodoxies. Wilson just had to deal with his own party, but Bush has had to deal with both. Ironically, one of the better moments of Bush's leadership (cutting the deal) was truly one of the worst moments in his presentation of self. That may well have reflected his need to bring along his own party (in the House at least) into the deal. His drop in approval was severe, but it was not clear how much of this drop was caused by the clumsiness of his public presentation, the deal itself, the juxtaposition of seemingly crass political jockeying with the brewing crisis in the Persian Gulf, or simply the growing concerns with the economy.

Events play a powerful role in evaluating any presidency, and in how a president responds to and manages them. Presidents benefit from favorable events, and even may have some influence over them. Presidents undoubtedly are adversely affected by negative events. What, then, are the events that seem to have significantly affected the Bush administration, and how do those events interact with the president's political circumstances?

THE EVENTS

For the first year and a half, George Bush was the beneficiary of an almost unrelieved stream of favorable news. The breakup of the Soviet empire, the cozy relationship with Mikhail Gorbachev, the Soviet withdrawal from Afghanistan, arms and troop cutbacks, the end of the cold war and the triumph of democracy and capitalism, the end of civil strife in Nicaragua and the surprising election of the U.S.-backed opposition coalition there—all these events played to what Bush saw as his great strength and his image as a judicious and prudent foreign-policymaker. Probably, without some resiliency in the economy, all these events would have mattered less. But without the anticipated buckling of the economy, Bush was in prime position to benefit from these favorable conditions and to allow them to bolster his image as a prudent foreign-policymaker.

There inevitably were downsides as well. The Exxon tanker's oil spill off the Alaska coastline failed to reinforce Bush's effort to characterize himself as the "environmental president." Exxon, however, managed to absorb most of the rap. The failure of the high-profile nomination of John Tower for secretary of defense to pass the Senate and that of the low-profile nomination of William Lucas for assistant attorney general for civil rights did not help the administration's image or repute for prowess. But the damage in these cases was well contained, affecting the nominees more than the administration that nominated them. Indeed, part of the containment of damage was that the administration proceeded to nominate well-regarded people to the positions for which the original nominees were turned down.[6]

Still, the overall picture until mid-1990 was that the Bush administration was sailing along without significant political problems. Indeed, its main political problem seemed to be the criticism of the president that he tacked to the slightest breezes of political opportunism rather than holding to a clear and steadfast course.

Given the momentous events occurring in the world, especially during the last part of 1989 and most of 1990, almost any grand strategy would have been rapidly outdated. Events outpaced any serious capacity for long-term thinking. While the world shook, it veritably can be said that Washington stood still. Of course, Bush came under attack for failing to respond more rapidly and dramatically to events. Yet, as David Hoffman reported in the *Washington Post* on 11 March 1990, Bush reputedly saw "no need to inject the United States into every new development, particularly when events seem to be moving in a favorable direction."[7] Bush's temperament as an old-fashioned Tory (adjusted to American conditions) and the favorable-events stream were conjoined. As Bush read it, the obvious prescription was to "do nothing, but do it well."

Old-fashioned Tories are, by definition, not in the vanguard for or against anything, but they are not necessarily in the rearguard either. When the nature of change becomes virtually self-revelatory is the time when conservatives of Bush's stripe find it useful to change course. The obvious eventually concentrates the mind of even the most skeptical, and Bush's beliefs, such as they are, are generally organized around whatever conventional wisdom is prevalent. But old-fashioned Tories are mainly empiricists, less likely to lead fashion than follow it. When fashion changed, Bush's posture also changed. Being more addicted to cold-war orthodoxies when he began his administration than Ronald Reagan was when he ended his, Bush's reaction to the powerful events around him was slow and cautious until it became clear that the old orthodoxy was crumbling. Once the obvious became obvious, the Bush administration moved accordingly, if unradically.

On the domestic scene, good news overrode bad, and Bush did little in the first year and a half to face up to the growing prospect of budgetary calamity—a calamity that the average citizen (and possibly leader) found impossible to understand in any straightforward way. As Paul Quirk points out in chapter 3 of this book, temporizing and using mirrors to reach agreements that everyone believed would deal with the politics of the moment, but not the policy problem, was a style preferred by both the Bush administration and congressional Democrats. Both parties found the costs of supplying policy greater than the costs of shirking. Beneath the surface, however, signs of trouble and difficult decisions were beginning to bubble.

Reaching budgetary agreements through mirrors and pseudo savings no longer would be possible once the dimension of the deficit and the Gramm-Rudman-Hollings reduction targets came into play for the next fiscal year and the out years. This dimension became apparent by early 1990, and it became public when the House Ways and Means chairman, Dan Rostenkowski, put forth proposals to cut spending and increase taxes in order to cut the deficit. Whereas Reagan might well have rejected the initiative out of hand, the Bush White House signaled a desire to continue discussions. Indeed, it is plausible, though hardly proven, that the Bush administration actually encouraged Rostenkowski's initiative as a trial balloon. In June, Bush reversed his "read my lips" pledge, fearing that the costs of a deep recession could endanger his reelection chances in 1992. What annoyed his party was that this fear overrode the costs of reneging on a pledge that had become the House Republicans' "McGuffin" (their hook for trying to gain a majority). The reversal also was viewed as diminishing the prospects of Republican candidates in the 1990 midterm elections. The outcome of these elections, further, did little to bolster Bush's standing within his party.

On 2 August 1990, the Iraqi invasion of Kuwait also turned the peaceful impetus that developed from the dissolution of the Soviet empire and the cold war into a set of circumstances that foreshadowed excruciatingly difficult decisions. Consensus easily developed around a strategy of passive defense, internationally agreed sanctions on Iraq, and deployment of defensive capabilities in Saudi Arabia. That consensus dissipated when the Bush administration decided to move immediately after the midterm election from the posture of a defensive *Sitzkrieg* to the prospect of an invasion to free Kuwait and possibly destroy Saddam Hussein's armaments and regime as well.[8] At this point, the consensus faltered, though the Democrats preferred to hang back with words and testimonials on behalf of caution, rather than legally impede the president from engagement either through invoking the War Powers Act or entertaining a resolution to support the president's use of force (which, of course, implies the freedom to reject such a resolution). Later, when the die was largely cast, the resolution, at the request of the administration, was forthcoming.

On the budgetary issue and the Persian Gulf threat, Bush was faced with what were truly the first two major crises of his presidency. Doing nothing well would not suffice. On the budget, Bush's instincts for policy reconciliation and his need to prevent alienation between his White House and the majority of the Republican minority in the House made his task particularly difficult. It is clear how Reagan would have resolved such a problem, though it is implausible to imagine that a need to reconcile the politics of governing with the politics of partisanship would have been perceived by him. The awkwardness of Bush's performance during the budget episode and the unpopularity of the compromise package hurt him with the public and in Washington. While Bush dropped sharply in the polls, he dropped from a level that was unusually high, and he proceeded to gain some of it back as the budget deal faded from public attention. The budget performance, however, began to stir hopes among Democrats that they could conceivably run effectively against Bush in 1992, as he came to look less invincible.[9]

Within months, these hopes seemed to be all but dashed by Bush's command performance in the Persian Gulf and the conclusive military victory of the U.S.-led forces. While congressional Democrats and peace movement organizers had expressed concern about the American military offensive buildup in the gulf, public opinion data consistently supported the president's position at levels up to about two-thirds.[10] After hostilities broke out, that support rose to three-fourths and more.[11] After the decisive military victory, the president was acclaimed almost unanimously. Bush's instincts in the Persian Gulf crisis clearly were those of a follower of *Realpolitik*, and in this regard it might be interesting to see how Carter would have responded in office. (We know his response out of office, which was akin to the congressional Democrats' skepticism about offensive operations.) The proper response to the Iraqi incorporation of Kuwait, which now seems obvious, was less so when the decisions were being formulated. Indeed, optimum short-term military resolution may well be incompatible with optimum long-term leverage in the region. The crisis reveals two powerful instincts of Bush as a decision maker and suggests a likely public and political response to a president with wide but not deep approval and with little personal political magnetism.

One instinct is that Bush's views of the world, as indicated, tend to follow a pattern of *Realpolitik*. Force and the credibility of its use are vital instruments to this perspective. Building coalitions of strange bedfellows (United States, Syria, and implicitly China and Israel) is based on the nature of common threat, rather than common values. The second instinct is that, as a decision maker, particularly in foreign policy where he makes his heaviest investments, Bush likes to work around a small set of decision makers with whom he is comfortable. If Jimmy Carter's problem was to comprehend and resolve the diversity he built around him, George Bush's problem is to create a diversity of perspectives around him. In foreign policy making, Bush is surrounded by people much like himself—pragmatic, skeptical, experienced, and political. They, like Bush, have difficulty articulating objectives publicly.

They, like Bush, may not avail themselves as widely as necessary of specialized experts from within the bureaucracy or from the outside academic and
research communities. In both the budget episode and the Persian Gulf crisis, it is apparent that Bush works best as a low-key version of Lyndon Johnson—cutting deals with other leaders. His is the insider game. His weakness
is in sensing outside perspectives and in extending the ambit of discussion
and debate. This is not because, like Reagan, Bush has strong passions about
the substance, but because his style of operation is fundamentally boardroom
politics and brokerage among "proper gentlemen," as traditional Tories con-
ceive it. "Proper gentlemen" do not include Saddam Hussein, and certainly
not Newt Gingrich. Boardrooms, as well, are notorious for erring on the side
of exclusivity.

   In less than six weeks, hostilities began and ended in the Persian Gulf.
The precise long-term outcome and costs are as yet uncertain. But in the
short term the results are abundantly clear. Bush's policy success has made
him politically successful, indeed seemingly invincible, at home. All presidents have their political standing affected by events, by judgments about
how they respond to those events or have them portrayed, and by their ability
to project a sense of confidence and leadership around them. Bush handled
good times well. In case that sounds self-evident, consult Carter's first two
years when he had difficulty dealing with a generally favorable environment.
Times of difficulty present all presidents with political problems, but they
present those who lack a core constituency—a George Bush, a Jimmy Carter,
a Gerald Ford—with special vulnerabilities. These presidents are apt to have
their political fortunes turn on circumstances more rapidly than others. Core
constituencies buffer this, to some extent, though they also set natural
boundaries on the extent to which presidents are likely to be approved. All in
all, two aphorisms from the sporting world, one from pugilism and the other
from baseball, may prove to be relevant to Bush. Each is mightily robust and
useful for all sports, including politics. The first says, "The bigger they are,
the harder they fall," which for Bush's approval ratings can be translated as
"The higher they go, the faster they fall." The second, attributed to the New
York Yankees' star pitcher of the 1930s, Lefty Gomez, says it's "better to be
lucky than good." In his first eighteen months, Bush had remarkable luck.
Now he is more dependent on his qualities as a decision maker and politician. Fortune is still vital to his choices, which in turn are vital to his chances.
But he is now faced with more excruciating choices to make, choices in
which satisfying the policy problem and the political problem simultaneously
may become increasingly difficult.

   On the domestic front, Bush has bought time with the budget deal and
even forced the ball back on the Democrats' court by essentially trading in

the Gramm-Rudman-Hollings broad-scale sequestrations for categorical spending cuts. On the foreign policy front, Bush has now acquired the mantle of leadership and virtually unheard of levels of popular approval. As with Eisenhower, popular approval mainly acquired in foreign policy may prove not to be fungible in domestic policy, a domain in which public skepticism about Bush persists. As with Eisenhower, to the extent that Bush can focus public attention on his image as a foreign policy maker, it is clearly to his advantage. His advantage diminishes to the extent that events conspire to focus attention on domestic matters, particularly if recessionary economic conditions persist.

Executive Style: The Presidency as Corporate Enterprise

Inside the Washington Beltway and among scatterings of political analysts in universities and the like, Jimmy Carter's presidency and, to a somewhat lesser degree, Ronald Reagan's, brought forth the claim that the prevailing system of presidential selection was rigged against experienced insiders. The inside view was that Carter could not work the system, whereas Reagan did not want the system to work. The key insider supposition has been that the demands of the selection system, indeed its very publicness and the long lead time required to gear up for it, work to discourage candidates for the presidency who have active governing responsibilities and whose basic political constituencies are other governing elites.

The concept of the Washington insider is remarkably ambiguous. Much like the late Justice Potter Stewart's standard for pornography (you know it when you see it), the concept of "the insider" may be mostly in the eye of the beholder. Lyndon Johnson was a congressional insider, and so was Gerald Ford. Each succeeded an unfinished presidency. In all likelihood, neither would have achieved the presidency on his own. Yet Ford could not get elected after finishing the term of the disgraced Richard Nixon, and Johnson was in no position even to contemplate a reelection bid after his first full term. Insiders, in short, do not necessarily succeed in the presidency. Johnson and Ford appear not even to have succeeded in holding together their own party. Moreover, the concept of the insider seems to emphasize congressional leadership experience—an experience useful for dealing with some, but hardly all, aspects of the presidency.

George Bush appears to be much more of an insider in the continental European, rather than American or even Westminster, meaning. His experiences include legislative and party roles. But they also include organizational and executive ones. Bush had a relatively brief career in the U.S. House of Representatives while challenging for (but losing) a seat in the U.S. Senate in

1970. He went on to a speckled career of holding offices as varied as ambassador to the United Nations, Republican party chairman, director of central intelligence and the CIA, and chief of mission to China in the period before
formal diplomatic recognition was bestowed at the ambassadorial level. Bush
then became a candidate for the presidency, losing the 1980 Republican nomination to Ronald Reagan, and accepted nomination for the vice-presidency,
to which he was elected. Bush's experience combines legislative background,
political operations, diplomacy, head of the U.S. intelligence apparatus, and
the vice-presidential role.

The variety of Bush's experiences does not inherently mean that he has
learned anything significant from them, of course. Most assuredly, that lies in
the eye of the beholder. The simple point to be derived from Bush's occupational history is that if experience means anything (and it might not), Bush is
a case worth examining. Unlike any president of modern vintage who comes
to mind, Bush has an unusually diverse repertoire of experiences. Again, we
need caution here about the dangers of overselling the potential impact of
résumés. First, it is almost always true that one's present role is more important than one's past roles. Second, it is possible merely to pass through experiences ungrazed—to be like the character in the Woody Allen film *Zelig*,
whose simple achievement was to be wherever the action was, neither influencing nor even absorbing it. Third, what these experiences mean for Bush's
presidency is not necessarily self-evident, even were we to assume that neither
of the first two considerations is important.

A consideration that goes beyond Bush's experiences needs to be added.
It is that the Bush presidency, not merely Bush as president, is well seasoned.
The Bush administration, for the most part, is notably devoid of missionary
zealots and, in the main, is addicted to insider politics. Two of the three most
important cabinet posts—state and treasury—are held by close and long-
standing Bush friends, James Baker and Nicholas Brady. Exceptions exist, of
course, as the case of John Sununu, the White House chief of staff, testifies.
By recent standards, though, few people needed to be acquainted with the
norms and ways of Washington or with one another. Since Republican administrations have been the norm over the past two decades and more, and a
corps of experienced individuals of the Republican persuasion has developed,
this familiarity might be expected. Alternatively, a new Democratic administration might be expected to have more problems in this regard. The Reagan
administration arrived on the scene desirous of making a statement that it
not only was different from the Carter administration but also from the
Nixon and Ford administrations. The Bush administration, to the contrary,
whether intended or not, sends a statement that establishment politics and
norms have resurfaced—a source of some despair for committed Reaganites.

The long-heralded search for the Washington insider and the insider administration thus appears to have culminated. Bush as president and the Bush presidency are as close to that ill-defined status as we are likely to find. If so, what are the possible consequences? Insiders are likely to be consensus mongerers and not "conviction politicians," as Margaret Thatcher, the former British prime minister liked to describe herself. Moreover, they are likely to want to operate secretively, to cut deals in small groups, and to avoid rocking boats. Further, they are likely to operate in incremental ways, to believe that the premises of the status quo provide the operative bases for future policy except under the most unusually compelling circumstances—until, in other words, it becomes abundantly clear that those premises no longer are viable. An insider presidency also is likely to place a great deal of emphasis on internal harmony and less on central command as the mechanism by which to achieve it. It is more apt to choose people with a large quotient of public self-control than to base personnel selections on ideological commitment. No doubt this description is idealized. The Bush administration has had its share of White House staffers whose mode of conduct is confrontational—John Sununu and, especially, Boyden Gray. It also has had some who envision themselves as "idea people," for example, the junior staffer James Pinkerton, who gained his fifteen minutes of fame by aligning himself with the wing of his party that espouses a market-oriented set of social policy reforms, known by the term "empowerment." In the cabinet, Jack Kemp, despite keeping a relatively controlled profile, also has been an apostle of activist but market-focused social policies.

Being an insider and a Tory evoke complementary rather than discordant images. Each leads to a preference for incrementalism, to the view that deals can be struck between reasonable players well versed in the game, and to a belief that secrecy is the best way to conduct delicate business. The prime players in the Bush administration appear to abide by these expectations. The deal looms larger than the deed, as Colin Campbell's analysis of Bush's management style in chapter 7 suggests. At its worst, this style induces confusion about goals and policies because goals and policies, for the most part, are secondary. At its best, as others have pointed out in this volume, the "Tory-insiderism" style provides space for deal making. The weaknesses of the visionless presidency are also its strengths, and vice versa. Its priorities, even more than most presidencies, are especially dictated by events. As the unloosening of the "no new taxes" pledge (or, for that matter, newfound toleration for those opposing legal restrictions on abortion) suggests, there are few ties that truly bind, whether in the form of policy or party commitments. The absence of principle, of course, cheapens the currency of policy positions that are escalated to seemingly high principle and then readily abandoned. It leads to cynicism, and ultimately to an ineffective articulation of where the president actually is. The conservative political analyst George Will has endlessly excoriated the Bush style on this score.[12] Ultimately, uncertainty at the top ripples throughout the organizations of government. At the same time, it provides space for others to be policy entrepreneurs and mediators.[13] In addition, and ironically, uncertainty provides opportunities to deal with issues whose high immediate costs have to be shared. Such opportunities clearly were foreclosed by the more principled Ronald Reagan. No one doubted where he stood, which is why, after the early burst of legislative success, government under Reagan essentially stood still.

Unlike Ronald Reagan, Bush is very much an active participant in his administration. His level of involvement on matters in which he is most interested is very high. As Bush himself has pointed out, he finds foreign policy a lot more interesting than domestic matters (a fairly common situation for Republican presidents) because it plays to what he thinks he knows best and is most confident at engaging. This confidence, in turn, contrasts markedly with the level of volatility found in many of his domestic policy ventures. Thus, one finds little volatility in his foreign policy behavior. His desire to ensure that relations with the Chinese government be sustained in the aftermath of the Tiananmen massacre was believed by Bush to be strategically necessary. It hardly was calculated to be politically popular, either domestically or in China. His engagement on that issue sprang from a firm belief that he, by virtue of his experience, best understood the situation there. Bush's personal diplomacy in putting together the coalition of forces to confront the threat of Saddam Hussein in the Persian Gulf also reflected a level of intense involvement reminiscent of Carter at Camp David when he hammered out the peace accord between Egypt and Israel. While Reagan was an inert president in an activist administration, Bush has been an active president in a largely reactive administration. Reagan drove his administration on the power of his ideas. When those ideas ran out of gas, so too did the administration. To the extent that Bush steers his administration, it is through his own engagement. That engagement is far more evident in foreign than in domestic affairs, and that is why *Time* could portray Bush as having two distinctive presidencies: a successful foreign policy one and a failing domestic one.[14]

The Bush administration has largely eschewed the ideological litmus tests of the Reagan White House or the personal loyalty tests of the Nixon White House. It has been relatively pacific and less openly conflictual than most recent administrations. Except for one air force chief of staff (Dugan) who may have said too much and one secretary of education (Cavazos) who may have said too little (each of whom was icily dispatched), the Bush administration has been remarkably tranquil by recent standards. All presidents want harmony, so Bush's interest in this is a constant across presidencies, rather than a variable. While uncertainty about policy often seemed to generate more potential for conflict during the Carter presidency, Carter's own penchant for playing the role of rational decision maker by listening carefully to everyone's case heightened the incentives for advocates to make cases in public. Reagan provided ideological tone and consistency throughout his administration, but he was lax when it came to dotting *i*s and crossing *t*s. Consequently, where ideals left off and application had to begin, guidance was gone, and going to the president was not much help in getting a resolution to problems that required a newly formed thought.

On the face of it, Bush's remarkable malleability actually should have increased incentives for conflict and public disarray within his administration. It is likely, of course, that with the passage of time internal discord will grow, especially between policy advocates such as William Reilly at EPA, Louis Sullivan at HHS, and Jack Kemp at HUD, and those, such as Richard Darman at OMB and Sununu, who seek to keep these advocates and their ambitions on a short leash. Perhaps an underlooked explanation for the relative absence of internal combat in the Bush administration rests on the White House's disinterest in policy, and a set of traditional agency constituencies thankful for such small favors. Under Reagan, policy meant threatening the status quo. Alternatively, under Bush, it has meant modest incremental adjustments of the more threatening Reagan-induced changes. Doing nothing (or at least little) seems better to many of the agency constituencies that had come to know doing something as doing something *bad* to them. Doing nothing neither arouses support nor stirs opposition. So far, the benign context of this agendaless presidency has been its saving grace. But that context has begun to recede, and as it does so, we probably can expect precisely the kinds of conflicts that damaged the Carter administration from within. Sooner or later, Bush's bona fides as a Republican will be questioned by the "ideas" wing of the party even more than at present. The empowerment entrepreneurs then may try to push the Bush administration off dead center, and require more of Bush than his mere verbal assent to their objectives.

Indeed, the relationship between Bush and his party may well be at the core of whatever disarray his presidency has been accused of. In trying to navigate between his party's policy entrepreneurs and his distinctly unentrepreneurial interests and instincts, he runs the risk of alienating much of his own party or decreasing the space available to cut deals with the Democratic majority in Congress. To cover himself, he will, as he already has, flip in one direction and then flop in the other in trying to reconcile his needs for coalition government with his needs to maintain his political base. Such a situation will make him look foolish because there is no obvious way for him to handle this conflict without alienating vital elements of his party. The budget episode of the autumn of 1990 could be a harbinger of things to come. From the standpoint of appearances, there is little doubt that Bush failed to handle that well. But there also was little room for him to be appreciably more agile. In order to keep his party's support in the longer run, he was induced to argue that the deal he made was one forced on him, rather than truly acceptable to him. For getting the chance to carve the basic structure of the budget deal, the Democrats found Bush's lamentations a small price to pay. The structure of the problems that Bush will have to navigate his way through, and the possibility of decreased party commitment to him, suggests that future tests of Bush's political agility will not be lacking. For now, though, the constraint of divided government and Bush's preferences for "directionless consensus" are mutually reinforcing.[15]

Personal Style

It is by no means an easy matter to translate a president's personal style into terms relevant to his conduct of the office. Not everything about personal style is equally important, and indeed many things are probably exceedingly unimportant. In spite of the inevitable temptations to wax on about it, one thing that probably is not doable at all is to get inside the president's head. At best, we can try to develop inferences from behavior and verbal conduct, mostly drawn from stories. My observations here are of the armchair variety. There may be less to them than meets the eye when these impressions are subjected to more thorough scrutiny. I readily concede tentativeness. The task of relating style to conduct also is made more complicated by the fact that most theories of personal style are vastly overdetermined, that is, style becomes too general to be an efficient explanation of conduct.

As with any personality, George Bush seems to have some noticeable traits. Individuals naturally differ in the extent to which their characteristics of personal style are more or less salient and more or less consistent. George Bush seems to be more difficult to figure out than Ronald Reagan. But is this because George Bush has a more ad hoc political style, or is it that he is an inherently more complex personality?

Since I am trying to do political analysis and not psychoanalysis, it is best to begin with categories that have to do with how Bush conducts his presidency. I suggest here three categories in which we might consider how elements of Bush's personal style relate to important aspects of presidential behavior. In no particular order, the first of these categories is that of *politi-*

cal/policy leadership. The second is *interpersonal relations*. Although this category does not seem inherently political, political skills are certainly related to how individuals deal with other people, especially other elites. The relevance of interpersonal to political skills is universally true, but has special salience in the American system where cooperation has to be continually solicited by political leaders and can virtually never be assumed. The third category is *decision making*. What elements of personal style become important to the ways in which individuals approach decisions?

It is clear that these present bigger issues than I can deal with authoritatively, at least at this point. But I can provide hints about how pieces of the Bush persona seem to connect to these aspects of his political style.

POLITICAL/POLICY LEADERSHIP

If inspiration is a part of one's definition of leadership, it is surely evident by now that George Bush is as inspiring as broccoli. Indeed, his expressed distaste for this "good for you" vegetable may have inspired children all over the country to resist parental pleas to eat the stuff. If so, it is probably as much inspiration as he has given.

The problem of the "vision thing," as Bush himself has put it with characteristic flair, is partly explained by the combination of several characteristics. First and foremost, as noted, is that Bush is a Tory; he is not a neoconservative or a Reaganite. He is not turned off by ideas, but he is equally not turned on by them either. A Tory's view of the world is imbued with skepticism about alterations to the status quo; it embodies the precept that doing nothing more likely is better than doing something. The difficulty with the "vision thing" that Bush experiences stems mainly from this traditional Tory perspective on the world. But this perspective is influenced by three other, interrelated factors. One is Bush's rhetorical deficiencies. It is not necessarily true that rhetoric and vision are the same. Rhetoric helps promote vision or may even substitute for it. Bush's rhetorical skills are neither dreadful nor very good. They seem about average, probably better than Ford's and Nixon's, for example. They pale by contrast, however, with those of his immediate predecessor, whose dramatic talents were honed over a lifetime. It so happened that Reagan's purity of vision and his capacity to project drama were symbiotic, though clearly one should not get carried away by a belief that the rhetorical and dramatic skills were fundamentally crucial to Reagan's successes. They probably were pretty important, however, to how he was written about and spoken of by journalists, just as Bush's inability to project a view (that he does not in any event have) is not at heart crucial to his successes or failures. Regardless of his rhetorical mechanics, it is basically difficult to capture hearts through the spirit of incrementalism. The low profile on rhetoric seems also to stem partly from Bush's upbringing, an upbringing that apparently deemphasized expressive values. It further may be related to Bush's conception of his presidential role as that of a discrete problem solver.[16]

The symptoms of this political style have been ridiculed by pundits. George Will, for example, sees the Bush political style stemming from his comfort with a small set of entitled decision makers and his disdain for the politics of public persuasion—a view, if true, that coincides neatly with the Tory profile of reactive adaptation and deemphasis on expressivism. As Will puts it:

> He discounts rhetoric because he discounts persuasion of the public. He is governing less by continuous acts of public consent than by a small elite's entitlement, the right of the political class to take care of business cozily. So, naturally, he has no need to do what Reagan did—argue, persuade, precipitate confrontations with Congress, force polarizing choices.[17]

Will's description is largely right, but not as devastating as he seems to think it is. The headline copyeditor, however, has it wrong. Will's article in the *Washington Post* was titled "It's Not Modesty, It's Arrogance." It is neither, of course. It is traditional Toryism, which is skeptical of grand ideologies and ambitious plans of action. Problems find you, in the Tory view; there is little reason to seek them out. Will's article, along with a plethora of others equally critical of Bush, appeared during the budget negotiations of 1990 when Bush, to be charitable, looked equivocal. One wonders what Will and his colleagues in the punditry business would have written of Eisenhower during the 1957 budget presentation when, in the face of different sets of criticisms from congressional Democrats, on the one hand, and his treasury secretary, George Humphrey, on the other, Eisenhower both backed his treasury secretary and defended and attacked his own budget? It provided Richard Neustadt with one of his prime cases for critiquing Eisenhower's purported incompetence as a politician.[18] Yet Ike's political situation was not all that different from Bush's; the Democrats wanted him to do more, the Republicans less, and he faced insurrection from within galvanized by a cabinet member.

While it is true that Reagan (whom Will coached for his 1980 debate with Carter) had ideas, Charles Jones speculates that it would have been better for someone else who had a different style of leadership to deal with the consequences of those ideas.[19] My purpose here is not to defend Bush but to understand him and how his style interacts with his political conditions. I believe that this style largely complemented the set of conditions in which he was placed. I conclude from this that Bush probably would not be best suited to lead a government that had Republican majorities in Congress that were anxious to define a policy agenda.

INTERPERSONAL RELATIONS

A key aspect of George Bush's familial socialization reputedly was to emphasize graciousness and considerateness in interpersonal relations. His climb to the top of the political heap has been assisted, to some degree, by his arduousness in courting goodwill. His penchant for scribbling thank-you notes in longhand symptomizes the effort to keep up good relations. These are little things, and they do not necessarily make for big differences in a president's success in the office. Their absence surely hurts, however. Nixon's support and Carter's, too, were so thin because too often the only sentiment either expressed toward other members of the political community was contempt.

Bush's manners seem to be those of the manner to which he was born: Be modest about yourself and considerate to others. In view of the political circumstances into which Bush had been cast, these seem to be a serviceable set of traits. He would have to work well with others to gain their cooperation. Whether or not he could do so would depend primarily on the interests and preferences of these other actors. But getting along with other members of the political community on a personal basis could do no harm and, in the margins, might do some good. As Colin Campbell notes in chapter 7 in this volume, Bush's presidency has not always been managed in a fashion conducive to this interpretation of Bush as a personality. It may be by intent or simply incidental, but some of the president's men, namely, John Sununu and Boyden Gray, have been cast in the role of Mr. Hyde to Bush's Dr. Jekyll. Thus the Bush White House is not so seemingly generous and gracious as Mr. Bush himself has been portrayed.

As with all of us, contradictory impulses are at work with Bush. If the conventional wisdom is that of the Bush who writes personal thank-you notes and reaches out, there also is a George Bush who is remarkably prickly and personality driven in his likes and dislikes. There are some people with whom he has had long-standing relationships and with whom he can communicate in an atmosphere of trust, whether they are in his party or not. The famous relationship between Bush's secretary of state, James Baker, has been remarked on.[20] But these relationships cut across party lines. Bush's close relations with the Democratic chair of the House Ways and Means Committee, Dan Rostenkowski, enabled Rostenkowski to take the first step in March 1990 in what could have been an elaborately choreographed dance to deal with the budget deficit. Bush also has had good relations with the Democratic House Speaker, Thomas Foley, who has been criticized by the rank and file within his party for many of the same things that Bush has (i.e., no ideas or vision and for being insufficiently partisan and confrontational). Yet, the House majority leader, Richard Gephardt, aroused Bush's ire with criticisms of his "failure to lead"—a set of criticisms that seemed directed to Bush's personal qualities as a leader.[21] For this, Gephardt was banished from White House events, at least for a while. There are other Bush episodes of personal defensiveness—the on-air spat with Dan Rather especially notable among them. Yet Bush lacks the deep paranoia that so much characterized Lyndon Johnson and Richard Nixon. Eventually, by virtue of Gephardt's help in resolving the budget deal, Bush's relations with him improved. Most notable, though, has been the way in which Bush and his minority leader in the Senate and former rival for the nomination, Robert Dole, have been able to cooperate. The two were notably cool toward one another after a bitter campaign, and Dole certainly does not easily forget. Yet the two have worked out a far more cooperative relationship than might have been imagined when Bush took office.

So, if Bush has prickly qualities to his personal judgments, they do not seem to generate lifelong grudges that make it impossible for him to cut deals at a later point. In a political system that depends to a larger degree than party governments do on the interplay of personal chemistries at the top, Bush seems more able than most presidents (probably the most since John Kennedy) to deal with other elites at the top of the system with confidence. In turn, this fits with Bush's notions of governmental deal cutting in small groups. This style may not fit George Will's tastes for principled actions, but it was Bush, not Ronald Reagan, who successfully moved to begin dealing with the budget deficit.

The two sides of Bush's personal style were captured by the political campaign of 1988. Bush reputedly resisted the strongly negative tactics urged on him by Lee Atwater and Roger Ailes until he became convinced that he probably could not win without wrapping himself in the flag and thereby associating Dukakis with flag burners or without tarnishing Michael Dukakis with the Willie Horton furlough episode, thereby associating Dukakis with crime and white fears.[22] At the point at which he became convinced that these themes were important to his case, however, he let all the chips (and ammunition) fall. Perhaps similar situations arose during the 1990 congressional session when Bush vetoed two bills, one a maternal-leave bill on a subject he promised to do much about during the election campaign, and the second a bill to strengthen affirmative action standards (in shorthand, the civil rights bill). Whatever the merits of either piece of legislation, Bush's talk of a kinder, gentler America was being put to the test here insofar as it meant reaching out to constituencies, especially in regard to the civil rights bill, that are not central to his party's base. Caught between party pressures, Republican (anti-quota) themes, and party-interest constituency links, on the one hand, and the outreach themes, on the other, Bush chose to forgo the outreach in order to strengthen his political base. Hence Bush reinforced prevailing notions among the nation's pundits that he had no fundamental beliefs or at least none that he would refuse to sacrifice for political expediency.

I do not know whether that proposition is any more true in Bush's case than in those of other presidents. The proposition itself would have to be clarified before it could be tested. Appearances, in any event, are more crucial than actual facts, whatever these might be. The appearance in Bush's case is that what makes for his flexibility and willingness to cut deals has a down side. And it is this: His personal principles of graciousness and considerateness and his political style emphasizing the role of social harmony and legitimacy do not ultimately seem to run deep. To the Republicans in Congress and to Republican challengers in the 1990 elections, a similar conclusion about their president could be (and was) arrived at, namely, there was no promise strong enough from which Bush could not find "wiggle" room when he felt he needed it. But if he was going to desert his party on taxes, he could not desert them on other things. As a general matter, he chose not to. Therefore, to Democrats, he reneged on their understanding of "kinder and gentler."

What this suggests is that circumstances influence personal choices, a hardly novel statement. But Bush seems to be not well anchored by a strong set of personal values that put him in control of his circumstances. Instead, he seems to be largely buffeted by circumstances, making his choices appear to be more susceptible to a raw calculus of what he personally has to lose or gain from them. Is George Bush idiosyncratic or typical of presidents in this regard? The answer to that question inherently will be debatable. From what has come before in this chapter, I would myself conclude that Bush is more similar to, than different from, other presidents.

DECISION MAKING

As in so many other aspects of his behavior, George Bush also seems to have irreconcilable elements to his decision-making style. While this early assessment no doubt will be modified by more detailed treatments later, after Bush has left the presidency, its basic outlines seem to capture much of the puzzlement that surrounds George Bush as a decision maker. On the one hand, there is the now-familiar risk aversion, caution, and prudence—the last characteristic being one that Bush likes to identify as part of his style as president. Alternatively, George Bush can be (and often is) an impulsive man, occasionally given to barroom language in lieu of the gentility in which he was raised. From time to time, he seems to feel the necessity to proclaim his manhood by "kicking ass"—first, the derrière of Geraldine Ferraro after she debated him in the 1984 election campaign, and second, that of Saddam Hussein (a more deserving one, to be sure) in the weeks leading up to the launching of the war against Iraq.

We often see in Bush, then, both a remarkable penchant for the coldly sober and risk-resistant path and stunningly bravado-like assertions from which little retreat seems possible. The nomination of David Souter to the Supreme Court exemplifies Mr. Bush's sober side superbly. Clearly, Bush made an effort to depolarize what had become a nasty confirmation process under Reagan. Whereas Reagan's penchant was to advertise for the Court to be remade in his own image, and to find controversial individuals who were likely to arouse opposition, Bush chose to find an individual without a substantial paper trail and about whom little was known for him to be called controversial or not. Yet Souter was not a G. Harrold Carswell (a failed 1970 "Who's he?" Nixon nominee to the Supreme Court) without a past, not simply a nonentity available to fit a presidential need by filling the "mediocrity seat" on the court.[23] In his confirmation hearings, Souter revealed an impressively agile but exceedingly discreet and nondoctrinaire bent of mind —the perfect depolarizing candidate for a president concerned with avoiding controversy.

But Bush's other side—an assertive, even defiant side—is notable at times. "No new taxes, read my lips" was no doubt not an uncalculated line, but it was a line calculated to make his life more difficult if he got elected. The sudden invasion of Panama and the rapid introduction of offensive forces into the Persian Gulf immediately after the 1990 elections seemed to reflect a willingness to take high-stake risks, ones that could easily have blown up in his face. The nomination of Dan Quayle for the vice-presidency struck many, too, as the work of a fundamentally impulsive man, as did the frenzied vacation of August 1990 following the Iraqi invasion of Kuwait. Bush's exercises at madcap golfing illustrated precisely the opposite of the calm and assurance he was trying to project.

Who, then, is the real George Bush? And what does it mean if we discover him? The serious answer, I am afraid, will have to be left to a later time, to be uncovered by individuals who have immersed themselves in a trail of documents. The casual speculation, which is what I can deliver from equally casual observation, is that, so far, George Bush, like most of us, is an individual with certain dominant yet nonetheless contrasting and conflicting qualities. Like many of us, he has impulsive qualities and is sensitive to slights. Given the opportunity to consider the second, third, or fourth thought, however, Mr. Bush seems to be a genuinely sober and cautious decision maker with propensities to defuse conflict. His presidency, if these observations are correct, will rest a great deal on how he has organized it for himself—whether it adjusts for his weaknesses and plays to his strengths. On the whole, he seems attached to his presidency and is an active player within it, in some contrast to his predecessor. Yet he is less frenetic about the need to control everything that is going on than Lyndon Johnson or Jimmy Carter were.[24] Unlike Ronald Reagan, who was no mystery at all, how we see George Bush depends a lot on the lenses we see him through. Insofar as Mr. Bush's dominant decision-making characteristics are concerned, I see him this way: a cautious incrementalist who works off the prevailing wisdom (when that has solidified) and is reluctant to depart from that prevailing wisdom until there is powerful evidence of its unworkability. Much more like Jimmy Carter than Ronald Reagan, Bush is more comfortable with facts than with theories, a virtue perhaps for decision making and a liability for cultivating party passions.

Conclusions

In the first year and a half of his administration, George Bush showed himself to be an effective maintaining president. He inherited favorable circumstances in all but his political situation. Stability, continuity, and incrementalism all played to his principal assets. When nothing was called for, it was done well. Good fortune in general helps presidents' political fortunes. That is an insipidly obvious conclusion. Presidents tend to look good when things are going well and bad when they are not. The period since the first year and a half, however, has been different.

Until the outcome of the Gulf War, things had gone less well for the country and for Bush. Increasingly, he had to give definition to his presidency. The Persian Gulf War, however, has markedly shaped public perception of Bush. The aftermath of the war will continue to affect these perceptions, positively or adversely. For now, Bush is at the crest of his foreign policy and national security leadership powers. The shelf life of approval based on his conduct of the foreign policy role, however, may be less durable than it now seems. For, in the end, judgments about Bush's presidency and the political fate of his presidency more likely will rest on matters he can less affect, namely, the economy and the belief that he is in control of things. This, too, remains to be seen. But these outcomes and beliefs more predictably will affect his presidency than will the stunning success achieved in the gulf.

As with most recent presidents of the Republican persuasion, Bush is apt to be party either to a grand coalition or a grand confrontation. Sometimes there will be elements of both. Bush needs his minority party for core support, but he will from time to time need the support of the Democrats in Congress as well. Although we can anticipate more than the usual level of political acrobatics under these conditions, by temperament, if not by political agility, Bush seems ably suited to be president in an environment emphasizing brokerage politics. Often forgotten is that Bush is merely one actor in a leadership cast that, with the exception of Newt Gingrich, also has a proclivity for brokerage politics. The forgotten part of the elite deal-making syndrome is that it also assumes leadership to be a collective enterprise. Such an environment will be short on inspiration and program. It will seemingly be devoid of clear purpose and ideals. But it may make the system work, if not to the optimal benefit of some particular sector of political opinion.

Bush is a president for some seasons, not all. He is Mr. Inside. The question is, Will he be able to cut the deals he needs to cut with a vision of the steps that remain ahead? The assessment of the budget deal produces no unequivocal judgment, though if one were a believer in "invisible hands," one readily could conclude that the outcome received more plaudits than did Bush himself. The uncertainties of reaching political agreements in the Middle East lie ahead, as do newfound concerns with the direction of the Soviet state. Bush feels on firmer ground on such issues, but big strategic thinking is not his style. Does this mean that present choices will be carefully reviewed for their effects on future choices? Or does it mean that Bush cannot strategically relate them? Either conclusion seems justifiable from the little we now know. Obviously, we need to know more, but what we need to know probably will not be accessible until some time in the future. For now, all we do know is that Bush prefers decisions to dogmas or, from a less charitable perspective, ad hoc responses to clear visions.

To those looking for social programs as a cure for some of the maladies afflicting American society, I suggest they devote their energies to electing Democratic presidents or, should one choose to be venturesome, to electing "empowerment" Republicans (to whom they should also attach a Republican Congress). Rounding, not sharpening, is Bush's style, one that perhaps is appropriate to a time and setting in which policy ideas have yet to congeal in either party.

Notes

1. For their contrasting views of Dwight Eisenhower's skills as a political leader, see Richard E. Neustadt, *Presidential Power* (New York: Wiley, 1960); and Fred I. Greenstein, *The Hidden-Hand Presidency: Eisenhower as Leader* (New York: Basic Books, 1982).

2. For further discussions of this thesis, see Larry Berman, "Looking Back on the Reagan Presidency," in *Looking Back on the Reagan Presidency,* ed. Larry Berman (Baltimore: Johns Hopkins University Press, 1990), 3–17; and Joel D. Aberbach and Bert A. Rockman with Robert M. Copeland, "From Nixon's *Problem* to Reagan's *Achievement:* The Federal Executive Reexamined," in Berman, *Looking Back,* 175–94.

3. See David Hoffman, "Bush: Making Himself Up as He Goes Along," *Washington Post,* 13 August 1989, B1, B4.

4. Despite opposition from right-wing gurus, Bush signed off on the appointment of former Dukakis adviser Lawrence Summers to chief economist of the World Bank. In the view of columnist David Warsh "Summers's appointment ... symbolizes faith on the part of the president that the mainstream economics consensus knows something, that politics is ultimately secondary to technique and the dispassionate search for truth. It is further evidence that what the Bush presidency is about is the rebuilding of the American establishment." David Warsh, "World Bank Appointment Shows Bush's Faith in the Dispassionate Search for Truth," *Washington Post,* 31 October 1990, B3.

5. Ann Devroy, "Defending Military Budget, Bush Calls for Cautious Response to Soviet Shifts," *Washington Post,* 8 February 1990, A30.

6. Nominated in Tower's place was a highly regarded member of the House of Representatives, Dick Cheney, and in Lucas's place, John R. Dunne, an experienced trial lawyer.

7. David Hoffman, "Bush's Evolution: Hesitation to Activism on Soviet Changes," *Washington Post,* 11 March 1990, A34.

8. *Sitzkrieg,* literally "sitting war," was the German word used to describe the passive military posture of British and French forces on the Western Front of Germany following the Anglo-French joint declaration of war on Germany that commenced with its invasion of Poland on 1 September 1939. The *Sitzkrieg* lasted until the Nazi forces invaded France nine months later.

9. See Robin Toner, "Democrats, Albeit Late, Ponder Presidential Bid," *New York Times,* 3 December 1990, A-16.

10. Looking at survey data on the public's attitudes toward the use of military force in support of President Bush's objectives to get Saddam Hussein to withdraw from Kuwait, Thomas Mann concludes that "when you do the breakdowns and when you follow up the sanctions question it indicates that a substantial majority, on the order of two-thirds, entertains the use of military force to get Saddam Hussein out of Kuwait." As quoted in Richard Morin, "Two Ways of Reading the Public's Lips on Gulf Policy: Differently Phrased Questions Seem to Yield Contradictory Results," *Washington Post,* 14 January 1991, A9.

11. "Initial Reaction Is Positive," *New York Times,* 18 January 1991, A11.

12. For a sampling, see among the columns of George F. Will, "Splitting Differences: This Democratic Nation Needs a Vigorous Argument, Not Judicial Fiat about Abortion," *Newsweek,* 13 February 1989, 86; "Wallowing in the Fine Print: In Just One Month Bush Has Punctured the Myth That the Media Are Carnivorous," *Newsweek,* 27 February 1989, 82; "Playing with Guns: Bush, Weather Vane of the Western World, Now Says: 'Ban Some Rifles, Pending a Study,'" *Newsweek,* 27 March 1989, 78; "The Pastel President: An Obsession with Miniaturized Ethics Floods in to Fill a Void of Public Purpose," *Newsweek,* 24 April 1989, 86; "The Winds of Words: Some People Who Deplore America's 'Imperial Overreach' Regret Today's Inability to Reach Noriega," *Newsweek,* 22 May 1989, 96; "Honey We Shrunk the Issues: Contentment Cooled Ideology in Europe but Heated It Up in America," *Newsweek,* 31 July 1989, 76; "Bush: Read My Polls—If Lithuania's Liberty Is Sold to 'Save' Gorbachev, What Is Not for Sale?" *Newsweek,* 7 May 1990, 76; "'Let Congress Clear It Up': Bush's Pratfalls Last Week Underscored the Evanescence of Presidential Power," *Newsweek,* 22 October 1990, 84; "Deals and Delusions," *Washington Post,* 11 October 1990, A23; and "It's Not Modesty, It's Arrogance," *Washington Post,* 12 October 1990, A21.

13. See Matthew Holden, Jr., "'Imperialism' in Bureaucracy," *American Political Science Review* 60 (December 1966): 943–51.

14. Indeed, *Time* portrayed Bush not as its "man of the year" but his dual confident foreign policy self and his stumbling domestic policy self as "men of the year." See "A Tale of Two Bushes: One Finds a Vision on the Global Stage; The Other Still Displays None at Home," *Time,* 7 January 1991, 18–33.

15. For the concept of "directionless consensus" (applied to the style of British civil servants), see Richard Rose, *The Problem of Party Government* (New York: Free Press, 1974).

16. Note these characterizations by *Newsweek* correspondents Tom DeFrank and Ann McDaniel: "The president's advisers are chosen to be team players. They are by and large gray suited and sober-minded, not flashy self-promoters. Like Bush, they tend to see themselves as problem-solvers and not ideologues." Furthermore, "Bush readily admits that he lacks the 'vision thing.' Instead, he regards himself as a problem solver. Though he does not hesitate to decide, he is essentially reactive, responding to events and pressures rather than plotting a long term course. His approach can be piecemeal and ad hoc." Thomas M. DeFrank and Ann McDaniel, "Bush: The Secret Presidency," *Newsweek,* 1 January 1990, 26–27.

17. Will, "It's Not Modesty, It's Arrogance."

18. See Neustadt, *Presidential Power.*

19. Charles O. Jones, "Ronald Reagan and the U.S. Congress: Visible-Hand Politics," in *The Reagan Legacy: Promise and Performance,* ed. Charles O. Jones (Chatham, N.J.: Chatham House, 1988). Another analyst, Thomas E. Mann, agrees, arguing that "subsequent presidents and Congresses cannot escape the Reagan legacy, but they may be able to manage better without him." See his "Thinking about the Reagan Years," in Berman, *Looking Back,* 29.

20. See, for example, Maureen Dowd and Thomas L. Friedman, "The Fabulous Bush and Baker Boys," *New York Times Magazine*, 6 May 1990, 34–67.

21. See Eleanor Clift, "Under His Skin: The Bush-Gephardt Feud," *Newsweek*, 26 March 1990, 16.

22. In describing how Bush came to adopt the Ailes-Atwater strategy, *Newsweek* claimed that Ailes and Atwater tried to focus Bush's attention on the Democrats' attacks on him at their convention. The claim was that "Bush was not a born street fighter [but] it was easier to get him down-and-dirty if you persuaded him that he was wronged and the manly thing to do was to fight back." "Waving the Bloody Shirt: Good George, Bad George," *Newsweek*, 21 November 1988, 117.

23. The "mediocrity seat" entered the lexicon in 1970 during the Senate debate over the confirmation of Judge G. Harrold Carswell for the Supreme Court. After Carswell's record was criticized for the number of reversals he had encountered at appellate levels and for the low quality of his opinions, one of his Senate defenders, Senator Roman Hruska of Nebraska, voiced an unusual theory of representation that he thought should apply to nominees for the Court. He claimed that since most people were mediocre, there should be someone on the Court to represent them. Thereafter, the object of Hruska's novel theory came to be referred to as the "mediocrity seat."

24. For a description of Bush's managerial role, see Joel Aberbach's chapter in this volume. Also see Ann Devroy, "Commander-in-Chief Leaves Military Details to Pentagon," *Washington Post*, 19 January 1991, A26.

2

Meeting Low Expectations: Strategy and Prospects of the Bush Presidency

Charles O. Jones

It's easy to underestimate George Bush because he's so damn genteel and nice. — Thomas Ashley

Bush is a genuine conservative, an American Tory. There are known characteristics of that breed: they care about the society and the government that is handed to them; they want to make small adjustments; they want to keep the boat afloat. Bush is a professional in public service, which means that he has respect for other professionals. — Nelson W. Polsby

In a postelection article entitled "Low Expectations," Burt Solomon of the *National Journal* explained that Bush entered the White House "with no obvious mandate and with a residue of bad feeling left from the unsavory campaign." Therefore, Solomon reasoned, "there's little expectation that Bush's first 100 days as President will rival Reagan's or Franklin D. Roosevelt's in 1933. Nor should they."[1] Solomon quotes Richard E. Neustadt as saying that he would not be surprised if Bush "tried to lower expectations."

This kind of analysis was typical in the aftermath of the 1988 election. No one concluded that Bush's forty-state win carried with it a mandate for specific action on the nation's agenda. George Bush had not spoken to the issues in the campaign, and the Democrats had retained virtually their same healthy margins in the House and Senate. It was not an inspiring election for those who believe in party government and who test the political system by its principles.

By the end of its first year, the lowered expectations of the administration had the approval of a near-record number of Americans. George Bush's

popular approval far exceeded that of Ronald Reagan at the end of his historic first year in office. It was also markedly higher than that of any other post-
World War II president except John F. Kennedy. And this record was
achieved in spite of low support in Congress by the standard measures. In
fact, Bush's presidential support score in Congress in 1989 was the lowest by
far for the first year of any postwar president—11 points below Richard
Nixon in 1969!

During the budget impasse in September and October 1990, President
Bush's popular approval ratings dropped significantly—the result both of
bad economic news and the prospect of a prolonged military presence in the
Persian Gulf. Yet his score remained substantially above that of Ronald
Reagan at the same point in his presidency—in spite of the fact that Bush's
legislative support scores in Congress dropped to new lows. And his popularity soared to record heights following the successful conclusion of the war
with Iraq.

Why should the popularity of a no-mandate, limited-action president
exceed that of a Ronald Reagan, whose political circumstances were better
suited to party government? This is one of the questions of central concern
in this chapter. I argue that the outcome in Bush's case fits the politics of our
time, a politics that meets none of the party government standards by which
it is typically tested. Put otherwise, the perplexity for analysts is reduced when
they shift their evaluative criteria from that of a party government perspective
to that of a mixed representational perspective of diffused responsibility.[2]

This chapter treats the following topics: expectations associated with the
responsible party and mixed representational perspectives; post-World War II
election results and their impact; what the voters thought they did in 1988;
the postelection "charge to the Bush administration"; first-year politics; second-year politics; and a concluding discussion that treats the president as a
representative, getting on with Congress in a two-branch government, and
the larger implications of split-party control or a mixed-representative system.
Special attention is paid throughout the chapter to a concept of "co-partisan"
policy politics, comparing it to patterns of unipartisanship. In summary,
this chapter seeks to place George Bush's presidency in the context of the
strategic advantages and disadvantages characterizing divided party government.

What to Expect: Comparing Two Perspectives

The dominant perspective in analyzing and judging the presidency and Congress is that of responsible party government. Outsiders might find that to be
curious, given that the United States has seldom had favorable conditions for

party government in the post-World War II period. What are those conditions? They are set forth most clearly in a classic statement, "Toward a More Responsible Two-Party System":

> An effective party system requires, first, that the parties are able to bring forth programs to which they commit themselves and, second, that the parties possess sufficient internal cohesion to carry out these programs....
>
> The argument for a stronger party system cannot be divorced from measures designed to make the parties more fully accountable to the public. The fundamental requirement of such accountability is a two-party system in which the opposition party acts as the critic of the party in power, developing, defining, and presenting the policy alternatives which are necessary for a true choice in reaching public decisions.[3]

Note the words and phrases in this summary: *party in power, opposition party, policy alternatives ... for choice, accountability, internal cohesion, programs to which parties commit themselves.* This report was heavily criticized when it was issued in 1950 as being insufficiently attentive to the realities of the American political structure.[4] But it persists as a touchstone for many analysts in judging the quality of elections and governmental performance.

By this accountability perspective, the good election is one that meets the following standards: publicly visible issues that divide the two parties, forthright party platforms that outline positions on major issues, candidate debates that clarify party differences, a significant win for the president in popular and electoral votes, a clear win for the president's party in Congress (sufficiently large so as to suggest presidential coattails—even issue congruity between presidential and congressional campaigns), a majority for the president's party in both houses of Congress, and declarations of support for the president by his party's congressional leaders. A review of post-World War II presidential elections shows only one election, that in 1964, that superficially meets all these criteria, though the elections of 1952 and 1980 met several criteria. When the conditions of party government are met, a mandate is typically declared by those self- or otherwise designated to make such judgments. The mandate—a policy or programmatic charge from the voters to the government—is the essence of responsible party government.

What of the mixed-representation perspective? For its understanding, we can turn to an earlier tract, *Federalist #51.* In reassuring the people of New York about the new constitution, James Madison and his co-authors reviewed the reasoning for and advantages of separated powers and checks and balances.

The great security against a gradual concentration of the several powers in the same department consists in giving to those who administer each department the necessary constitutional means and personal motives to resist encroachments of the other....

A dependence on the people is, no doubt, the primary control on the government; but experience has taught mankind the necessity of auxiliary precautions....

In republican government, the legislative authority necessarily predominates. The remedy for this inconvenience is to divide the legislature into different branches; and to render them, by different modes of election and different principles of action, as little connected with each other as the nature of their common functions and their common dependence on the society will admit. It may even be necessary to guard against dangerous encroachments by still further precautions. As the weight of the legislative authority requires that it should be thus divided, the weakness of the executive may require, on the other hand, that it should be fortified.[5]

A review of the Constitution shows that the founders were successful in developing auxiliary precautions. Separate elections, staggered terms, bicameralism—these and other features contributed to a mixed-representative system exactly suiting the requirements of a government controlling itself. Thus the constitutional realities are that we will seldom experience a "party in power" or an "opposition party ... presenting the policy alternatives." And mandates will be rare.

The potential for divided-party government has been there from the start. With a two-party system and single-member districts in place, nothing in the constitutional structure prevented any one of the following combinations:

Combina-tion	Democrats Win	Republicans Win
1	White House, House, Senate	No branch
2	White House, House	Senate
3	White House, Senate	House
4	White House	House, Senate
5	No branch	White House, House, Senate
6	Senate	White House, House
7	House	White House, Senate
8	House, Senate	White House

As it has happened in this century, divided government was infrequent during the first forty-six years and very frequent since. Here is the record:

Combina-tion	1901–47	Number of years	1947–93	Number of years
1	1913–19, 1933–47	20	1949–53, 1961–69, 1977–81	16
2	—		—	
3	—		—	
4	1919–21	2	1947–49	2
5	1901–11, 1921–31	20	1953–55	2
6	—		—	
7	1911–13, 1931–33	4	1981–87	6
8	—		1955–61, 1969–77, 1987–93	20

The results show forty years of unified-party government (i.e., same party control of both branches) in the first forty-six years of this century (87 percent), or only six years of divided-party government. Just as the American Political Science Association created its Committee on Political Parties in 1946, however, politics began to change. In the years since, we have had unified-party government for eighteen years and divided-party government for twenty-eight years (61 percent). More dramatically, there has been divided government for twenty-six of the thirty-eight years 1955–93 (68 percent) and twenty of the twenty-four years 1969–93 (83 percent).

There has to be a message here someplace. It may be clarified by acknowledging that these post-World War II election outcomes are neither unconstitutional nor necessarily dysfunctional. They are allowable under the rules for governing as set forth initially and as these rules have been adapted through the decades. And any charge that split-party outcomes interfere with proper governing must at least engage the arguments in favor of separation set forth in *The Federalist Papers* and the Constitution.

The advantages of the mixed-representative system have not altered very much through time. They include variable geographic or regional representation of interests, a second chance for those who lose in one arena, public display of policy alternatives, encouragement of policy innovation, and competitiveness among contending forces to represent all interests. That good may result from conflict, criticism, and competition is hardly a new idea in democratic theory. And, in fact, one sees it as fundamental to the thinking of the responsible party advocates when they speak of the need for the "opposition party" to act "as the critic of the party in power, developing, defining, and presenting the policy alternatives that are necessary for a true choice in reaching public decisions."

Cannot the same advantage be realized even more dramatically in a legislature controlled by one party acting to criticize an executive controlled by the other? Why, in fact, would that outcome not be even more advantageous, since the criticism comes from a group with real power to force compromise? After all, an opposition party under the responsible party format can do little more than talk and say no. It has no representation in the White House and is in the minority in both the House and the Senate. The experience in frustration of House Republicans (in the minority since 1955) is instructive on this point. That frustration is well expressed in the title of a book written by one House minority leader, John J. Rhodes of Arizona: *The Futile System.*[6]

In summary: (1) The Constitution permits, indeed encourages, divided government; and (2) American voters have decided in recent years to exercise that option on a regular basis. These facts should promote an analysis of what has happened, not invite perplexity or wishful thinking. In so doing, we may even find a political system at work.

What the Voters Have Done and Whether They Like It

A closer look at the post-World War II national election results shows even greater confusion than is indicated by the split-party results. Consider the following patterns:

For the Democrats:

- [ ] President wins narrowly, House and Senate Democrats realize substantial gains (1948).
- [ ] President wins narrowly, House and Senate Democrats retain majorities but either lose seats (1960) or stay the same (1976).
- [ ] President wins in a landslide, House and Senate Democrats realize significant gains (1964).

In each of the four elections, the Democrats won control of both ends of Pennsylvania Avenue. But there were ample reasons in three elections (1948, 1960, and 1976) to question the extent to which the voters were endorsing a "party in power" concept. There were reasons in each case for congressional Democrats to act independently of the president. Only in 1964 might one be justified at the superficial level of congruous election results to declare a mandate for the "party in power." That is, in 1964 Lyndon Johnson and congressional Democrats won overwhelmingly in an election with strong ideological overtones, thus seemingly meeting primary conditions for responsible party government. Parenthetically, it might be observed that even in that situation one must question whether all criteria of the party responsibility model were met, since the Republicans were spoken of as a dispirited and ineffective opposition.

For the Republicans:

- ☐ President wins in a landslide, House and Senate Republicans win bare majorities (1952).
- ☐ President wins in a landslide, House and Senate Republicans realize substantial gains, achieving majority status in the Senate (1980).
- ☐ President wins in a landslide, House and Senate Republicans (as the minority) stay the same (1956, 1988) or House Republicans realize small gains and Senate Republicans realize slight losses (1972, 1984).
- ☐ President wins narrowly, House and Senate Republicans (as a minority) realize small gains (1968).

These variations, too, fail to satisfy the conditions for responsible party government. The Eisenhower and Reagan victories came close. In the Eisenhower case, however, the Republicans went outside the party in order to nominate a winner (Taft being the "responsible party" choice). In the Reagan case (1980), the Senate win was stunning, but a Democratic House majority allowed for a special kind of divided-government politics that does not well suit responsible party criteria.

There are other indications of voter preference for sending mixed political messages. For example, thirty-four states have been won by Republican candidates in at least five of the last six presidential elections (twenty-one states were won by the Republican in all six). In contrast, in twenty-five states during the same period Republicans won the governorship and majorities in both houses of the legislature no more than 20 percent of the time. Remarkably, among these twenty-five states were fourteen that voted for the Republican presidential candidate in at least five of six elections.[7]

Still other evidence of the voters' contribution to split-party results comes in the increasing number of congressional districts won by one party for the House and the other for the presidency. Though the trend is not straight-line, the data show significant increases in the number of split results in this century—from less than 15 percent of the districts on the average before 1948 to over 30 percent on the average since that time (and reaching a high of 45 percent in 1984).[8]

Then there is the matter of election results at the state level. The toleration of divided government is not limited to the national level. In 1974, one party won the governorship and majorities in both houses of the legislature in twenty-nine states. By 1988, the number of states meeting that condition had fallen to eighteen, with thirty-one states (63 percent of those with partisan, bicameral legislatures) having one or the other form of divided government (eighteen with the split between the governor and the legislature, thirteen with a split between the two houses of the legislature).

Are voters pleased with these results? The fact that they continue to produce split-party control is at least partial evidence that they are not consciously moved to make the corrections desired by the party responsibility advocates. But there is more direct evidence. In a *Wall Street Journal*/NBC poll taken in January 1990, voters expressed a preference for divided government by a margin of 63 to 29 percent, better than two to one.[9]

Clearly, such results are deeply disturbing to advocates of unified and responsible party government. In reflecting on recent developments in Eastern Europe and the Soviet Union, James MacGregor Burns concluded that these nations have little to learn from us beyond our Bill of Rights and an opposition party. In fact, "we can, paradoxically, learn from them."[10] Burns then listed a standard set of party responsibility reforms. Here is an excellent example of the dissatisfaction among the party responsibility advocates with the American people and their political system. What the voters want, apparently, is not good for them. It is hard to know exactly what part of democratic theory one turns to for support of that proposition.

What the Voters Thought They Were Getting in 1988

Whether it is legitimate to interpret an election as having conveyed a mandate, we now have ample evidence on what voters thought about the choice facing them in 1988. These thoughts have relevance in regard to viewing the president as a representative. How did voters perceive Candidate Bush? Who did they think he was? What did they think he favored? Which groups liked which candidates? The answers to these questions should help us understand whether President Bush met their expectations. They may even explain subsequent public approval ratings.

Consider, first, that Americans do not like being placed on an ideological scale. Therefore it is not surprising that, when asked, large numbers place themselves in the middle. Among those who are willing to identify themselves, conservatives consistently outnumber liberals in recent years. At no time during the 1980s did the number of liberals come close to matching the number of conservatives, as measured in three major polls. The averages through 1988 were as follows:[11]

	Liberals	Conservatives
National Opinion Research Center	24.5%	33.4%
CBS News/*New York Times*	19.1	34.0
Roper Organization	20.4	43.4

This conservative advantage may be said to be amplified in politics by the interesting disjuncture between how the public views societal and personal ideological trends. According to one 1988 survey, 52 percent of respondents judge that American society is more *liberal* now than twenty years ago, while only 17 percent of the respondents considered themselves to be more liberal than in the past (29 percent judged themselves more conservative).[12] That the country has moved left while voters are moving right is a familiar Republican campaign theme.

Asked by a Harris poll in August 1988 whether they "prefer a president who is a conservative, a moderate, or a liberal," respondents split as follows:[13]

A conservative	40%
A moderate	41
A liberal	13

Taken together, these data clearly suggest a campaign strategy in an open race, one requiring that each candidate's image must be fixed in the voters' minds. Barbara Farah and Ethel Klein point out that

> Michael Dukakis declared that he did not like labels and that his campaign would focus on competence, not ideology; the Republicans put ideology squarely on the campaign agenda.... By early September the "L word" had become a major theme of the Bush campaign, and the role that ideology was to play in the campaign was evident.[14]

As Farah and Klein show, the strategy worked. In May, 27 percent of the electorate considered Dukakis a liberal; by election day, 56 percent rated him that way. Of those who so categorized Dukakis, over 60 percent then voted for Bush.[15]

Next, consider the groups that supported George Bush and those that supported Michael Dukakis. Table 2.1 provides an overview. It holds few surprises, to be sure. But it confirms the moderate-to-conservative basis of Bush's support. Among the social, economic, and religious groupings, Bush scored best with married men, the middle-aged, the college educated, white-collar workers, homemakers, high-income voters, whites, and Protestants.

TABLE 2.1

SOURCE OF SUPPORT, BUSH AND DUKAKIS, 1988

	Bush supporters		Dukakis supporters	
	50–55%	56% +	50–55%	56% +
Party				
Republicans		☒		
Democrats				☒
Independents	☒			
Sex and marital status				
Married men		☒		
Married women	☒			
Unmarried men	☒			
Unmarried women				☒
Age				
18–29	☒			
30–44	☒			
45–59		☒		
60+	☒			
Education				
Not HS graduate				☒
HS graduate	☒			
Some college		☒		
College graduate		☒		
Postgraduate	☒			
Occupation				
Professional/manager		☒		
White collar		☒		
Blue collar			☒	
Teacher/student			☒	
Unemployed				☒
Homemaker		☒		
Retired	☒			
Union household				☒
Income				
Under $ 10,000				☒
$10,001–19,999			☒	
$20,000–29,999	☒			
$30,000–39,999		☒		
$40,000+		☒		
Race and region				
White		☒		
East	☒			
Midwest		☒		
South		☒		
West		☒		

TABLE 2.1 — *Continued*

	Bush supporters		Dukakis supporters	
	50–55%	56% +	50–55%	56% +
Black				☒
Hispanic				☒
Religion				
White Protestant		☒		
Catholic	☒			
Jewish				☒
Fundamentalist or				
White Evangelical		☒		
Community size				
Large cities				☒
Suburbs/small cities	☒			
Rural/small towns		☒		

SOURCES: Compiled from data in Gerald M. Pomper, *Election of 1988: Reports and Interpretations* (Chatham, N.J.: Chatham House, 1989), 133–34.

His average support among these groups was 59 percent. He also did extremely well in the South and had impressive showings in the Midwest and West. Though retaining 56 percent of the rural and small-town vote, his majority was substantially below that of Reagan in 1984 among these voters. The composite profile of the Bush voter is that of an individual who is privileged in American society, probably anxious to preserve present advantages, and unlikely to support new welfare programs.

In contrast, the groups heavily supporting Dukakis had ample reasons to ask more of government. They included unmarried women, the less educated, the unemployed, union households, low-income voters, blacks, Hispanics, and those living in large cities. The average support for Dukakis among these voters was over 60 percent.

Candidate awareness of the group basis of support should then determine the nature of the rhetoric on each side. Marjorie Randon Hershey analyzed the content of the two debates.[16] The results are as follows:

	First Debate		Second Debate	
	Bush	Dukakis	Bush	Dukakis
Mentions of domestic issues	40%	88%	8%	36%
Mentions of foreign/defense issues	26	23	24	24

As is evident, Bush emphasized domestic issues more than foreign and defense issues in the first debate; he reversed those priorities in the second. Dukakis overwhelmingly emphasized domestic issues in the first debate, with fewer mentions in the second debate, but still greater than mentions of foreign and defense issues. In neither debate did Bush offer a "wish list" of government programs, which is not surprising.

The logical next questions to consider in evaluating what happened in 1988 between the voters and George Bush are these: What did voters like about Bush? What did they not like about Dukakis? What issues were important in voting for each candidate? Table 2.2 (*page* 49) provides the answers, based on data in the Cable News Network/*Los Angeles Times* poll.[17] Bush voters primarily liked his experience, competence, and vision. Among the positive characteristics, these three contributed 73.6 percent to his vote (39.7 percent of the 53.9 percent received by Bush). They did not like Dukakis's liberalism, his personality, the risk of making a change, and the possibility that he would not stand up for America. Among the negative characteristics, these four contributed 64.9 percent to Bush's vote (35 percent of 53.9 percent).[18]

What of the issues? Bush scored particularly well among voters for whom defense, abortion, crime, taxes, and trade were important issues; he scored less well among those for whom the deficit, ethics, drugs, unemployment, and the environment were important issues. Consider these results in terms of how active Bush was likely to be once in office. He was expected to support a strong defense, "stand up for America." The president has limited responsibilities in regard to abortion or crime policy, Bush's tax statement was to hold the line, and a comprehensive trade bill had just recently passed the Congress. Those who wanted a more activist government in regard to drugs, environmental protection, and unemployment voted in greater numbers for Dukakis.

A second poll, that by ABC News/ *Washington Post,* reinforces these conclusions. Bush voters considered national defense, the economy, taxes, and foreign affairs to be most important; Dukakis voters judged the problems of the poor, the economy, health care, the deficit, and taxes to be most important.[19]

There appear to be several consistent messages from the preceding review:

1. In recent years, more Americans have moved right than left in the political spectrum, yet conclude that the society may have moved left.
2. An overwhelming majority of Americans favored a moderate or conservative in the White House, presumably one who is less active in expanding government.

3. Those groups supporting George Bush favored the status quo, thus maintaining present advantages.

4. Issue voting in 1988 did not support an activist program for President Bush. He was expected to maintain a strong defense, low taxes, and a strong economy.

TABLE 2.2

WHY VOTERS VOTED AS THEY DID IN 1988

	Percent mentioning	Percent voting for	
		Bush	Dukakis
Most positive Bush characteristics			
More experience	34	97	3
More competent	27	73	26
Vision of future	17	52	46
Impressive in debates	7	54	46
Avoid a recession	4	80	19
More likable	3	52	42
Most negative Dukakis characteristics			
Too liberal	28	94	6
Personality	19	55	43
Too risky a choice	15	76	24
Won't stand up for America	8	65	33
Won't be elected	4	63	34
Issues important to Bush voters			
National defense	23	84	15
Abortion	20	63	36
Crime	18	67	31
Taxes	15	70	29
Trade	5	57	42
Issues important to Dukakis voters			
Budget deficit	25	39	60
Governmental ethics	17	31	67
Drugs	14	41	58
Unemployment	10	35	64
Environment	11	28	70

SOURCES: Compiled from data in Gerald M. Pomper, *The Election of 1988: Reports and Interpretations* (Chatham, N.J.: Chatham House, 1989), 143; and *National Journal*, 12 November 1988, 2854.

The Postelection Charge to George Bush

The 1988 results were probably as predictable during the last month of the campaign as in any recent election. Close observers pretty much knew what was going to happen in both the presidential and aggregate congressional returns. As a consequence, it was a dull election night for the analysts, one with few of the surprises that television, in particular, likes to cover.

Postelection interpretations were uniformly pessimistic about what to expect from a Republican president and Democratic Congress. Editorial writers at the *Economist* were quite blunt:

> After eight years in the shadows, he has his own presidency. But George Bush will never enjoy the popularity of Ronald Reagan ... nor will he have the same opportunities to shine. This new president ... will find that ruling is often a mocking word whose substance will elude him for much of the next four years.[20]

Most commentary was a variation on a doubting theme. Looking back on what had happened, all agreed that there was no mandate. Looking ahead to the new administration, most expressed apprehension. The result was a rather gloomy forecast: An untested president, lacking the popular image of his predecessor, faced having to cope with a demanding agenda without a mandate and sharing power with a Democratic Congress. Here is a sample of postelection headlines:

> "Rough Road: Election Results Show Lack of a Consensus About President's Role" 			(*Wall Street Journal*, 9 November 1988)
> "Challenges for Bush: An Uncertain Agenda and a Wary Congress"
> 				(*New York Times*, 10 November 1988)
> "President-elect Starts Move Toward a 'Bush Revolution': But Failure to Bolster GOP Position in Congress Will Make It Harder to Lead"
> 				(*Christian Science Monitor*, 10 November 1988)
> "What to Expect: The Outlook for the Bush Years: Reaganism Without Ideology, Persistence without Brilliance—and Serious Trouble with Congress" 			(*Time*, 21 November 1988)
> "The Tough Tasks Ahead: George Bush Wins a Decisive Victory and a Personal Vindication, but No Clear Mandate"
> 				(*Newsweek*, 21 November 1988)

Columnists and editorial writers produced slight variations in what were otherwise virtually interchangeable reviews. For Richard Cohen of the *Washington Post*, George Bush now had "to prove that his character is a match for his ambition," a matter not resolved by a "dirty campaign" and no "clear mandate."[21] Albert C. Hunt concluded that had Bush "tried to lay out an agenda, it would have made his task over the next four years considerably easier." Now he had to campaign further just to have a mandate.[22] Lou Cannon judged that there were "obstacles left and right," but "Bush's best insurance against a successful challenge from his right is to have Reagan in his corner."[23] Haynes Johnson described the 1988 election as "issueless, avoid-pain, postpone-decisions, float-along-America." "With Democrats more strongly in control of Congress, Bush faces potentially greater opposition on Capitol Hill than has the more popular Ronald Reagan."[24] "George Bush is no Ronald Reagan," Fred Barnes discovered. Reagan set an ideological tone, Bush's campaign issues "are irrelevant to the way he intends to govern as president."[25]

One of the most balanced efforts to look back in order to see ahead was an editorial in the *Washington Post.* It is worth quoting at length.

> The truth of the matter is that the whole argument over the nature of Mr. Bush's mandate is in a sense merely incidental to a much larger and more immediate issue: How, on the basis of his campaign rhetoric and whatever the voters consider his mandate to be, a newly installed President Bush will handle the challenge of creeping Gramm-Rudman deadlines, burgeoning federal government costs and a Democratic Congress not exactly bursting with enthusiasm to help him out of the fiscal and financial pressures that are intensifying. His mandate in this poorly focused election may not have been to fix the budget deficit, but until he does, he can do little else. Given all this, we expect Mr. Bush's plans cannot be grandiose; his claims and demands will not be dramatic. He will reveal himself as a man whose hope is to make the so-called Reagan revolution work, to somewhat extend its social sympathies and to vindicate the past eight years in the next four. He will also be doing a lot of bailing out. If you will pardon the expression, in this context we think the Bush presidency is more likely to be about competence than ideology.[26]

However realistic this analysis, and its implicit advice, may be, following it carried substantial risks in a political world dominated by a party responsibility or unified-government perspective. That is, the president is expected to lead, no excuses accepted. Thus, moving from postelection to preinauguration analysis was likely to be based on the president-as-activist-leader set of expectations. By mid December, the columnist Tom Wicker judged that "President-elect Bush has hit the ground limping." He found that Bush was "hedging on major program decisions, still damaging by delay his supposed choice to head the Pentagon, and still assembling an administration dominated by familiar faces."[27] And by his inauguration, the new president was advised to become a symphony conductor.

> He must find a way to persuade, cajole and stimulate the mighty institutions of government, the vast electorate and, perhaps most important, the rest of the world, to follow his lead, to respond to his cue, to make a thundering symphony out of disharmony at the flick of his conductor's wand.[28]

The president with no mandate was soon to be criticized for moving too cautiously; indeed, for permitting the world symphony to play without him. However rational it might have been in the postelection period to exercise prudence, doing so invited failure by the tests of the responsible party model president.

The First Year: Doing Well by Doing Poorly

> The new Bush Administration was marked by a preference for competence, not ideology. The President's style was one of reactive problem solving, not strategic vision. His approach to Congress ... was one of compromise, not confrontation. His approach to policy disagreements was personal communication and diplomacy rather than "going public" to bring pressure to bear.... The Bush presidency in its first year might be characterized as one of consolidation, seeking a "new balance," not confrontation and change.[29]

This positive evaluation is of particular interest because it comes from the author of *The Strategic Presidency: Hitting the Ground Running*. In that book, James P. Pfiffner points out that a new administration has to move quickly.

> They must shift gears from campaigning to governing, and they are faced with the gigantic task of taking over the U.S. government. They want to take advantage of the "mandate" from the voters and create a "honeymoon" with Congress.... Early victories may provide the "momentum" for further gains. The desire to move fast is driven by the awareness that power is fleeting.... The need to "hit the ground running" is also important because of what scholar Paul Light calls the cycle of decreasing influence.[30]

So how is it that the Bush presidency can get a high first-year rating while seemingly violating the strategy recommended by Pfiffner and many others? The answer appears to lie in the fact that the requisite conditions for "hitting the ground running" were not met. Bush did not have a mandate;

lacking a marriage, there was no honeymoon; power had already fled; therefore, influence was unlikely to cycle down, as predicted by Paul C. Light.[31] In other words, Pfiffner discovered in the Bush presidency a different kind of White House, one that required new criteria for measuring success.

Much of the difference in 1989 is captured in the concept of *co-partisanship*. A unified government is properly tested by the criteria of unipartisanship, that is, whether those who claim affiliation with the majority party support their leaders in the White House and Congress. The important test is this: Can a president realize the potential of his party's congressional majorities? Presidents can be expected to vary in their personal and political capacities to do so; for example, compare Lyndon Johnson with John Kennedy or Jimmy Carter. But the test itself is reasonable enough. And the argument stands that the president should move quickly, since the midterm elections are less than two years away.

As explained, the 1988 election did not produce a majority government. Both parties won. One interpretation even had it that "Democrats in Congress are approaching their relationship with President-elect Bush not so much with rancor as with confidence that they share his mandate to govern."[32] Several leaders were quoted as saying that they expected many areas of cooperation. But they also made it clear that cooperation would be based on negotiation among equals. "The people who will be sitting down with George Bush were also winners in the election" is the way House Democratic Whip Tony Coelho of California put it. Speaker Jim Wright of Texas understandably agreed: "If there is a mandate, it clearly is for Bush as president and a Democratic Congress to build upon the constructive program we embarked on last year."[33] Winning, under the circumstances, clearly required a carefully developed strategy, one suited to the conditions of co-partisanship.

As used here, co-partisanship refers to a situation in which each political party has independent sources of power to the extent that (1) the power will be used to participate broadly in the policy process (including initiating proposals), and (2) negotiation carries rewards for both sides. Co-partisanship is naturally associated with divided government—a president of one party, a Congress of the other (one house or both). Depending on advantages, however, one branch may be more powerful, thus reducing the need to negotiate, or one branch may be uncertain as to who benefits, possibly inducing a stalemate. Thus, if the congressional Democrats have a veto-proof majority, they may prefer to ignore the president's preferences; or if no one knows for certain what are the political and economic effects of a budget solution, each side may thwart the other. As suggested, then, co-partisan agreements may be the outcome for some issues, stalemate the outcome for others.

A critical precondition to co-partisan politics is the independent but variable power base for each of the contending forces. There has to be a reason for one side to negotiate with the other. Each institution begins with impressive constitutional status. Seldom can one act independently of the other, though the president's authority as commander-in-chief gives him a significant edge in foreign and defense issues. The more intangible sources of power can vary dramatically, as has been outlined by many presidential and congressional scholars.

As to George Bush, the postelection analysis of his weaknesses was reviewed above—dirty campaign tactics, no program, no mandate, no honeymoon, untested as the "top banana." And so there was work to be done if the Democratic Congress was not to run roughshod over him. Far from being in a position to dominate Washington politics, George Bush had to prove himself worthy of co-partisan negotiation. He had to create and maintain an independent power base that was not conferred by his forty-state win. Thus were the strategic imperatives of his first year identified. He could do well in interbranch, co-partisan politics by doing poorly in meeting the standard party responsibility criteria.

In the previews of his assuming office, three issues in particular were listed as absolutely requiring attention, and each would result in high conflict between Bush and Congress: the budget, aid to the *contras,* and the savings-and-loan disaster. Bush sought to defuse these conflicts by reaching agreements with congressional Democrats, taking a conciliatory initiative that was hard for the Democrats to counter. Bush began with this tactic in his Inaugural Address:

> To my friends—and yes, I do mean friends—in the loyal opposition—and yes, I mean loyal: I put out my hand.
> I am putting out my hand to you, Mr. Speaker.
> I am putting out my hand to you, Mr. Majority Leader.
> For this is the thing: This is the age of the offered hand.
> And we can't turn back clocks, and I don't want to. But when our fathers were young, Mr. Speaker, our differences ended at the water's edge. And we don't wish to turn back time, but when our mothers were young, Mr. Majority Leader, the Congress and the Executive were capable of working together to produce a budget on which this nation could live. Let us negotiate soon—and hard. But in the end, let us produce.[34]

What President Bush failed to add was that, rhetorically, he had taken his listeners back to an era when divided government was the exception, not the rule. Never mind. He wanted to establish a conciliatory, cooperative posture toward those who, by some interpretations, shared his mandate.

The record shows that a significant measure of cooperation was achieved in the early months of the administration for each of the three contentious issues. Following an initial, bruising fight over the nomination of former Senator John Tower to be secretary of defense, budget makers at both ends of Pennsylvania Avenue reached an agreement that then passed both houses in the form of a budget resolution. A bipartisan accord was reached on Central American policy that "drained most of the political poison for the year out of debates."[35] And Bush offered a recovery plan for the savings-and-loan association that formed the basis of a bill passed in Congress by late summer. Thus the legislative, if not the appointive, record of the early period seemingly accomplished the strategic goal of avoiding debilitating political and policy struggles. The Bush administration hit the ground conciliating.

Contributing to the success of this strategy was a crisis of leadership among congressional Democrats that surely reduced their confidence and effectiveness, providing the cautious president with the latitude to frame his strategy. First, and with the least significant effect, was the election of a new Senate majority leader. Having served since 1977, Senator Robert C. Byrd (D-W.Va.) decided not to seek another term as leader. In a somewhat surprising result, George J. Mitchell (D-Me.) defeated two opponents for the position. The president's advantage was that of working with a new leader, one striving to develop a style that would gain him support. The president could help or hinder that process.

A second early advantage for Bush was created by a pay bill. A public furor developed over the size of the increase and the manner by which it was to go into effect. Traditionally skittish about voting themselves pay hikes, members of Congress created a blue-ribbon commission to make recommendations for all three branches. The commission proposed sizable increases, which were endorsed by both Presidents Reagan and Bush. Beyond the amount, a 51 percent hike, was the procedure that authorized the increase unless Congress voted to kill it within thirty days. After a great deal of wrangling and devastating media and public reaction, both the House and Senate voted against the increases. Newt Gingrich (R-Ga.) concluded that "this [pay hike controversy] has sparked a level of anti-Congress feeling that is more intense than any political feeling since Watergate."[36] Staggering from self-inflicted wounds, Democrats in Congress were in no position to take advantage of Bush's weakness and lay claim to national policy leadership.

The controversy over the pay raise had several unfortunate effects for congressional Democrats: It drew attention to honoraria received by members speaking to outside groups, set the House against the Senate, and questioned the leadership capability of Speaker Jim Wright of Texas. Wright was heavily criticized for his handling of the issue at the very time that he was under investigation by the Committee on Standards of Official Conduct (the ethics committee). And the matter of pay focused attention on exactly the charges being leveled against the Speaker—that he had sought to circumvent House rules on honoraria limits through the sale of books to groups to which he spoke.

Meanwhile, the House Democratic Whip, Tony Coehlo of California, was under investigation for questionable investments. Thus, two of the top three House Democratic leaders were hampered by serious charges of ethical lapses. Coehlo was the first to resign, avoiding a full investigation. Five days later, on 31 May, in a dramatic resignation before a packed House, Speaker Wright spoke to his colleagues:

> Let me give you back this job you gave me as a propitiation for all of this sea-
> son of bad will that has grown up among us.... I will resign as Speaker of the
> House effective upon the election of my successor and I'll ask that we call a
> caucus on the Democratic side for next Tuesday to choose a successor. I don't
> want to be a party to tearing up the institution. I love it.
>
> To tell the truth, this year, it has been very difficult for me to offer the
> kind of moral leadership that the organization needs because every time I have
> tried to talk about the needs of the country ... the media have not been inter-
> ested in that. They wanted to ask me about petty personal finances. You need
> somebody else. So I want to give you that back.[37]

On 6 June, Thomas S. Foley of Washington was elected Speaker, and over the next two weeks a completely new House Democratic leadership team was put in place: Richard A. Gephardt of Missouri, majority leader; William H. Gray of Pennsylvania, Whip; Steny H. Hoyer of Maryland, caucus chairman; and Vic Fazio of California, caucus vice-chairman. All these members had had leadership experience *but not in these positions and not as a team.*

Thus the House Democrats began the summer having to accommodate new faces in new places. The effect was positive for President Bush's cautious and consolidative strategy for building support and creating his own presidency. He did not have to be concerned that congressional Democrats would fill the vacuum by assuming control of the agenda and of policy development. The outcome might have been very different had Speaker Wright not been crippled by ethics investigations, since Wright was a policy-oriented, New Deal Democrat anxious to participate actively in agenda setting and policy development.

The advantage for President Bush in congressional Democratic preoccupation with leadership problems should not be overstated. It bought him time by directing attention to the disarray among the opposition party on

Capitol Hill. It did not place him in command of policy politics in Washington. This point is illustrated by the president's effort to cut the capital gains tax, thus fulfilling a campaign promise. The president succeeded in the House with help from Democrats in the Committee on Ways and Means. But it was a costly win. Senate Democrats pressed for compensatory tax hikes on the affluent, eventually preventing the capital gains cut from being voted on and succeeding in having it removed from the reconciliation bill in conference with the House.

The presidential support score for Bush at the end of his first year was the lowest of any first-year president since the *Congressional Quarterly* has been producing that measure (i.e., since World War II). Bush's score was 63 percent—11 points below Nixon's first year in 1969 and nearly 20 points below Reagan's.[38] But it was difficult to interpret exactly what that score meant. Probably it suggested the need for analysts to consider the political and policy conditions of the time, as well as the variation in what it is presidents want Congresses to do. President Bush was clearly interested more in foreign and defense than domestic policy. And his action in Panama seemed to enhance his public status.

Then there is the matter of how well a president does otherwise by getting high support scores on Capitol Hill in his first year. Bush needed to establish an independent advantage so as to participate actively in co-partisan politics. He was unlikely to gain that advantage merely by doing what was necessary to get an impressive support score, since to do so would require acquiescence to Democratic initiatives *if they were, in fact, forthcoming from the new leadership team.* This point is different from that made earlier about a conciliatory posture so as to avoid early confrontations with Congress. In those cases, the administration took the initiative with proposals designed to get Democratic support.

More promising for creating advantages was the consolidation of the administration's team (separating itself from the Reagan presidency) and seeking a broader base of public approval than was forthcoming in the 1988 election. If successful in these moves, then the White House would have positioned itself strategically to bargain more effectively in subsequent cross-partisan policy-making.

The record shows that both these goals were achieved during 1989. The administration was criticized for moving too slowly in filling important subcabinet positions (and the rejection of John Tower to be secretary of defense was not the recommended way to begin forming a team). But the criticism was typically based on the accepted theme of "hitting the ground running." In fact, as noted earlier, there were good reasons not to adopt that pace. Further, the Bush administration was the first elected since 1928 to follow one of the same political party and the first since 1836 to have a vice-president succeed through election. The importance of these facts is simply that George Bush had to move carefully to create his own presidency. He had to do so without damaging the party or the presidency of his predecessor. By historical record, there were not readily available precedents for accomplishing these goals. And surely the concept of "hitting the ground running" was less applicable.

There is further evidence in public opinion polls that an activist president who scores well with Congress may not be viewed as doing that well otherwise. Consider the following poll results, as reported in the *Washington Post* in January 1990:

1. The president's approval rating reached nearly 80 percent.
2. The Congress's approval rating was half of that, just under 40 percent.
3. Many more respondents judged that Congress "has the most power in Washington" (53 percent compared to 15 percent identifying the president as having the most power).[39]

Thus the president ended his first year in office having improved his approval rating while receiving a poor support score from a Congress with a low public approval rating (while seemingly being held responsible as the most powerful branch of government). One lesson would seem to be that doing well with Congress was not required for President Bush to do well with the public. A second lesson may have been that Congress would be held responsible for national policy-making, not a pleasing prospect for Democrats during a period of budget containment.

To summarize, co-partisanship in 1989 resulted in postponement of many issues because of a lack of clear direction. In fact, the results were not wholly unlike those of the 1988 election. Senate Minority Leader Robert Dole of Kansas put it this way: "There hasn't been any demand, any mandate in the Congress and executive branch for major changes. We've done some sort of nibbling around the edges." House Democratic leaders essentially agreed. Majority Leader Gephardt stated that "we're usually a reactive institution. It's very hard for Congress to lead."[40]

The year ended with international events taking center stage. U.S. forces invaded Panama on 20 December and Eastern European regimes fell like dominoes as the new year began. Though the president did not escape criticism inside Washington—it was said that he was too aggressive in Panama and insufficiently involved in Eastern Europe— presumably an international agenda provides many more advantages for him than a domestic one.

The Second Year: Waiting for Saddam

It seems to me that Bush is two personalities. There is the personal presidency and there is the policy presidency. The personal presidency is remarkably pro-active, almost over active. This guy gets up at five in the morning, goes out and he jogs five miles and then he comes back and has four meetings and then he writes 50 personal notes to people and then he goes out and runs around town, prepares for another trip.... It is almost impossible to imagine George Bush taking a nap in the afternoon, waking up at nine A.M., falling asleep in an audience with the Pope.

The policy presidency of George Bush is reactive, not quite passive, anything but proactive. His instinct when it comes to issues is to say: "Let's let things germinate." Not, there's a problem, we better solve it; or, there might be a problem, let's do something before it becomes a problem.... Maybe the problem will go away. Maybe it will turn out to be less severe than we thought. If it does turn out to be worse and the time has come to act, then I'm perfectly comfortable looking at the alternatives and making a decision. It is not that I'm reactive because I don't want to deal with this [problem].[41]

These comments by a seasoned Washington political analyst suggest a virtual war between proactive personal behavior and reactive policy behavior. The evidence seemingly supports this analysis. Can the two behaviors be reconciled in a way to assist in understanding the president's strategy of decision making? I think they can, and the second year shows how. The second-year strategy was no more satisfying to the advocates of an activist presidency. Whereas the first year could be explained by political and policy conditions, the second year was more revealing of the melding of these conditions with personal style for explaining White House strategy.

The proactive personal behavior does carry over to politics and policy-making, but not necessarily to problem solving. It shows up in a remarkably energetic effort to stay in contact with those with whom the president must negotiate should problems develop. Thus there is almost a boy-scoutish "Be Prepared" approach that, as suggested above, awaits events and then acts to resolve a sure thing. By this approach, the president's strategy is, if you will, to be actively, not passively, reactive. That may even be what the analyst quoted above means by his modification "and not quite passive."

This style as strategy can be illustrated in both domestic and foreign policy in 1990. On the domestic front, the analysts were not encouraging: "Vulnerable to Events," "Stalemates of Last Decade Haunt Agenda for 1990," "[State of the Union] Address Reflects Modest Bush Agenda," "With the Issues Emotional and Elections Near, Bush-Congress Budget Fight Is Likely to Be Nasty."[42] There were few optimists and little reason for optimism.

As they had for nearly a decade, virtually all the domestic issues were dealt with in the context of the budget deficit. Basically, short of an economic crisis, the budget process worked to the president's political advantage, particularly a cautious president with a limited "proactive" social agenda. The advantage works like this. Under the Gramm-Rudman-Hollings procedure, the president is told what his budget must be. For fiscal year 1991, the budget could be unbalanced by $64 billion (plus a fudge factor of $10 billion). The Bush administration proposed a budget with a $64.7 billion deficit, well within the prescribed limits. The president acts first in the process and therefore can manage economic indicators, revenue estimates, and savings on expenditures to his advantage. Put otherwise, he can produce what he is told to produce by managing the numbers.

In co-partisan politics, it is then predictable that congressional Democrats will declare the president's budget to be unrealistic, often "dead on arrival." In making that declaration, Democratic leaders are essentially stating that they are then prepared to offer an alternative that is realistic. And in 1974, members of Congress put in place a budget process at their end of the avenue. So, as the clock moves inexorably toward the end of the fiscal year, attention naturally shifts to Capitol Hill where partisan wrangling dominates the debate. The president can deal himself in or out of this battle. But the setting is there—in Congress—not in the White House. And the president can assume the posture of cooperating, cajoling, or condemning—all the while reminding the public that it is Congress, not the president, that must ultimately approve the budget.

This script was followed in 1990 with variations to suit the changing circumstances.

> President Bush's $1.2 trillion budget for fiscal 1991 got predictably bad reviews when it reached Congress Jan. 29: It can't be taken seriously, snapped the Democratic majority....
> Democratic leaders dismissed the budget with familiar complaints that it would spend too much on defense and too little on domestic programs, do little to combat chronic deficits without new taxes, and meet the $64 billion deficit limit for 1991 mainly by relying on overly favorable economic forecasts.[43]

It is not necessary to review the very long story of budget making in 1990. Suffice it to say that the protracted struggle resulted in severe criticism of both White House and congressional leaders. The president did deal himself back into the process when new forecasts projected an economic downturn. A budget summit was convened once the Democrats had passed a budget resolution, and President Bush even went so far as to rescind his campaign pledge not to raise taxes. Still, a budget agreement proved elusive over the summer. Negotiations resumed after the August recess, finally producing a package on the last day of the fiscal year.

Unfortunately, the initial agreement reached between the White House and the leaders of Congress was not acceptable either to the left among the House Democrats or the right among House Republicans. The co-partisan goal was to have at least half of each party vote for the package—130 Democrats and 89 Republicans for a 219-vote majority. Early on the morning of 5 October, neither party achieved the 50 percent goal. The package was defeated, 179–254, with 40 percent of Republicans and 42 percent of Democrats in favor.

Neither Bush nor congressional leaders were seemingly prepared for this outcome, in spite of signals that it might occur. Nor was it likely that either was capable of a preparedness sufficient to the task of preventing intense partisan clashes. The impasse reflected the intractability of the deficit issue and illustrated the potential for stalemate in co-partisan politics. To propose increasing taxes and cutting programs is to touch the nerve ends of party differences. The achievement of getting a plan at all was overshadowed by its defeat on the House floor.

The president's veto power is clearly an important resource in co-partisan politics. By summer 1990, President Bush had established this authority as an important weapon in checking the initiatives of congressional Democrats. He had vetoed thirteen bills by that time, and Congress was unable to override any one of them. The further threat of vetoes for legislation carried over to the final weeks of the second session (one list cited eighteen bills for which a veto was recommended) added weight to the president's influence. Richard A. Roe (D-N.J.) observed that "every time we go to the bathroom around here somebody says, 'Check on the White House. They are going to veto.' "44

Practically the whole government appeared to be in suspended animation prior to the August recess. Few major bills had passed, the only appropriations measure to pass was a supplemental bill for fiscal year 1990, and a budget agreement seemed as illusive as ever. And with an election pending, Congress returned in September to an extraordinary workload to be handled in a brief time.

September and October 1990 were among the more remarkable months in contemporary national policy-making. As one might expect, the White House and Congress were consistently criticized as being ineffective. Yet the record shows the passage of the largest deficit-reduction package in history (including election-year tax increases), consequential reform of the budget process, and enactment of several significant measures (e.g., reauthorizations for farm, housing, and Head Start programs; a tough clean-air plan, immigration reform, a crime bill, and a new child-care program). The concentration of effort in round-the-clock sessions was bound to invite criticism, even ridicule, of the system. There was virtually no positive commentary on either the process or its product once Congress adjourned.

In foreign policy, events early in 1990 moved so swiftly that the president could hardly do anything but "Be Prepared." Developments in Eastern Europe and the Soviet Union dominated the news. The president was criticized for not playing a more active role in responding to or even managing these events. Senate Majority Leader George Mitchell advised President Bush to go to the Berlin Wall, many members of Congress and media analysts proposed more tangible support for Lithuania in its struggle for independence, others were critical of the president for not offering more economic aid to Eastern Europe. The president's strategy throughout was one of "watch and wait," while maintaining the closest ties to the relevant foreign leaders. Since the developments themselves were overwhelmingly favored by most Americans, including most members of Congress on both sides of the aisle, there were few political costs to the president's strategy.

The situation in the Middle East was quite different. The growing tension between Iraq and its neighbors, Kuwait in particular, certainly required careful monitoring. But, as it happened, "waiting for Saddam" turned out to be considerably more engaging for the United States. When the wait was over, and Iraq invaded Kuwait, the president moved swiftly to activate the communication network he had built up during the period of his presidency and before. Whether he should have waited is a debatable issue that I will not review here, except to take note of the criticism in Congress and elsewhere by those who believed that the administration sent misleading signals to Saddam Hussein before the invasion. The point I wish to make is that President Bush's actively reactive strategy was well illustrated by the Iraqi invasion and his subsequent efforts to mobilize a worldwide response.

The Iraq-Kuwait situation significantly altered domestic politics once Congress reconvened in September. In particular, the budget summiteers had to reconsider proposed cuts in defense as well as aid to Arab nations that supported the UN sanctions. Broad support for American actions in the Persian Gulf translated into short-term support for President Bush as well. His public approval ratings increased once again, in spite of a limited record in working with Congress, then declined with the threat of recession and the prospect of an extended stay in the Middle East, then recovered somewhat during the final months of 1990, and skyrocketed with the national euphoria that accompanied the war with Iraq.

The Bush strategy in the Persian Gulf was to mobilize a broadly based international coalition against Iraq. This approach included a series of resolutions in the United Nations, leading to one authorizing "all necessary means" if Iraq failed to withdraw from Kuwait by 15 January 1991. This international effort proceeded without a parallel action on Capitol Hill. President Bush consulted with congressional leaders, but he did not seek, nor did he believe he required, a resolution to take the actions he believed necessary. Some members of Congress proposed that it be called back into session to debate such an action. No such session was held. Congressional leaders were perplexed as they sought to define the legislative role in authorizing the use of military force, particularly, as in the Persian Gulf, where war seemed inevitably to follow. Meanwhile, the White House was anxious to preserve the flexibility judged necessary for world leadership in contemporary times. A resolution authorizing presidential use of force was a first order of business for the 102nd Congress. Following a vigorous debate, the resolution passed both houses despite the opposition of Democratic congressional leaders.

Conclusions

Study of the Bush presidency is fruitful for revealing the dynamics and strategies of co-partisan government. It provides a better case even than the Reagan administration as a result of the need for Bush to improve his political position following the 1988 election. He entered office with limited "political capital," relatively few "political advantages," and therefore a weak "strategic position."[45] The prospects were for a possible loss of control to congressional Democrats. Bush's potential advantage was that of low expectations—not a very impressive "chip" in the politics of high stakes.

The argument here is that the president's strategy has been one of trying to compete for and maintain his share of authority. To accomplish this goal, he has had to seek the public support that was not evident in the election. He has had to press his outside advantage, primarily in foreign and defense policy, while initially benefiting from a failure of the congressional Democrats to capitalize on their inside advantage of greater numbers and leadership of both houses. Public support is not typically a reliable advantage for presidents. It is subject to many interpretations, and it can change quickly. But everything is relative. Lacking other resources, public approval will be viewed as a significant source of support. In co-partisan politics, a president will turn to whatever advantage is available.

Comprehending co-partisan government begins with accepting its legitimacy and understanding its dynamics. To do otherwise typically encourages the analyst to propose recommendations for institutional reform. As co-partisanship is at present practiced in Washington, both the Bush White House and the Democratic Congress compete for shares of power in the national policy process. Their capacity to compete effectively varies with the advantages they have available (e.g., Bush's public support, his status as a world leader; Congress's constitutional role in declaring war, the 1990 election results as slightly favoring the Democrats). The resulting conflict produces considerable anxiety as the contending forces press their advantages and play for time. The lengthy budget summit in 1990 is a particularly dramatic example of co-partisanship at work; its failure shows the intensity of interbranch competition on fiscal issues. The carryover of many major bills to the final weeks of the second session is also illustrative, as is the passage of several of these bills.

Focusing only on the delay involved, or the compromises made, or the stalemate that results, fails to acknowledge the change in politics that has occurred. Thus, for example, an executive-congressional budget-making process was at work in 1990. It was not a pretty sight, especially for the advocates of unipartisan or responsible party government. But one should not miss the historic nature of the event. In fact, a cross-institutional budget process has been developing for some time—a forest that many bark and leaf fanciers have simply missed.

One final note as we look forward in the Bush administration. In its present form, co-partisanship is characterized by a Republican president and a Democratic Congress maintaining sufficient independent support to set the bargaining condition. Successful bargains can defuse election issues, starve challengers of campaign talk (and money), return incumbents (possibly by lower turnout from a cynical or bored voting population), and thus perpetuate divided government. Neither side particularly wants split-party control of government. James L. Sundquist is no doubt correct in arguing that the partisan instinct favors competition. "[Political parties] are and should be organized for combat, not for collaboration and compromise."[46] As it has happened in the post-World War II period, however, the competition often has occurred within the context of institutional balance, with each party rather solidly staked out at each end of Pennsylvania Avenue. The message here is that policy and political processes have adjusted to that reality. It is time that we understand what those processes are, since they characterize contemporary American politics.

Acknowledgments

This chapter benefits from research I am doing on post-World War II presidential-congressional relations, supported by the Brookings Institution, the University of Wisconsin Graduate School, and the research funds of the Hawkins Chair in Political Science, University of Wisconsin-Madison. I benefited from the comments of Leon D. Epstein. John Bader provided research assistance and also offered useful comments.

Notes

1. Burt Solomon, "Low Expectations," *National Journal,* 12 November 1988, 2838.

2. In comments on this chapter Leon D. Epstein made a distinction between "party government" and "responsible party government," the latter being associated with the doctrinal school of the report of the American Political Science Association (see below). The distinction is a useful one; primary emphasis here is on many of the preferences drawn from the responsible party school.

3. American Political Science Association, Committee on Political Parties, "Toward a More Responsible Two-Party System," as reprinted in Henry A. Turner, *Politics in the United States* (New York: McGraw-Hill, 1955), 234.

4. See Turner, *Politics,* 240–62.

5. *The Federalist Papers,* No. 51 (New York: Modern Library, 1937), 337–38.

6. John J. Rhodes, *The Futile System* (Garden City, N.Y.: EPM Publications, 1976).

7. Data developed from Harold W. Stanley and Richard G. Niemi, *Vital Statistics on American Elections* (Washington, D.C.: CQ Press, 1988), 105–6.

8. Data from Norman Ornstein, Thomas Mann, and Michael Malbin, *Vital Statistics on Congress, 1989–1990* (Washington, D.C.: CQ Press, 1990), 62.

9. Reported in "Washington Wire," *Wall Street Journal,* 19 January 1990, 1.

10. James MacGregor Burns, "U.S. Model for Eastern Europe?" *New York Times,* 8 February 1990, A21.

11. "Opinion Roundup," *Public Opinion,* November/December 1988, 30.

12. Ibid., 31.

13. Ibid., 34.

14. Barbara G. Farah and Ethel Klein, "Public Opinion Trends," in *The Election of 1988: Reports and Interpretations,* ed. Gerald M. Pomper (Chatham, N.J.: Chatham House, 1989), 110–11.

15. Ibid., 111.

16. Marjorie Randon Hershey, "The Campaign and the Media," in Pomper, *Election of 1988,* 90.

17. Cable News Network/*Los Angeles Times* exit polls reported in William Schneider, "Solidarity's Not Enough," *National Journal,* 12 November 1988, 2855.

18. Gerald M. Pomper, "The Presidential Election," in Pomper, *The Election of 1988*, 143. Also reported in Schneider, "Solidarity's Not Enough," 2854.

19. As reported in "Opinion Roundup," *Public Opinion*, January/February 1989, 33.

20. *Economist*, 12 November 1988, 9.

21. *Washington Post*, 10 November 1988, A23.

22. *Wall Street Journal*, 11 November 1988, A10. The *Journal*'s panel of political experts agreed with the dire forecasts. "'George Bush's lack of a mandate is an enormous problem,' says Kevin Phillips.... Worse, he figures Mr. Bush will be in the White House 'when the chickens finally come home to roost.'" 11 November 1988, A12.

23. *Washington Post*, 14 November 1988, A2.

24. *Washington Post*, 18 November 1988, A2.

25. *New Republic*, 28 November 1988, 8.

26. *Washington Post*, 14 November 1988, A10.

27. *New York Times*, 16 December 1988, 39.

28. David Hoffman, "George Bush Takes Up the Baton," *Washington Post National Weekly Edition*, 16–22 January 1989, 6 ff.

29. James P. Pfiffner, "Establishing the Bush Presidency," *Public Administration Review*, January/February 1990, 70.

30. James P. Pfiffner, *The Strategic Presidency: Hitting the Ground Running* (Chicago: Dorsey Press, 1988), 7.

31. Paul C. Light, *The President's Agenda* (Baltimore: Johns Hopkins University Press, 1982), chap. 2.

32. Susan F. Rasky, "Democrats See Reason to Work with President," *New York Times*, 13 November 1988, 1.

33. Quoted in Tom Kenworthy, "Wright Vows 'Cooperation' with Bush," *Washington Post*, 11 November 1988, A8.

34. Text of address in *Congressional Quarterly Weekly Report*, 22 January 1989, 143.

35. Janet Hook, "New Leaders Felt Their Way Gingerly through Session," *Congressional Quarterly Weekly Report*, 12 December 1989, 3299.

36. Quoted in Janet Hook, "Pay Raise Is Killed, but the Headaches Persist," *Congressional Quarterly Weekly Report*, 11 February 1989, 263.

37. Text of address in *Congressional Quarterly Weekly Report*, 3 June 1989, 1347.

38. Janet Hook, "Bush Inspired Frail Support For First Year President," *Congressional Quarterly Weekly Report*, 30 December 1989, 3540.

39. As reported in the *Washington Post*, 21 January 1990, A1.

40. Quoted in Hook, "New Leaders Felt Their Way Gingerly through Session," 3284.

41. Personal interview, 21 July 1989.

42. Headlines, in sequence, from *National Journal*, 6 January 1990, 6; *Congressional Quarterly Weekly Report*, 6 January 1990, 9; *Washington Post*, 1 February 1990, A1; *Wall Street Journal*, 29 January 1990, A20.

43. Jackie Calmes, "Bush Dealing from Strength as Budget Season Opens," *Congressional Quarterly Weekly Report*, 3 February 1990, 299.

44. As quoted in Janet Hook, "Avalanche of Veto Threats Divides Bush, Congress," *Congressional Quarterly Weekly Report*, 22 September 1990, 2991.

45. Terms used respectively by Light, *President's Agenda;* Richard Neustadt, *Presidential Power and the Modern Presidents* (New York: Free Press, 1990); and George C. Edwards III, *At the Margins: Presidential Leadership of Congress* (New Haven: Yale University Press, 1989).

46. James L. Sundquist, "The New Era of Coalition Government in the United States," *Political Science Quarterly*, Winter 1989–90, 629.

3

Domestic Policy: Divided Government and Cooperative Presidential Leadership

PAUL J. QUIRK

In a memorable passage in his acceptance speech at the 1988 Republican National Convention, presidential nominee George Bush distinguished his domestic policy from the hard-line conservatism of President Ronald Reagan, promising to strive for a "kinder, gentler America." A Bush government, he suggested, would be more compassionate toward those in need and would protect values, such as community, that were at risk in an America devoted to free enterprise. He stated his intention to be an education and environmental president. Although without giving any signs of overly great confidence or determination, he also promised substantial reductions of the federal budget deficit.[1] After the election, when it became certain that the Democratic party would continue to control both chambers of Congress, Bush and his staff spoke of plans to set aside the confrontational style of the Reagan presidency and work toward a cooperative relationship with the legislative branch.[2]

After two years in office, the point at which most presidents have their most significant domestic achievements already behind them, Bush had little to show for his fine intentions. The most significant domestic policy change during this period was the savings-and-loan rescue bill, which committed vast federal funds merely to contain a financial disaster whose costs were dimly appreciated, if at all, at the outset of the administration.[3] Because of those costs, efforts to cut the budget deficit lost ground. Few major administration initiatives were adopted in the areas of education, the environment, or social policy. In all, President Bush arguably had the least domestic policy achievement in his first two years in office of any president since the 1920s.

This chapter considers what accounts for such a poor showing. Was it, in the first place, Bush's fault? Did he genuinely intend a cooperative presidency and a "kinder, gentler America," or was that empty rhetoric, designed to confuse opponents of a do-nothing domestic presidency? If his stated intentions were sincere, did Bush or his staff fail to execute a cooperative strat-

egy with adequate skill? Or were the circumstances of Bush's presidency—
including divided government and the desperate financial condition of the
federal government—utterly hostile to domestic achievement? Finally, and
the most disturbing possibility, did Bush's domestic failure demonstrate the
sheer unworkability of American political institutions in the current era? Before we proceed to review Bush's domestic performance, let us briefly discuss
why this last possibility suggests itself for consideration.

Divided Government and the Cooperative Presidency

The Bush administration tests in some distinctive ways the potential for bipartisan presidential leadership and a cooperative presidency. The very notion of such a presidency, however, is unorthodox and theoretically problematic.

As James L. Sundquist has pointed out in a provocative essay, until very
recently nearly all modern discussion of the role of the president in American
government was based on the theory of party government.[4] According to that
theory, the complex, fragmented constitutional structure designed by the
founding fathers is incapable of providing effective government, at least under modern conditions, unless its parts are brought into harmony through
the binding force of a political party. For the government to act effectively in
circumstances that require innovative or decisive measures, the president and
Congress must go beyond checking and balancing one another and agree on
a course of action. If the president and majorities of the House and Senate
belong to the same party, it is natural for them to do so. The president and
the House and Senate majorities not only have similar policy goals but also
have partisan electoral incentives to seek agreement. But if the president and
the majority in one or both chambers are of different parties, they will find
agreement more difficult. They will have conflicting policy goals, and their
electoral incentives will encourage each to embarrass or defeat the other. In
short, American government can function effectively when the president can
lead Congress because the House and Senate majorities are bound together
by party ties.

Through most of the twentieth century, this situation of unified government usually obtained. The preponderance of the electorate cast straight
party votes, and each party's fortunes rose or fell in both branches at the same
times. Sundquist observes that from 1897 to 1954, a condition of divided government prevailed only 14 percent of the time, and always in the last half of a
president's term.[5]

As the experience of the past two decades has made abundantly clear,
however, unified government is no longer the norm. Around one-quarter of

the electorate typically splits its vote for president and senator or representative. In fact, many analysts now believe that the Democrats have a lock on the House of Representatives and a strong advantage in the Senate, and yet the Republicans have a comparable advantage with respect to the presidency. In the thirty-six years from 1955 through 1990, divided government has prevailed for twenty-four years, or two-thirds of the time.[6] One cannot draw firm conclusions about the relative strength of the parties in presidential elections. The entire period from 1952 to 1988 encompasses only ten elections, with only six different Republican candidates and seven Democrats. But divided government clearly is no longer any surprise, and it may be the new norm.

These developments have prompted scholars, commentators, and political figures to call for more analysis of the performance of divided government and the prospects for cooperative, bipartisan presidential leadership. Indeed, Sundquist has demanded that political scientists either formulate a new theory of how American government functions or else, as he evidently prefers, openly acknowledge that it no longer does function adequately and set about the task of considering remedies.

I do not presume to offer a new theory of American government.[7] On the basis of some recent work on the cooperative resolution of policy conflict, however, I offer several observations for such a theory.[8] First, the reasons for expecting rivalry between the parties notwithstanding, bipartisan cooperation obviously does, in fact, occur. In recent years the failure to reduce federal budget deficits has demonstrated, disastrously, the barriers to such cooperation. But the passage of the historic Tax Reform Act of 1986 is an important counterexample. As Sundquist admits, it is hard to make a compelling case for or against party government by discussing cases.

Second, there are straightforward reasons why party rivalry may be less destructive than advocates of unified party control suppose. For one thing, both parties in a divided government seek to avoid blame for blocking policy change.[9] Congressional Democrats can get away with obstructing the initiatives of a Republican president, therefore, only if they can somehow obscure their responsibility for the failure to act. With Republican candidates always ready to level charges in the next campaign, they often cannot adequately do so. During congressional action on the tax reform bill, for example, both parties wanted to avoid blame for defeating reform, so they collaborated to pass a strong measure. In addition, members of Congress mainly seek individual, rather than party, electoral success; and that depends mainly on their individual records and service to constituencies, rather than party records or presidential success. All incumbents can prosper together. Thus members of Congress are unlikely to withhold support, for partisan reasons, from a measure that serves their individual political interests. If, for such reasons, divided government does not lead to overly destructive party rivalry, the apparent advantages of a fragmented system, such as moderation and stability, may outweigh the costs.

Third, divided government calls for an approach to presidential leadership that stresses mediation and cooperative negotiation.[10] The principal skills of such leadership are not those of using conflictual rhetoric and other means to rally partisan or factional supporters. Instead, effectiveness in cooperative presidential leadership has two principal requirements. One is the ability to induce cooperative dispositions among potential opponents, especially leaders of generally unsupportive interest groups (such as labor unions for a Republican president or business groups for a Democrat) and members on the wrong side of the aisle in Congress. This ability depends, among other things, on interpersonal skills, willingness to invest effort in cultivating relationships, ability to inspire trust, and skill in using rhetoric to elicit concern for common interests. It is not enough to proclaim such interests; for example, when President Jimmy Carter told the public of an energy crisis that was "the moral equivalent of war," his bland delivery persuaded few.

The second requirement is to choose positions and strategies that promote agreement on terms that are favorable for the president's constituencies and serve broader interests. To be effective, any negotiator must avoid making excessive demands or appearing unwilling to make concessions. Such behavior will cause negotiations to break down. Thus a president seeking cooperative policy change must exercise restraint in the promises he makes to partisan constituencies. Yet an effective negotiator also must avoid making overly large or rapid concessions, which will lead to agreement on unfavorable terms. And he must keep from promoting "lowest common-denominator" agreements, which minimize salient concessions for both sides without much genuine gain for the common interests at stake.

A useful summary statement of this strategic requirement, derived from general negotiation theory, is the notion of "flexible rigidity."[11] On this conception, a negotiator must be *flexible about means*, that is, willing to consider alternative proposals, and yet relatively *rigid about ends*, that is, unwilling to give up ultimate goals quickly or easily. Such a strategy is not easily maintained: The distinction between means and ends is often lost in political conflict. And it is sometimes hard to impose any subtle strategic notions on a loosely organized executive branch.

In assessing the domestic performance of the Bush administration, therefore, we need to keep in mind both the special requirements of cooperative presidential leadership and the deeper questions about the workability of divided government.

George Bush and Cooperative Presidential Leadership

From the outset of his term, President Bush's plan for domestic policy was precisely to attempt cooperative policy change. Unfortunately, the circumstances of his presidency were not propitious for significant domestic policy achievement.[12] In addition, although Bush was in many ways personally suited to a cooperative strategy, there were major flaws in his execution of it.

The time was ripe for inaction. The Reagan-era agenda of reducing the size and cost of government was exhausted. There was scant public support for further reductions. In fact, by the end of the Reagan administration, polls showed that majorities of the public favored expansion of government efforts to deal with crime, drugs, education, poverty, the environment, and other problems.[13] Nor was there congressional support for more cuts. Bush faced a larger Democratic congressional majority than had ever previously been held by the opposition party in the beginning of a presidential administration.

Instead of carrying forward Reagan's agenda, most of Bush's promises of new initiatives in domestic policy represented revisions or outright reversals of Reagan's policies; and they implied expanding the scope of government. Bush proclaimed the goals of being considered "the education president" and "the environmental president." He promised major advances in overcoming drug abuse. In general, as we have seen, he offered the vision of a kinder, gentler America—meaning one with more compassion for the needy. Such promises were well adapted to eliciting cooperation from the Democratic Congress.

They were not well adapted, however, to the grim facts of the federal budget. Although by 1989 the federal deficit had shrunk in relative terms to about $170.2 billion, or 3 percent of gross national product (GNP), down from about 6 percent of GNP in 1982, it was still much larger than either historic peacetime norms or any level that most economists considered sensible. There was a broad consensus that further reductions were necessary. More specifically, the 1987 Deficit Reduction Act (also known as Gramm-Rudman-Hollings II) had set mandatory deficit-reduction targets that no one advocated revising upward. It set a target deficit of $100 billion for fiscal 1990, a reduction of $28 billion from the projected 1990 deficit under policies in force in 1989.[14] The prominence of deficit cutting on the federal agenda militated against major spending increases for domestic programs; it meant that such increases would be defensible, economically and politically, only in the event of a major tax increase or drastic reductions in defense spending.

In addition, the prospects for major domestic policy change were diminished by several unforeseeable developments. During the crucial first one-hundred days of Bush's term, the White House wasted several precious weeks in an acrimonious controversy over the nomination, ultimately rejected by the Senate, of John Tower as secretary of defense. The administration prolonged the agony and increased the political costs of the defeat by choosing to treat the nomination as a test of the president's power. By the time the White House could turn its attention back to the legislative agenda, the opportunity to exploit the traditional first-year "honeymoon" with Congress had passed.

Moreover, the major item on the legislative agenda was not one of Bush's choosing; it was the governmental response to a rapidly deepening financial crisis in the savings-and-loan industry. Having largely failed to anticipate the magnitude of the industry's financial losses, the White House and Congress were forced to hammer out a plan to liquidate or salvage the insolvent S&Ls, protect the investment of federally insured depositors, and pay the bill. With estimated costs mounting to $148 billion over an eleven-year period, the S&L rescue package absorbed vast chunks of White House, congressional, and public attention, and raised additional barriers to significant achievement in domestic policy.[15]

Finally, the entire domestic agenda, including the S&L rescue, was eclipsed by extraordinary developments in foreign affairs. From the outset of his term, Bush had to deal with the wave of economic and political reform and ultimate collapse of communism in the Soviet Union and Eastern Europe and with the development and then violent suppression of a reform movement in China. Even though the United States had at best marginal influence on these events, the White House had to monitor closely what were by far the most important developments in world politics since the emergence of the cold war. In August 1990, when the White House and Congress would otherwise have been in the last stages of negotiating several important bills, the Iraqi invasion of Kuwait plunged the nation into the most serious military crisis since the Vietnam war.

To obtain significant achievements in domestic policy, therefore, the Bush administration had to overcome the distractions of the Tower affair, the savings-and-loan crisis, the collapse of communism, and the Iraqi invasion and find areas of common interest with congressional Democrats—without producing major increases in federal expenditure. There were some obvious candidates: One compelling interest that Bush shared with the Democrats was to reach a budget agreement that would shrink the deficit and meet the Gramm-Rudman-Hollings targets. Another common interest was to update and reform environmental and regulatory policies, especially by renewing the Clean Air Act, overdue for reauthorization since 1981.

Other issues held less promise for constructive bipartisanship. In a series of controversial decisions interpreting civil rights laws, the Reagan Supreme Court had imposed new constraints on affirmative action programs, putting civil rights policy squarely on Congress's agenda.[16] The Democrats wanted to reverse the Court and strengthen affirmative action, while the Republicans, including Bush, wanted to block any bill that would result in quotas. Both Bush and the congressional Democrats wanted to improve education, help the homeless, rationalize welfare, and combat illicit drugs and the crime associated with them. But meaningful action in pursuit of any of those goals, unlike environmental or civil rights legislation, would require major new federal expenditures. The various opportunities for cooperative presidential leadership were obviously linked. The more success was achieved in reducing the deficit, the greater would be the fiscal capacity for achievement in other areas.

More emphatically than any other modern president, Bush set out to cooperate with Congress and specifically with the rival party. Although he had some particular aptitudes for cooperative leadership, his execution left much to be desired. An affable, patrician gentleman who disliked confrontation, Bush excelled in the skills of encouraging a cooperative disposition among potential opponents. Having served in the House and presided over the Senate as vice-president, Bush was well known and generally liked in Congress. To maintain his relationships and show respect for the institution, he came to Capitol Hill for personal visits with congressional leaders. In a period of a few months he invited every senator and most of the representatives to the White House. Through countless phone calls and handwritten personal notes, he kept in touch with members of Congress of both parties and a host of other Washington acquaintances. Two of Bush's senior aides —the White House Chief of Staff John H. Sununu and Budget Director Richard Darman—sometimes interfered with the good feelings by taking positions in a manner that members of Congress found arrogant. But after the incessant hostilities of the Reagan years, members of Congress and especially Democrats appreciated the atmosphere of harmony.[17]

Yet Bush often failed to take positions and adopt strategies well suited to a cooperative approach. Instead of maintaining the appropriate posture of flexibility about means and rigidity about ends, Bush vacillated—and so was, by turns, flexible and rigid about everything. At times he quickly gave up whatever was needed to get a deal. As the price for peace with Congress on Nicaragua, for example, he struck an agreement that gave each of four committees a veto over aid to the *contras*. As we will see, this relaxed attitude about ends also led Bush to promote lowest-common-denominator agreements in domestic policy.

At other times, Bush refused to make significant concessions, even on minor issues or ones where he lacked the leverage to make his demands stick. Some of his occasional rigidity was perhaps a matter of acting tough just to show his capacity to do so—a way of dealing with the "wimp" factor. In the spring of 1989, for example, after making major concessions to congressional Democrats on strategic weapons and aid to the Nicaraguan *contras,* Bush unexpectedly vetoed a minimum-wage bill over a difference of thirty cents an hour.[18] A more important source of rigidity was Bush's effort to keep his incautious campaign promises about tax policy—a pledge to restore special tax treatment of capital gains and a seemingly unconditional promise not to accept a tax increase. These promises were problematic from the standpoint of budgetary realities; more important, they ignored the need to work with a Democratic Congress. At bottom, Bush's failure to adopt a consistent and flexibly rigid negotiating strategy may have been connected with his lack of much interest in ideas or ideology, criticized as shallowness by such critics as the conservative columnist George Will. An excess of pragmatism may have made it difficult for Bush to focus sufficiently on ultimate objectives.

Finally, in a damaging oversight, Bush overlooked an elementary and essential task of legislative leadership, that of identifying a few major proposals as principal initiatives.[19] The Reagan administration had elevated to a fine art the long-established practice of concentrating congressional and public attention on a few measures defined as central presidential objectives. Remarkably, Bush did not attempt to repeat the performance. Apart from the problematic demand for a capital gains tax reduction, he did not define a legislative program, but allowed Congress or events to set the agenda. As a result, only issues with their own intrinsic necessity—the budget negotiations and the savings-and-loan bailout—acquired prominence or were treated with special urgency. This was a debilitating failure for any form of presidential leadership, cooperative or otherwise.

In short, then, Bush's leadership in domestic policy was hampered by divided government, adverse budgetary and political circumstances, and deficiencies in his execution of a cooperative strategy. To examine the effects of these obstacles, let us review his performance in some central areas of domestic policy.

The Budget Deficit

The central test of Bush's cooperative strategy was whether the administration could reach agreement with Congress on a budget policy to reduce the federal deficit substantially. As the preponderance of economists held, deficit reduction was crucial to the nation's long-term economic health. It was also pivotal to the prospects for cooperative policy change in other areas of domestic policy; only if existing revenues and expenditures could be brought into closer balance could the president and Congress seriously contemplate any significant new expenditures. Moreover, because the failure to act on the budget deficit during the eight years of the Reagan administration was by far the leading current source of concern about divided government, the ability to reduce the deficit was the main test of whether cooperative presidential leadership could make such government work. Arguably, the difficulties under Reagan resulted from the special circumstances of his presidency—the intensity of partisan and ideological conflict and the president's lack of realism about fiscal policy. The results on the deficit under Bush would indicate whether a moderate, pragmatic president pursuing a cooperative strategy would get a better result.

In fact, the Bush administration made bipartisanship a central feature of its budgetary strategy in both 1989 and 1990; but in neither year was shaping the budget a successful exercise in cooperative policy-making. Among other causes of difficulty, Bush was at times flexible about ends (especially deficit reduction) and rigid about means (especially capital gains)—just the opposite of the recommended strategy.

In the development of Bush's first budget, for fiscal 1990, the administration engineered a lowest-common-denominator agreement with the Democratic Congress that avoided hard choices and deferred until future years making genuine progress to reduce the deficit. The Gramm-Rudman Act called for a fiscal 1990 deficit of $100 billion, with a $10 billion cushion, so that projected deficits over $110 billion would result in automatic spending cuts. Reaching the lower figure would require a reduction of $28 billion from the projected 1990 deficit.

While seeking to achieve or at least project that reduction, Bush declined to modify his stand on taxes. (His lips, so to speak, had not yet begun to quiver.) Indeed, despite intense opposition by Democrats, he continued to push for a reduction in the capital gains tax to a maximum rate of 15 percent, from the 28 percent maximum for other income. He argued that the measure would stimulate investment and, by encouraging investors to cash in long-accumulated gains, would increase tax revenues by about $5 billion per year in fiscal 1990 and fiscal 1991.[20] Democrats countered, with better economic evidence, that the reduction would have a minimal effect on investment and pointed out that it would substantially reduce tax revenues and complicate deficit-cutting in the long run.[21] With estimates that most of the benefits would go to taxpayers with annual incomes over $1 million a year, they attacked Bush's proposal as a windfall for the rich.[22]

The administration's initial budget plan, introduced in February, relied largely on one-time savings, highly optimistic economic assumptions, and other shaky devices to project a fiscal 1990 deficit of $91 billion, comfortably below the statutory target. It spelled out spending increases in popular areas, such as education and the space program. But it promised spending cuts without listing them. In short, it denied or covered up the necessity for painful choices and proposed, in effect, to leave the real budget deficit virtually untouched for another year. OMB Director Richard Darman argued that Congress would have declared a more specific budget "dead on arrival," as it had frequently done with Reagan's budgets.[23] But the columnist David Broder, alluding to one of Bush's campaign advertisements that was widely condemned as deceptive, referred to the plan as the "Willie Horton budget."[24]

Although the Democrats criticized Bush as using smoke and mirrors to give the impression of deficit reduction, they did not insist on a more conscientious effort. Instead, both Democratic and Republican congressional leaders joined the White House in summit negotiations to work out a common budget plan, with the president's proposal as the starting point. After nine weeks of private meetings, the White House and congressional leaders announced an agreement that maintained and extended the president's choice to take the easy path to bipartisan cooperation. The plan purported to cut deficits by $28 billion. Said Democratic Senator J. Bennett Johnston: "This budget involves no pain, involves no difficulty, involves no political sacrifice—and it fools no one."[25] A cornerstone of the agreement was $5.3 billion of unspecified revenue increases. Even though everyone knew that not much genuine deficit reduction was being accomplished, the resulting budget resolution sailed through Congress on bipartisan votes with little difficulty.

The process of implementing the budget resolution in revenue, appropriations, and reconciliation bills, however, was made conflictual and uncertain by Bush's refusal to consider tax increases and especially his concerted effort to defeat the Democratic leadership on capital gains. Throughout the summer and early fall, the administration turned up the pressure for the capital gains tax cut. Partly because of the expected short-term revenue gains (which could be used to protect programs or pay for additional tax breaks), some Democrats—including a pivotal group on the House Ways and Means Committee—were willing to support the measure. The resulting standoff between the White House and the Democratic leadership rekindled partisan hostilities and delayed passage of the reconciliation bill.[26]

Nor did the capital gains effort succeed. In October, the new fiscal year began without a reconciliation bill, and the president was required to order $16 billion in across-the-board spending cuts under the Gramm-Rudman law. As intended, the sheer crudeness of those cuts created heavy pressure to reach an agreement that would supersede them. In November, as the congressional session drew near to a close, Bush faced the reality of the vote counts and the likelihood of a Democratic filibuster in the Senate and punted—agreeing to set aside capital gains for the year.[27]

The president used his remaining leverage—enhanced by a threat to veto the reconciliation bill and leave the automatic cuts in place—to pressure Congress to produce a reconciliation bill that would achieve as much as possible of the deficit reduction agreed to in the spring summit. Enacted with broad bipartisan support at the close of the session, the final bill still obtained only about half of that reduction—$14.7 billion—much of it by accounting gimmicks.[28]

In the end, therefore, Bush had managed to secure some outward manifestations of a cooperative budget process—a summit agreement on the concurrent resolution in the spring and a bipartisan final budget package in the fall. But that appearance was misleading. The fight over capital gains had made most of the intermediate steps intensely conflictual. More important, the substance of a constructive agreement was largely lacking. Agreement had been reached, not by resolving differences in a manner that served long-term common interests, but by sweeping difficult choices under the rug. Such a process had not been inevitable. "If there were some leadership somewhere," observed political scientist Allen Schick, "I think people would be willing to talk."

In the following year's deliberations on the fiscal 1991 budget, Bush no longer was in a position to avoid hard choices on the deficit. Congressional budget leaders had warned that the deficit cutting charade of the fiscal 1990 budget could not be repeated for 1991. Indeed, many Democrats had indicated that a second bipartisan agreement would be impossible without a tax increase.[29] But Bush had spent a year reinforcing his campaign pledge not to accept one, which had encouraged many Republican congressmen to make, and frequently repeat, the same pledge. Bush was torn, therefore, between wanting to keep his antitax campaign promise and wanting to work out a deal with the Democrats for significant deficit reductions. Unfortunately, he never made a choice that he was willing to live with. Instead, he went through a series of gyrations that left the budget process in chaos, damaged his party's standing with the voters, and compromised the credibility of his presidency.

Bush's fiscal 1991 budget proposal was an ambitious, partisan starting point for negotiations—with substantial spending cuts for Medicare and other programs favored by Democrats, small defense cuts (despite the rapid evaporation of the cold war), no tax increase, and a new version of the capital gains tax reduction.[30] Again using optimistic economic estimates, the proposal promised a deficit in the modest amount of $36.5 billion—under the Gramm-Rudman target of $64 billion.

Within a few months, however, budget policymakers were facing the prospect of 1991 deficits more than three times that amount. Mostly because of the rapidly escalating costs of salvaging the savings-and-loan industry, OMB's estimates of the 1991 deficit grew from $100 billion in February 1990 to $138 billion in May and then shot up to $231 billion in July.[31] With projected deficits at these levels and accumulating evidence of an approaching recession, few advocated meeting the 1991 Gramm-Rudman target, which would have required tax increases or spending cuts so large that they could push the economy over the edge. Instead, a consensus formed on a revised goal of producing a long-term measure that would cut the deficit by $50 billion in 1991 and $500 billion over a five-year period.[32]

To accomplish deficit reduction of that magnitude, Bush again asked for bipartisan summit talks, which would allow him to avoid taking sole responsibility for the painful proposals that were in the offing. To persuade the Democrats to join the negotiations, however, he was forced to modify his position on taxes. Bush first stated his willingness to negotiate with "no preconditions," a vague expression meant to bring the Democrats to the table without taking responsibility for initiating discussion of a tax increase.[33] This evidence of a more flexible stance was enough to alarm conservative Republicans, some of whom held a news conference to reaffirm their antitax principles. But it was not enough to satisfy the Democrats, who continued during the summit talks to demand a more forthright statement by the president. Finally, in June, Bush openly acknowledged that he was unable to keep his campaign promise and announced, unambiguously, that he would support a negotiated budget package that included a tax increase. Rank-and-file Republicans were outraged at Bush's switch; in fact, the House Republican Conference broke ranks with the president and adopted a nonbinding resolution opposing any tax increase.[34]

Notwithstanding the concession by Bush, the summit talks moved toward agreement at a glacial pace. Represented by Sununu and Darman, the administration continued to insist on a capital gains provision; the Democrats, led by Senate Majority Leader George Mitchell and House Majority Whip Richard Gephardt, demanded a compensating tax increase for high-income families. The negotiators used various procedural techniques to subdue conflict and protect both sides from exploitation: a moratorium on partisan criticism, a requirement that the Republicans and Democrats make major proposals at the same time, and a stipulation that each party would have to deliver a majority of its members in Congress to support the agreement. Nevertheless, the talks were suspended for the August congressional recess with little progress to show for three months of negotiation.[35] Eventually, under pressure of compelling deadlines—the approach of the new fiscal year and the triggering of a massive sequestration of funds under the Gramm-Rudman Act—the administration again abandoned the capital gains tax reduction, and the summit negotiators put together a package of tax increases and spending cuts that the leaders of both parties were willing to support.[36]

Instead of an orderly implementation of the agreement, however, there ensued a period of budgetary chaos. Even with a televised presidential address and a week of intense lobbying by the administration and the bipartisan congressional leadership, it was impossible to sell the budget package to a congressional majority. Some rank-and-file members resented the summit process, which had cut them out of participation. But the main objections were substantive: Conservatives were appalled by the inclusion of a sizable tax increase and the absence of a cut for capital gains, while many liberals were equally outraged by some of the spending cuts, especially a large one for Medicare.[37] When House Republican Whip Newt Gingrich publicly rejected the president's request for support, failure was imminent. Five days into the fiscal year, the summit agreement went down to defeat, 179–254, on the House floor. In the subsequent apportioning of blame, members of Congress complained that the negotiators had failed to assemble a fair package and that arrogant, condescending treatment by Sununu and Darman had alienated potential supporters.

In the aftermath of the defeat, the federal government lacked a budget for almost a month, and Bush, seemingly confused, lacked a strategy. The automatic, across-the-board Gramm-Rudman spending cuts had gone into effect with the beginning of the fiscal year. Nevertheless, to increase the pressure on Congress to pass a budget, Bush vetoed a stopgap spending bill, briefly closing down the government. But he soon relented and allowed the government to continue operating for the duration of the crisis. He also gave conflicting signals about his demands. With the summit disbanded, Bush was forced to react to Democratic proposals—and had difficulty deciding what to do. He changed his mind three times in two days on whether he would accept tax increases for high-income families—leaving congressional leaders confused and causing speculation about the disintegration of his presidency.[38]

Partly because the administration kept up the pressure for major deficit reductions, congressional negotiators did not abandon the summit package, but merely trimmed some of the rough edges—in particular, restoring funds for Medicare and shifting more of the tax burden to high-income families. By the end of October, they had pieced together a modified package of tax increases and spending cuts that claimed 1991 deficit savings of $40 billion and five-year savings of $492 billion. Referred to as Gramm-Rudman III, the measure also established new budget procedures designed to improve future enforcement of deficit targets. Under the circumstances of manifest urgency, both chambers approved the bill by comfortable margins. In the end, there were differing assessments of what had occurred. Senator Warren Rudman expressed a widespread alarm about the chaotic process: "What we are seeing is a very good illustration that divided government doesn't work anymore." Others, like House Speaker Thomas S. Foley, were impressed by the nearly $500 billion in deficit savings: "We ought to have some credit for the fact that this is not an agreeable or easy thing to do."[39]

Few, if any, were impressed by President Bush's performance. In a sense, he deserved a share of the credit that Speaker Foley claimed for Congress; after all, he had certainly taken his share of the political heat. But in a larger sense, he had been a major source of all the difficulties: Both by his own rigidity and by the effect of his rhetoric on other politicians, he had driven federal budgeting to a new level of contention and uncertainty.

A Kinder, Gentler America

Aside from the problem of the budget deficit, the Bush administration had opportunities for cooperation with the Democratic Congress in several other areas of domestic policy. Bush and many congressional Republicans shared with the Democrats an interest in promoting certain social goals as part of keeping his commitment to a "kinder, gentler America." But he also had important differences with them in that he was less willing to cut defense spending or impose additional burdens on taxpayers or industries in order to serve those goals. On such issues Bush negotiated with Congress quite effectively—taking firm and consistent positions and keeping ultimate objectives in focus.

EDUCATION, DRUGS, AND WELFARE

In most areas of domestic policy—including education, antidrug programs, and welfare—significant policy achievements were almost certain to require substantial expenditures. Hard pressed to control budget deficits, Bush in these areas often proclaimed lofty goals, but in fact he supported only modest expansion of federal activities.

With his campaign promise to be the "education president," Bush responded to widespread anxiety about the declining performance of American education and about the ramifications of that decline for the problems of poverty, crime, and international economic competitiveness. He argued, however, that the failures of education were not caused by lack of funds and that the best chances for improvement lay primarily in making better use of existing funds. His education platform consisted mainly of offering modest federal support for a variety of innovations, such as open enrollment, incentive pay for outstanding teachers, and rewards for schools that improve performance with underprivileged children.[40]

Bush's principal education initiative was a fall 1989 education summit conference with the nation's governors in Charlottesville, Virginia. Amid much fanfare, the summit agreed that the White House and the governors would establish national performance standards for education. Combined with a strategy and the necessary resources to achieve those standards, this approach had some promise of fostering improvement. But the effort to implement the standards foundered, with critics pointing to a lack of commitment and leadership by the White House.[41]

In keeping with his campaign doctrine, Bush proposed a modest education program, with $441 million in new funds. Congressional Democrats mostly endorsed the president's proposals, but sought to raise the ante with additional measures of their own. House Education and Labor Committee Chairman Augustus F. Hawkins, for example, introduced a $3.7 billion proposal that responded more fully to the governors. Although Republican committee members were initially angered by the summary dismissal of the president's bill and boycotted the committee meetings for six weeks, a compromise was eventually reached. Representative William D. Ford (D-Mich.) brought together Hawkins and the committee Republicans and worked out an omnibus bill that combined their proposals in a more moderate measure.[42] Considering the stringent budgetary circumstances, Bush's promotion of national education standards and his qualified support for growth in education programs were creditable steps toward fulfilling his campaign promise on education.

There were, if anything, even greater anxieties about drug abuse, especially the rapid spread of crack cocaine and the upsurge in violent crime associated with it. Traditionally, the federal response to drug abuse has emphasized interdiction of supplies and the capture and punishment of drug suppliers—a strategy that, whatever its substantive merits, has much appeal to the electorate. Unfortunately, all efforts to block the distribution of illicit drugs have failed. As experts like Peter Reuter have pointed out, the only antidrug strategies with any real promise are treatment and education, which succeed with some individuals.[43]

The Bush administration partly converted to this view, but neither Bush nor the Democrats advocated funding for treatment or education on a scale that would fully implement it. In August 1989 the president approved the outlines of a $7.5 billion antidrug program, which included a $200 million funding increase for state and local governments and $295 million in economic and military aid for Peru, Bolivia, and Columbia.[44] Critics observed that Bush's request would not sustain a real war on drugs.[45] Moreover, he proposed to pay for it by shifting funds from certain programs with strong Democratic support, including the Economic Development Administration.[46] Just as with education, the Democrats demanded more spending. With the Senate adding $900 million to Bush's proposal, they managed to obtain a certain amount of it. The resulting program approximately doubled federal antidrug spending, but it still assigned state and local governments most of the responsibility and left drug-policy experts unimpressed with the federal effort.[47] Indeed, federal policymakers did not discuss the expensive option of making treatment available to all addicts who are willing to attempt it.

Instead of actual funds and programs, however, Bush's drug strategy relied largely on persuasion and publicity, the portfolio of his outspoken drug czar, William J. Bennett. Using his office as a pulpit, Bennett went around the country giving speeches against drug abuse and threatened to issue report cards on the drug-fighting achievements of state and local governments.[48] Bush's antidrug policy went beyond past federal efforts, but fell short of a program one could expect to produce noticeable results.

Whereas on education and drugs budget difficulties set sharp limits to Bush's initiatives, on welfare policy they kept him from acting at all. Despite reforms enacted in 1987, welfare policy in the late 1980s was by most accounts incoherent, with little coordination across means-tested programs; inequitable, with huge variations in benefit levels across states; and stingy, with average payments having shrunk drastically in real terms during the Reagan administration. There had been no progress in overcoming chronic dependency. To do anything about it, however, was a controversial and expensive proposition. The White House Domestic Policy Council spent months sifting proposals and in August 1990 produced a fifty-page options paper for the president. Judging from reports, the paper did not recommend a presidential initiative on welfare.[49] In any event, none was attempted.

CIVIL RIGHTS AND ENVIRONMENTAL PROTECTION
In some areas of domestic policy—including, notably, civil rights and environmental protection—the issue was not federal spending but the rights and duties of private parties, including industry. The absence of major effects for the federal budget gave the president room to maneuver, but he was still determined to control private-sector costs.

With respect to civil rights, it was ultimately unclear whether the Bush administration and the Democratic-controlled Congress had compatible interests. Civil rights was on the agenda because of a series of Supreme Court decisions, the most important of which was *Wards Cove Packing Co.* v. *Antonio* (1989), that had weakened the legal position of employees seeking redress for alleged employment discrimination. With majorities supplied by Reagan appointees, the Court had ruled, among other things, that employees who claimed that an employer's practices had a "disparate" racial or gender impact had to identify the specific practices at fault (that is, they could not merely point to differential results) and then had to demonstrate that the practices did not serve a legitimate business purpose.[50]

The Democrats, led by Senator Edward M. Kennedy, sought to overturn the decisions and restore the burden of proof to the employer. Some conservatives, led by Senator Orrin Hatch, defended the Court's decisions. Bush, a civil rights moderate with unusual black support for a Republican, was caught in the middle. On the one hand, he had stated his support for affirmative action. On the other hand, he argued that requiring employers to prove that all their employment practices are nondiscriminatory would virtually force them to adopt a quota system; he promised to use his veto power, if necessary, to prevent that outcome.

The result of these conflicts and Bush's ambivalence was a year of difficult negotiations between the White House and Senator Kennedy over the terms of a bill that the president would sign. On a few occasions Bush or Sununu announced prematurely that agreement was at hand and that the president expected to sign a bill.[51] One obstacle to reaching agreement was the sometimes inadequate coordination among the president's staff; Kennedy complained in July 1990 that he had worked out a deal with Sununu only to receive a conflicting offer the same day from White House counsel C. Boyden Gray.[52] The major difficulty, however, was the lack of a basis for mutual accommodation. Because either employers or employees had to bear the burden of proof, one side had to win. Nor was it entirely clear that Bush and Kennedy both wanted to reach agreement; some argued, in particular, that Bush would benefit politically from a veto by solidifying the support of southern and blue-collar whites. At any rate, the two sides did not agree: After adopting only marginal changes to meet the administration's objections, the House and Senate, with support from civil rights groups, passed essentially the Democratic version of the bill. Making good his threats, the president vetoed it. Bush had failed to cooperate with the Democratic Congress, but they may have had nothing to cooperate about.[53]

Probably Bush's principal self-initiated domestic policy accomplishment—one not driven (like deficit reduction and the savings and loan bailout) by impending disaster—was the renewal of the Clean Air Act. It was also a paradigmatic example of cooperative presidential leadership: The administration not only reached agreement with congressional Democrats but helped resolve difficult disputes that cut across party lines.

Subject to periodic reauthorization, the Clean Air Act of 1970 was renewed on schedule in 1977; but the next renewal, scheduled for 1981, failed to occur during the Reagan administration because the White House and Congress had incompatible basic objectives for a revision and because Congress itself was deeply divided.[54] Despite a number of efforts to break the logjam, the country's most important environmental law had to be kept in effect by continuing resolutions for nine years.

There were three major areas of conflict: urban smog (with measures to reduce automobile pollution); toxic air pollution (with measures affecting chemical manufacturers and other industries); and acid rain (with measures limiting industrial furnace emissions, especially from electric power plants). Because of the popularity of environmental control, there was strong support in Congress for tougher standards in each of these areas. But powerful opposition came from the automobile industry, whose chief defender, Representative John Dingell, was chairman of the House Commerce Committee, with jurisdiction over the act; midwestern electric utility companies and the eastern coal industry, which faced potentially massive costs of preventing acid rain; and industry and conservatives in general. In fact, regional and sectoral conflicts were so intense and complicated that some doubted that any bill could obtain a majority in Congress.

Partly to substantiate his campaign promise of environmental leadership, Bush decided early to give high priority to renewing the Clean Air Act. To develop a proposal, the administration assembled a working group with senior officials from several affected agencies, and it consulted elaborately with congressional leaders and spokesmen for industry, environmental groups, and other interests. Introduced in the summer of 1989, the Bush bill sought to strengthen environmental protection without imposing excessive costs on industry. It was relatively easy on the automobile industry, but tougher on toxic air pollution and quite severe with midwestern utilities, which were called upon to pay the piper for a decade of resisting responsibility for acid rain. Of special importance, from the standpoint of cooperation, the bill proposed to expand the use of market-oriented regulatory strategies, such as so-called marketable emissions permits, which economists argued would lead to better environmental protection at lower cost than traditional regulatory methods. Because of their unfamiliarity, among other reasons, market-oriented strategies have been hard to sell to politicians and interest groups. But to the extent that they become politically feasible, they can make possible enormous gains for both environmental and industry interests at the same time.

The introduction of the Bush bill resurrected congressional interest in renewing the Clean Air Act and created an expectation that some bill would pass. It still was not easy; and the Bush administration repeatedly supplied new impetus. At end of 1989, Bush criticized Congress for a lull in activity on the bill. The administration negotiated with Senate liberals to hold down cleanup costs; and it pressured the conservative Dingell and his leading environmentalist opponent, Representative Henry Waxman, to find compromise solutions to several long-standing disputes. Despite numerous amendments, the bill maintained the basic structure of the president's proposal, including the innovative use of market principles. Finally cleared by the conference committee and enacted into law in the fall, the bill was widely greeted as a major achievement.

Implications

On the whole, the record of domestic policymaking in the first two years of the Bush administration is cause for, if anything, added concern about the effectiveness of divided government. As a political moderate with instincts for negotiation, Bush seemed the ideal president to provide cooperative, bipartisan leadership—the only kind of leadership with a chance of success in circumstances of divided-party control. Yet his accomplishments were decidedly modest. Only one major law—the renewal of the Clean Air Act—was crucially a presidential initiative. The budget process nearly broke down. By the summer of 1990, Bush's public approval had dropped sharply, especially for his handling of domestic issues. After the fall budget crisis, it dropped further.[55] One might ask, if George Bush could not make divided government work, who could?

But this view oversimplifies the lesson of Bush's domestic performance and overstates the case against divided government. Three observations should qualify any dire conclusions about the efficacy of government under divided party control. First, domestic policymaking under Bush worked reasonably well in some respects. In the end, the president and Congress adopted a large and well-balanced package of deficit cuts, and they established new procedures to encourage greater budget discipline in the future. The Clean Air Act reauthorization was widely regarded as a success. Additional accomplishments were very limited. But in most other areas of domestic policy, there was little opportunity for significant action. With respect to education, drug abuse, and welfare, policy change was constrained by lack of resources; in civil rights, it was constrained by lack of agreement that change was needed. None of these cases provides strong grounds for an indictment of divided government or the contemporary American political system.

Second, despite Bush's seeming suitability for cooperative leadership, the modesty of his domestic achievements partly reflected his own limitations of style and strategy: his failure to establish a legislative agenda, his willingness to promote lowest-common-denominator agreements, and above all, his penchant for rigidity and rhetorical excess, especially on taxes. In the end, in other words, it is not so difficult to suppose that another president who had set out to attempt cooperative leadership could have accomplished more than Bush did.

Third, to the extent that structural defects in the American political system have contributed to the budget stalemate, it is unclear whether the main problem was divided government or the lack of responsible policy debate in contemporary election campaigns. Bush's rigidity and incautious rhetoric on taxes were a legacy of the 1988 election campaign and his ostensibly unconditional promise to prevent a tax increase. In a period when massive budget deficits, strong public support for domestic programs, and Democratic control of Congress made intense pressure for tax increases foreseeable, a reasonably thorough campaign debate would have made that promise appear simplistic and dubious and rendered its political payoff problematic. That Bush found the promise useful to his election prospects resulted in part from the poverty of debate and criticism in the campaign.[56] In a word, simplistic promises and other kinds of superficial rhetoric work, and work well, in contemporary American electoral politics.

The main structural causes of the impoverished discourse in presidential campaigns are widely recognized. They include, among other things, the concentration by the news media on the strategy and tactics, rather than the substance, of a campaign; the infrequency and brevity of formal presidential campaign debates; and the candidates' heavy reliance on short, often visually oriented television advertisements to address the voters.[57] Under these conditions, voters have an opportunity to learn a good deal about where each candidate stands on a variety of issues. But they receive very little supporting or critical information by which to judge the credibility of those stands. Put differently, the candidates' claims are subjected to minimal reality testing.

Presidential campaigns that trade in wild claims, unrealistic promises, and other careless rhetoric are likely to cause difficulties for the performance of government regardless of whether party control is divided or unified. Under divided-party control, such campaigns will lead to conflict and stalemate, as the president's extreme or irresponsible positions are blocked in Congress. Under unified control, they will lead to extreme or irresponsible *policies,* as a compliant Congress puts the same presidential positions into effect. It is not clear which situation is worse.

If this account is correct, the urgent task in seeking to improve the structural conditions for government performance is not to promote unified-party control. It is to ensure that presidential and other electoral campaigns include coherent and penetrating debate about the major issues facing the nation. Unfortunately, the latter task appears no easier than the former.

Acknowledgment

Energetic and highly competent research assistance by Cheryl Sklar was instrumental in the development of this chapter.

Notes

1. Paul J. Quirk, "The Election," in *The Elections of 1988,* edited by Michael Nelson (Washington, D.C.: CQ Press, 1989), 64–92.

2. John Felton, "Will Bush-Hill Honeymoon Bring Bipartisanship?" *Congressional Quarterly Weekly Report,* 18 February 1989, 332–37.

3. John R. Cranford, "Bush's Thrift Plan Greeted with Caution on Hill," *Congressional Quarterly Weekly Report,* 11 February 1989, 255–58.

4. James L. Sundquist, "Needed: A Political Theory for the New Era of Coalition Government in the United States," *Political Science Quarterly* 103 (1988): 613–35.

5. Ibid., 613.

6. Ibid., 614.

7. For a useful discussion of the potential strengths of divided government, see James P. Pfiffner, "Divided Government and the Problem of Governance," in *Divided Democracy,* edited by James Thurber (Washington, D.C.: CQ Press, 1991), 39–60.

8. Paul J. Quirk, "The Cooperative Resolution of Policy Conflict," *American Political Science Review* 83 (1989): 902–21.

9. Timothy J. Conlan, David R. Beam, and Margaret T. Wrightson, *Taxing Choices: The Politics of Tax Reform* (Washington, D.C.: CQ Press, 1989).

10. Quirk, "Cooperative Resolution of Policy Conflict"; Roger Fisher and William Ury, *Getting to Yes: Negotiating Agreement without Giving In* (Boston: Houghton Mifflin, 1981); William I. Zartman and Maureen R. Berman, *The Practical Negotiator* (New Haven: Yale University Press, 1982).

11. Dean Pruitt, *Negotiation Behavior* (New York: Academic Press, 1982).

12. See George C. Edwards III, "Nowhere to Go and No Way to Get There: Congressional Relations in the Early Bush Administration," *Political Science Teacher* 2 (Summer 1989): 2–4.

13. Murray Weidenbaum, "Facing Reality in the George Bush Era," *Society,* March/April 1989, 25–28.

14. David Rapp, "House, Senate Adopt Versions of $1.17 Trillion Plan," *Congressional Quarterly Weekly Report,* 6 May 1989, 1026–28.

15. John R. Cranford, "Bush Faces Powerful Foes as Bailout Battle Nears," *Congressional Quarterly Weekly Report,* 18 February 1989, 303–5.

16. The major case was *Wards Cove Packing Co.* v. *Antonio* (1989). See Joan Biskupic, "Deal on Civil Rights Measure Stymied by 'Quota' Issue," *Congressional Quarterly Weekly Report,* 14 July 1990, 2225–26.

17. Richard E. Cohen, "The Gloves Are Off," *National Journal,* 14 October 1989, 2508–12.

18. Janet Hook and Chuck Alston, "Mixed Signals, 'Agenda Gap' Plague Bush's First Year," *Congressional Quarterly Weekly Report,* 4 November 1989, 2921–26.

19. James P. Pfiffner, "Establishing the Bush Presidency," *Public Administration Review* 50 (1990): 64–73.

20. "Highlights of President Bush's Budget Proposal," *Congressional Quarterly Weekly Report,* 11 February 1989, 251–54.

21. Ibid.

22. Elizabeth Wehr, "Revenue Package Stalled by Capital Gains Fight," *Congressional Quarterly Weekly Report,* 29 July 1989, 1932.

23. David Rapp, "Bush Sets Course with $1.16 Trillion Budget," *Congressional Quarterly Weekly Report,* 11 February 1989, 250.

24. David S. Broder, "A 'Willie Horton' Budget," *Washington Post,* 15 February 1989, A25.

25. David Rapp, "Bipartisan Pact Lets Everyone Be a Winner—For Now," *Congressional Quarterly Weekly Report,* 22 April 1989, 880.

26. Jackie Calmes, "Bipartisan Pact Set the Stage for Easy Going in the Fall," *Congressional Quarterly Weekly Report,* 2 September 1989, 2245–47.

27. Jackie Calmes, "Bush Drops Gains Tax Drive, Shifts Focus to Deficit," *Congressional Quarterly Weekly Report,* 4 November 1989, 2927–30.

28. Jackie Calmes, "Bush, Congress Reach Deal on Deficit-Reduction Bill," *Congressional Quarterly Weekly Report,* 25 November 1989, 3221–23.

29. Lawrence J. Haas, "Back to the Trenches," *National Journal,* 3 February 1990, 274–76.

30. Jackie Calmes, "Bush Dealing from Strength as Budget Season Opens," *Congressional Quarterly Weekly Report,* 3 February 1990, 299–303.

31. Pamela Fesler, "Summit Talks Go in Circles as Partisan Tensions Rise," *Congressional Quarterly Weekly Report,* 21 July 1990, 2278.

32. Pamela Fesler, "Pressure Mounts for Action When Summiteers Return," *Congressional Quarterly Weekly Report,* 26 May 1990, 1635.

33. Pamela Fesler, "Read My Lips: No Conditions, Bush Tells Democrats," *Congressional Quarterly Weekly Report,* 12 May 1990, 1457–63.

34. Pamela Fesler, "Negotiators Go into Recess No Closer to Compromise," *Congressional Quarterly Weekly Report,* 4 August 1990, 2484.

35. Pamela Fesler, "Negotiators Stuck in Neutral as August Recess Nears," *Congressional Quarterly Weekly Report,* 28 July 1990, 2383–85.

36. The package saved $40 billion in deficits. For the terms, see John R.

Cranford, "Budget Deal Claimed Real Savings: The Devil Lay in the Details," *Congressional Quarterly Weekly Report,* 6 October 1990, 3194.

37. *New York Times,* 6 October 1990.

38. *New York Times,* 10 October 1990; *New York Times,* 11 October 1990.

39. *New York Times,* 28 October 1990.

40. Julie Rovner, Macon Morehouse, and Phil Kuntz, "Bush's Social Policy: Big Ideas, Little Money," *Congressional Quarterly Weekly Report,* 10 December 1988, 3459–65.

41. Burt Solomon, "Vulnerable to Events," *National Journal,* 6 January 1990, 6–10; Dick Kirschten, "Designated Taxers," *National Journal,* 31 March 1990, 774–77.

42. Jill Zuckman, "Measure Grows as House Gives Bush a Lesson in Addition," *Congressional Quarterly Weekly Report,* 21 July 1990, 2317–20.

43. W. John Moore, "Analyzing Strategy for the War on Drugs," *National Journal,* 6 January 1990, 29.

44. *Washington Post,* 8 August 1989.

45. *Washington Post,* 7 September 1989.

46. Lawrence J. Haas, "Battling Is Over Priorities, Not Costs," *National Journal,* 16 September 1989, 2272.

47. Solomon, "Vulnerable to Events."

48. Burt Solomon, "It Takes More Than a Bully Pulpit ... to Wage a War on Drugs," *National Journal,* 13 January 1990, 82–83.

49. Burt Solomon, "On the Domestic Front ... This President Is Aiming Low," *National Journal,* 11 August 1990, 1971.

50. Joan Biskupic, "Partisan Rancor Marks Vote on Civil Rights Measure," *Congressional Quarterly Weekly Report,* 21 July 1990, 2312–16; Dinah Wisenberg, "House Panel Adds Its Stamp to Civil Rights Measure," *Congressional Quarterly Weekly Report,* 28 July 1990, 2418.

51. *Washington Post,* 15 May 1990.

52. Biskupic, "Partisan Rancor Marks Vote on Civil Rights Measure."

53. *Washington Post,* 18 October 1990; *Washington Post,* 19 October 1990; *Washington Post,* 23 October 1990.

54. Margaret E. Kriz, "Politics in the Air," *National Journal,* 6 May 1989, 1098–1102.

55. "Opinion Outlook," *National Journal,* 28 July 1990, 1856; *New York Times,* 14 October 1990.

56. See Quirk, "The Election."

57. Thomas E. Patterson, *The Mass Media Election* (New York: Praeger, 1980).

4

Bush and the Post-Cold-War World: New Challenges for American Leadership

LARRY BERMAN

AND

BRUCE W. JENTLESON

Watch and learn, maybe I'll turn out to be a Teddy Roosevelt.

There is a new world of challenge and opportunities before us, and there's a need for leadership that only America can provide.

No one is more determined to seize from battle the real peace that can offer hope, that can create a new world order. When this is over, the United States, its credibility and its reliability restored, will have a key leadership role in helping to bring peace to the rest of the Middle East. — President George Bush

When scholars look back on the Bush presidency, they will probably note the extraordinary events that characterized President Bush's first twenty-four months in office. The political and military transformation of Europe placed a cap on the post-World War II cold war and the ideologies that sustained it. The breakdown of communist systems in Eastern Europe, the unification of Germany, and the concomitant disintegration of the Warsaw Pact appeared to confirm the inaugural phrases of President Bush that the day of the dictator was over and the totalitarian era was passing. In the words of the new president, "a new breeze" was blowing throughout a world "refreshed by freedom." Yet, despite President Bush's admonition that only America could provide the kind of leadership necessary for this new world of challenges and opportunities, no Bush doctrine or grand design existed for meeting the collective security needs of a new world order—until, that is, the war in the Persian Gulf.

It was then that Bush began to speak of a "new world order," as both the rationale for justifying the massive American military intervention and the vision for the world that would replace the cold war. Undoing the illegal annexation of Kuwait was part of what Bush defined in his 1991 State of the Union Address as "a defining hour." In the president's lexicon, "what is at stake is more than one small country, it is a big idea—a new world order where diverse nations are drawn together in common cause to achieve the universal aspirations of mankind: peace and security, freedom and the rule of law. Such is a world worthy of our struggle, and worthy of our children's future."[1]

It is relevant, if not ironic, to recall that immediately prior to Iraq's 2 August 1990 invasion of Kuwait, President Bush's leadership in foreign policy tended to be characterized as more *reactive* than *proactive;* more *adrift* than *imaginative*. One observer referred to the Bush administration (distinct from the events that surrounded it) as the Revlon presidency, a reference to the President's inclination to identify serious problems but offer only cosmetic solutions.[2] Bush as the "reactive president," first labeled by the columnist David Broder, posed the danger of becoming increasingly "constrained by circumstances not of his making. His leadership will inevitably come to be questioned. To exercise the full range of his constitutional powers, a president must be able to launch and sustain initiative of his own, not just wait for 'others' and then figure out how to react."[3] *U.S. News & World Report* titled its first-year appraisal of the Bush presidency "The Year of Living Timorously." Bush was characterized as "reluctant"; a "nonideological caretaker."[4] In a similar first-year assessment of the Bush presidency, the *National Journal* noted that "in these topsy-turvy times, George Bush—more than most other Presidents—may see events fix his fate. His could be a memorable presidency—or be ignored by history."[5]

Saddam Hussein guaranteed that George Bush would not be ignored by history. In January 1991 *Time* identified the George Bush of foreign policy as its "Man of the Year" for displaying "a commanding vision of a new world order."[6] By the end of January, the president had become a war leader, and public approval of his leadership stood at unprecedented levels. In the war's immediate aftermath, President Bush basked in broad domestic and international approval for his handling of the crisis. Yet ambiguities in the new world order as well as the disorderliness of the postwar peace have raised questions bearing on history's ultimate judgment of the Bush presidency. Which George Bush is the real foreign policy one: the reactive president of 1989 and April 1991 or the commanding-vision president of 2 August 1990–

26 February 1991, the footnote-to-history president or the central actor in a new world order? Let us look first at the content and context of the global transition and then go on to issues of process and policy between 1989 and 1991.

The Global Transition

Dean Acheson titled his memoirs *Present at the Creation;* George Bush might title his memoirs "Present at the Collapse." The cold war has ended, and a post-cold-war world has begun to emerge. The break with the past is not to-tal—it never is—but the transition is as profound as any that has occurred since the late 1940s, involving the very structure of the international system, the sources of international power and influence, and the composition of the global agenda.

In structural terms, world politics is no longer about two blocs squaring off. In 1989 and 1990 the United States and the Soviet Union, the two former irreconcilable adversaries, demonstrated a degree of cooperation not seen since their World War II alliance against Hitler. Moreover, on the one side, the Soviet bloc simply no longer exists, and the future of the Soviet Union itself is questionable, mired as it is in an economic quagmire and torn by secessionist movements, with the country looking less like a superpower and more like an Ottoman "sick man of Europe." On the other side, the Western alliance is showing signs of its own period of transition. While the United States, Western Europe, and Japan continue to share fundamental interests, the strains and tensions of policy conflicts and mutual misunderstanding are increasing.

Related to this structural transformation is the shift in the relative value of military and economic "currencies" of international power. Military power remains a valuable currency, as the war in the Persian Gulf again demonstrated. It always will. But the fact remains that the end of the cold war has devalued military power somewhat in relative terms. Economic power, in contrast, has appreciated in value, becoming more of a "hard power" currency as a function of ever increasing global interdependence. Yet, as reflected in George Bush's statement in his Inaugural Address that "we have the will, but not the wallet," the United States is strapped by its largely self-inflicted triple deficit in its budget, its trade balance, and its international financial position. "The changes in power," observes Stanley Hoffmann, "limit the ability of the United States to set the rules and to provide the solutions."[7]

The third key aspect of the global transition can be seen in the new issues added to the global agenda. Again, it no longer is nuclear deterrence and anticommunist containment with all else subsumed as "low politics." The global environment, the international drug trade, the persisting and impover-ishing Third World debt crisis, hunger, and development—while pushed to the background by the Gulf War—are issues likely to reexert pressure for greater attention from U.S. foreign policy.

These foreign policy changes of a transitional age have constituted the context in which the Bush administration has pursued its foreign policy. As we see in this chapter, in some instances they have demanded precisely the strengths George Bush brought to the presidency, especially his skills as a cri-sis manager and deft diplomat. Yet, in other respects they have drawn out Bush's foreign policy flaws and failings, particularly with respect to the need for adaptation and innovation and for strong domestic political and policy leadership.

The Domestic Side of Bush Foreign Policy
POLITICAL CONTEXT FOR EVALUATING BUSH'S LEADERSHIP

> So far today, I've said the Pledge and I haven't joined the ACLU and I haven't furloughed any murderers. I've delivered on my entire mandate, and it isn't even lunch yet.—*Doonesbury* cartoon on Day 1 of the Bush Presidency

George Bush is the first sitting vice-president to succeed to the presidency since Martin Van Buren did so in 1837. The election of 1988 marked the first time since 1928 that the country did not change political parties when it changed presidents. The aftermath of the election left the legislative branch firmly controlled by Democrats, who would increase their numerical advan-tage in the 1990 midterm election. In many respects the Bush agenda *was* the Reagan legacy.[8] That legacy included Reagan's shift from cold warrior to pre-sider over the cold-war's eleventh hour. President Reagan received his strong-est popular approval ratings in the area of reducing the chances of nuclear war with the Soviets. Images of Ronald Reagan and Mikhail Gorbachev strolling together through Red Square in May 1988 in the bliss of *glasnost* and *perestroika,* as well as their five summit meetings, had a profound impact on public perceptions and expectations, and on the perceptions of the vice-presi-dent in fashioning his agenda for leadership.

The public expects its leaders to be ideological and noncompromising, pragmatic and flexible. It can be a no-win situation for a president, a funda-mental paradox of presidential leadership. Throughout the 1988 presidential election, Democratic candidate Michael Dukakis urged voters to support him because the election was about "competence, not ideology." He was correct; neither candidate could lay claim to the title of ideologue. The 1988 election was waged over taxes, prison furloughs, death sentences, and the Pledge of Allegiance. There were also the images of Willie Horton leaving prison and Michael Dukakis riding in a tank, but there was very little articulation of a foreign policy blueprint for the next decade.

During the 1988 presidential campaign, Vice-President George Bush promised to "stay the course"; once in office, President Bush started off by attempting to stabilize and build on Reagan foreign policies. Bush, unlike Reagan, chose not to wage *ideological* warfare in choices over policy or personnel appointments. The new president had no mandate to dismantle his predecessor's legacy; instead, he was expected to extend it. As one aide put it, "Prudence is the president's anchor and democracy his sail."[9]

The nonideological context of the Bush administration did not seem to trouble the American public, which consistently approved of Bush's handling of the job. Approval ratings during his first year hovered well above 70 percent, and by most accounts, Bush is extremely attentive to these polls. Personal diplomacy replaced or at least stood in the place of a clearly articulated doctrine for foreign policy; critics called it rudderless, but it simply lacked an ideological base (eventually causing a rift between conservative Republican leaders and the more moderate Bush). "If ideology was the engine of the Reagan foreign policy," wrote Maureen Dowd and Thomas L. Friedman, "instinct drives the Bush foreign policy. Bush instinct and Baker instinct. Over the years, both men have often seemed at a loss when pressed to articulate what issues they hold dear or what they believe in. Peace, they might answer, or fairness. Their foreign policy vision, in essence, amounts to 'we know best.' They regard themselves as good people who will do the correct thing and, if circumstances permit, the right thing."[10]

PRESIDENTIAL POWER

In his seminal contribution to our understanding of presidential leadership, political scientist Richard Neustadt focused on the power problem that confronted the person inside the White House.[11] The president's formal powers, Neustadt maintained, are really no guarantee of influence; successful leadership requires that the White House occupant be an expert politician (persuasion is bargaining, in the sense that the president needs to convince others that they ought to do what the president wants because it is in their interest to do so). These "others" are important constituencies that include members of Congress, political parties, the general public, foreign leaders, the media, and the executive branch. A president must zealously guard his power prospects by making certain that the advisory process does not insulate him from frank and objective debate about options. The president must always nurture his relationship with the Washington and international communities because, as president, he needs their cooperation in order to get what he wants done actually to be done. The president need not bargain or persuade on every issue of policy because the presidency as an institution often inspires its own kind of loyalty. Moreover, as Bush has demonstrated by the frequency of his use of the veto, the president possesses a wide range of unilateral command powers that may be used to accomplish policy objectives. Nevertheless, in a divided and fragmented political system, the president often resembles a large Gulliver tied down by thousands of cords.[12] Neustadt's framework still provides useful clues for helping us understand the keys to presidential leadership.

What are we to make of George Bush? First, as the opening quotation from the president reveals, Bush sees himself in the mode of a strong steward president, like Teddy Roosevelt. Indeed, Bush has replaced the cabinet room portrait of Calvin Coolidge with that of the first and only Republican Roosevelt. Sidney Blumenthal notes in his comparison of Bush and Roosevelt that "in the Oval Office itself, Bush strategically placed not one but two sculptures of his new hero—as if to suggest the two roles through which Roosevelt so skillfully defined his glittering public career: the dude and the Rough Rider."[13] Like Roosevelt, Bush is a strong protector of presidential prerogatives, especially in foreign affairs. As we show in a later section, Bush has been willing to challenge Congress with the threat and use of the veto. As America's first modern president, Teddy Roosevelt fashioned an independent foreign policy in the role of commander-in-chief. George Will recently observed that Bush, "who recently blurted out that he much prefers dealing with foreign policy than with people and problems here at home, may get his implicit wish: he may become, essentially, Secretary of State."[14]

President Theodore Roosevelt, it should be recalled, deployed military forces abroad without the full (if any) consultation with Congress, "took Panama," sent the U.S. fleet around the world, secretly agreed to recognize Japan's hegemony in Korea and Manchuria, and won the 1906 Nobel Peace Prize. With respect to his uncompromising worldview, Roosevelt believed that "peace cannot be had until the civilized nations have expanded in some shape over the barbarous ones." Compare this view with President Bush's articulation of U.S. goals in the Persian Gulf: "to defend civilized values around the world ... a world where the rule of law supplants the rule of the jungle."[15] Following a ten-day retreat to Camp David some two weeks prior to war in the gulf, President Bush attended a 2 January 1991 senior staff meeting and told his aides, "I've had a lot of time to think about the situation in the Middle East, I've reconciled all the moral issues. It's black versus white, good versus evil."[16] Indeed, it can be argued that Bush the pragmatist all but disappeared in his war of words with Saddam Hussein. Suddenly the president was on a moral crusade, much like Teddy Roosevelt. In a 29 January 1991 speech to the National Association of Religion Broadcasters, the president invoked the Bible, Lincoln, and Thomas Aquinas in justifying that the coalition was "on the side of God." In Bush's words, "the first principle of a just war is that it support a just cause. Our cause could not be more noble."

STYLE

In foreign policy, George Bush's operating style has been characterized as one of "Rolodex" diplomacy—the President works the phone much as Lyndon Johnson did, and has learned that the fundamental operating principle of a politician is dividing any number by two and adding one.[17] Believing that "goodwill begets goodwill," Bush many times demonstrated his flexibility—for example, by backing off from one of the cardinal principles of his predecessor in not negotiating with terrorists. Thus he sent a personal card to Iranian President Rafsanjani and placed calls to Kings Hussein, Hassan, and Fahd; Prime Ministers Ozal and Thatcher; Chancellor Kohl; and Presidents Mubarak and Bendjedid; and the pope—all in the span of a day with the intent of securing the release of U.S. hostages.

The Bush style is also one of sheer energy and personal warmth. With respect to energy, none of his predecessors has traveled as much or as far in pursuit of personal diplomacy. By the end of 1990, Bush had visited twenty-nine countries, almost as many as Reagan did after eight years in office (see table 4.1). As of 23 January 1991, Bush had traveled 267,072 miles, a number that may well have been higher except for the president's "grounding" during the Gulf War.[18]

There is a general consensus that George Bush tends to be cautious and pragmatic, having earned the childhood nickname "Have Half." The selections of James Baker III as secretary of state, Brent Scowcroft at the National Security Council, and John Tower/Richard Cheney at the Defense Department were based on pragmatic and friendship criteria, not ideology. "I would hate to be President without friendships ... not just the loneliness of it, but the barrenness of it...." Bush told the *New York Times*.[19]

Bush is clearly more decisive than Jimmy Carter and more in charge than Ronald Reagan. As the Gulf War strategy proceeded, it became evident that Bush does not micromanage decision making; neither does he overdelegate responsibility. He did not become a prisoner of the White House, as did Lyndon Johnson and Jimmy Carter.

THE BUSH TEAM: PROFESSIONALS AND BUDDIES

Bush's principal foreign policy appointees have two characteristics in common: (1) They all are professionals, with substantial previous foreign policy or

TABLE 4.1
BUSH AND FOREIGN TRAVEL: THE FIRST TWO YEARS

1989

24–29 February   Bush travels to the Far East to attend the funeral of Emperor Hirohito of Japan. Visits Japan, China, and South Korea. Meets with nineteen national leaders gathered for the funeral. Included were Juan Carlos of Spain, Corazon Aquino of the Philippines, Hosni Mubarak of Egypt, Chaim Herzog of Israel, Noburo Takeshita of Japan, Deng Xiaoping and Zhao Ziyang of China, and Roh Tae Woo of South Korea.

Mid-June   Bush travels to Brussels, Belgium, for NATO alliance summit. Meets with most Western European (NATO) leaders and introduces proposal on short-range nuclear forces.

Mid-July   Bush travels to France, Poland, and Hungary. Meets with Eastern bloc leaders to discuss the future of American aid. Attends the "green" summit in Paris as well as the bicentennial celebration of the French Revolution. At that summit were most European leaders.

2–3 December   Bush travels to Malta to meet with Mikhail Gorbachev and discusses a wide variety of issues regarding superpower relations, troop cuts in Europe, and the future of Eastern Europe. Following the meeting in Malta, Bush flies to Brussels to meet with NATO leaders and brief them about the summit.

1990

15 February   Bush travels to Cartagena, Colombia, for a one-day drug summit with South American Presidents Barco (Colombia), Garcia (Peru), Paz Zamora (Bolivia). On the agenda was the signing of the Declaration of Cartagena, a document designed to create a framework for fighting the drug war.

10 April   Bush meets with Canadian Prime Minister Brian Mulroney in Toronto. The leaders discuss East-West relations, trade, free trade, Eastern Europe, NATO, and Mulroney's recent trips to Mexico and the Caribbean.

Early July   Bush attends the NATO summit in London to discuss that organization's future in the light of changes in Europe and the coming of 1992.

Mid-September   Bush meets with Mikhail Gorbachev in Helsinki, Finland, for a weekend summit to discuss the Persian Gulf crisis and other issues.

TABLE 4.1 — *Continued*

Thanksgiving	Bush travels to Europe and then to the Middle East to drum up support for a UN resolution supporting the American efforts against Saddam Hussein and to spend the holiday with troops stationed there. While there, he meets with Syrian President Assad to bolster his support.
26–27 November	Bush spends time in Mexico negotiating U.S.–Mexican relations with President Salinas.
4 December	Bush goes to Brazil and meets President Fernando Collor de Mello; goes to Uruguay and meets President Luis Albert Lacalle.
5 December	Bush goes to Argentina and meets with President Carlos Menem.
6 December	Bush goes to Chile and meets with President Patricio Aylwin.
7–8 December	Bush goes to Venezuela and meets with President Carlos Andres Perez.

SOURCES: *Time, Newsweek, U.S. News & World Report,* and *Congressional Quarterly.* See Richard Reeves, "On the Road with George Bush," *Sacramento Bee,* 7 December 1990, B10.

other relevant governmental experience; and (2) they all are long-time friends or associates of George Bush. This mix of "professionals and buddies" has had both benefits and drawbacks for the administration's decision making and agenda setting.

Bush wasted no time in nominating James Baker to be secretary of state; the announcement was made the morning after election day. Few were surprised, and few were critical. The Bush-Baker friendship goes back over twenty years and includes Baker's roles as campaign manager of Bush's 1980 presidential bid and campaign chairman in 1988. Theirs is virtually a kinship; they share a combination of patrician ideals of public service with partisan competitiveness and personal ambition— "steel with an overlay of tennis," as two journalists aptly characterized it.[20] Baker also had won substantial praise from the press and from Democrats in Congress for being the pragmatist among ideologues in the Reagan White House. Baker's stint as treasury secretary in the second Reagan term gained him some experience in international affairs.

As national security adviser, Bush appointed Brent Scowcroft. Scowcroft boasted impeccable credentials: national security adviser in the Ford administration (to which his relationship with Bush dates), retired air force lieutenant general, Ph.D. from Columbia University, chairman of the 1983 Scowcroft Commission on the MX missile and arms control, member of the 1987 Tower Commission investigating the Iran/*contra* affair. Scowcroft's reputation in press, political, and even academic circles as a respected strategist contrasted nicely with the questionable credentials of such Reagan appointees as Richard Allen, Robert McFarlane, and John Poindexter. His low-key, behind-the-scenes operating style also played much better than the more abrasive and contentious styles of predecessors Henry Kissinger and Zbigniew Brzezinski.[21]

Bush's major appointment blunder was John Tower. The fight over Tower's nomination as secretary of defense hurt Bush politically, although the costs were contained by the shrewd political stroke of nominating Richard ("Dick") Cheney to replace Tower. Cheney also is a man with a long résumé: White House chief of staff in the Ford administration, congressman from Wyoming since 1978, member of the House Intelligence Committee, ranking member of the House Iran/*contra* investigative committee, and newly elected House Republican Whip (a position into which Newt Gingrich then moved). The Senate unanimously confirmed Cheney within a week of his nomination.

The fourth key team member is the chairman of the Joint Chiefs of Staff, General Colin Powell. Powell emerged during the Reagan years, first as a top Defense Department aide and then as the national security adviser appointed in the wake of the Iran/*contra* scandal, as a man in uniform who stood for everything that Oliver North did not. Powell was so highly respected and popular that some Republican strategists touted him in 1988 as a possible vice-presidential nominee. His highly favorable reviews in the Gulf War prompted comparisons to General Dwight Eisenhower and speculation about a future presidential candidacy.

As a team, Bush and his appointees generally have been regarded as competent and cohesive, especially in comparison to recent administrations. Even those who disagree with their decisions do not question their competence. Nor have there been any deep and bitter fissures, such as Kissinger vs. Rogers or Vance vs. Brzezinski or Weinberger vs. Shultz. Yet there have been some internal conflicts. For example, through at least mid-1990, there was a Cheney vs. Baker split over policy toward the Soviet Union. Defense Secretary Cheney took an only slightly modified hard line of continuing concern about the Soviet military threat and persisting skepticism about the durability of the changes in Soviet politics and policy. Secretary of State Baker, although hardly an advocate of disarmament or entente, put much greater emphasis on the significance of the changes that had taken place and was much more eager to take steps to continue to improve relations. Others also entered the fray, notably Robert M. Gates, the deputy national security adviser, whose hard-line speech Baker suppressed in late October 1989, and CIA Director William Webster, who testified to Congress in March 1990 that best intelligence estimates were that even if Gorbachev fell, the Soviet Union would not pose a serious military or political threat for the foreseeable future.[22]

Another intra-administration conflict has been over global environmental policy. Here the principal rivals have been White House Chief of Staff John Sununu and Environmental Protection Agency Administrator William Reilly. Sununu's reputation as an anti-environmentalist dates back to his support for the Seabrook nuclear power plant when he was governor of New Hampshire. In October 1989 he rejected Reilly's proposal that the United States host the next international conference on global warming. The conference instead was held in Geneva the following year, and Reilly was forced to go carrying a White House-written list "of caveats and weakening amendments."[23] This issue has continued to be a contentious one.

Beyond such specific policy conflicts, there has also been concern that the Bush team is too tightly drawn and too homogeneous. Bush may see himself as using his close friends/top advisers, as he put it, as "a catalyst for decision making or bull sessioning."[24] The less-positive view, as expressed by James David Barber, is that "Bush wants twins around him and that can be dangerous."[25] Even the conservative columnist William Safire remarked on the "absence of creative tension [which] has generated little excitement or innovation ... as a result of the Bush emphasis on the appearance of unanimity, we miss the Rooseveltian turbulence that often leads to original thinking."[26] (We note here that Safire is referencing the second Roosevelt, the model of Neustadt's classic chapter, "Men in Office.") A further problem is that the smallness of the circle shuts expertise and information out of the decision-making process. This has been a particular criticism of Baker and his small circle of aides within the State Department, largely closing out experienced career foreign service officers and other experts. This partly explains the administration's weaknesses in policy innovation. And while it has yet to happen, the concern remains that too closed and tightly drawn processes for policy formulation and decision making could produce seriously flawed and even disastrous policies.

BUSH AND CONGRESS

In his relations with Congress, George Bush has appeared torn between two conflicting sides of his political persona. There is George Bush the politician: nonconfrontational, nonideological, pragmatic, willing to learn to live with divided government. But there also is George Bush the presidentialist, the jealous guardian of executive prerogatives in the conduct of foreign policy, who by December 1990 had vetoed twenty public bills. We have seen evidence of each of these dispositions during Bush's first two years.

When Ronald Reagan called for bipartisanship in foreign policy, for "Republicans and Democrats standing united in patriotism and speaking with one voice," the one voice was meant to be his, with Congress merely joining in at the refrains. George Bush tried to change the tune right from the start. "We've had a chorus of discordant voices," he stated in his Inaugural Address. "We need harmony," an objective toward which he pledged that this was to be "the age of the offered hand." He even tried to include Congress in his "buddy-ship," showing up at the House gym for a workout and inviting key congressional Democrats to private dinners at the White House.

The same theme was struck by the secretary of state designate, James Baker, in his confirmation hearings. "Simply put," Baker stressed in his prepared remarks, "*we must have bipartisanship to succeed.*" Baker went on to emphasize three "principles" of a bipartisan foreign policy: "First, *trust* that we each have the public interest in mind.... Second, *consultation,* that we are trying to communicate.... Third, *consistency,* that our decisions and agreements once arrived at, are, in fact, decisions and agreements that will be kept." Baker, too, put this forward more as a compact than a threat.[27]

The Reagan-Bush contrast was especially evident on Nicaragua and South Africa, with compromise replacing confrontation. Nicaragua during the Reagan years stands along with Vietnam as one of the most bitter cases in U.S. history of interbranch conflict over foreign policy. It was not only the constant battle over *contra* aid but also the tone and tenor of the debate, as when White House Communications Director Patrick Buchanan posed an upcoming vote as a patriotism litmus test of whether Democrats stood "with Ronald Reagan ... or Daniel Ortega."[28] And then, of course, there was the Iran/*contra* affair, the essence of which was an executive branch willing intentionally to deceive the legislative branch, even to the point of breaking the law of the land.

The lesson Bush and Baker learned from all this was that Nicaragua had to be gotten off the agenda as quickly as possible if it was not to get relations with Congress off to a wrong start. They thus negotiated with, rather than bashed, their congressional opponents. And, within two months, they had worked out a bipartisan compromise agreement on *contra* aid. Concessions were made on both sides, the Bush administration giving up on military aid and Congress agreeing to continue to fund the *contras* at all. And the benefits went beyond the specifics of Nicaragua policy. As Congressman David Obey (D-Wisc. and chairman of the House Foreign Operations Appropriations Subcommittee) put it, "It's nice to sit down with an administration official ... and not be considered an enemy of your country."[29]

A second contrast can be seen in the politics of South African sanctions. From the outset, the Reagan administration hailed its new policy of "constructive engagement" as being about "old friends ... who are getting back together again."[30] Critics, however, saw nothing constructive about it. In 1986 Congress passed the Anti-Apartheid Act, which included broad mandatory trade sanctions. Reagan vetoed the bill, despite the urgings of key Republican congressional leaders to work out a compromise. And for the first time in thirteen years, since President Nixon's veto of the War Powers Resolution, Congress overrode a presidential veto on a foreign policy issue.

As vice-president, Bush had toed the Reagan administration line. But here too, as president he showed his pragmatism. A deal was struck in October 1989 in which congressional proponents of additional sanctions deferred their legislation, and the Bush administration pledged not to seek to lift, and to enforce more conscientiously, existing sanctions (on which the Reagan administration had been intentionally lax). There even was acknowledgment by the assistant secretary of state for African affairs that the sanctions had been effective, that "sanctions have played a role in stimulating new thinking within the white power structure."[31] Then, when Nelson Mandela came to the United States in June 1990, after having been freed from prison four months earlier, George Bush was prominent among those to greet and hail him.

Yet, on a broad range of other issues, Bush has been willing to confront Congress and assert executive authority. The reasons have been a mix of policy conflict and claims of institutional prerogatives. This was especially evident, as we discuss in more detail later in the chapter, in the conflict over China policy following the Tiananmen Square massacre. But this was not strictly an isolated episode. Bush vetoed numerous other foreign-policy-related bills. He vetoed the congressional resolution restricting the FS-X deal with Japan, accusing Congress of exceeding its constitutional power to regulate foreign commerce and of having "intrude[d] into areas entrusted by the Constitution exclusively to the executive."[32] He vetoed the 1989 foreign-aid appropriations bill on the grounds that its restriction of Iran/*contra* "leveraging" of aid to get foreign governments to take actions that the U.S. government could not was an infringement of the executive's right to conduct diplomacy. He also pocket-vetoed the fiscal year 1991 intelligence authorization bill, asserting that its tightened reporting requirements for contacts with foreign governments related to possible covert actions "could have a chilling effect on the ability of our diplomats to conduct highly sensitive discussions."[33] And in the midst of the buildup to war with Iraq, even when he was stressing the threat of Iraqi chemical weapons, he vetoed a chemical weapons sanctions bill, claiming that it would hurt U.S. exports, that it would offend some of our partners in the anti-Iraq multinational coalition, and that its mandatory nature would unduly constrain presidential authority. (The next Congress passed a virtually identical bill in February 1991, in the middle of the war; this time the President signed it.)

Then there was the tension over war powers in the Iraqi crisis. Congress was strongly supportive of the initial deployments of Operation Desert Shield. When Bush delivered a televised speech to the nation on 12 September, the House majority leader, Richard Gephardt, served up the Democratic party's response: "In this crisis, we are not Republicans or Democrats. We are only proudly Americans. The President has asked for our support. He has it." Even traditional liberals, such as Senate Foreign Relations Committee Chairman Claiborne Pell, initially took the position that to invoke the 1973 War Powers Resolution "would upset the applecart." Instead, in early October, both chambers overwhelmingly passed resolutions supporting "the deployment by the President of the United States Armed Forces to the Persian Gulf region in response to Iraq's military aggression" (380–29 in the House, 96–3 in the Senate).[34]

The tensions with Congress emerged when Bush announced on 8 November a doubling of U.S. forces, to over 400,000 troops, and a shift in strategy to mounting "an adequate offensive military option." Part of the problem was procedural. Up to this point, the Bush administration had consulted reasonably closely with Congress, yet this major shift in strategy was revealed without any prior consultation with the congressional leadership and two days after the midterm election, as a "November surprise." But the conflict also was a substantive one over strategy. Even in its earlier resolutions, Congress had qualified its support as intended for a strategy that, while coercive, emphasized "the use of *diplomatic* and other *nonmilitary* means while maintaining credible United States and multinational *deterrent* military force" (emphases added). The economic sanctions were working, contended a number of key congressional Democrats (including Senate Armed Services Committee Chairman Sam Nunn, Senate Majority Leader George Mitchell, House Speaker Thomas Foley, and Majority Leader Gephardt), and would achieve our objectives if we just gave them more time. Senator Nunn's committee held major hearings, bringing in a number of prestigious witnesses (including two former chairmen of the Joint Chiefs of Staff) in support of the stick-with-sanctions position.

The issue came to a head in early January 1991. The Bush administration had pushed a resolution through the UN Security Council setting a 15 January deadline for Iraqi withdrawal from Kuwait and authorizing any member state to use "all necessary means" after that date (Resolution 678, the twelfth UN resolution since the crisis began to support the U.S. position).

Bush claimed that with the UN resolution in hand and on the basis of his constitutional authority as commander-in-chief, he could go to war after 15 January without a formal declaration of war by Congress. It was politically risky to do so, though, without even the semblance of congressional authorization.

Right up to the eve of war, the American public was ambivalent about going to war. But criticisms also were mounting of Congress as politically spineless for not taking a position one way or the other. For the Democrats in Congress, the political dilemma was a particularly tough one. Did sanctions really still have a chance to get Iraq out of Kuwait? Or did the "stiff arm" (Bush's phrase) given to Secretary Baker at Geneva by Iraqi Foreign Minister Tariq Aziz mean that war truly had become a last resort? And, politically, should the Democrats again take a stand against the use of force and as "the party of peace," or did they risk further reinforcing their post-Vietnam "wimp" image?

Finally, on 11 and 12 January the House and Senate voted on identical resolutions "to authorize the use of United States Armed Forces pursuant to United Nations Security Council Resolution 678." The resolutions passed by votes of 250–183 in the House and 52–47 in the Senate. The Democratic leadership in both chambers opposed the resolutions, and their party voted 179–86 and 45–10 against them. Enough Democrats supported the President, though, to give him the political base he needed. The first attacks on Baghdad came on 16 January.[35]

In sum, in Bush's relations with Congress, we have a president who on the one hand is a pragmatic, mainstream man with political instincts for making deals and avoiding confrontation, yet on the other hand has strong and deep presidentialist inclinations and sees executive imperatives in the conduct of foreign affairs. This has been a much less bitter mix than with previous administrations, but one that still has made for interbranch relations consistent with Edward Corwin's classic characterization of "an invitation to struggle ... for the privilege of directing American foreign policy."[36]

Major Foreign Policy Issues

Rather than attempt to cover all foreign policy issues of the first two years of the Bush administration, we focus on four key areas: China, Latin America (particularly Panama and Nicaragua), Soviet Union/post-cold-war Europe, and the Gulf War. These issues have had major importance in their own right and illustrate some of the broader patterns discussed in preceding sections of this chapter.

CHINA

Bush's pragmatism or penchant for splitting the difference manifested itself when the administration confronted its first major international crisis in June 1989 as Chinese soldiers marched on Tiananmen Square and killed hundreds of prodemocracy protesters. The massacre occurred less than six months after Bush entered office and took place in a nation dear to the president. Bush had served as American envoy in China during the mid-1970s.

The government crackdown came at a time when the breakdown of communism was making its way across Europe. A visit by Gorbachev to China about one month before the 3–4 June massacre seemed to incite the (mostly) student-led protests. The government, led by Deng Xiaoping, retaliated hard against the protesters, with military action resulting in hundreds of deaths. Additionally, access to the Voice of America was cut off, and official Chinese news censored any transmissions of the urban-based events to the hundreds of millions of peasants living in the countryside.

The initial American reaction was to issue a criticism of the Chinese actions, provide sanctuary to dissident Fang Lizhi and his wife, suspend military sales and high-level official contacts, express opposition to international loans to China, and issue advisory notices for American tourists heading to China. Bush also extended for twelve months the visas of the 70,000 Chinese students studying in the United States.

But these rather severe penalties later were amended by Bush's pragmatic approach to postcrisis relationships. The president clearly views China as a vital part of the American foreign policy structure. The Chinese government's outrage at the extension of the student visas was expressed to the American ambassador to Beijing. On 30 November 1989, President Bush vetoed a bill sponsored by Representative Nancy Pelosi of California that would have extended the students' stay for up to four years. Despite much criticism of the veto, Bush explained that his issuance of an administrative order would provide for basically the same privileges, but allow him to keep control of foreign policy making. "I want to keep control of managing the foreign policy of this country as much as I can. And I didn't think that legislation was necessary.... I do not want to isolate the Chinese people.... We have contacts with countries with egregious records on human rights, so I'm going to keep looking for ways to find common ground."[37]

The impetus for Bush's statement was a secret mission by Brent Scowcroft and Lawrence Eagleburger to Beijing with the hopes of moving toward the establishment of renormalized relations. While Bush readily acknowledged China's human rights violations, he also argued that its influence in the region with regards to Afghanistan and Cambodia mandated the attempt to make U.S.-China relations "business as usual." Professor Arthur Waldron provided a perceptive analysis of Bush's convictions on China: "One, American intervention can make a difference in China's future, particularly if it takes the form of personal diplomacy. Two, the possibility of making such a difference is important enough to justify accepting substantial political damage at home. China holds primacy in Asia and has the potential to be a world superpower. Three (a carefully hedged but nevertheless detectable belief), China is somehow different enough to be partially exempted from the moral considerations that increasingly guide and constrain American policies everywhere."[38]

The initial public steps taken by Bush, coupled with the low-key attempts to reestablish normal relations, possessed the markings of the Bush imprint: Practical politics came first. A presidential news conference illustrates this key point:

> *Q:* Do you have any second thoughts about the approach that you took ... and your sending of your high-level envoys there, and any thoughts that this policy must now change because of the lack of response from the Chinese?
>
> *A:* No. But I'm not happy with the evolution of reform in China but I have no regrets about that. And I'm reinforced by—by a lot of expert opinion that feels that the approach I took, accomplishing something by executive order that the Congress wanted to do dramatically later on through legislation, was the proper approach. And I—so I hope—hope our policy will bear more fruit. But no, I am not happy with the status quo.
>
> *Q:* Well, Mr. President, if you're not happy with the status quo, why not change your policy now to take a tougher line toward the Chinese regime?
>
> *A:* Because I'm familiar with China and I think we're on the right track.[39]

PANAMA, NICARAGUA, AND LATIN AMERICA

Taken at face value, Latin America can be considered the home of some major Bush foreign policy victories. A U.S. invasion deposed and captured Manuel Noriega of Panama. Free elections were held in Nicaragua, and the Sandinistas were defeated. Democratic elections also were held in eight other Latin American countries, some, such as Chile, for the first time in almost twenty years. Bush ventured to Cartagena, Colombia, and met with the presidents of Colombia, Bolivia, and Peru in a much-heralded drug summit. New debt and trade initiatives (the Brady Plan, Enterprise for the Americas, the U.S.-Mexico Free Trade Agreement) were launched. As we noted elsewhere, Bush even took the time out amid the Persian Gulf crisis to visit several Latin American countries.

Yet it is precisely in these victories and initiatives that the limits of the traditional American approach to Latin American can be seen. Consider Panama. Noriega had supplanted Iran's Ayatollah and Libya's Qaddafi at the top of American international demonology. He also had been an acute political embarrassment to Bush during the presidential campaign and in October 1989 when Bush's unwillingness to support a coup attempt revived the old "wimp" charges. The U.S. invasion, dubbed "Operation Just Cause," was greeted by upward of 85 percent approval in public opinion polls, and it sent Bush's overall approval ratings from 55 to 73 percent (an all-time record for a president at the beginning of his second year in office). George got his man!

Since then, the great victory has begun to appear less complete and less sweet. Noriega is gone, replaced by a duly elected government led by President Guillermo Endara, but Panama is anything but stable and prosperous. A coup attempt in December 1990 was put down only with the help of U.S. troops. The original plan to pull the 10,000 U.S. troops still on Panamanian soil back to their bases was scrapped for fear that, without the U.S. presence, the next coup might succeed. The economy is still in a shambles, with unemployment by some estimates at over 25 percent of the workforce. Corruption remains rampant, and the drug trade persists. U.S. aid has been much less than promised, not even equal to the direct damages caused by the invasion, according to a former U.S. ambassador.[40] Disturbing reports also have surfaced, telling of far greater death tolls and destruction having been inflicted by the invasion.[41]

The fundamental roots of these problems arguably go back to the old presidential portrait that now hangs in the Bush cabinet room. As President Teddy Roosevelt observed when discussing the acquisition of the Panama Canal, "We stole it fair and square." The evidence of ties directly to Noriega go back to the early 1970s and include his having been on the CIA payroll under CIA Director George Bush. As part of the war against the Sandinistas, the relationship had grown even closer and had led the Reagan-Bush administration to look the other way even when Noriega assassinated political opponents. When sanctions were imposed in 1986, when Noriega's dangers as a drug runner outweighed his value as an anticommunist operative, Reagan-Bush got caught further in the contradictions of their policy. The sanctions were the economic equivalent of the neutron bomb: They destroyed the economy but left the leader standing. And even when Noriega was finally deposed, it was amid a devastated landscape that the new government had to attempt to rebuild.

Similarly, in Nicaragua the victory, while hailed in the short term, came with no guarantees and lots of problems. Here, too, the economy was in a shambles and the body politic bitterly fractured. Would the new government of President Violeta Chamorro be a stable one? Nor was it only from the Sandinistas that the challenges came. The UNO coalition that Chamorro headed in the election campaign against the Sandinistas encompassed numerous political parties and factions. Holding them together, especially in the hard times of economic reconstruction and democratic institutionalization, has been difficult. More ominous were reports of bands of "re-contras," disenchanted with the democratic process and taking up arms again. As to U.S. aid, even in the euphoric days immediately following Chamorro's election, the gap between promises and payout was a wide one, as Congress both delayed and cut aid for the new government.

Bush also has taken other initiatives, as noted, in trying to deal with the drug problem and the debt crisis and to stimulate hemispheric trade. The very fact of these initiatives is to his credit, following the Reagan obsession with Nicaragua to the virtual exclusion of other issues. But in the longer term it is real progress that matters. The international drug cartel has yet to be broken. This has domestic repercussions for the United States and even more so for countries such as Colombia, where the violence continues to undermine the solvency of fundamental political institutions and to tear at the nation's societal fabric. The Brady Plan, while providing some debt relief, has not provided nearly enough. For all its soaring rhetoric, it is not only skeptics who are reminded by the Enterprise for the Americas initiative of the great but dashed expectations of the Alliance for Progress. And the free trade agreement with Mexico has aroused substantial opposition from labor and other interest groups in the United States.

Thus, for Bush, the risk in Latin America is that the rewards will be short lived, with difficult reckonings lying ahead.

THE SOVIET UNION, EUROPE, AND THE END
OF THE COLD WAR

Anyone who claims to have predicted the events of 1989 in Europe and the Soviet Union, as a noted French scholar and strategist privately remarked, is a liar or a charlatan or both. How many of us ever included German reunification among the "alternative futures" scenarios in our international relations courses? Imagine the odds one could have gotten in Las Vegas on a wager that every single communist government in Eastern Europe would fall in less than a year and without a single shot being fired by NATO or Warsaw Pact forces, not to mention a nuclear war. Such profound peaceful changes in the international order are historically unprecedented. On the day France, the United States, Great Britain, and the Soviet Union relinquished all occupation rights in Germany, former Soviet Foreign Minister Eduard A. Shevardnadze offered the following assessment of these extraordinary events: "September 12 will go down in history as a date important in many ways for both Europe and the world at large ... we have drawn a line under World War II and we have started keeping the time of a new age."[42]

Thus, while it is difficult to count crises that are avoided, we must not be smug about what could have happened as the Berlin Wall came down and the communist empire crumbled. In this respect, Bush's lack of a penchant for rhetorical flourish (a handicap in other respects) was beneficial. He eschewed the temptation to make "we won, you lost" statements or to take actions that would have made the decisions not to intervene as the Soviet empire unraveled, one country after another, even more difficult for Gorbachev, both psychologically and politically. "I'm not going to back off my principles because it [*sic*] might offend Mr. Gorbachev," Bush stated on what he described as a "delicate" visit to Poland in July 1989. "But I'm not going to try to put him in a box by throwing strains on the Warsaw Pact."[43]

On other issues as well, Bush and Baker practiced a skilled diplomacy with their Soviet counterparts, Gorbachev and Shevardnadze. Bush and Gorbachev held an unprecedented three summits in the first two Bush administration years, and Baker met more often with Shevardnadze (until his abrupt and worrisome resignation in December 1990) than with any other foreign minister. Their list of achievements was substantial: progress toward both a Conventional Forces in Europe (CFE) agreement and a Strategic Arms Reduction Treaty (START); close consultations and negotiations on German reunification; a virtual de facto alliance against Iraq and improved relations on other Middle East issues, including a U.S.-sponsored meeting in Washington between Shevardnadze and Israeli Prime Minister Yitzhak Shamir; progress on the major persisting regional conflicts in Angola, Cambodia, and Afghanistan. Perhaps the highest compliment is that U.S.-Soviet diplomatic relations were normalized. Not all conflicts were settled, and not all interests have converged, but the process of diplomacy among leaders of these two former adversaries was regularized.

This was the way both George Bush and Jim Baker liked to do business. Person-to-person, talk things through, take the tough positions when necessary, add a touch of friendship here and there. The December 1989 Malta Summit, with its emphasis more on nurturing personal rapport than on a working policy agenda, embodied the classic Bush script. The goal was "to create a relaxed setting where the two leaders could get a sense or a feel for one another and what's on their minds, and their way of doing business, so they could see where the other was coming from."[44]

In other respects, the Bush administration has appeared uncertain and even confused as to what new relationship it seeks with the Soviet Union. Time and again over the first two years, even before the January 1991 violent crackdown in the Baltics, it repeatedly resisted opening up economic relations. In COCOM (Coordinating Commitee–Consultative Commission), it has had to be dragged along by the Western European allies to liberalize cold-war export controls. As to economic aid for the Soviet Union, when House Majority Leader Gephardt proposed it in a speech in March 1990, the Bush administration denounced him as naive and woolly-headed. When West German Chancellor Helmut Kohl proposed it at the 1990 Western summit, Bush first tried to quash the proposal and then said the Germans were free to do what they wanted, as the United States would (or would not, as the case may be). But then in December 1990, when food shortages and overall economic crises in the Soviet Union were no longer deniable, the Bush administration finally realized that within the borders of the Soviet Union, bread mattered more than personal summitry and diplomatic achievements.

Moreover, with Shevardnadze gone and Gorbachev increasingly weakened by opposition from a more restive and assertive right wing, more questions have been raised about this leader-centric diplomacy. Would ministerial negotiation and coordination work as smoothly without Shevardnadze? Pledges of a steady course were made by Gorbachev, but even if that proves true, it would be difficult to build anew the personal rapport and trust Baker and Shevardnadze clearly shared. And how unequivocal should U.S. support for Gorbachev be, especially as doubts mount about his commitment to further economic reform and political democratization? Was it now more than ever that our friend needs our support? Or might Gorbachev become the next shah or Somoza, a strongman leader increasingly unpopular at home, close links to whom could carry a dangerous price down the road? Neither of the conclusions indicated by the January 1991 military crackdown in the Baltics, where Gorbachev either gave the order to shoot unarmed civilians or lacked the power to prevent it, was particularly comforting.

The Bush administration has shown a similar sense of confusion and lack of direction toward Eastern Europe after the revolution. It was one thing to welcome Lech Walesa to the White House and hail the velvet revolution. But the gap between expressions of support and such more tangible manifestations of support as economic aid was a wide one indeed. The Bush administration "offered millions when we need billions," as a Solidarity newspaper put it.

There also have been uncertainties as to what a post-cold-war security order means for U.S. relations with its traditional Western allies. The Bush approach to NATO has been one of reluctant flexibility. For example, back in the spring of 1989, the administration pushed the NATO allies to resist Gorbachev's arms-control proposals for a "third zero" on short-range nuclear missiles and instead to deploy the new-generation Lance missiles. It did finally shift policy, but only on the eve of the NATO summit and when a major rift might otherwise have resulted. The same reluctance but then flexibility came the following year when Bush first fought a "rearguard action" to preserve NATO "first use" doctrine even after the Warsaw Pact had ceased to exist in anything more than name, and then led the-cold-war-is-over chorus in the July 1990 NATO communiqué.[45]

As the new European security order has begun to take institutional shape, the debate has gone beyond NATO doctrine and the specific issue of arms control to the broader question of the overall role and place of NATO in a post-cold-war Europe. As Robert Tucker has observed, "when alliances lose their common adversary, their normal fate is to break up."[46] While no European nations are about to resign their membership, it is questionable whether they still see NATO in as central a role as the United States does. "NATO should remain in being only as long as necessary to create the conditions that would allow it to be dissolved," stated Sir James Eberle, retired admiral and former NATO field commander.[47] And the Europeans are no longer willing to be confined to junior-partner status, especially not on continental affairs. Accordingly, much of the action has been shifting to enhanced political-military roles for such institutions as the Conference on Security and Cooperation in Europe (CSCE), in which the United States is not as much the senior partner, and the European Community (EC) and Western European Union (WEU), in neither of which is the United States even a member.

Nor have tensions been evident only on security matters. Trade conflicts between the United States and Western Europe are not new, but the clash in late 1990 over agricultural subsidies led to the breakdown of the Uruguay Round of GATT negotiations and much animosity on both sides of the Atlantic. The European resentment was expressed by Roy Denman, former head of the EC delegation in Washington: "Negotiations by megaphone and at gunpoint do not work in an era of a proudly uniting Europe."[48] Similarly, in U.S.-Japanese relations, increased tensions are palpable at many levels, from the burden sharing of the Gulf War to ongoing trade disputes to the disturbing increase in societal resentments expressed by Japan bashing on one side and America bashing on the other.

Thus, in relations with our former cold-war adversaries and our Western allies, we can see more of the mix of strengths and weaknesses of Bush the reactive president. His skills and savvy in diplomacy have been vital to managing some crises and potential crises. They have gotten into his in-box, and Bush has dealt with them. But on less apparently pressing and more long-term issues, he has been slow to change and has not provided strong leadership. The United States has been more dragged along than leading the way in shaping a post-cold-war order in Europe.

PRESIDENTIAL LEADERSHIP IN THE PERSIAN GULF WAR

President Harry Truman once remarked that a Truman foreign policy would not have existed "but for Joe Stalin." From George Bush's perspective, perhaps Saddam Hussein provided a historical parallel for building a framework of policy by which to secure the president's vision of post-cold-war collective security arrangements in the Middle East. Following the 2 August 1990 invasion of Kuwait by Iraqi troops, President Bush was quite successful at forging an effective international coalition against Iraq, first in support of UN economic sanctions and then a series of resolutions authorizing the use of force to remove Iraq from Kuwait and the conditions under which the coalition would cease its war efforts. In the early days of the crisis, some critics still focused on "the 'Carterization' of Bush,"[49] but the successful diplomatic maneuvering and coalition building that produced UN sanctions as well as Resolution 678 and the subsequent release of all U.S. hostages in Iraq constitute a considerable testament to Bush's leadership skill. Bush wanted the hostages freed, but he did not ask Americans to burn candles or pray for their freedom. Bush did not do for Hussein what Jimmy Carter did for the Ayatollah by making the hostages the issue.

In building the international coalition, Bush proved to be a skillful bargainer by trading advantages in return for support for international sanctions against Iraq. The administration canceled Egypt's $7 billion debt, convinced Saudi Arabia to give $1 billion in aid to Moscow, allowed Turkey to ship 50 percent more textiles to U.S. markets, ended China's eighteen-month diplomatic isolation (by agreeing to welcome the Chinese foreign minister in Washington), shipped new weapons to Israel, and brought Hafez Assad of Syria into the anti-Iraq coalition (with a visit from President Bush). And, for the first time, the Soviet Union joined the United States as an ally in Middle East policy formulation. Regardless of Soviet motives and despite the fact that the Soviets had yet to allow totally free immigration, President Bush agreed to suspend the Jackson-Vanik amendment in order to respond favorably to a Soviet request for credit guarantees for purchase of agricultural commodities. As David Hoffman observed, "although such diplomatic gameship is not a new phenomenon, it has become a particularly distinctive feature in this pragmatic, non-ideological administration and its handling of the Persian Gulf crisis."[50]

Although President Bush was extraordinarily skillful in putting together and maintaining the broad international and domestic coalition against Hussein and defending Saudi Arabia from attack, his most formidable challenge was to rally and maintain public support for beginning and sustaining what might have become a prolonged military conflict. When the president told the nation and the world that Iraq's aggression "would not stand," he meant it. Very few political observers took the full measure of George Bush's intentions. The president repeatedly promised that, should war come to the Persian Gulf, it would be "no Vietnam." The president explained, "If there must be war, we will not permit our troops to have their hands tied behind their backs, and I pledge to you there will not be any murky ending. If one American soldier has to go into battle, that soldier will have enough force behind him to win and then get out as soon as possible.... In our country I know that there are fears of another Vietnam. Let me assure you, should military action be required, this will not be another Vietnam. This will not be a protracted, drawn-out war."

Operation Desert Shield became Operation Desert Storm, and allied air attacks quickly destroyed virtually all Iraqi air defense and many other key military targets in Iraq and Kuwait. The United States deployed 527,000 troops into the theater of operations. The number of sorties approached 100,000, averaging 2800 every twenty-four hours. U.S. and allied forces controlled the skies over Iraq and Kuwait, and there was an exceptionally low number of allied military casualties. The war soon became the professional military's therapeutic revenge for the political restraints imposed during the Vietnam war. Looking back at his Vietnam experience, for example, retired Admiral Thomas Moorer observed: "This is so different from Vietnam, it's out of this world."[51] Where President Lyndon Johnson used to brag that his planes "can't even bomb an outhouse without my approval," President Bush confidently turned such decisions over to his generals. By 28 February 1991, in just a hundred hours of a ground war and six weeks of an air campaign, the United States and its coalition partners achieved, in the words of President Bush, "a quick, decisive and just victory."[52]

President Bush provided several public justifications for the U.S. presence in the gulf. These objectives tended to shift in their priority and emphasis giving rise to initial speculation that the president had either not clearly articulated the real reasons for entering into war or, like a fox, had cleverly disguised his military objectives. The initial U.S. military response was clearly aimed at protecting Saudi Arabia from Iraqi assault. "The independence of a sovereign Saudi Arabia," President Bush pledged, "is of vital interest to the United States." Speaking at the U.S. Marine outpost in northeastern Saudi Arabia during Thanksgiving 1990, President Bush tried to leave little doubt about the U.S. presence: "Why are we here? It's not all that complicated. There are three key reasons why we're here with our UN allies making a stand in defense of freedom. We're here to protect freedom, we're here to protect our future and we're here to protect innocent life."

During the six months of U.S. deployments in the gulf, several justifications were given by the administration:

1. "A mad dictator" who wants to control "the economic well-being of every country in the world." "A classic bully who thinks he can get away with kicking sand in the face of the world." "A dictator who has gassed his own people, children, unleashing chemical weapons of mass destruction, weapons that were considered unthinkable in the civilized world for over 70 years."

2. "Oil-lifeline threatened." "Our mission is about protecting national security which is to say protecting our future because energy security is national security for us and, indeed, for every country."

3. "It is aggression." "Protecting freedom means standing up to aggression. You know, the brutality inflicted on the people of Kuwait and on innocent citizens of every country must not be rewarded, because a bully unchecked today is a bully unleashed for tomorrow.... The invasion of Kuwait was without provocation, the looting of Kuwait is without excuse, and the occupation of Kuwait will not stand."

4. "Iraq's aggression is not just a challenge to the security of Kuwait and the other gulf neighbors but to the better world we all hope to build in the wake of the cold war. We're not talking simply about the price of gas. We are talking about the price of liberty." "No president is quick to order American troops abroad. But there are times when any nation that values its own freedom must confront aggression. Czechoslovakia, they know first-hand about the folly of appeasement. They know about the tyranny of dictatorial conquests. And in the World War that followed, the world paid dearly for appeasing an aggressor who should and could have been stopped. We're not going to make that mistake again. We will not appease this aggressor. As in World War II, the threat to American lives from a seemingly distant enemy must be measured against the nature of the aggression itself."

5. "It is the national security." "It is a world order that is threatened."

6. "If you want to sum it up in one word, it's jobs."

7. "Restore rulers to Kuwait."

8. "Nuclear threat." "And let me say this, those who would measure Saddam Hussein's, those who would measure the timetable for Saddam's atomic program in years may be seriously underestimating the reality of that situation and the gravity of the threat." "Every day that passes brings Saddam one step closer to realizing his goal of a nuclear weapons arsenal.... You know, no one knows precisely when this dictator may acquire atomic weapons, or exactly who they may be aimed at down the road. But we do know this for sure: He has never possessed a weapon that he didn't use. What we're confronting is a classic bully who thinks he can get away with kicking sand in the

face of the world. So far I've tried to act with restraint and patience. I think that's the American way. But Saddam is making the mistake of his life if he confuses an abundance of restraint, confuses that with a lack of resolve."

In the showdown over Iraq's invasion of Kuwait, the president at times appeared to have raised the stakes of losing face by engaging in public ridicule and challenge. We say "appeared" because it is possible that the president anticipated Saddam's response to personal insults. Indeed, the conflict sometimes looked like a personal dispute, with Bush calling Saddam "another Hitler" and deliberately mispronouncing the Iraqi leader's name, and Saddam calling Bush "Satan in the White House." When Saddam threatened that "the sands will run red with the blood of Americans and their Arab running dogs, and all their bones will bleach in the desert sun forever," Bush and his generals developed a brilliant military strategy to avert the outcome. When Secretary of Defense Dick Cheney promised that Saddam would "go back to Baghdad with his tail between his legs," he was not bluffing.

The combination of skillful diplomacy and extraordinary military planning made the ground war much less of a high-stakes gamble than many feared. Saddam chose not to use chemical weapons presumably because he either could not deploy them or feared a tactical nuclear strike against Baghdad. On the eve of the ground war the president rejected a Soviet peace proposal, leaving the impression that he had gambled "on a violent and potentially unpopular ground war than risk the alternative: an imperfect settlement hammered out by the Soviets and Iraqis that world opinion might accept as tolerable."[53] Conventional wisdom was wrong; Bush wanted and fully expected a win that would destroy Iraq's military capacity. He kept the coalition together and, buttressed by public approval ratings in the 80 percent range, politely but firmly rejected the Soviet proposal and prevented Saddam Hussein from using diplomacy to achieve a political victory. Hussein had miscalculated the political will and military power of his enemy. There would be no opportunity to ascertain whether the American public would tolerate large numbers of casualties. In the words of General H. Norman Schwarzkopf, Saddam Hussein "is neither a strategist nor is he schooled in the operational art nor is he a tactician nor is he a general nor is he a soldier."[54] We might add that following the war no one seemed to be calling President Bush a "wimp."

DETERRENCE FAILURE: COULD THE CRISIS HAVE BEEN AVOIDED?
A further question that still needs to be asked is whether the whole crisis could have been avoided in the first place. Without in any way exonerating

Saddam Hussein's aggression and illegal annexation of Kuwait, historians and policy analysts will certainly address the issue of "deterrence failure." "I think the suggestion that somehow the United States was responsible for or contributed to Saddam Hussein's invasion of Kuwait is ludicrous," stated Secretary Baker. Only "with the benefit of 20/20 hindsight," he contended, could one say that things should or even could have been done differently.[55] There are, however, substantial reasons, given U.S. policy toward Iraq both in the immediate period preceding the invasion and more generally dating back to 1982, for not being content with this rationalization.

It is axiomatic that effective deterrence requires accurate threat assessments and credible threat signaling.[56] Both the capabilities and the intentions of an adversary must be assessed on an ongoing basis and must be responded to in a manner that seeks conciliation where possible but also poses confrontation where necessary. The Bush policy did not fulfill these criteria. Instead, as stated in a recent report by a distinguished study group, "it is unlikely that Iraq's Saddam Hussein would have invaded Kuwait had he not calculated both that the regional balance of power stood in his favor and that local and outside powers would not react vigorously."[57]

Much of the controversy regarding the administration's immediate handling of the crisis surrounded the 25 July meeting between Saddam and U.S. Ambassador April Glaspie. According to the partial transcript released by Iraq, and not commented on by the Bush administration for over six months, Ambassador Glaspie's response to Saddam's threat to invade Kuwait was "we have no opinion on Arab-Arab conflicts, like your border disagreement with Kuwait." When Ambassador Glaspie was finally permitted to comment publicly at congressional hearings on 20 and 21 March 1991, she claimed that these statements were taken out of context and that she had issued "clear and repeated warnings that we would support our vital interests." Yet her counterclaim itself had at best partial credibility. One senior administration official privately commented that "if you read her cable you would not say that the entire Iraqi transcript was phoney baloney." And, as Representative Lee Hamilton (D-Ind.) remarked, the record "confused me, it confused this subcommittee, it confused much of the Washington press, and it is not unreasonable for me to think it might confuse Saddam Hussein as well." When Representative Hamilton asked, "Did you ever tell Saddam Hussein, 'Mr. President, if you go across that line into Kuwait, we're going to fight?'," Ambassador Glaspie replied, "I did not."[58]

Nor was it just a matter of a single meeting or a single misstatement. The previous day, Margaret Tutwiler, one of Baker's closest aides, very clearly emphasized that "we do not have any defense treaties with Kuwait, and there are no special defense or security commitments to Kuwait." Later in the week, in fact just the day before Iraq invaded, when asked in a congressional hearing where the United States stood, Assistant Secretary of State John Kelly stated, "We have no defense treaty relationships with any of the [gulf] countries," and "we have historically avoided taking a position on border disputes."[59]

One respected journalist called these and other Bush administration statements "the most disastrous disavowals of U.S. responsibility towards a threatened, friendly nation since Dean Acheson's public declaration in 1950 that South Korea lay beyond the U.S. defense perimeter in Asia."[60] There even was some evidence of intelligence warnings on 28 July of major troop movements—the "logistics trail," as one Pentagon official put it, that proved Saddam "was lying (about invading)."[61] Admittedly the evidence was not absolutely clear, but it was deemed serious and credible enough for both the CIA and DIA to shift their estimates of an Iraqi invasion from "possible" to "likely." But the warning was not heeded.

Plenty of explanations can be offered: The administration was distracted by events in Europe and the Soviet Union and simply was not able to pay enough high-level attention; or such trusted Arab leaders as Egyptian President Mubarak and Saudi Arabia's King Fahd kept reassuring the administration that Saddam would not invade. But explanations are not justifications. One has to ask whether Saddam really would have invaded Kuwait if the United States had signaled a firmer and less equivocal position, say, for example, if George Bush had reaffirmed the Carter Doctrine?

Moreover, going back well before the immediate crisis period, the kindest characterization of the Bush policy toward Iraq is that it was overly conciliatory. One has to go back to March 1982 when the Reagan administration began pursuing its anti-Iran alliance of convenience with Iraq. This was said to be classic balancing strategy: The enemy of my enemy is my friend. But with Iraq, the Reagan and Bush administrations did not just tilt, they lunged. They did not just begin a limited, tactical relationship, as truly classic balancing strategy would have dictated, with further improvements conditioned on further demonstrations of shared interests. Iraq was taken off the list of terrorist nations, even though it still supported terrorism. Full diplomatic relations were restored in November 1984, and while some protests were made in ensuing years, they tended to be more plaintive and couched than tough and assertive. Not in August 1988 (*after the war with Iran was over*) when Iraq used chemical weapons against the Kurds. Not in February 1990 when, at an Arab summit, Saddam warned against new U.S. efforts to dominate the region and called on all "good" Arabs to undermine U.S. influence. Not in April 1990 when Saddam threatened to "burn half of Israel." Not when Saddam massed his troops on the Kuwaiti border.

Meanwhile, billions of dollars in official credits were extended to Iraq, and export controls were relaxed so much that hundreds of millions of dollars worth of dual-use high technology, including such potent weaponry as fuel-air explosives, were exported. Especially given the emphasis placed after the invasion on Iraq's nuclear weapon potential, one has to wonder why export controls were so loose for so long. When economic sanctions against Iraq were proposed in Congress, the Reagan and then the Bush administrations opposed them. This was true in August 1988, following revelations of Iraqi use of chemical weapons against the Kurds. It also was true in July 1990, on the eve of the crisis, when Bush threatened to veto a sanctions bill.[62]

Of course, one could argue that this was a war which should not have been avoided, that U.S. interests were well served by the disarming of such a dangerous aggressor as Saddam. At minimum, that is a coldly realpolitik view, which would simply dismiss the human suffering and environmental damage wreaked by the war. But it also is a questionable calculation even in strict realpolitik terms, which may depend as much on postwar policies as on the war itself.

Thus, for a president who put so much emphasis on credible threats in his crisis management, it seems altogether warranted to hold him to the same standard in assessing his precrisis policy. Saddam Hussein, analytically speaking, behaved quite rationally, albeit ruthlessly so. In 1980 he calculated that the internal weakness and international unpopularity of his prey made the time ripe to attack Iran. His attack on Kuwait appears to have been similarly strategized. Kuwait was even weaker than Iran militarily. With American officials sending such extraordinarily weak signals—we have no opinion, it's your border dispute, we come only in friendship—would it have been rational, given his objectives, for him *not* to invade? This is a crisis that could have been avoided. Deterrence did not have to fail. The Bush administration by no means carries full responsibility for the failure to deter an Iraqi invasion of Kuwait. But it surely carries an ample share.

CONCLUDING OBSERVATIONS: THE MORNING AFTER THE WAR
"By God, we've kicked the Vietnam syndrome once and for all," George Bush exclaimed to a group of state senators in the White House.[63] Such was the prolix state of American political rhetoric in the war's immediate aftermath. Yet, even with such an overwhelming *military* victory, the postwar cessation of hostilities did not bring political resolutions. Failing to anticipate the internal consequences of the Kurdish uprising on both its scope and intensity, George Bush wavered in peace until pressured by world leaders and domestic opinion to aid the refugees. In an astute assessment of Bush's staggering, Andrew Rosenthal observed that "Mr. Bush is once again facing

the questions that characterized his presidency before the war: Does he operate from moral principle or from political pragmatism?"[64]

Not wanting unilaterally to intervene militarily in an Iraqi civil war, the Bush administration chose initially to do nothing for the fleeing Kurds. The administration continued to speak of a new world order in the Middle East even as Iraqi helicopter gunships slaughtered thousands of Kurds. With Saddam still in power, the Kurds and Shiites of Iraq were left to their own defenses. A Gallup poll in early April revealed that a majority of Americans, 56 percent, believed that "the United States and its allies should have continued fighting until Saddam Hussein was removed from power." Only 36 percent disagreed.[65]

Scholars of the presidency were not the only ones to ask why President Bush did not go to the United Nations with the same moral fervor and diplomatic deftness that characterized his post–2 August leadership. Why did the president respond so slowly to the glaring need for a major humanitarian effort to assist the refugees, who had answered Bush's call and had received CIA encouragement to overthrow Saddam? Moreover, in the Gallup poll cited above, 78 percent of 1002 adults interviewed favored "providing food and medical supplies to rebels" in Iraq. Why did an administration which clearly knew how to take initiative in crisis choose to remain inert during the war's immediate aftermath?

Midterm assessments of first-term presidents are more status reports than predictions. For example, writing in 1983 for a volume similar to this one on the evolution of Reagan foreign policy at midterm, political scientist I.M. Destler concluded: "In Moscow, the emerging post-Brezhnev regime was proving—by initial appearances—more aggressive and imaginative diplomatically, though whether its prime goal was disruption of NATO or a serious deal on arms control was not yet clear.... Was Ronald Reagan, the man, up to this demanding leadership challenge?"[66] Five years later, we knew the answers, but few of us could have forecast the broad dimensions and depth of the Reagan legacy in foreign affairs.

After two years in office, George Bush took his nation to war and achieved a brilliant military victory. Throughout the crisis, it was said that the fate of the Bush presidency was inexorably tied to the success of Operation Desert Storm. With his huge victory, the president sat atop extraordinary approval ratings and held the respect of the international coalition of nations. He has sought to convert these into a renewed bipartisan spirit in Congress encompassing a broad range of issues in foreign policy. When in January 1991 *Time* placed a double image of George Bush on its cover with the title "Men of the Year," it lauded the man who displayed a "commanding vision of a new world order" and drubbed the other man, who "showed little vision for his own country."[67] It is on the global stage and over the issue of war or peace that George Bush seems likely to be judged by history.

Yet Bush seems not to appreciate adequately some of the forces that must be reckoned with in the building of the heralded new world order. Perhaps more than ever before, foreign policy strength in the 1990s is going to require a solid domestic core. A nation with a $250+ billion budget deficit cannot provide very much assistance to the new democracies of Eastern Europe and Latin America. A nation that allows its economic competitiveness to decline cannot do very much about its $100+ billion trade deficit. A nation that continues without an energy policy will continue to be vulnerable to new crises in the Persian Gulf. A nation that allows its social problems to mount—its educational system to decline, its once-great cities to decay, its crime rate to shoot up, its race relations to fester—may find its claim to moral leadership and the attractiveness of its ideals to be increasingly questioned by other people around the world. The fate of the foreign policy George Bush may be much more closely intertwined with the domestic policy George Bush than he, who would much rather lead the world than the nation, would prefer.

Domestic politics also is likely to pose challenges in a different sense, namely the international spillover from civil wars and other internal conflicts in other states. The greatest threats to world peace, as well as the most profound ethical dilemmas, in the next few years may well emanate from conflicts within rather than between countries. Yet the Bush record, as with the Kurds in Iraq and with Lithuania, has shown more confusion than coherence. Reassessments of traditional strategies and development of alternative ones, particularly multilateral ones, will be needed.

Finally, for all its strength, the Bush style, with its emphasis on personal relationships, pragmatic policy-making, and evolutionary decision making, is a reactive agent willing to absorb the gamut of change and then (and only then) create policy accordingly. It worked brilliantly in building the coalition in the Persian Gulf in *response* to Saddam; it has been much less effective in *anticipating* the new Europe. Times of crisis usually demand exceptional performances from leaders, and George Bush is governing during such a time. But, after the war, Bush's vision of a new world order in the Middle East and Europe will need some recalibrating. Hafez Assad of Syria, Hashemi Rafsanjani of Iran, Mikhail Gorbachev of the Soviet Union, to name only a few, will each make claims to a role in shaping the new world order.

Throughout his career, Bush has given ample evidence of flexibility and compromise when it was politically necessary to do so. Bush the pragmatist may very well be up to the task, but the challenge is perhaps the greatest of our century. The postwar order must include new security arrangements in a region torn by war and one that rarely has known a stable balance of power capable of deterring aggression; arms-control agreements that will constrain the rebuilding of chemical/biological and nuclear arms plants; economic reconstruction; renewed efforts to settle Israeli-Palestinian and Arab-Israeli disputes; and a comprehensive strategy by the United States to reduce its dependence on oil and deal with other pressing domestic problems. The morning after the war provides President George Bush with the formidable task of implementing the broad dimensions of his plan of a new world order. This is no longer "the vision thing." How well the president succeeds will depend as much on his leadership skills as on the willingness of leaders in today's world order to share the president's objectives and goals of a new order.

Acknowledgments

We want to acknowledge especially the assistance of Scott Hill, a graduate research assistant at the U.C. Davis Institute of Governmental Affairs. We also thank political science undergraduates Hiram Patel and Dorene Rodriguez. Our colleagues Emily Goldman, Miroslav Nincic, Donald Rothchild, and Paul Zinner provided many helpful suggestions for the chapter.

Notes

1. "Text of President Bush's State of the Union Message to Nation," *New York Times,* 30 January 1991, A8. See also Morton Kondracke, "The Fine Print," *New Republic,* 25 February 1991, 13. Kondracke maintains that "nothing about the New World Order is entirely clear, of course, because it's still more slogan than strategy. The administration says it means good things: promotion of democracy, collective security, arms reductions, settlement of regional disputes, cooperation among industrialized nations, and free trade. But many Americans fear it means that this country will be the world's policeman, and many foreigners see it as a post-cold-war American grab for hegemony."

2. Attributed to Georgetown University Law Center Associate Dean Peter Edelman, in Burt Solomon, "Vulnerable to Events," *National Journal,* 6 January 1990, 6–10.

3. David Broder, "The Reactor President," *Washington Post,* 19 August 1990.

4. Gloria Borger, "The Year of Living Timorously," *U.S. News & World Report,* 13 November 1989, 26.

5. Burt Solomon, "Vulnerable to Events," *National Journal,* 6 January 1990, 6–10.

6. "Men of the Year, A Tale of Two Bushes," *Time,* 7 January 1991.

7. Stanley Hoffmann, "A New World and Its Troubles," in *Sea-Changes: Amer-*

ican Foreign Policy in a World Transformed, edited by Nicholas X. Rizopoulos (New York: Council on Foreign Relations Press, 1990), 287.

8. See Larry Berman, ed., *Looking Back on the Reagan Presidency* (Baltimore: Johns Hopkins University Press, 1990). See also Sidney Blumenthal, *Pledging Allegiance: The Last Campaign of the Cold War* (New York: HarperCollins, 1990).

9. "Annual Check-Up," *New Republic,* 21 January 1990, 7.

10. Maureen Dowd and Thomas L. Friedman, "The Fabulous Bush and Baker Boys," *New York Times Magazine,* 6 May 1990, 36.

11. See Richard Neustadt, *Presidential Power and Modern Presidents: The Politics of Leadership From Roosevelt to Reagan* (New York: Free Press, 1990); see also R.W. Apple, Jr., "Presidential Reward," *New York Times,* 12 December 1990, A9.

12. See Thomas E. Mann, ed., *A Question of Balance: The President, The Congress and Foreign Policy* (Washington, D.C.: Brookings Institution, 1990); James Thurber, *Divided Democracy: Cooperation and Conflict between the President and Congress* (Washington, D.C.: CQ Press, 1991).

13. Sidney Blumenthal, "Bull Mouse," *New Republic,* 7 and 14 January 1991, 11–16.

14. George Will, "Flippant Style, Trivial Pursuits," *Newsweek,* 5 November 1990.

15. See George Bush, "Why We Are in the Gulf," *Newsweek,* 26 November 1990, 28–29; Thomas Friedman, "No Compromise on Kuwait, Bush Says," *New York Times,* 24 October 1990, A6. See also excerpts from presidential news conference, 1 December 1990, *New York Times,* 4; "Excerpts from Speech by Bush at Marine Outpost," *New York Times,* 23 November 1990.

16. Fred Barnes, "Brave New Gimmick," *New Republic,* 15 February 1991, 15–16.

17. See David Hoffman, "George Bush and the Power of the Thank You Note," *Washington Post, National Weekly Edition,* 21–27 August 1989, 22; Michael Duffy, "Mr. Consensus," *Time,* 21 August 1989, 16.

18. Maureen Dowd, "Bush at War: Seeking To Be Not Too Detached, Yet Not Gripped by Detail," *New York Times,* 23 January 1991.

19. See William Safire, "Bush's Cabinet: Who's Up," *New York Times Magazine,* 25 March 1990, 31–34, 63–67; Morton Kondracke, "Blind Men's Bluff," *New Republic,* 6 March 1989, 20; Andrew Rosenthal, "National Security Adviser Redefines the Role, Drawing Barrage of Criticism," *New York Times,* 3 November 1989, A12; Burt Solomon, "Bush's Passion for Friendship Abets His Diplomatic Policy," *National Journal,* 8 December 1990, 2986–87.

20. Dowd and Friedman, "Fabulous Bush and Baker Boys," 36.

21. "Virtually everyone who knows Mr. Scowcroft uses the same adjectives to describe him: quiet, calm, conciliatory, self-effacing." Rosenthal, "National Security Adviser Redefines the Role," A16.

22. What made this especially grating for Cheney was that he had no advance warning of Webster's testimony, yet he was testifying the same morning to another congressional committee. Baker, however, reportedly got to screen Webster's testi-

mony. Patrick E. Tyler, "Cheney Finds CIA Director Is No Comrade in Arms," *Washington Post,* 6 March 1990, A21.

23. Michael Weisskopf and William Booth, "In West, U.S. Stands Alone on Warming Issue," *Washington Post,* 6 November 1990, A5.

24. Quoted in Rosenthal, "National Security Adviser Redefines the Role," A8.

25. Quoted in Andrew Rosenthal, "For Bush, Life on the Run Catches Up," *New York Times,* 6 July 1990, A6.

26. Safire, "Bush's Cabinet," 32.

27. *Department of State Bulletin,* April 1989, 11. Emphases in original.

28. Patrick J. Buchanan, "The Contras Need Our Help," *Washington Post,* 5 March 1986, A19.

29. Robert Pear, "Bush's Courting Splits Democrats," *New York Times,* 16 March 1989, A8.

30. Glenn Frankel, "There's Really Not Much the U.S. Can Do About South Africa," *Washington Post, National Weekly Edition,* 24 December 1984, 24.

31. Testimony by Assistant Secretary of State for African Affairs Herman J. Cohen to the Senate Foreign Relations Committee, cited in John Felton, "Congress Is Willing to Defer Imposing New Sanctions," *Congressional Quarterly Weekly Report,* 7 October 1989, 2659.

32. Chuck Alston, "Bush Crusades on Many Fronts to Retake President's Turf," *Congressional Quarterly Weekly Report,* 3 February 1990, 291–95. This article also mentions instances in which Bush did not veto bills but otherwise dissented. In November 1989 he signed an appropriations bill (H.R. 2989—P.L. 101–36) despite a provision seeking to forbid the Treasury Department and other agencies from requiring employees to sign secrecy agreements and then proceeded to ignore it in practice. In signing a defense spending bill (H.R. 3072—P.L. 101–65), he stated his right not to abide by the earmarks contained in the accompanying committee report, asserting that "any such language has no legal force."

33. Memorandum of Disapproval on S. 2834, reprinted in *Congressional Quarterly Weekly Report,* 8 December 1990, 4119. The previous year, Bush had objected to intelligence bill language requiring notification within 48 hours of the initiation of a covert operation. The Senate Intelligence Committee agreed to compromise, deleting the specific time limit in exchange for a letter from Bush explaining how he would handle the existing requirement for "prompt notification."

34. Bruce W. Jentleson, "The Domestic Politics of Desert Shield: Should We Go to War? Who Should Decide?" *Brookings Review* 9 (Winter 1990–91): 22–28.

35. It also should be noted that these resolutions were not formal declarations of war and thus left the constitutional questions surrounding war powers even murkier than before this crisis. Further adding to the uncertainties as to the precedents set was the court ruling on the judicial order sought by Congressman Ronald V. Dellums (D-Calif.) and 54 other members of Congress to stop the president from going to war without a formal congressional declaration of war. While the injunction was denied, as it had been in previous cases, such as during the 1987–88 Iran-Iraq war, in this case the judge stated in his opinion the interpretation that Article I

of the Constitution intended that a president could not go to war without congressional approval. For one view of the historical debate over war powers, see Michael J. Glennon, *Constitutional Diplomacy* (Princeton: Princeton University Press, 1990).

36. Edward Corwin, *The President: Office and Powers, 1787–1957* (New York: New York University Press, 1957).

37. "Bush Bid to Fix Beijing Ties Strains Those with Hill," *Congressional Quarterly Weekly Report*, 16 December 1989, 3435.

38. Arthur Waldron, "Bullish on Beijing," *New Republic*, 9 April 1990, 20.

39. Excerpts from a news conference, quoted in *New York Times*, 14 March 1990, A8.

40. Ricardo Chavira, "Meanwhile, Back in Panama," *Newsweek*, 26 November 1990, 38.

41. "Victims of Just Cause," segment of "60 Minutes," 30 September 1990.

42. "Four Allies Give Up Rights in Germany," *New York Times*, 13 September 1990, 1.

43. Maureen Dowd, "Bush in Warsaw on 'Delicate' Visit to Push Changes," *New York Times*, 10 July 1989, A1.

44. Maureen Dowd, "Two-Summit Plan Reflects Bush Style: Intense (Relaxed) Personal Diplomacy," *New York Times*, 6 November 1989, A10.

45. Characterization made by John D. Steinbruner, director of foreign policy studies at the Brookings Institution, cited in Michael R. Gordon, "Nuclear Strategy Shift," *New York Times*, 3 July 1990, A11.

46. Robert W. Tucker, "1989 and All That," in Rizopolous, *Sea-Changes*, 218.

47. Craig Whitney, "Amid Cold War's End, Questions about NATO," *New York Times*, 26 December 1990, A10. See also Alan Riding, "The New Europe," *New York Times*, 20 November 1990, A4.

48. Roy Denman, "Why the Trade Talks Fizzled," *New York Times*, 20 December 1990, A31. U.S. Agriculture Secretary Clayton Yeutter responded that Denman's arguments were little more than "a nifty two-step." Yeutter accused the Europeans of lacking the political will to do anything more than "nibble only at the edges of reform." See his "Letter to the Editor," *New York Times*, 9 January 1991, A20.

49. Eleanor Clift, "The Carterization of Bush," *Newsweek*, 22 October 1990, 28.

50. David Hoffman, *Washington Post, National Weekly Edition*, 3–9 December 1990.

51. See *Wall Street Journal*, 24 January 1991.

52. See Leo Rennert, "Bush: Gulf Less Risky Than Vietnam," *Sacramento Bee*, 19 December 1990, A20; see also "'No Vietnam,'" *Newsweek*, 10 December 1990, 24–231; see also Bob Woodward, *The Commanders*, New York: Simon and Schuster, 1991.

53. Maureen Dowd, "Bush Moves to Control War's End Game," *New York Times*, 23 February 1991, 1.

54. "Excerpts from Schwarzkopf News Conference on Gulf War," *New York Times*, 28 February 1991, A8.

55. Thomas L. Friedman, "Baker Seen as a Balance to Bush on Crisis in Gulf," *New York Times*, 3 November 1990, 6.

56. See, for example, Robert Jervis, *Perception and Misperception in International Relations* (Princeton: Princeton University Press, 1976); and Alexander L. George and Richard Smoke, *Deterrence in American Foreign Policy: Theory and Practice* (New York: Columbia University Press, 1974).

57. *Restoring the Balance: U.S. Strategy and the Gulf Crisis*, Initial Report of the Washington Institute's Strategic Study Group (Washington, D.C.: Washington Institute for Near East Policy, 1991), 13.

58. Jim Hoagland, "... And the Tale of a Transcript," *Washington Post*, 17 September 1990, A16; Jim Hoagland, "Transcript Shows Muted U.S. Response to Threat by Saddam," *Washington Post*, 12 September 1990, A33; Thomas L. Friedman, "U.S. Revises Image of Envoy to Iraq," *New York Times*, 22 March 1991, A9.

59. Elaine Sciolino and Michael R. Gordon, "U.S. Gave Little Reason Not to Mount Kuwait Assault," *New York Times*, 23 September 1990, 1, 18; Paul A. Gigot, "The Great American Screw-Up: The U.S. and Iraq, 1980–90," *National Interest*, Winter 1990/91, 3–10.

60. Hoagland, "And the Tale of a Transcript."

61. Patrick J. Sloyan, "Bush Ignored Satellite Tip-Off of Invasion," *Cleveland Plain Dealer*, 21 September 1990, 1A, 4A.

62. Nor, however, should Congress be let off the hook on sanctions. Substantial opposition remained, notably from farm-state members. See Douglas Waller, "Glass House," *New Republic*, 5 November 1990, 13–14. See Morton Kondracke, "Saddamnation," *New Republic*, 7 May 1990, 9–12; "The Most Dangerous Man in the World," *U.S. News & World Report*, 4 June 1990.

63. See "The Reward of Leadership," *Newsweek*, 11 March 1991, 30.

64. Andrew Rosenthal, "Can Bush Regain Momentum?" *New York Times*, 21 April 1991, sec. 4, p. 1.

65. Michael R. Kagay, "War's End Hasty, Americans Say," *New York Times*, 10 April 1991, A7.

66. I.M. Destler, "The Evolution of Reagan Foreign Policy," in *The Reagan Presidency: An Early Assessment*, edited by Fred Greenstein (Baltimore: Johns Hopkins University Press, 1983), 157.

67. See also David Hoffman, "The Two Presidents Running the U.S. Gulf Policy," *Washington Post, National Weekly Edition*, 7–13 January 1991, 23.

5

George Bush and the Public Presidency: The Politics of Inclusion

George C. Edwards III

George Bush's relations with the American public have been one of the most unanticipated aspects of his presidency. A president who lacks the manipulative public relations instincts and skills of his immediate predecessor found himself at higher levels in the polls than Ronald Reagan ever reached. After a year in office, the Gallup poll found that 40 percent of the people could not name anything in response to a question regarding Bush's greatest achievement in office.[1] At the same time, the president enjoyed record approval levels.

Unraveling these apparent paradoxes is one of the goals of this chapter, which focuses on Bush's relations with the public in his first two years in office. It explores both the nature of his public support and the explanations for it.

Mandate

The first time that the nation collectively evaluates a president is in the election itself. Every newly elected president prefers to come into office with a "mandate," a sense that the people have spoken and support his policies. The most effective means of setting the terms of debate on many issues at once and overcoming opposition is by creating the perception of an electoral mandate, an impression that the voters want to see the winner's programs implemented. Indeed, large-scale changes in policy virtually never occur in the absence of such perceptions, such as those of 1932, 1964, and 1980.

Mandates can be powerful symbols in American politics. They accord added legitimacy and credibility to the newly elected president's proposals. Concerns for representation and political survival encourage members of Congress to support the president if they feel the people have spoken. And members of Congress are susceptible to such beliefs. According to David

Mayhew, "nothing is more important in Capitol Hill politics than the shared conviction that election returns have proven a point."[2] Members of Congress also need to believe that voters have not merely rejected the losers in elections but have positively selected the victors and what they stand for.

More important, mandates change the premises of decision. Following the presidential election of 1932, the essential question became not whether government should act to fight the Great Depression but *how*. Similarly, following the election of 1964, the dominant question in Congress was not whether to pass new social programs but how many programs to pass and how much to increase spending.

In 1981, the tables were turned. Ronald Reagan's victory placed a stigma on big government and exalted the unregulated marketplace and large defense budgets. More specifically, the terms of the debate over policy changed from which federal programs to expand to which ones to cut; from which civil rights rules to extend to which ones to limit; from how much to regulate to how little; from which natural resources to protect to which to develop; from how little to increase defense spending to how much; and from how little to cut taxes to how much.

In 1980 Ronald Reagan carried forty-four states, won 51 percent of the popular vote, 71 percent of the House districts, and 489 electoral votes; and he scored a 10 percent margin of victory over Jimmy Carter in the popular vote. In 1988 George Bush carried forty states, won 53 percent of the popular vote, 69 percent of the House districts, and 426 electoral votes, and he achieved a 6 percent margin in the popular vote. Although the results seem to be reasonably similar, they were interpreted very differently.

Whereas Reagan entered office widely perceived as having received a mandate to govern,[3] the conventional wisdom at the time of Bush's inauguration was that he had received no mandate in the election. This view was evidently shared even by the president-elect, who declined to engage in the ritual of claiming a mandate no matter how close the election.

The conditions of Bush's electoral victory undermined any claims that the White House could make as to having received a mandate. The new president's popular vote percentage was a respectable but unimpressive 53 percent, and his party lost seats in both houses of Congress. He actually ran *behind* the winners in 379 of the 435 congressional districts. Thus there was little basis for members of Congress inferring presidential coattails.

Other factors that might encourage the perception of a mandate were also missing in 1988. The press did not engage in the hyperbolic analyses that characterized coverage of the 1980 election results, and since Bush had led in the polls throughout the entire postconvention period, his victory lacked the psychological advantage of surprise. Moreover, Bush emphasized continuity, not change, in his campaign and did not offer bold new initiatives. Instead, the campaign was marked by a notable lack of focus on issues—as well as a dearth of civility.

Thus the new president's strategic position was one in which he was not able to structure the choices of Congress as being for or against a chief executive who had the support of the people.

Public Approval

Perhaps the biggest political surprise of the Bush administration has been the president's high standing in the polls. This section briefly describes his impressive approval ratings and then focuses on explaining them.

BUSH IN THE POLLS

As table 5.1 (page 132) shows, George Bush did not begin his tenure with a love affair with the American people. Instead, his approval rating in the first Gallup poll after he took office was only 51 percent, the first time a modern president has received a lower approval rating than the percentage of the popular vote he received in his election.[4] A month later, his approval rating rose to a comfortable 63 percent, but in March, April, and May it fell back to the 50s—unusually low levels for a new president. The June poll found his approval rating at 70 percent, however, a figure his predecessor never reached, and it remained at about that level through the rest of 1989.

In 1990 Bush soared to 80 percent approval, a figure exceeded in the Gallup poll since World War II only by the poll following the invasion of the Bay of Pigs in 1961. For the rest of the year, he obtained support at an average level that had not occurred since the days of John F. Kennedy.

Some raised the question whether Bush's approval was as strong as that of his predecessors. We lack sufficient data to reach a definitive conclusion on the issue. But the Gallup poll did compare the strength of Bush's approval in November 1989 with that of Reagan's in November 1981. The results are shown in table 5.2 (page 133). Reagan had a higher fraction of his supporters approve "strongly," but he also had a much lower approval level than Bush and a lower percentage of the population approved strongly of his performance in office. It is possible that Reagan's support was more intense, but the primary political consequence of less committed support, a decline in approval, did not occur in Bush's first two years in office.

The supposedly beloved Ronald Reagan, the "Great Communicator," was expected to be a difficult act to follow. How could his successor enjoy a much higher standing in the public opinion polls, especially when the Bush administration did not stress public relations activities?

TABLE 5.1
PUBLIC APPROVAL OF GEORGE BUSH

	Ap- prove	Disap- prove		Ap- prove	Disap- prove
1989			*1990 continued*		
24–26 January	51%	6%	10–11 September	76%	16%
28 Feb.–2 March	63	13	14–16 September	73	17
10–13 March	56	16	27–30 September	67	20
10–16 April	58	16	3–4 October	66	25
4–7 May	56	22	11–14 October	56	33
8–11 June	70	14	18–21 October	53	37
6–9 July	66	19	25–28 October	54	36
10–13 August	69	19	1–4 November	58	32
7–10 September	70	17	8–11 November	58	34
5–8 October	68	20	15–18 November	54	33
2–5 November	70	17	29 Nov.–2 Dec.	61	29
7–10 December	71	20	6–9 December	58	33
			13–16 December	63	30
1990					
4–7 January	80%	11%	*1991*		
8–11 February	73	16	3–6 January	58%	31%
15–18 February	73	16	11–13 January	64	25
8–11 March	68	18	17–20 January	82	12
15–18 March	74	15	19–22 January	80	14
5–8 April	68	16	23–26 January	83	13
19–22 April	67	17	30 Jan.–2 Feb.	82	15
17–20 May	65	20	7–10 February	79	18
7–10 June	67	18	14–17 February	80	14
15–17 June	69	17	21–24 February	80	13
6–8 July	63	24	28 Feb.–3 March	89	8
19–22 July	60	25	7–10 March	87	8
9–12 August	74	16	14–17 March	86	9
16–19 August	75	16	21–24 March	84	10
23–26 August	76	16	28–30 March	82	11
30 Aug.–2 Sept.	74	17	4–6 April	83	12

SOURCE: Gallup polls.

TABLE 5.2

THE STRENGTH OF PUBLIC APPROVAL

	Ronald Reagan *November 1981*	*George Bush* *November 1989*
Approve "strongly"	25%	32%
Approve "not strongly"	24	38
Overall approval	49	70

SOURCE: Larry Hugick, "Bush Rates High on Eastern Europe, 'Nice Guy' Image; Lower on Economy and Other Domestic Issues," *Gallup Report*, November 1989, 5.

EXPLAINING BUSH'S APPROVAL

To understand Bush's standing in the polls, we must first understand public evaluation of the president in general. I have written at length on this elsewhere[5] and address the subject of presidential approval in briefer fashion here.

Personality. One factor commonly associated with someone's approval is personality. In common usage the word "personality" refers to personal characteristics such as warmth, charm, and humor that may influence responses to an individual on a personal level. It is not unusual for observers to conclude that the public evaluates presidents more on style than substance, especially in an era in which the media and sophisticated public relations campaigns play such a prominent role in presidential politics. In other words, some argue that the public evaluates the president by how much they may like him as a person.

George Bush has a congenial personality. He is warm, sincere, relaxed, and secure. In other words, he is a person most people "like." The Gallup poll found that 84 percent of the people approved of Bush as a person in November 1989 (only 73 percent approved of Reagan as a person at a similar point in his term).[6] Table 5.3 (page 134) shows some specific qualities the American people attribute to President Bush.

Although the public may "like" a president, it still may not approve of the way he is handling his job. Ronald Reagan provides a good test case of the role of personality in presidential approval. Some, especially the president's detractors, ascribed Reagan's standing in the polls primarily to his personal charm and telegenic good looks, his stage presence and professional skills as a television performer (the "Great Communicator"), the White House's extensive "packaging" of the president's public appearances, or to a

TABLE 5.3

PERSONAL QUALITIES OF GEORGE BUSH

"Please tell me which word or phrase better describes your impression of George Bush."

Warm, friendly	84%
Confident	76
Sincere	75
Steady, reliable	72
An active president	70
A leader	67
Intelligent	66

SOURCE: Gallup poll, 6–8 July 1990.

Teflon coating that insulated him from accountability for problems of governing and public policy. In contrast, Richard Wirthlin, the president's primary pollster, argues that the president's standing in the polls was not the result of his "nice" personality.[7]

A comparison of the results of asking the same people whether they approved of President Reagan's handling of his job and whether they approved of him as a person found the average difference between approval of Reagan as a person and approval of his performance as president was 21 percentage points, representing over a fifth of the public.[8]

It is plausible that there is some relationship between personal approval and job approval. The relationship is probably reciprocal. The president's appealing personality may buttress his job-approval ratings. It seems equally likely, however, that when Reagan's job performance ratings fell, as during the recession of 1982, they had a negative influence on his personal approval evaluations. In general, however, Americans appear to compartmentalize their attitudes toward the president. They have little difficulty in separating the person from the performance.

What may be a greater influence on presidential approval is the way the public evaluates the job-related traits it attributes to the president. Assessments of characteristics such as the president's integrity, reliability, and leadership ability (as opposed to attributes such as personal warmth and charm) significantly influence the approval ratings of presidents.[9]

Recent research on voting behavior in presidential elections has found that characteristics voters ascribe to candidates, such as moral character and leadership competence, are important influences on their votes. This finding holds for persons of all education levels.[10] Individual presidents or candidates are easier for people to focus on than complex policy issues, and this inclination is reinforced by the orientation of media coverage toward the personalization of politics.[11]

George Bush, as table 5.3 shows, is seen as an intelligent, industrious, cautious, solid leader. Such perceptions have certainly not hurt him in the polls. At the same time, there is a danger that the way the public perceives presidential traits may change as new problems arise or in relation to the president's past performance. Certain characteristics may become more salient in response to changing conditions. For example, when the Iran/ *contra* affair became news, President Reagan's decision-making style became a prominent issue, and many people evaluated the same behavior, namely, his focus on the "big picture" and detachment from the details of governing, in a different light. At midterm, President Bush had escaped such problems.

Issue Salience. Understanding presidential approval requires identifying what is on the minds of Americans. If a matter is not *salient* to people, it is unlikely that it will play a role in their evaluations of the president. The relative weight of values and issues in evaluations of the president also varies over time. Valence, or style, issues are values such as patriotism, morality, and a strong national defense, on which there is a broad public consensus and which are more basic than a position on a specific policy question. The president's articulation of valence issues, directly and in the symbols he employs in his actions and speech, can affirm the values and beliefs that define citizens' political identities. As a result, valence issues may be powerful instruments for obtaining public support, for presidents often prefer to be judged on the basis of consensual criteria with which they can associate themselves.

There is reason to believe that valence issues augmented Ronald Reagan's standing in the polls. People liked the values he articulated more than they liked his stands on specific policy questions. Americans are conservative in their basic values, such as religion and morality, pride in country, and strong national defense, and are skeptical about the government's ability to solve social and economic problems; they responded positively to the president's broad themes. As long as values and the symbols used to represent them were more salient than issues, Reagan did well in the polls. When issues were more salient, as during the recession of 1982 or in the wake of the Iran/*contra* scandal, he slipped.

There is experimental evidence that network news helps provide a frame of reference for some issues; when it does, this affects evaluations of presidents. For example, if people saw poverty as a systemic outcome, rather than dispositional, they were less likely to evaluate Ronald Reagan highly.[12] Another experiment found that President Carter's overall reputation and, to a

TABLE 5.4
APPROVAL OF BUSH'S HANDLING OF VARIOUS AREAS
OF PUBLIC POLICY

"[Do] you approve or disapprove of the way President Bush is handling _____?"

	Approve	Disapprove
Federal budget deficit	32%	53%
Poverty and homelessness	30	59
Economic conditions	40	51
The drug problem	53	41
Environmental issues	46	40
Abortion issue	38	45
Education policy	53	35
Foreign policy	65	21
The situation in Eastern Europe	63	16
Relations with the Soviet Union	81	11
The situation in Central America	40	39

SOURCE: Gallup poll, 9–12 November 1989.

lesser extent, his apparent competency, were affected by network news. The standards people used in evaluating the president, what they felt was important in his job performance, seemed to be influenced by the news they watched on television.[13] When the news media began covering the Iran/*contra* affair, Ronald Reagan's public approval took an immediate and severe dip as the public applied new criteria of evaluation.[14]

George Bush has been lucky. At the beginning of his term, divisive issues such as the nomination of John Tower as secretary of defense and the savings-and-loan crisis dominated the news. During this period, Bush had unusually low levels of approval for a new president. Then he went to the NATO summit and came away with rave reviews. Foreign policy, and what is more important, *consensual* foreign policy dominated the news. His approval rating zoomed to 70 percent.

Then came his best luck of all: the collapse of communism in Eastern Europe. For months, the premier issue of public policy was the disintegration of the Soviet bloc, the overthrow of communist regimes, and the liberalization of the Soviet Union, symbolized most powerfully by the destruction of the Berlin Wall and the unification of Germany.

Bush got to preside over the end of the cold war, what many characterized as the *winning* of the cold war. It is difficult to imagine a more consensual policy (like containment in 1950s and early 1960s). The voices of the few detractors who complained that the administration was reacting to events and not dominating them were drowned in a joyous chorus of relief and praise for the president's prudent stewardship, coupled with anticipation of a peace dividend.

The importance of the salience of issues is clear from an examination of the data presented in table 5.4, based on a Gallup poll in November 1989. The president's overall approval rating was 70 percent. Yet his performance was not rated highly on a large number of objectively important policies ranging from the federal deficit to abortion. It did not matter. As long as the public approved of Bush's handling of what was salient at the time, matters of foreign policy (where he also has strong credentials), it accorded him high overall approval.

Then, at the end of 1989, the United States invaded Panama and arrested Manuel Noriega. Since Noriega had few supporters and since the costs of the incursion were low, this policy was widely supported (see table 5.5), and gave the president another, although short, boost in the polls, raising him to the 80 percent mark in January 1990. No other modern president has ever begun his second year that high in the polls.

TABLE 5.5

SUPPORT FOR THE INVASION OF PANAMA

"Do you think the United States was justified in its invasion of Panama, or not justified?"

Justified	74%
Not justified	19

SOURCE: CBS News/ *New York Times* poll, 13-15 January 1990.

By July 1990 some of the bloom was off the rose. The collapse of communism was becoming old news, and Bush was being dragged down in the polls by doubts about his handling of divisive domestic issues such as the economy and the savings-and-loan scandal.[15] The erosion of approval was strongest among blacks and white conservative Democrats, perhaps those we would expect to be most sensitive to concerns about the economy and most susceptible to economic downturns.[16]

In early August the prominence of issues changed again, this time in response to the Iraqi invasion of Kuwait. The president's policies of sending

American troops to protect Saudi Arabia and to take the lead in an embargo of Iraq were widely supported by the American people, and the president benefited from what is commonly referred to as a "rally event," in which the public increases its support of the president in times of crisis, at least in the short run, because he is the symbol of the country and the primary focus of attention at such times. Moreover, people do not want to hurt the country's chances of success by opposing the president, and the president has an opportunity to look masterful and evoke patriotic reactions among the people. Thus the president's approval levels shot up once again into the 70s.

Once more, the rally effect was short lived. The end of September brought new domestic policy problems for the president as he entered into intense negotiations with Congress over reducing the federal budget deficit. He suffered an embarrassing defeat on his first proposal and then made matters worse by switching his stand on taxes, including a switch on increased taxes on the wealthy over a period of twenty-four hours. With the budget as the most salient issue and the public negatively evaluating the president's performance in reducing the deficit, Bush's approval ratings took a tumble.[17]

His approval ratings rose somewhat after a budget was passed and Congress adjourned, peaking at 63 percent in the last Gallup poll of 1990. In the last quarter of 1990, however, the crisis in the Persian Gulf became more controversial than it was in the summer and threatened to diminish the president's public support. Once questions were raised in Congress and the press about the wisdom of going to war with Iraq, the crisis became a more divisive one and weakened the impact of the rally effect. In mid-December 62 percent of the public thought sending troops to Saudi Arabia was the right thing to do, but 30 percent felt the United States should have stayed home.[18] Correspondingly, approval of the way in which the president was handling the crisis fell.[19]

This dissension continued until the eve of the Gulf War. Then everything changed. Once the actual fighting began, the president experienced the largest rally in presidential approval since the end of World War II, 18 percentage points. By the time the shooting stopped at the end of February 1991, Bush had climbed to the highest rating, 89 percent, ever reached in a Gallup presidential approval poll.

Once the war was over, attention turned to new issues, ranging from the recession to the plight of the Kurds in Iraq. With the national agenda changed once again, the president's approval rating began to fall in the polls.

Responsibility. Even if a matter, such as the economy, is salient to the public, it is not likely to affect people's evaluations of the president unless they hold him responsible for it.[20] Despite the prominence of the chief executive, there are several reasons why people may not hold the president responsible for all the problems they face personally or for some problems that they perceive confront the country.

Most people do not politicize their personal problems, and most of those concerned about personal economic problems do not believe the government should come to their assistance.[21] If people perceive that their economic problems are the result of their own failings or those of their immediate environment, then their personal economic circumstances should not necessarily lead to discontent with national political figures or institutions. A study asking who is "most responsible" for "economic problems" found that only 11 percent chose the president; 67 percent chose big business and big labor.[22]

Some people may feel that those who preceded the president or who share power with him are to blame for important problems. During the 1982 recession, for example, Ronald Reagan was spared the wrath of those who felt economic problems were more the fault of President Carter's administration than of Reagan's, that the president had little control over the causes of inflation and unemployment, and that past presidents had been unable to control these same problems.[23] A poll taken on election day in 1982 found that 41 percent of the voters blamed Ronald Reagan for the recession, but 44 percent blamed the Democrats.[24]

Similarly, there is evidence that voters are sophisticated enough to recognize that current conditions are not necessarily reflective of either present or future economic performance.[25] Although 36 percent termed Reagan's economic policies a failure at the midpoint of his first term and only 6 percent claimed they were a success, 49 percent felt the president's program needed more time to work.[26] Thus, the president is not automatically blamed for hard times.

Perceptions of salience and responsibility may combine to influence presidential approval. A study of the 1984 presidential election found that perceived changes in personal economic circumstances affected candidate evaluations only for those who were doing worse (a small percentage) and who held government responsible.[27]

George Bush took office facing a set of problems left over from the previous administration. The necessity of balancing the budget, bailing out savings-and-loan institutions, cleaning up nuclear power plants, interdicting illicit drugs, wringing corruption from federal housing programs, and caring for the homeless, for example, were all part of the agenda already in place when Bush assumed office. Much of his administration's efforts focused on these issues, and the public seems to have disassociated him from the cause of the problems.

A July 1990 poll found that only 3 percent of the public blamed Bush for the problems with the savings-and-loan industry.[28] An August 1990 poll found that half the public felt the country was in a recession, but only 13 percent blamed Bush.[29] In March 1991, 48 percent of the public placed much of the blame for the recession on the Reagan administration compared with only 15 percent who placed the blame primarily on the Bush White House.[30]

Another national poll in the late summer of 1990 found that the public blamed congressional leaders more than President Bush for the lack of progress in reducing the budget deficit.[31] Yet another poll found that if Bush agreed to a deficit-reduction plan that included a tax increase, only 18 percent of the public would think less of him, while 14 percent would think more of him, and it would make no difference for 65 percent.[32]

A September 1990 ABC News/ *Washington Post* poll found nearly half the public blamed Congress for the deficit, but only a fourth named Bush.[33] After weeks of feuding over the budget between Congress and the White House, an October 1990 CBS News/*New York Times* poll found that only 6 percent of the respondents blamed only Bush for the fiscal impasse, just a fourth as many as blamed only Congress.[34]

Thus the president typically received the benefit of the doubt from the American people. He also helped himself by often staying above the fray and letting party and congressional officials respond to attacks on his administration. He also has used others as surrogates to shield him from the criticism that could be expected in response to controversial decisions and unpopular proposals. For example, Treasury Secretary Nicholas Brady first proposed a deposit fee to pay for the savings-and-loan bailout, Defense Secretary Dick Cheney made the announcement about a compromise proposal on the MX and Midgetman missiles, Secretary of State James Baker revealed the decision regarding the limited sanctions against China, and Vice-President Dan Quayle was given the assignment of touting the Strategic Defensive Initiative.

Although blame for problems is the most commonly discussed side of the responsibility question, credit is an equally interesting issue. The American people may be slow to ascribe blame to the president, but they appear equally unwilling to award laurels. For example, few gave Bush much credit for the collapse of communism in Eastern Europe (see table 5.6). But the public did not think that his high approval ratings were simply the product of his good fortune.

Performance. For matters that are salient to the public and for which it holds the president accountable, the quality of the president's

TABLE 5.6

A QUESTION OF CREDIT

"How much credit do you think George Bush deserves for the changes taking place in Eastern Europe?"

Most	3%
A lot	9
Some	62
No credit	22

"President Bush is mainly popular because . . ."

He inherited a good economy and a good international situation he had little to do with	33%
Of the things he has done and the way he has handled himself.	64

SOURCES: CBS News/*New York Times* poll, 13-15 January 1990; ABC News/ *Washington Post* poll, 1-4 February 1990.

performance becomes a factor in presidential approval. Yet the criteria by which the public evaluates presidential performance are not clear. A discussion of the most often cited issue area influencing presidential approval, the economy, will help illustrate the dimensions of the question.

The state of a nation's economy has a pervasive influence on the lives of its citizens. Their sense of self-esteem, social status, and optimism about the future are often related to the economy. So are their lifestyles and the opportunities for their children.

The conventional view is that people's evaluations of the president are affected strongly by their personal economic circumstances. That is, they are more likely to approve of the president if they are prospering personally than if they feel they are not. According to Richard Neustadt, "the moving factor in [presidential] prestige is what men outside of Washington see happening to *themselves*."[35] Lyndon Johnson believed that "the family pocketbook was the root-and-branch crucial connection to all his plans and hopes for the future."[36]

Many studies have focused on the question of the impact of economically self-interested behavior in voting for candidates for Congress or the presidency, with a wide variety of results.[37] In recent years, however, an impressive number of studies have found that personal economic circumstances are typically subordinated to other, broader considerations when people evaluate government performance or individual candidates.[38]

More specifically, some scholars have argued that citizens evaluate the president on the basis of broader views of the economy than their narrow self-interests. In other words, rather than ask what the president has done for them lately, citizens ask what the president has done for the *nation.*[39]

There are strong theoretical reasons to have confidence in such findings. On a wide range of issues, including federal tax policy, busing schoolchildren for racial integration, the Vietnam war, energy policy, national health insurance, law and order, and unemployment, scholars have found little relationship between the self-interest of respondents and their policy preferences or voting behavior.[40]

Furthermore, people differentiate their own circumstances from those of the country as a whole. For example, in a Gallup poll taken in July 1990, only 45 percent were satisfied with the way things were going in the nation, but 81 percent were satisfied with the way things were going in their personal lives.[41]

Thus, when the public evaluates the president in terms of the economy, it is likely to look beyond narrow self-interest and personal problems. The question then is whether people rely on the overall performance of the economy as their criterion for evaluating his performance or whether they employ a more general notion of how he is handling economic policy. The two criteria are related, but the latter may give the president more leeway.

The public may be less harsh in its evaluations of a president who is struggling with a difficult situation, even if he is not meeting with short-term success. Franklin D. Roosevelt may have enjoyed the public's tolerance in 1933 and 1934 not only because he could not be held responsible for the depression but also because he was seen as doing the best that could be done under trying circumstances.

An extensive cross-sectional analysis showed that people's perceptions of their personal finances, experiences with unemployment, the effects of inflation, business conditions, and nation's economy did not correlate highly with presidential approval. Perceptions of presidential performance in economic policy, however, had strong relationships with more general evaluations of the president. Although one might conclude that perceptions of the president's handling of economic policy were simply a product of more general evaluations of the president, this proved not to be true.[42]

Thus, although the performance of the economy during Bush's first two years in office was lackluster at best, his approval rating did not suffer much in the polls. Nor was it inevitable that it should. The nature of the public's evaluation of presidential performance, combined with the importance of issue salience and attributions of responsibility provided him an important cushion against a worsening economy.

TABLE 5.7

EXPECTATIONS OF THE BUSH ADMINISTRATION

"Do you think the Bush administration will or will not be able to do the following":

	Will	*Will not*
Reduce the federal budget deficit?	39%	46%
Get the drug crisis under control?	36	51
Improve the quality of the environment?	62	26
Keep America prosperous?	74	16
Keep the nation out of war?	77	11
Reduce the crime rate in the U.S.?	39	49
Improve educational standards?	74	18
Increase respect for the U.S. abroad?	74	15
Improve the lot of minorities and the poor?	53	36
Avoid raising taxes?	29	64

"Here are some things George Bush says he wants to do as President. Please tell me whether you think he will, or will not, be able to do them. Do you think George Bush will, or will not, be able to ... "

	Will	*Will not*
Significantly improve the environment in this country?	49%	44%
Significantly improve education in this country?	62	30
Improve relations with the Soviet Union?	69	21
Significantly reduce the drug problem this country?	35	56
Balance the federal budget in the next four years?	17	75
Significantly reduce the problem of homelessness?	37	55

"Do you think George Bush will ask Congress to increase taxes in the next four years?"

Yes	73%
No	22

SOURCES: Gallup poll, 24-26 January 1989; CBS News/*New York Times* poll, 12-15 January 1989.

Expectations. Perhaps contributing to the seeming lack of importance attached to the president's performance on a wide range of domestic issues were the expectations of the public (shown in table 5.7, page 143). The expectations the American people had of the Bush presidency were decidedly mixed on a range of important issues. Only modest percentages of the public felt Bush would make progress on controlling illicit drugs, reducing crime and homelessness, and balancing the budget. Expectations were especially low regarding the president's most famous campaign promise: not to raise taxes (see table 5.8).

These low expectations were encouraged by the modest agenda of the Bush administration. A *Doonesbury* cartoon published before his inauguration had Bush on his first day in office declaring: "So far today, I've said the Pledge and I haven't joined the ACLU and I haven't furloughed any murder-

TABLE 5.8

EXPECTATIONS REGARDING TAXES

"Do you think George Bush will be able to keep his campaign promise of no new taxes, or not?"

Yes	22%
No	71

"Will Bush raise taxes?"

Yes	77%
No	22

"While President Bush is in office, do you think taxes will probably be raised or probably not be raised to reduce the deficit?"

Be raised	70%
Not be raised	22

"Do you think George Bush will ask Congress to increase taxes in the next four years?"

Yes	73%
No	22

SOURCES: NBC News/*Wall Street Journal* poll, 14–17 January 1989; ABC News poll, 12–16 January 1989; Yankelovich Clancy Shulman for *Time* and Cable News Network, 9–10 January 1989; CBS News/*New York Times* poll, 12–15 January 1989.

ers. I've delivered on my entire mandate, and it isn't even lunch yet." At the end of Bush's first year in office, George Will summarized it with "Bush Promised Little; We Got What He Promised."[43]

These low expectations may have been a boon to Bush. Since he began with such low expectations, it was more difficult to disappoint the public. When he had to agree to tax increases in 1990, few were shocked. Moreover, low expectations are relatively easy to exceed. Apparently, that is exactly what happened. In February 1990, an ABC News/*Washington Post* poll found that 67 percent felt that George Bush was "turning out to be a stronger President than I expected."[44] In a July 1990 Gallup poll, 50 percent of the public responded that Bush "is doing a better job as President than I expected."[45]

Leading the Public

Certainly leading the public is an important component of leadership in the modern presidency. What is particularly interesting about the Bush administration is the contrast between its efforts at public relations and those of the Reagan administration.

PROJECTING A VISION

The conventional wisdom is that one of Ronald Reagan's greatest strengths was his ability to project a vision of where he wanted the country to move. George Bush, in contrast, has been repeatedly criticized for either lacking such a vision, failing to articulate one effectively, or both. This stewardship of competence without a compass, it is said, detracts from his ability to build a strong image and associate himself with the values of his supporters.

It is true that Bush rarely conveys a sense of motivating principle, that he does not project a clear vision of who he is. Moreover, he believes saber-rattling is counterproductive, and he is uncomfortable in the bully pulpit. As he proclaimed in his Inaugural Address, "Some see leadership as high drama, and the sound of trumpets calling. But I see history as a book with many pages and each day we fill a page with acts of hopefulness and meaning."

George Bush lacks rhetorical talent, and he knows it. As he told interviewer David Frost, when it comes to certain issues, especially emotional ones, "I'm not good at expressing the concerns of a nation—I'm just not very good at it."[46] Because he understands his limitations as a communicator, especially before mass audiences, and because of his own orientation toward politics, the president prefers to move incrementally toward solutions to discrete problems rather than engage in conceptual, strategic thinking and grand oratory. He goes public as much as anyone before him, but he is more comfortable building consensus one-on-one, behind closed doors.

He did not hold his first prime-time news conference until 8 June 1989 and waited until 6 September 1989 for his first televised Oval Office speech. This speech focused on illicit drugs, and the president displayed a bag of cocaine purchased across the street from the White House. The purchase turned out to be contrived, so the president was upstaged by his own prop.

Bush made only four prime-time addresses from the Oval Office in his first two years. None can be said to have had much impact. The short speech he made regarding the proposed budget agreement for fiscal year 1991 was especially disappointing. Rather than producing a groundswell of support, it seemed only to increase public awareness of the agreement's painful provisions. He suffered an embarrassing defeat in Congress shortly thereafter.

The president's message is often garbled. For example, rather than face the decision to raise taxes squarely, portraying it as an act of courageous political leadership, the White House tried to be cute and simply tacked onto a White House bulletin board the president's statement that the deficit problem required, among other things, "tax revenue increases." But the press seized on it as major news, while the president hid for three days and a large number of Republicans threw a fit. A majority of House Republicans signed a letter to Bush opposing any increase in tax rates; they felt betrayed, and the surprise of the president's change in policy only made it worse.

Everyone was left wondering just what the president was saying. Republicans tried to put a positive face on the issue. Representative Gerald Solomon thought Bush was talking about "tax revenue increases based on continued economic growth"; Representative Robert S. Walker thought Bush might be referring to *cuts* in capital gains taxes; and Senator Pete V. Domenici did not see it as a change in policy at all, at least not regarding income taxes.

The Democrats read the president's lips a bit differently. Speaker Thomas Foley, Senate Majority Leader George Mitchell, and others made it clear, albeit in a low-keyed manner, that they viewed the president's statement as his conclusion that tax increases were necessary.

The White House was not telling. Marlin Fitzwater responded to reporters' requests for clarification by announcing that "we aren't willing to give definition to any of these terms."[47]

In keeping with his style, Bush's 1990 State of the Union message was a patchwork, unfocused and verbose, reflecting a confusion of priorities. His address to the nation regarding the crisis in the Persian Gulf also included distracting comments on other policies, including the budget.

It is one thing to describe Bush's limitations as a public communicator. It is something quite different to attribute significance to it. One of the lessons of the Bush administration seems to be that you do not have to be an actor to obtain public support.

Whatever the critics may say about the "vision thing," the public seems less concerned. As table 5.9 shows, polls have repeatedly found that the public has not found Bush wanting in the area of vision. Although critics complained that he failed to explain carefully the purpose of the Persian Gulf action, most American disagreed, even in August 1990.[48]

IMAGE MANAGEMENT

If Bush's efforts at communicating directly with a mass audience are unremarkable, his broader public relations efforts are often viewed as even worse. He disdains image making and "handlers" such as Michael Deaver. The president is comfortable essentially being seen as himself, even when his message may be blurred in a whirl of activity.

TABLE 5.9
BUSH'S VISION

"Do you approve or disapprove of the job President Bush has done so far in explaining his policies and plans for the future to the American people?"

Approve	65%
Disapprove	28

"Do you approve or disapprove of the job President Bush has done so far in explaining his policies and plans for the future to the American people?"

Approve	53%
Disapprove	37

"Do you think George Bush has a vision of where he wants to lead the country?"

Yes	80%
No	14

"Regardless of your overall opinion of him, do you think George Bush has a clear idea of what he wants to do as President, or don't you?"

Has clear idea	63%
Doesn't have clear idea	29

SOURCES: Gallup polls, 28 February–2 March 1989 and 4–7 May 1989; CBS News/*New York Times* polls, 12–15 January 1989 and 13–16 April 1989.

This is not to say that Bush has ignored public relations and symbolic manipulation. The president wore a plain business suit for his inaugural speech, walked part of the parade route, and invited all comers to a White House reception the next day. He unveiled his proposal for a constitutional amendment banning flag burning in front of the Iwo Jima Memorial, and the introduction of his proposal to renew the Clean Air Act was followed by a press conference with the Grand Tetons as a backdrop. In October 1989, when the president's image was seen as too fuzzy, the White House hired Sig Rogich, a Las Vegas advertising and public relations executive, as the president's new image maker.

Yet, in general, the Bush White House has given lower priority to public relations efforts than did his predecessor. In fact, one of the ironies of Bush's first year in office was the criticism he received from the press for his administration's lack of skill at using the media for his purposes. The theme of the day and the systematic stage management of the Reagan administration were out, improvisation was in. There was much less effort at manipulating the networks to obtain fifteen or thirty seconds on the evening news with specific coverage favorable to the White House.[49]

PRESS RELATIONS

President Bush has adopted a highly successful approach in dealing with the press—without the use of manipulative techniques. Rather than use the media to develop a coalition for policy reform, he has used it to demonstrate his performance in office. The president is accessible and friendly to journalists and seeks them out, whether calling them to come over for lunch or other social occasions on an individual basis or through unannounced visits to the press room to see if reporters might have some questions for him. He held more press conferences in his first year and a half in office than Ronald Reagan held in eight years.

The news conference is the centerpiece of Bush's media strategy. Conferences are built around what Bush considers his greatest asset: face-to-face, personal contact. Most are rambling sessions, held without warning, reflecting the president's penchant for informal, unpressured settings. Since there is often little or no warning of the press conferences, there are no expectations to live up to, no carefully prepared questions, and less chance of the president getting nervous on television. Instead, there is a friendly, open president in command of detail and trying to impress on the press corps that it is a part of the White House team.

Unlike those in the Reagan years, Bush press conferences are typically aimed at newspapers, not television. He does not use the press corps as a prop to speak to the American people, as other presidents have. He talks to the press, not over it. Most of his press conferences have been held during the day when only CNN puts them on the air. There has usually not been a prepared statement, and there is often news on several subjects in the same conference.

The result is that the press corps generally likes and respects Bush. One reporter argued that Bush's personal graciousness earned him the benefit of the doubt. "He's not the sort of human being you want to pursue."[50] The press is not looking for gaffes, despite the president's often tortured syntax, when it appears Bush is a hands-on chief executive who is clearly up to the job of president.

Nevertheless, the president devours everything printed and broadcast about him and seems to take criticism personally. His testiness in February 1990 following criticism in the press for misleading statements from the White House designed to protect top-secret plans, such as meeting Gorbachev in Malta, the trips of high-level officials to China following the massacre at Tiananmen Square, and the four-power conference on a united Germany, raised a momentary ripple but did not seem to leave lasting bitterness on either side.

The Politics of Inclusion

In general, George Bush has practiced the politics of *inclusion*. His is a term devoted to consolidating the gains of the Reagan administration and dealing with the problems it left behind, rather than mobilizing a coalition behind bold new enterprises. From the beginning, Bush dampened expectations of major domestic proposals and said he would go slow on international initiatives. Thus his administration has been characterized to a large degree by a general spirit of moderation, openness, and bipartisanship.

He named one of his opponents for the Republican presidential nomination and the wife of another to his cabinet. He has tried to broaden the Republican umbrella to include a wide range of views on abortion—perhaps our most divisive issue. He has identified himself with environmentalists and civil rights, proposing a Clean Air Act and making clear his desire to sign a civil rights bill (even though he vetoed the bill that Congress passed). Bush also appointed people to the civil rights division of the Justice Department and the Civil Rights Commission who were more sensitive to the concerns of the black community than were those appointed by Ronald Reagan, and a few days before taking office he made a speech honoring Martin Luther King, Jr., on the celebration of the civil rights leader's birthday.

Blacks have been more likely to think that Bush cared about their problems than that Reagan did.[51] And majorities of Democrats and blacks approved of the administration's working to broaden the concept of civil rights so that it encompassed issues related to the disabled, the elderly, and people who have been diagnosed as having AIDS.[52]

George Bush has not let space open between him and the Democrats, just the opposite of the polarizing approach of Ronald Reagan. The latter sought to change policy through conflict, while Bush seeks to employ compromise. From a distance, which is how most Americans view politics, differences of opinion are likely to look like haggling over details rather than principles.

As a consequence, Bush has consistently received high levels of approval, for a Republican president, from Democrats and nonwhites, frequently obtaining majority support from each. This performance is especially impressive when one considers that from 1970 through 1988 there is no record of majority black approval for a Republican president in Gallup or CBS News/*New York Times* polls. Ronald Reagan received an average of only 30 percent approval from Democrats and 22 percent approval from nonwhites.

This blurring of ideological differences with the Democrats has been beneficial to Bush's standings in the polls, but it is not without costs for Republicans in general, who are left without clear issues on which to contest elections. Thus the president campaigned for Republicans in the 1990 midterm elections on the basis of party rather than issues.

The Far Right has been especially distressed with the president's moderation. He failed to condemn the Chinese government's repression of the democracy movement with sufficient vigor to satisfy them, and he similarly failed to support the secession movements in the Soviet Baltic states in any tangible way. Bush's support for environmental legislation, civil rights, higher taxes, Puerto Rican statehood, relaxation of restrictions on high-tech exports to Eastern Europe, rights for the disabled, a lack of restrictions on the National Endowment for the Arts, and Bush's civil orientation toward homosexual groups has disappointed many conservative Republicans.[53] The desertion of conservative House Republicans on the vote on the president's hard-won budget compromise in October 1990 was one of the low points of the Bush administration.

Many conservatives argued that Bush should appeal more to the public and force polarizing choices, losing some points off his approval ratings but solidifying a committed core of the public to serve as the base for changes in policy.[54]

Aside from the notable limitations on any president mobilizing the public,[55] such advice is beside the point. An administration with a modest agenda and a consensus-seeking president who distrusts public rhetoric is unlikely to rely heavily on the public presidency to govern.

Notes

1. 8–11 February 1990.

2. David R. Mayhew, *Congress: The Electoral Connection* (New Haven: Yale University Press, 1974), 70–71.

3. The 1980 election and perceptions of mandates in general are discussed in George C. Edwards III, *At the Margins* (New Haven: Yale University Press, 1989), chap. 8.

4. George C. Edwards III, *Presidential Approval* (Baltimore: Johns Hopkins University Press, 1990), 123–25.

5. See ibid., chaps 1–3.

6. Larry Hugick, "Bush Rates High on Eastern Europe, 'Nice Guy' Image; Lower on Economy and Other Domestic Issues," *Gallup Report,* November 1989, 5.

7. Interview with Richard Wirthlin, Princeton, New Jersey, 4 April 1987.

8. Edwards, *Presidential Approval,* 131–32.

9. George C. Edwards III, *The Public Presidency* (New York: St. Martin's Press, 1983), 239, 243.

10. George E. Marcus, "The Structure of Emotional Response: 1984 Presidential Candidates," *American Political Science Review* 82 (September 1988): 737–62; Arthur H. Miller, Martin P. Wattenberg, and Oksana Malanchuk, "Schematic Assessments of Presidential Candidates," *American Political Science Review* 80 (June 1986): 521–40; David P. Glass, "Evaluating Presidential Candidates: Who Focuses on Their Personal Attributes?" *Public Opinion Quarterly* 49 (Winter 1985): 517–34.

11. For a review of the literature on this issue, see Edwards, *Public Presidency,* chap. 4.

12. Shanto Iyengar, "Television News and Citizens' Explanations of National Affairs," *American Political Science Review* 81 (September 1987): 815–31.

13. Shanto Iyengar, Mark D. Peters, and Donald R. Kinder, "Experimental Demonstrations of the 'Not-So-Minimal' Consequences of Television News Programs," *American Political Science Review* 76 (December 1982): 848–58.

14. Jon A. Krosnick and Donald R. Kinder, "Altering the Foundations of Support for the President through Priming," *American Political Science Review* 84 (June 1990): 497–512.

15. Poll by Market Opinion Research, a Republican firm, cited by Michael Oreskes, "Bush Regains Record Rating in Crisis," *New York Times,* 22 August 1990, A10.

16. See, for example, George Gallup, Jr., and Frank Newport, "Bush Approval Down, Especially among Blacks," *Gallup Poll Monthly,* July 1990, 2–9.

17. Michael R. Kagay, "In Poll, Both Bush and Congress Faulted for Crisis," *New York Times,* 9 October 1990, A11.

18. Michael Oreskes, "Poll Finds Americans Divided on Sanctions or Force in Gulf," *New York Times,* 14 December 1990, A1, A8.

19. See, for example, the Gallup poll of 15–18 November 1990.

20. See, for example, Jon Hurwitz and Mark Peffley, "The Means and Ends of

Foreign Policy as Determinants of Presidential Support," *American Journal of Political Science* 31 (May 1987): 236–58.

21. Richard A. Brody and Paul Sniderman, "From Life Space to Polling Place," *British Journal of Political Science* 7 (July 1977): 337–60; Paul Sniderman and Richard A. Brody, "Coping: The Ethic of Self-Reliance," *American Journal of Political Science* 21 (August 1977): 501–22. See also Stanley Feldman, "Economic Self-Interest and Political Behavior," *American Journal of Political Science* 26 (August 1982): 449–52; Kay L. Schlozman and Sidney Verba, *Injury to Insult: Unemployment, Class and Political Response* (Cambridge, Mass.: Harvard University Press, 1979).

22. K. Jill Kiecolt, "Group Consciousness and the Attribution of Blame for National Economic Problems," *American Politics Quarterly* 15 (April 1987): 203–22.

23. Mark Peffley and John T. Williams, "Attributing Presidential Responsibility for National Economic Problems," *American Politics Quarterly* 13 (October 1985): 393–426.

24. NBC News-Associated Press poll discussed in William Schneider, "Reaganomics Was on the Voters' Minds, but Their Verdict Was Far from Clear," *National Journal*, 6 November 1982, 1892–93. Also see John R. Petrocik and Frederick T. Steeper, "The Midterm Referendum: The Importance of Attributions of Responsibility," *Political Behavior* 8, no. 3 (1986): 206–29.

25. William R. Keech and Henry W. Chappell, "A New View of Political Accountability for Economic Performance," *American Political Science Review* 79 (March 1985): 10–27.

26. NBC News-Associated Press poll discussed in Schneider, "Reaganomics Was on the Voters' Minds." Also see Petrocik and Steeper, "The Midterm Referendum."

27. Alan I. Abramowitz, David J. Lanoue, and Subha Ramesh, "Economic Conditions, Causal Attributions, and Political Evaluations in the 1984 Presidential Election," *Journal of Politics* 50 (November 1988): 848–65.

28. Peter D. Hart and Robert M. Teeter poll for NBC News/ *Wall Street Journal*, July 1990, cited in "Opinion Outlook," *National Journal*, 28 July 1990, 1856.

29. Market Opinion Research poll cited in Richard Morin, "Look Out, Incumbent Rascals: You May Get Fired," *Washington Post, National Weekly Edition*, 17–23 September 1990, 37.

30. Robin Toner, "Poll Finds Postwar Glow Dimmed by the Economy," *New York Times*, 8 March 1991, A11. The poll is a CBS News/ *New York Times* poll of 2–4 March 1991.

31. Richard L. Berke, "Congress Returning to Its Tasks With No Sign of Budget Accord," *New York Times*, 4 September 1990, A1.

32. Hart and Teeter poll for NBC News/ *Wall Street Journal*, July 1990, cited in "Opinion Outlook," 1856.

33. Morin, "Look Out, Incumbent Rascals," 37. In addition, most of the respondents replied that they trusted Bush to do a better job than Congress in reducing the deficit.

34. Robin Toner, "Sour Views of Congress Emerge From Survey," *New York*

Times, 12 October 1990, A11. Poll dates were 8–10 October 1990. This poll found that the public had more confidence in Congress than in Bush to reduce the deficit.

35. Richard E. Neustadt, *Presidential Power: The Politics of Leadership from FDR to Carter* (New York: Wiley, 1980), 73.

36. Jack Valenti, *A Very Human President* (New York: Norton, 1975), 151.

37. For a guide to the early literature on this question, see Edwards, *Public Presidency,* 263–64n. 35.

38. Lee Sigelman and Yung-mei Tsai, "Personal Finances and Voting Behavior: A Reanalysis," *American Politics Quarterly* 9 (October 1981): 371–400; Pamela Johnston Conover, Stanley Feldman, and Kathleen Knight, "Judging Inflation and Unemployment: The Origins of Retrospective Evaluations," *Journal of Politics* 48 (August 1986): 565–88; Pamela Johnston Conover, "The Impact of Group Economic Interests on Political Evaluations," *American Politics Quarterly* 13 (April 1985): 139–66; Stanley Feldman, "Economic Self-Interest and the Vote: Evidence and Meaning," *Political Behavior* 6, no. 3 (1984): 229–52; M. Stephen Weatherford, "Evaluating Economic Policy: A Contextual Model of the Opinion Formation Process," *Journal of Politics* 45 (November 1983): 866–88; D. Roderick Kiewiet, *Macroeconomics and Micropolitics: The Electoral Effects of Economic Issues* (Berkeley: University of California Press, 1983); William Schneider, "Opinion Outlook: A National Referendum on Reaganomics?" *National Journal,* 9 October 1982, 1732; M. Stephen Weatherford, "Economic Voting and the 'Symbolic Politics' Argument: A Reinterpretation and Synthesis," *American Political Science Review* 77 (March 1983): 158–74; Jeffrey W. Wides, "Perceived Economic Competency and the Ford/Carter Election," *Public Opinion Quarterly* 43 (Winter 1979): 535–43; Gregory B. Markus, "The Impact of Personal and National Economic Conditions on the Presidential Vote: A Pooled Cross-Sectional Analysis," *American Journal of Political Science* 32 (February 1988): 137–54; John R. Owens, "Economic Influences on Elections to the U.S. Congress," *Legislative Studies Quarterly* 9 (February 1984): 123–50; Michael S. Lewis-Beck, *Economics and Elections;* (Ann Arbor, Michigan: University of Michigan Press, 1988); Donald R. Kinder, Gordon S. Adams, and Paul W. Gronke, "Economics and Politics in the 1984 American Presidential Election," *American Journal of Political Science* 33 (May 1989): 491–515; Donald R. Kinder and Walter R. Mebane, Jr., "Politics and Economics in Everyday Life," in *The Political Process and Economic Change,* ed. Kristen Monroe (New York: Agathon, 1983), 141–80.

39. See, for example, Donald R. Kinder, "Presidents, Prosperity, and Public Opinion," *Public Opinion Quarterly* 45 (Spring 1981): 1–21; Richard Lau and David O. Sears, "Cognitive Links between Economic Grievances and Political Responses," *Political Behavior* 3, no. 4 (1981): 279–302.

40. See, for example, Michael R. Hawthorne and John E. Jackson, "The Individual Political Economy of Federal Tax Policy," *American Political Science Review* 81 (September 1987): 757–74; David O. Sears, Richard R. Lau, Tom R. Tyler, and Harris M. Allen, Jr., "Self-Interest vs. Symbolic Politics in Policy Attitudes and Presidential Voting," *American Political Science Review* 74 (September 1980): 670–84; David O. Sears, Carl P. Hensler, and Leslie K. Speer, "Whites' Opposition to 'Bus-

ing': Self-Interest or Symbolic Politics?" *American Political Science Review* 73 (June 1979): 369–84; David O. Sears, Tom R. Tyler, Jack Citrin, and Donald R. Kinder, "Political System Support and Public Response to the Energy Crisis," *American Journal of Political Science* 22 (February 1978): 56–82; Douglas S. Gatlin, Michael Giles, and Everett F. Cataldo, "Policy Support within a Target Group: The Case of School Desegregation," *American Political Science Review* 72 (September 1978): 985–95; Richard R. Lau, Thad A. Brown, and David O. Sears, "Self-Interest and Civilians' Attitudes toward the War in Vietnam," *Public Opinion Quarterly* 42 (Winter 1978): 464–83; John B. McConahay, "Self-Interest versus Racial Attitudes as Correlates of Anti-Busing Attitudes in Louisville: Is It the Buses or the Blacks?" *Journal of Politics* 44 (August 1982): 692–720; Donald R. Kinder and D. Roderick Kiewiet, "Economic Discontent and Political Behavior: The Role of Personal Grievances and Collective Economic Judgments in Congressional voting," *American Journal of Political Science* 23 (August 1979): 495–527; Kinder and Mebane, "Politics and Economics in Everyday Life"; and sources cited therein.

41. *Gallup Poll Monthly,* July 1990, 17.

42. Edwards, *Public Presidency,* 226–53. See also Edwards, "Comparing Chief Executives," 54.

43. George Will, Bryan–College Station *Eagle,* 21 January 1990, 8A.

44. 1–4 February 1990.

45. 6–8 July 1990.

46. Quoted in R.W. Apple, Jr., "Capital," *New York Times,* 6 September 1989, 15.

47. "Perfectly Clear," *Congressional Quarterly Weekly Report,* 30 June 1990, 2031.

48. Michael Oreskes, "Bush Regains Record Rating in Crisis," *New York Times,* 22 August 1990, A10; CBS News/ *New York Times* poll, 16–19 August 1990.

49. As a result, President Bush has received less coverage on the network news than did Ronald Reagan at comparable points in their administrations. See S. Robert Lichter and Richard E. Noyes, "Bush at Midpoint: In the Media Spotlight," *American Enterprise,* January/February 1991, 50–51.

50. Burt Solomon, "Bush Cultivates the Press Corps ... Hoping for a Harvest of Goodwill," *National Journal,* 5 May 1990, 1104–5.

51. CBS News/ *New York Times* poll, News Release, 12 April 1990, 2.

52. Diane Colasanto, "Public Wants Civil Rights Widened for Some Groups, Not for Others," *Gallup Poll Monthly,* December 1989, 13, 15.

53. See, for example, Richard A. Viguerie and Steven Allen, "To Bush: The Right Has Other Choices," *New York Times,* 14 June 1990, A15.

54. See, for example, George Will, "535 Political Rookies Surely Can't Be Any Worse Than Present Bunch," Bryan-College Station *Eagle,* 14 October 1990, A8.

55. See Edwards, *At the Margins,* chap. 7.

6

Governing Unheroically (and Sometimes Unappetizingly): Bush and the 101st Congress

Barbara Sinclair

Political commentators frequently imply that the failure of the president and Congress to solve the major problems facing the country is the result of personal character flaws, that the reprehensible practice of "playing politics" and a lamentable lack of backbone on the part of one, the other, or both are the primary barriers to their coming to grips with the federal deficit and other problems facing the nation. Get the right people into office, the implication is, and all will be well.

This chapter, in contrast, argues that structural and other contextual factors are much more important determinants of the character of presidential-congressional relations and of policy outputs than are the personal characteristics of the individuals involved. The behavior of the president and members of Congress is shaped and constrained by the context in which they act; what commentators interpret as playing politics or a lack of backbone is, given the context, often the best strategy for a president or member of Congress. That is, it is the best way to advance the politician's goals of policy results and electoral success.

While some may argue that the goal of electoral success *is* disreputable and that what is needed are principled public officials indifferent to being voted out of office, this argument ignores the crucial role that wanting to be reelected plays in keeping public officials responsive to the wishes of the electorate that chose them. Within democracies, elections are the mechanism we rely on to assure that those we elect have an incentive to be responsive to our policy preferences, and that mechanism works only as long as most elected officials desire reelection.

Understanding the relationship between a particular president and Congress and the policy outputs that ensue requires understanding how incentives and behavior are shaped by context. During the first two years of the Bush administration, this chapter argues, the incentives for the president and

Congress to cooperate were as strong as they are ever likely to be under conditions of divided control. And cooperation produced some notable policy successes: the Clean Air Act, for example. Yet context-determined barriers to cooperation and incentives to pursue other strategies also existed and in the critical budget area came very close to preventing agreement. Furthermore, the prolonged, arduous, and convoluted process of reaching a deficit-reduction accord was costly to both the president and Congress, for it further eroded public confidence in these institutions. This period may well delineate both the possibilities and the limits of cooperative policymaking under conditions of divided control.

The Contextual Determinants of Presidential and Congressional Strategies

The Constitution establishes a relationship of mutual dependence between the president and Congress. The president depends on Congress not just for new programs but also for money to carry out existing programs, for approval of top-level personnel to staff the administration, and for acquiescence in many of the decisions he makes that Congress, through legislation or less formal means, could hinder. While the Constitution and the weak, decentralized party system it fostered provide the president with no basis for commanding Congress, they do give him leverage. Through the veto, his control of the executive branch, and his access to the media, the president can advance or hinder the goals of members of Congress. Given his dependence on Congress, his inability to command yet his potential capacity to influence, every president needs a strategy for dealing with Congress—a plan for getting Congress to do what he wants and needs it to do in order for him to accomplish his goals.

A president's strategies in dealing with Congress are shaped and constrained by his legislative goals and the resources he commands. The extent to which a president's policy preferences and those of a congressional majority coincide or conflict influences how a president sets out to get what he wants from Congress, as well as his probability of success. So, too, do the resources the president commands for eliciting support beyond that based purely on policy agreement.

A substantial partisan majority in Congress is generally considered the single factor contributing most to a president's probability of success.[1] Even within the weak party system in the United States, members of a party tend to share policy preferences; consequently, when members of the president's party make up the congressional majority, they and the president will often agree, at least on the general thrust of policy. Furthermore, the members of his party have an interest in the president's success that transcends any specific legislative battle. Because many such members believe a strong president will be able to help them attain various of their goals in the future, they may be willing to support the president even when their policy preferences do not coincide with his. To the extent that presidential success in the legislative arena breeds a perception of strength that translates into future success, a member of the president's party may believe supporting the president today will pay off in terms of the passage of preferred legislation in the future. To the extent that presidential success has an electoral payoff—increasing the chances of holding the White House or increasing congressional representation—a fellow party member has an incentive to provide support for the president beyond that based purely on policy agreement. Congressional leaders of the president's party are especially likely to see presidential success as in their best interest; thus, when the president's party is in the majority, the very considerable institutional and procedural advantages of control of the chamber are usually available to the president.

Members of the other party, in contrast, are likely to see a strong, successful president as a threat to their future goal advancement. They are less likely to share his policy preferences, so an increase in his legislative effectiveness may threaten their policy goals. Their electoral goals are diametrically opposed to his; the president wants his party to hold the White House and increase its congressional representation, attaining or holding control. To the extent that the president's legislative success advances his party's electoral success, contributing to that success is costly for members of the other party.

For the president to elicit support from members of the opposition party beyond that based purely on policy agreement, such members must be persuaded that the costs of opposing the president are higher than the costs of supporting him. The most likely basis for doing so is via a threat to the member's personal reelection chances. Circumstances that make that threat credible provide a president with significant resources for influencing Congress.

A RESOURCE-POOR PRESIDENT AND
A STRENGTHENED CONGRESS

George Bush began his presidency in a weak strategic position vis-à-vis Congress. Democrats controlled both houses of Congress, the Senate by a margin of ten, the House by eighty-five seats. Although Bush had won with a respectable 54 percent of the vote, Republicans had lost seats in both houses of Congress. The rare loss of seats by the party winning the presidency and the issueless character of the campaign produced a consensus that the election carried no policy mandate. Consequently, Democratic members of Congress felt they had nothing to fear from Bush. In 1981, in the wake of an issue-oriented campaign in which significant numbers of incumbent Democrats were defeated, many Democrats believed that their constituents wanted them to support Reagan's policy departures and that they risked defeat if they opposed him.[2] The 1988 election carried no such message.

A resource-poor president, Bush confronted a Congress better equipped to exert influence on policy under conditions of divided control than the Congress Nixon faced when first elected in 1968 or even the Congress Reagan confronted in the early 1980s. Internal reforms of the 1970s and adaptive changes in the 1980s resulted in a Congress more capable not only of playing an independent policy-making role but also of challenging the president, even in foreign and defense policy areas.[3]

A major expansion in personal and committee staffs in the 1960s and 1970s made members of Congress much less dependent on the executive for information and expanded members' and committees' legislative and oversight capabilities. The upgrading of the Congressional Research Service and the General Accounting Office, and the establishment of the Congressional Budget Office (CBO) and the Office of Technology Assessment in the 1970s gave Congress access to expertise in key areas that was independent of the executive. The Budget and Impoundment Control Act of 1974, which created the CBO, limited the power of presidents to impound—or refuse to spend—funds appropriated by Congress, a power that many presidents had occasionally exercised and that Nixon had attempted to expand. More important, the act set up a mechanism by which Congress can make decisions about the overall level of spending, taxes, and the deficit, as well as about spending priorities, and consequently made it possible for Congress to challenge the president's recommendation in a comprehensive rather than piecemeal manner.

During the 1980s, especially after 1982, congressional Democrats who had been badly split during the 1970s began showing increasing ideological homogeneity. Both a convergence in the character of southern and northern Democrats' election constituencies and a narrowing of the feasible issue space during a conservative period seem to have contributed to high voting cohesion among Democrats. During the 100th Congress, the average Senate Democrat voted with his party colleagues on 85 percent of recorded votes that split Democrats and Republicans; the average House Democrat voted with his colleagues on 88 percent of such party votes.[4]

In the House of Representatives, which Democrats controlled throughout the 1980s, the decline in the ideological heterogeneity of the Democratic membership made increasingly strong party leadership possible.[5] The reforms of the 1970s had enhanced the leadership's resources. Thus, when the Speaker was given the power to nominate all Democratic members of the Rules Committee, the leadership attained true control of the legislative floor schedule and an invaluable tool for structuring the choices members face on the floor. In the 1980s, under pressure from a conservative confrontational president who threatened their policy and election goals, Democrats became increasingly willing to allow their leadership to make aggressive use of such resources. During the 100th Congress, the House Democratic leadership put forth its own policy agenda, and using the Rules Committee advantageously to structure members' floor choices and the party's large and increasingly effective Whip system to mobilize votes, it enacted into law the entire agenda, often over the president's objections and sometimes over his veto. Thus, when Bush became president, he confronted a cohesive Democratic party and a Democratic party leadership experienced at building coalitions in opposition to the president.

THE BUDGET DEFICIT AS A CONSTRAINT

In addition to legislative goals and election-based and institutional resources, previous policy choices contribute to defining the context and affect the choice of strategy. The large budget deficits that were the legacy of Ronald Reagan's policy successes pervasively influenced the behavior and strategies not only of the president but also of Congress. The 1981 tax cut and the enormous defense-spending increases of the early Reagan years produced a sizable gap between revenues and expenditures even during periods of healthy economic growth. In response to Reagan's urging and out of concern with the deficit, Congress made substantial cuts in discretionary domestic spending, but the impact on the deficit was relatively minor.

By the middle of Reagan's presidency, stalemate had been reached. Reagan's adamant opposition ruled out new taxes as part of the solution; such legislation could not be passed over the president's veto. Furthermore, after the 1984 campaign, many Democrats believed advocating taxes when the president opposed them was an electoral kiss-of-death. Republicans, in contrast, believed Democrats had used Republican proposals to cut social security cost-of-living increases in a demagogic fashion in the 1982 campaign and shied away from any such changes. In the mid- and late 1980s, Reagan's budgets proposing further cuts in domestic discretionary spending were "dead on arrival"; even most Republicans were unwilling to make more cuts in popular programs. Given these constraints and fundamental differences in budget priorities between Reagan and congressional Democrats, the Gramm-Rudman-Hollings Act, which mandated a phased reduction in the deficit over several years, only encouraged the president and Congress to engage in "smoke and mirrors" economic forecasting and accounting gimmickry.[6]

By 1988, a consensus was emerging among Washington policymakers that certain national problems—the crumbling infrastructure, education, child care—needed to be addressed and that doing so adequately depended on getting a handle on the deficit. Polls suggested that the public agreed. Yet no sense of crisis or urgency existed to provide impetus to policy innovation. On the public's willingness to sacrifice to meet these needs, evidence was at best ambivalent. Seemingly in response to this national mood, Bush, during the campaign, had promised increased attention to education, child care, and similar programs, but also no new taxes.

PRESIDENTIAL AND CONGRESSIONAL STRATEGIES

A president who commands a large stock of resources can attempt to impose his will on Congress, as Reagan did in 1981. For a president with meager resources, such an aggressive strategy would be doomed to failure. Limited resources suggest a strategy with much more emphasis on compromise. Of course, the feasibility of compromise-based strategies depends on the extent to which the president's policy preferences and those of a congressional majority coincide or conflict. The further the president is to the right or left of the congressional center of gravity, the costlier is the compromise needed to get agreement. At some point, the president will prefer the status quo and a campaign issue to legislation.

The available evidence indicates that George Bush's personal policy preferences are more moderate, and therefore somewhat closer to those of a congressional majority, than Ronald Reagan's. More important, although ideologically murky, the 1988 campaign with its "kinder, gentler" slogan also suggested that Bush intended to take more moderate positions than his predecessor, at least on education and the environment. To be sure, on many issues the distance between Bush's preferred outcome and that of congressional Democrats was considerable. Yet it seemed typically not so great as to preclude the possibility of a compromise.

Bush's strategy vis-à-vis Congress can be largely explained in terms of these factors. Facing a Congress firmly in the control of the opposition party, unable credibly to claim a policy mandate, and constrained by the big deficit, Bush proposed a modest legislative agenda. He proposed some modest new education programs, an increase in funding for the war on drugs, child-care legislation and a rewrite of the Clean Air Act, which were on Congress's agenda in any case, plus legislation to bail out the savings-and-loan insurance fund and clean up nuclear weapons plants.[7]

Given the modest character of most of Bush's legislative goals, his appeals to bipartisanship and for constructive compromise made sense. As soon as the campaign was over, Bush began a concerted campaign to build and rebuild bridges to members of Congress. As a former member of the House and a long-time Washington political insider, Bush had a broad circle of acquaintances, which he nurtured by sending handwritten notes and making phone calls. He made a special effort to cultivate the Democratic leaders of Congress. As a courtesy, he went to Capitol Hill to confer with the Democratic party leadership. In instructions to his cabinet nominees, Bush said, "We're going to have some fights with Congress, but we're not going to approach it as though we're dealing with the enemy."[8]

For congressional Democrats, circumstances also dictated a strategy weighted toward compromise. Congressional Democrats did not fear Bush electorally; they did not believe he had a policy mandate that superseded their own. Yet Bush possessed the veto, and Democrats knew that mustering the two-thirds needed to override would seldom be possible. Also, many Democrats believed that the public wanted any new president to be given a chance, that a confrontational attitude would hurt their standing with the public. Furthermore, although some resentment about the campaign lingered, Democrats' dominant emotion was relief that the new president was not Reagan but someone who believed that, sometimes at least, government could contribute to the solution of societal problems. The Democratic leadership strongly believed that were stalemate to develop, it must not be the Democrats' fault. The leadership was convinced that, given the president's greater access to the media and thus the public, his version of any ambiguous reality was likely to prevail.

They, like Bush, sent out repeated messages about their willingness to work with the president in a bipartisan spirit. In the Democrats' reply to President Reagan's radio address on 12 November 1988, Speaker Jim Wright offered "sincere congratulations" to Bush and pledged cooperation.[9] In the Democratic response to Bush's first address to Congress, the Speaker reiterated the Democrats' willingness to work with the new president.[10]

In fact, given the Bush agenda, Democrats had every reason to believe a strategy of compromise would work to their benefit. Many of the issues on Bush's agenda, such as education and child care, were long-time Democratic issues. Because these issues were on the president's agenda, Republicans and other opponents could not easily kill recommended legislation through delay. Democratic proponents could hope at minimum to get reasonable legislation through compromise with the administration; also possible was forcing the president to accept a stronger bill than he preferred so as to avoid the embarrassment of vetoing popular legislation.

A more aggressive posture vis-à-vis the president was precluded by the problems that beset congressional Democrats during the first half of 1989. After a vigorous three-way contest, Senate Democrats elected a new majority leader in late 1988, and George Mitchell understandably required some time to consolidate his political position and become conversant with the job. House Democrats underwent a series of traumas: an extremely bitter and divisive fight over a pay raise, the protracted ethics investigation of Speaker Jim Wright, and ethics charges against Democratic Whip Tony Coelho. The new leadership team of Speaker Thomas Foley, Majority Leader Richard Gephardt, and Whip Bill Gray included only one member with experience at the top ranks of House leadership.

Both for the new president and for congressional Democrats, the best strategy for dealing with the other was cooperation and compromise. Bush lacked the resources to run over the Democrats in Congress. Given the veto and the president's ability to command media attention, congressional Democrats could not hope regularly to impose their legislative will on Bush.

But although Bush is as moderate a presidential candidate as the Republican party is likely to nominate, differences in policy preferences between Bush and congressional Democrats were frequently substantial. Bush is not as ideologically conservative as Reagan, but on most issues he advocates positions well to the right of the Democratic center of gravity. Like any Republican president, Bush must be responsive to core party constituencies such as business; moreover, he must be sensitive to the party's right wing, an increasingly important component of the Republican party and one that has been suspicious of him. Bush's no-new-taxes stance, one that for many Republicans had become the central defining difference between the parties, was diametrically at odds with the dictates of responsible public policy in the view of most Democrats.

The differences in policy preferences also meant that sometimes no compromise that both sides preferred to the status quo existed. Under such circumstances, the president is likely to veto rather than make further concessions, while congressional Democrats are willing to provoke a veto rather than compromise beyond a certain point.

When control of Congress and the presidency is divided, compromise can have electoral costs. When a president of one party and a Congress of the other work together and produce legislation through compromise, issue differences between the parties become blurred and responsibility for outcomes obscured. Some members of both parties, but especially those of the party controlling Congress, fear that this works to their electoral detriment. Why should voters choose a Democratic presidential candidate if the Democratic party offers no clear alternatives? The president's party will in any case get the credit among those satisfied with government performance.

In general, both parties are understandably concerned with the assignment of credit and blame for what the government does and does not do.

When control is divided, there is a great deal of uncertainty about how the public will assign credit and blame as well as great efforts to influence those judgments. And in this the interests of the president and the majority party in Congress are diametrically opposed. Yet, the desire to claim credit and avoid blame can work as either an encouragement or a barrier to compromise. Conflicts over strategy within the White House and among congressional Democrats during Bush's first two years were strongly influenced by differing assessments of how the public would make judgments regarding credit and blame.

In sum, although compromise was the preferred strategy for Bush and for congressional Democrats, it was dictated more by limited resources than by a broad-ranging coincidence of interests. Consequently, deviations from the strategy of compromise were frequent. Tension between the imperative to compromise in order to enact legislation—to get *a* bill—and incentives to defect from that strategy characterized relations between Bush and Congress during the 101st Congress.

The First Year: Cooperation, Conflict, and Conspiracy

Bush's early moves in his relations with Congress actually carried a somewhat mixed message. His agenda was modest and, by and large, nonconfrontational; some items were also on the agenda of congressional Democrats. Bush's initial moves on the budget, however, were read by Democrats as irresponsible political posturing. In fact, Bush's "no new taxes" campaign pledge presented the administration with a complex strategic situation in meeting the deficit-cutting targets mandated by Gramm-Rudman. Any further cuts in discretionary spending were bound to be unpopular; all the easy cuts had been made years ago. Getting the deficit under control and paying for needed social programs and infrastructure repair, most independent experts believed, required new revenues. But backing away from clear and salient campaign promises is never easy. For Bush, reneging on his "no new taxes" pledge would alienate the potent right wing of his party. Furthermore, backing down would be interpreted as a sign of weakness, which a resource-poor president can ill afford.

One of the earliest policy decisions a new president must make concerns the budget. His predecessor will have prepared a budget, but he is expected to and usually has every reason to alter it and make it his own. Boxed in by irreconcilable promises, seeking to avoid blame for unpopular program cuts, yet wanting to influence congressional budget decisions early in the process, the administration presented to Congress a list of additions it wished to have made in the Reagan budget, but refused to specify where the cuts should come. Although the speech in which the proposal was presented to Congress was couched in conciliatory and inclusive language, many Democrats interpreted the proposal as a continuation of the blame-avoidance budget games of the Reagan years. As Democratic Representative Charles Schumer said, "He picks the increases and lets us make the cuts—that's not very bipartisan."[11]

In his 9 February address to a joint session of Congress, Bush called on Congress to put forward its proposals and negotiate with the administration. Many Democrats believed negotiating on the basis of the president's partial budget plan was simply letting Bush off the political hook. In the end, however, congressional Democrats had no choice but to negotiate. When the president makes the request, the opposition party in Congress cannot refuse to talk. Given the president's greater media access, congressional leaders would find explaining a refusal to the American public almost impossible. Furthermore, Democrats could not produce a politically viable budget resolution on their own. Given the Republican campaign to tar them as the party of high taxes, Democrats had no intention of playing into Republican hands by including a general tax increase in their budget resolution. Yet without a substantial tax increase, the Gramm-Rudman deficit-reduction target could be met only through draconian cuts in defense or domestic spending or through accounting gimmickry. The cuts could not pass the House or Senate and were politically suicidal. Accounting gimmicks required sanction from OMB, which is under the president's control. The Democrats agreed to talk.

If, in the budget area, the administration's early moves maximized the potential of a weak hand, the Senate confirmation battle over John Tower showed the meagerness of Bush's resources. When the Senate rejected Bush's nomination of Tower to be secretary of defense, it was the first time any president had lost an initial cabinet nominee. The defeat clearly indicated that the Democrats did not fear Bush. The debate further suggested that many senators no longer believed that Congress owed the president almost complete deference in the choice of officials subject to Senate advice and consent. Republicans argued that it is the president's right to have whomever he wants, unless an indubitable "smoking gun" is found. Democrats argued for a greater reliance on their judgment and thus, by implication, for a broader congressional role. "If a senator has a serious doubt, he should err on the side of safety," Democratic Senator John Breaux said.[12]

The Tower battle and what Democrats saw as administration budget games did less than one might have expected to sour relations between Bush and congressional Democrats. Both had too much at stake in bipartisan cooperation. The widespread perception that voters "are tired of the bickering

... they want us to work together"[13] meant that both the president and congressional Democrats had a strong incentive to talk bipartisanship. And the relative balance of resources gave both an incentive to pursue compromise seriously on a number of issues.

On 24 March, after four weeks of intensive negotiations, Bush and congressional leaders agreed on a *contra* aid package that provided continued nonmilitary aid. Bush, in essence, abandoned the Reagan administration policy of attempting to oust the Nicaraguan Sandinistas by military force, a policy bitterly opposed by Democrats and one lacking a congressional majority. In return, Democrats gave Bush sufficient nonmilitary aid to protect him against right-wing attacks that he had abandoned the "brave, freedom fighting" *contras*.

A snowballing crisis provided the impetus for cooperation and compromise on a bill to restructure and refinance the thrift industry and its deposit-insurance system. In the House, Democrats provided greater support than Republicans for the tough provisions Bush requested and the savings-and-loan industry opposed.

FROM COOPERATION TO CONFLICT TO CONSPIRACY: CAPITAL GAINS AND MORE BUDGET POLITICS

On 14 April Bush and a bipartisan group of congressional leaders announced that a budget agreement had been reached. "This is not a heroic agreement," Speaker Jim Wright conceded.[14] Indeed, as the nonpartisan publication *Congressional Quarterly* pointed out, the deal was based on the administration's overly rosy economic assumptions, and a good part of the spending cuts were attained by "one time windfalls or other accounting gimmicks that would not carry over into future years."[15] Furthermore, the agreement called for at least $5.3 billion in new revenues from unspecified sources that the Bush administration insisted could be achieved without Bush's reneging on his no-new-taxes pledge.

The deal's attraction to Bush was that it offered him the possibility of getting through his first year without breaking that pledge or exceeding the Gramm-Rudman limits and thus precipitating automatic spending cuts. Congressional Democrats avoided the blame that would be heaped on them when they were unable to pass legislation meeting the Gramm-Rudman limits, as they surely would fail to do on their own. In addition, Democrats hoped that the modest agreement was only the beginning and would lead to a more significant deal later in the year. Bush's OMB director, Richard Darman, was talking about the "deal of the century," which would tackle the deficit in a serious and comprehensive fashion. The new spirit of cooperation, many hoped, would pave the way for such an agreement in the fall.

Instead, the pact led to confrontation rather than cooperation. When the House Ways and Means Committee went to work drafting tax provisions to meet the budget agreement's new revenue figures, conservative Democrat Ed Jenkins proposed a cut in the capital gains tax, and when five other Democrats and all committee Republicans joined him, the committee voted out such a provision over its chairman's objections. Bush had advocated a capital gains tax cut during the campaign and in his budget speech to Congress. The Democratic leadership opposed the cut and believed that Bush had agreed, as part of the budget pact, not to pursue it in 1989. Because this change in tax law would actually increase revenues for the first year or two, its appeal to Bush was enormous. Passing it would enable him to keep two of his major campaign pledges simultaneously.

On 28 September President Bush won a major victory on the House floor when the Democratic leadership's alternative was defeated and the Jenkins provision passed the House. The new leadership team had started its countermobilization effort too late and came up short. In the Senate, however, the Finance Committee reported a reconciliation bill without the provision, thereby giving opponents a procedural advantage on the floor. Supporters needed sixty votes to cut off a filibuster before the tax cut could come to a vote on the floor, and Majority Leader Mitchell held sufficient Democrats to prevent such a vote.

After a good deal of heated rhetoric—the White House accused Mitchell of abusing Senate rules—and with automatic spending cuts going into effect, an agreement was reached. Republicans dropped their attempts to add the capital gains tax cut to the reconciliation bill, and Democrats agreed to strip such extraneous provisions as child care from the legislation. A modest deficit-reduction package was finally enacted just before Thanksgiving. Not only had no progress toward the "deal of the century" been made, the spirit of cooperation had been badly frayed.

The capital gains and budget battles fueled a controversy among Democrats about party strategy vis-à-vis Bush. The strategy of cooperation and compromise that their leaders had adopted and that most had supported came under attack from those who believed its principal beneficiary was Bush. The capital gains battle convinced many Democrats that Bush was not serious about real deficit reduction. Bush's soaring popularity persuaded many that their leaders' conciliatory and statesmanlike public statements were giving Bush a free ride. In the fall of 1989, in response to members' demands, Democratic leaders adopted a more aggressive public stance toward the president, attacking Bush's policies on Eastern Europe and China, his capital gains proposal, and his unwillingness to back up his "kinder, gentler" rhetoric with money.

Capitol Hill had no monopoly on strategy conflict or frustration. By the end of his first year, Bush had learned that no amount of sweet talk or writing notes would compensate for the election-based resources he lacked. Like most presidents with opposition Congresses before him, he went public and sharply criticized Congress, saying Congress deserves "an editorial pounding to get them to do what they ought to do—support the President as he tries to move the country forward ... and not let them dominate debate by blocking everything I try to do."[16]

During the first year of his presidency, then, Bush and Congress cooperated to produce some significant policy agreements, but in the critical budget area, only a "slide-by" deal was attained. Although large, mindless across-the-board spending cuts were avoided, the difficult decisions were put off. The budget agreement, in effect, represented a conspiracy to avoid making hard and unpopular choices. Moreover, acrimony and distrust characterized the process more frequently than bipartisan goodwill.

A serious budget-reduction package had to include significant revenue increases. Yet the centrality of the tax issue to the parties' images and therefore their electoral fates made compromise increasingly difficult. Attempting to shake the high-tax image that Republicans had successfully pinned on them, Democrats refused to take the initiative—and the blame—in proposing new taxes. A great many Republicans believed that their no-new-taxes image accounted for their party's electoral success, and Bush had pledged himself to that course during the campaign. As they saw it, Republicans had a great deal to lose by a compromise that included reneging on new taxes.

Social Welfare, Environment, and Civil Rights Policy: The Varieties and Limits of Compromise

If the conditions necessary for serious compromise were lacking in budget discussion, the social welfare, environment, and civil rights areas seemed to offer better prospects for fruitful cooperation. Bush had expressed support for legislation in these areas during the campaign; Democrats had long advocated action. Yet the strategic situation was complex. In many instances, despite agreement on the need for legislation, Bush's and congressional Democrats' views on the form that legislation should take diverged sharply. In addition, the parties' conflicting electoral goals complicated the strategic calculus.

Bush's goal was to obtain passage of legislation so as to redeem his campaign promises and reap credit with the target population as well as with the general public, but to keep the legislation weak enough so as not to alienate key Republican constituencies, particularly business and the party's right wing. Congressional Democrats, in contrast, wanted to force Bush to accept strong legislation; they would thereby satisfy their own and their constituencies' policy goals and force Bush to alienate important segments of his party. Alternatively, were it not possible to maneuver Bush into accepting legislation stronger than he preferred, Democrats wanted to force him into publicly opposing the legislation, which would presumably cost him support among target populations and the general public. Forcing strong legislation on a reluctant president (publicly kicking and screaming) would be best of all from congressional Democrats' point of view. Congressional Democrats would get the legislation and the credit.

Republicans were not well positioned to shape legislation to Bush's liking. In the House, the Democrats' margin was large enough and their cohesion high enough that, when combined with the great advantages procedural control gives the majority party, Republicans were seldom able to build a winning coalition behind their preferred approach. The narrower partisan balance and rules that give the minority greater powers allowed Senate Republicans to influence legislation to a greater extent. Yet, while they could sometimes extract concessions, Senate Republicans could seldom deliver legislation in the form Bush preferred. Nor did they always agree with the president and use their influence on his behalf.

Thus, Bush was forced to rely heavily on the veto as his major weapon. As of September 1990, the Bush administration had issued 120 veto threats.[17] Almost every major bill in the social welfare, environment, and civil rights areas, including many that were part of Bush's agenda, were under threat of veto at some time during their progression through the legislative process. In most, though not all, cases, Bush's purpose in threatening a veto was to force substantive concessions from congressional supporters of the legislation.

CASES IN CONFLICT AND COMPROMISE

The first major social-welfare legislation to be considered was an increase in the minimum wage. Reagan had refused to countenance any increase, but Bush agreed to support a modest one. After trying and failing to reach a mutually acceptable compromise with the administration when Bush refused to budge from his initial position, Democrats passed legislation that met only some Republican concerns. Bush vetoed the bill immediately. In addition to satisfying his right wing, which opposes the minimum wage altogether, Bush was concerned about reestablishing his reputation in the wake of the Tower defeat; hanging tough on this issue seemed necessary in order to avoid being seen as a pushover.

Democrats were unable to override the veto, nor could they arouse much public indignation over the issue. The labor unions were extremely unhappy, but the general public expressed little interest. Late in the year, Congress passed a somewhat more modest bill, which Bush signed. No longer needing to show toughness at all costs and reluctant to give Democrats another shot at rousing public opinion, Bush agreed to a compromise somewhat closer to the Democrats' than to his initial position. In essence, the result was a draw. The Democrats got a bill they preferred to no legislation, but little political benefit. Bush got legislation he could live with and avoided a political cost in an area potentially difficult for Republicans.

The circumstances surrounding the enactment of clean air legislation were similar only in that it, too, had been stymied by the Reagan administration. Clean air legislation was on George Bush's agenda; it was a less partisan issue and one with broader public appeal than the minimum wage. But it was also one in which business had an enormous stake; a tough bill would cost industry much more than an increase in the minimum wage would.

The Senate committee in late 1989 reported a bill considerably stronger than the administration's. When Majority Leader Mitchell brought the legislation to the floor in early 1990, opponents mounted a filibuster. Unable to muster the sixty votes required to break the filibuster, Mitchell and other supporters of the bill entered into extended negotiations with the administration and key Senate opponents. A compromise bill was agreed to, and Mitchell and Minority Leader Robert Dole fended off all "deal-breaker" amendments and secured Senate passage.

In the House, committee leaders, over an extended period of time, forged a series of agreements on most contentious issues. Their compromise passed on 23 May by a vote of 401–21. Although reasonably content with the bill's environmental sections, Bush opposed the provision of special unemployment and retraining benefits to workers who lost their jobs because of the new law, and the White House warned of a veto.

After a long and difficult conference, a compromise bill emerged during the last days of the session. The administration accepted tougher regulations than it had initially proposed as well as a pared-down program of worker benefits; congressional environmentalists accepted automobile pollution provisions that were less strict than they had hoped to get. Neither Bush nor congressional supporters of strong legislation wanted to see the bill die, and so both were willing to give ground. The resulting legislation is probably the premier domestic policy achievement of the 101st Congress and the Bush administration.

Child-care legislation illustrates still another variety of presidential-congressional relationship. Although child care was a central element of Bush's agenda, his and congressional Democrats' approaches differed radically. Bush favored a tax-credit approach and threatened to veto the Senate Democrats' bill, which included grants to the states for subsidies to child-care providers and payments to parents. Despite the threat, the Senate rejected an administration-backed substitute and passed the Democratic bill in mid-1989. House Democrats took still another approach, routing new child-care funding through the existing Social Service Block Grant instead of setting up a new program. On the House floor, the administration backed a substitute that went well beyond its original proposal. Democrats nevertheless defeated the substitute and passed their bill despite Bush's threat to veto.

Differences among the positions of the administration, the Senate, and the House made prospects of an agreement seem bleak. Yet at the last moment a deal was worked out and included in the budget agreement put together in the final days of the Congress. Tax credits and grants to the states were included. Congressional Democrats agreed to funding levels much below their initial preferences, but the administration gave considerably more ground when it agreed to the creation of a new grant program for the states and the inclusion of a limited set of standards for child-care providers, both of which it had vehemently opposed.[18]

Although civil rights legislation was not on Bush's agenda, he certainly did not want to be only the third president in history (after Andrew Johnson and Ronald Reagan) to veto a civil rights bill. Civil rights advocates were determined to overturn a number of adverse Supreme Court decisions including several that made proving job discrimination much more difficult. Initially, Bush's Justice Department opposed any legislation, but in response to criticism the administration altered its position to support some mild changes. The bills that emerged from the House and Senate were much stronger than Bush wanted; Republican supporters of the president failed in both chambers to alter the legislation to his liking. Bush reiterated his veto threat, claiming the bills would lead to hiring quotas. Efforts by House and Senate conferees to reach a compromise that the administration could accept revealed an unbridgeable gulf. Congress passed the strong bill the conferees agreed on, the president vetoed it, and the Senate failed by one vote to override the veto. Bush thus prevailed in policy terms and pleased his business constituency, which strongly opposed the legislation. But the victory was costly; he alienated the minority community and tarnished his civil rights credentials with the broader public.[19]

THE VETO STRATEGY AND THE LIMITS OF DOMESTIC POLICY CHANGE UNDER CONDITIONS OF DIVIDED CONTROL

No Bush veto was overridden during the 101st Congress. By threatening vetoes, the president frequently extracted substantive concessions from congressional Democrats. Yet the frequency with which Bush found it necessary to threaten vetoes and the number of significant bills he actually did veto are indicators of weakness, not strength. A resource-poor president, Bush was forced to fall back on the primary weapon given to every president by the Constitution. The veto is, however, more effective in blocking legislation the president opposes than in forcing Congress to produce legislation the president wants. When Bush wanted legislation, he generally had to make major compromises himself to get it. Moreover, because of Republican weakness in Congress, Bush was forced to employ the veto in instances where doing so entailed considerable political cost. Had the president's preferences prevailed, Congress would have sent him a civil rights bill he could sign and would not have sent him the family and medical leave bill at all.

The record of Bush and the 101st Congress in nonbudget domestic policy probably delineates the possibilities, character, and limits of policy change under conditions of divided control and no strong public demand for action. The policy preferences of president and congressional majority were probably as similar as they are likely to be under divided control. Nevertheless, on major legislation, policy differences were frequently very large, and budgetary stringency worked against the passage of major new legislation. The end result was a respectable but unheroic record. Clean air, child care, a major housing bill, and the Americans with Disabilities Act (legislation to protect the disabled against discrimination) were the premier achievements. In each of these cases, the process of enactment was long and difficult; in most, it was fraught with conflict between congressional majorities and the president and required often agonizing compromises. Yet sufficient common ground existed to make agreement possible. When the president's and congressional Democrats' divergent policy and electoral goals did not provide sufficient common ground, no compromise was possible. Thus, civil rights and family and medical leave bills were killed by presidential vetoes; major education legislation died in conference.

Foreign Affairs and Defense Policy

During his presidency, Ronald Reagan and Congress were at loggerheads on a series of foreign and defense policy issues: defense spending, arms control, policy toward Central America and South Africa. Bush and congressional Democrats had strong incentives to change the tenor of that relationship. Democrats and Republicans agreed that mutual suspicion and constant confrontation did not make for good policy and were unpleasant besides. "I sense a weariness of the acrimonious debate and the impugning of character that have become common," Republican Senator John McCain said, adding that there is "a growing awareness that some of these issues cannot be addressed unless there is bipartisan agreement."[20] Democratic Representative Sam Gejdenson, a frequent liberal critic of Reagan, said, "Everybody here is tired of having to look at the other branch of government as some enemy post, where you have to shackle them so they will do what the law says."[21]

In addition to concerns about the quality of foreign policy made in such an atmosphere, Bush's political weakness and Democrats' concern about their party's image dictated a bipartisan approach. As a resource-poor president, Bush had a better chance of accomplishing his goals by working with Congress than by futilely attempting to impose his will on it. Democrats feared that constant confrontations over foreign and defense policy were more likely to harm their party's image than the president's.

The *contra* aid agreement worked out in the first months of the Bush presidency illustrated the incentives for cooperation in a particularly exaggerated fashion. During the last year of the Reagan administration, the lack of a congressional majority for further military aid became absolutely clear. Bush certainly did not possess the resources to alter that balance of forces; consequently, he had good reasons to cut his losses. The Democratic leadership was willing to provide him with a face-saving way of doing so because they feared that, were Congress simply to cut off all aid, any subsequent adverse developments in Nicaragua would be blamed on them.

As in domestic policy, barriers to cooperation also existed. Some policy differences between Bush and congressional Democrats were substantial. Moreover, during the long period of confrontation between Congress and the president, not only Reagan but also Nixon, Ford, and to some extent even Carter, congressional Democrats had become accustomed to exercising influence over foreign and defense policy in ways that presidents considered micromanagement and an illegitimate encroachment on executive prerogatives. Bush, urged on by the Republican right wing, declared his determination to reassert presidential prerogatives.[22]

In 1989, Bush agreed to substantial defense spending cuts to get a budget agreement. But that agreement did not avert battles over weapons systems that were similar to those during the Reagan years. When the smoke had cleared, Congress had significantly slowed the production rate of the Stealth bomber and had made a very large cut in Bush's SDI funding request, for the first time reducing spending below the previous year's level. Bush's political weakness, combined with events in Eastern Europe and the Soviet Union that reduced the perception of threat, deprived him of the leverage necessary to sustain his defense policy. Democrats, and some Republicans as well, followed their own policy preferences and judgment, rather than defer to the president.

On aid to Poland and Hungary, Congress also followed its own judgment. In response to the momentous events in those countries, Bush proposed an aid package that many in Congress believed inadequate. Criticism forced Bush to up his request several times; even so, Congress approved considerably more than he wanted.

Bush's meager aid request specifically and his cautious wait-and-see attitude toward changes in the Soviet Union and Eastern Europe occasioned a series of attacks by congressional Democrats. Senate Majority Leader Mitchell, House Majority Leader Gephardt, and many other Democrats criticized Bush as hesitant, overcautious, and lacking in vision. Bush's unwillingness to take a strong stand in response to China's brutal crackdown on dissenters was attacked by Republicans as well as Democrats.

By and large, however, events worked to dampen conflict between Congress and the president. Bush's invasion of Panama was popular with the public and Congress. In the Nicaraguan elections, the U.S.-supported opposition won. The South African government released Nelson Mandela from prison and seemed headed for talks. Bush's initial response to Iraq's invasion of Kuwait received widespread praise from members of Congress.

Sparring between Congress and the president certainly continued. The most serious point of controversy was over the defense budget. In response to the declining threat from the Soviet Union, the administration several times revised its budget request downward during 1990. Democrats nevertheless believed the request to be excessive and, in the House budget resolution, cut it further. The Persian Gulf crisis altered the political atmosphere enough to prevent the enormous cuts the administration had feared; nevertheless, decreases were significant, and Congress again slashed the SDI and Stealth bomber budgets and mandated a reduction in U.S. troop levels.

Congress continued to include directives in its legislation that the president believed encroached on his prerogatives. In response, Bush vetoed several bills and, in 1990, said he would ignore nine provisions of a State Department authorization bill he had signed.[23] To get the aid to Nicaragua and Panama he had requested, Bush was forced to accept nonrequested funding for a variety of programs and projects.

In sum, the first two years saw no major confrontations between Bush and Congress over foreign policy. Geopolitical events were the most important determinant of relatively tranquil relationships. The seeds of future confrontation, however, may have been sown with Bush's campaign to reassert presidential prerogatives.

Certainly Congress shows no sign of retreating from its assertive foreign and defense policy role. Genuine policy agreement, as well as the desire to display a united front in a time of crisis, underlay members' strong initial support for Bush's policy toward Iraq. Nevertheless, the resolutions of support passed by Congress were carefully worded so as to avoid giving the president a blank check. Majority Leader Mitchell repeatedly warned Bush that "under the American Constitution, the president has no legal authority —none whatsoever—to commit the United States to war. Only Congress can make that grave decision." And in its adjournment resolution Congress included an authorization for its leadership to call Congress back into session "as necessary" after adjournment.[24] When, two days after the midterm elections, Bush ordered a huge increase in American troop levels in the Persian Gulf, congressional criticism began in earnest.

Budget Battles, 1990

In 1990, all the participants knew, the budget would again provide the most severe test of the limits of policymaking under divided control. President and Congress, Democrats and Republicans intensely wanted to avoid large automatic spending cuts, and doing so dictated cooperation. But deep policy differences and election-related political calculations acted as major barriers to compromise.

For Bush, the strategic situation in early 1990 was unchanged from that of the previous year; he wanted to avoid triggering the Gramm-Rudman cuts without proposing new taxes. The budget Bush submitted to Congress on 29 January called for higher defense spending and lower domestic spending than the majority Democrats preferred; it reached the Gramm-Rudman target for deficit reduction through economic assumptions much rosier than those of most independent analysts, by accounting gimmicks, and by domestic cuts that Congress had rejected repeatedly in the past.[25] In an otherwise conciliatory State of the Union address, Bush again promised no new taxes and reiterated his call for a capital gains tax cut—statements greeted with thunderous applause by congressional Republicans and grim silence by Democrats.

By sending Congress a budget that did not, in reality, make the hard choices necessary to cut the deficit, Bush put the ball in the congressional Democrats' court, hoping to force them into making unpopular proposals or showing that they were incapable of producing any budget at all. While Democrats were united in their dislike for Bush's budget, drafting their own would not be easy. Although Bush had in fact included $21.1 billion in new revenues (but not, he claimed, taxes) in his budget, many Democrats were leery of supporting any new revenues without Bush's explicit support; and Democrats had no hope of achieving the Gramm-Rudman targets unless they also adopted the administration's overly optimistic economic assumptions.

Congressional Republicans pushed for an immediate summit with the administration, believing that this would give them a stronger hand. The Democrats were reluctant. The rank and file, including those on the Budget Committee, had felt left out of the process in 1989 and did not want a repeat of that experience; the leadership believed it had been burned by administration officials, especially Darman. Almost everyone realized that eventually some talks would be necessary, but most believed that the further along the congressional budget process was when talks did start, the greater the Democratic leverage.

MANEUVERS AND NEGOTIATIONS: MAY–SEPTEMBER

On 2 May House Democrats passed their budget resolution. The resolution specified the same amount in new revenues as Bush's budget, but to alleviate concerns that Republicans would again skewer Democrats as big taxers, the report stated that the House would not act on the proposed tax increase "unless and until such time as there is bipartisan agreement with the President of the United States on specific legislation to meet or exceed such reconciliation requirements." [26] The same day, the Senate Budget Committee reported out its budget resolution.

Almost immediately thereafter, Bush invited the congressional leadership to the White House for preliminary talks. Estimates of the deficit were rising, the economy showed signs of slowing, and the forward movement in the Democratic-dominated congressional budget process threatened to decrease the president's leverage. Democrats were wary about another summit, but again their leadership could not refuse the president's request to talk. Democrats did publicly and repeatedly push the president to define the problem that necessitated the summit: "The president needs to clarify for the country what the problems are and how he thinks they should be resolved," said House Budget Committee Chairman Leon Panetta.[27]

After the president stated that there were "no preconditions," Democrats agreed to talk. Although this concession was clearly necessary to get talks started, many Republicans were upset. Conservative Republicans in the House and Senate held press conferences, wrote letters, and took to the floor urging the president to stick to his no-new-taxes pledge.[28]

Budget negotiators held their first meeting on 17 May and sessions continued through much of June. Estimates of the likely size of the deficit continued to increase, but no progress was made toward a plan to deal with it.

A serious deficit-reduction plan would entail highly unpopular proposals; neither Republicans nor Democrats wanted to lay out a plan first and thus receive the blame for originating painful policy options. Democrats argued that only the president with his "bully pulpit" could explain to the public the magnitude of the problem facing the country and could convince people that sacrifices were necessary. In a 17 May press conference, Bush responded to congressional Democrats urging him, as president, "to lead the country on this issue" by saying:

> Democrats did come down—some of them—saying, "Well, you should go first." I said to them, "Wait a minute, who appropriates all the money? Where's the revenue? Who's got the obligation under the Constitution to raise the revenues? So let's not talk about going first."[29]

But Democrats had been tarred as high taxers too often; they were united in their unwillingness to propose increasing taxes. In late June, congressional leaders told the president that unless he was willing to make a stronger statement on taxes, there was no hope of the talks succeeding. With the economy looking increasingly shaky and the amount of the automatic spending cuts that would occur soaring if there were no deal, the costs to the president of a breakdown rose sharply. The health of the economy, Bush's extraordinary popularity, and even his reelection were potentially at stake.

On 26 June 1990, Bush issued a statement that read, in part: "It is clear to me that both the size of the deficit problem and the need for a package that can be enacted require all of the following: entitlement and mandatory program reform; tax revenue increases; growth incentives; discretionary spending reductions; orderly reductions in defense expenditures; and budget process reform.... The bipartisan leadership agree with me on these points."[30] The president still did not propose any specific deficit-reduction plan and certainly no specific tax increases.

The reaction made it clear why Bush had stuck with his initial budget strategy as long as he could. The media played the statement as a huge story and stressed Bush's reneging on his campaign promise. Some editorials commended Bush for finally recognizing reality, but headlines and TV news stories emphasized that Bush had broken his promise. Lynn Ashby, of Bush's hometown *Houston Post,* asked, "Was he lying or did he just not understand the situation?"[31] Many of the stories, by implication or directly, asked the same question. Republican candidates reacted with dismay, and an appreciable number of Republican members of Congress vowed to vote against any deal that included new taxes. Meanwhile, and less noted, over a hundred House Democrats wrote the Speaker saying any new taxes should be levied on the wealthy.

THE FIRST BUDGET AGREEMENT: 30 SEPTEMBER–4 OCTOBER
On 30 September, the day before the beginning of the fiscal year when a new budget must be in place to keep the government functioning, the president

and the congressional leadership announced a deal had been reached. Although Bush's late-June statement had seemed to jump-start the negotiations, differences over taxes and domestic spending cuts had continued to block progress. After the August recess, negotiators met for ten days of intensive talks at Andrews Air Force Base, away from the media and the distractions of Capitol Hill. When that meeting failed to produce an agreement, the negotiating group was pared down to include only the top party leaders. The primary barrier to an agreement, Democrats claimed, was Bush's continued insistence on a cut in the capital gains tax without an offsetting income tax rate increase for the wealthy. Media attention increasingly focused on the capital gains issue and Bush's opposition to a rate increase for the rich.

Despite the president's phenomenal popularity in the wake of the Persian Gulf crisis, he was unable to prevail on capital gains. The Democratic leadership refused to give in. And nervous Republican congressional leaders, perceiving that the Democrats were winning the media war on the issue of a tax break for the wealthy when everyone else was being asked to sacrifice, began to back away from a capital gains tax change. Bush capitulated.

The agreement included neither a capital gains tax cut nor an increase in income tax rates for upper-income groups; it relied instead on excise tax hikes, including increased taxes on gasoline and home heating oil. A large proportion of the domestic spending cuts came out of Medicare, requiring sharply higher payments by the elderly.[32]

None of the principals to the negotiated agreement were enthusiastic. It was an unpalatable package but, given the deep policy differences between the sides, the best they could do. And it was better, they contended, than the alternative of severe across-the-board spending cuts.

After leaders had briefed their members in party caucuses, prospects for passage in the Senate appeared favorable; majorities of both Republicans and Democrats seemed prepared to support the agreement. House passage would be much more difficult. Republican Whip Newt Gingrich, one of the original group of negotiators and a leader of the right wing, on 1 October came out against the package because it included new taxes. Democratic liberals were upset with the big Medicare cuts and the regressive nature of the new taxes.[33]

From early in the talks, it had been understood that, for an agreement to go into effect, majorities of all four party-chamber groupings would be required, thus spreading the responsibility and the blame. To get the support of a majority of House Republicans would require an extraordinary presidential effort. In July, the House Republican Conference had passed by a 2–1 margin a resolution opposing new taxes. The president began working the phones 1 October, calling House Republicans and asking for their support.

In the succeeding days, groups of Republicans were brought to the White House to meet with Bush. At the administration's request, former Presidents Reagan and Ford also made some calls. Overly vigorous lobbying by high administration officials, however, may have backfired. White House Chief of Staff John Sununu, never known for his tact, offended members when he threatened retaliation for a negative vote. Bush would come into their districts and embarrass them before their constituents, Sununu warned.[34]

At the urging of Democratic and Republican supporters of the budget agreement, Bush went on television to attempt to sell the package to the American people. The already substantial constituent opposition to the painful provisions of the accord swelled appreciably in the aftermath of the president's speech. Bush's first attempt to mobilize public opinion to pressure Congress was a dismal failure. Even stratospheric presidential popularity ratings cannot automatically be translated into policy support, Bush learned.

When the House vote was taken 4 October, the budget resolution incorporating the summit agreement was voted down 179–254 with majorities of both parties voting in opposition. The House Republicans' desertion of Bush was devastating. He could not persuade even a majority of fellow partisans in the House to support him.

Heavily criticized by the White House, House Republicans contended that it was Bush who had deserted them when he reneged on the no-new-taxes pledge. Many believed that not only was that good policy but it was also the party's best hope of becoming a majority in the House and Senate. Some believed that, in order to assure a good economy by 1992 for his own reelection, Bush had decreased Republican congressional candidates' chances in 1990. Basically, for a majority of House Republicans, both their policy and their electoral goals dictated voting against the president. Even arguments that a defeat would severely undermine the president's strength as a leader on the world stage and at home were insufficient to alter many members' calculus.

THE SECOND BUDGET AGREEMENT: 5–28 OCTOBER

In order to pressure Congress to act and in the hopes of repairing his battered leadership image, Bush vetoed the continuing resolution providing temporary funding for the government and shut the government down. Congress, remaining in session over the Columbus Day weekend, passed a stripped-down budget resolution; in response to this indicator of progress, Bush relented and signed a new continuing resolution, funding the government through 19 October.

By this point, the character of the public debate over taxes had clearly changed; as the media portrayed it, no longer was the question whether or not there would be new taxes but on whom the new taxes would fall most heavily. Moreover, the budget was *the* big story, receiving intensive media coverage and eliciting a high level of attention by the public.

As Congress got to work on a budget plan to replace the defeated bipartisan package, Bush sent out a stream of mixed signals as to what he would accept, especially with respect to a possible tradeoff of a cut in capital gains for an increase in rates for the wealthy. Headlines about the president's flip-flopping appeared across the country: "Flap over flip-flop may hurt in '92" and "'Wimp' factor back in news" headlined an article on the possible political fallout of Bush's contradictory statements.[35] Public opinion polls showed the budget imbroglio taking a toll on Bush's job rating, which fell by 19 points between mid-September and mid-October, according to an ABC News-*Washington Post* poll.[36]

House Democrats moved swiftly to put together their own budget plan. Bush's agreeing to a package that included new taxes inoculated Democrats against the charge that they alone were high taxers, many Democrats believed; and most thought that in the public exchange over which taxes would be levied, Democrats were the clear winners. Consequently, Democrats were able to agree on and quickly pass a package that included no new gas tax, a significantly decreased cut in Medicare, and higher tax rates on the wealthy. The House approved the Democratic reconciliation bill 16 October by 227–203, with 217 Democrats and 10 Republicans voting for it.[37]

Many Senate Democrats also found the House package appealing; for them, as for their House party colleagues, it seemed to combine good policy and good politics. But because rules give the minority much more power in the Senate than in the House, the Democratic leadership knew it could not pass a bill without Republican support, and the House plan was anathema to congressional Republicans and to Bush. Promising their members that they would attempt to move toward the House provisions in conference, Majority Leader Mitchell and Finance Committee Chair Lloyd Bentsen worked with their Republican counterparts to pass a bipartisan bill much more similar to the original package than the House bill. It included a sizable gasoline tax, a bigger cut in Medicare than the House bill, and only a minor increase in taxes on the wealthy, to be accomplished not through a rate hike but through a limitation on deductions.

After the defeat of the summit package, Bush had publicly kept his distance from attempts to come up with new legislation. "I think it's very important that our able team ... stay in touch" with House and Senate negotiators, Bush said. "But we're not going to force our way in. This is the business of the Congress. The American people know that. They know the president doesn't pass the budget, and doesn't vote on all this stuff. It's the Congress that does."[38] Bush thus attempted to return to his earlier strategy of refusing to take a position and distancing himself from hard choices. But while he could maintain this hands-off posture publicly, he had too large a stake in getting an acceptable agreement really to withdraw. Bush supported the Senate package and worked behind the scenes for its passage. He also signed another continuing resolution, to fund the government through 24 October.

The conference to work out differences between the House and Senate bills began on 19 October, with administration officials integrally involved. The resulting bill had to be acceptable to the president; otherwise, he could veto it. Yet the strategic situation had shifted significantly since the earlier budget negotiations. Now, a liberal House-passed version with higher tax rates for the wealthy was one of the two proposals on the table; it had considerable support among Senate Democrats as well, and any package that emerged from conference would have to command the support of a large majority of House Democrats. Few House Republican votes were likely. The defeat of the summit agreement consequently had the effect of moving the center of gravity to the left. If Democratic votes would have to pass any package in the House, the compromise would have to be one that House Democrats favored and that meant one in which the rich bore more of the tax burden. In essence, it meant a package much less to the president's liking than the initial summit agreement.

The compromise that emerged included a hike in the tax rate on high-income taxpayers, a proposal Bush had bitterly opposed, and other provisions that indirectly raised the taxes the better-off would pay; capital gains taxes were not cut. Gas taxes were increased less and Medicare cut less than in the summit agreement. At 7 A.M. Saturday, 28 October, only hours after final agreement on the five-year, $490 billion deficit-reduction bill was reached, a weary House voted approval 228–200. Democrats split 181–74 in favor; Republicans, 47–126 against. That Saturday afternoon, by a vote of 54–45, the bill passed the Senate, with 35 Democrats and 19 Republicans supporting it.

WHY BUSH LOST

In the short term at least, the 1990 budget battle was a disaster for the president. Bush was forced to accept provisions he had fought against vigorously and publicly, and he did not get the provision—a cut in the capital gains tax—about which he seemed to care most. His leadership image took a severe battering, and the terms in which the issue was discussed had altered to favor the Democrats. Only days before the congressional elections, the president's popularity was falling precipitously and Republicans everywhere were put on the defensive. Why was the outcome so unsatisfactory for Bush?

Bush, in the budget area as in most others, of necessity had relied heavily on the president's media access and the veto to influence outcomes. A president's greater media access gives him an enormous advantage in having his interpretation of complex and abstruse matters accepted by the public over that of his congressional critics. Thus Bush could submit budgets that finessed the hard choices, he could claim that budget responsibility belongs solely to Congress, without eroding his leadership image. A president has many opportunities to project an image of leadership and can create more at will, by, for example, inviting foreign leaders to the White House. The congressional Democrats' complaint that the president had abdicated his leadership role could not compete with pictures of Bush entertaining Gorbachev at the White House. Since Democrats could not force Bush to lay out a proposal that actually made the hard choices or pass a plan of their own over his veto, they were forced to bargain with Bush. Furthermore, as long as he needed only a minimalist deal, as in 1989, Bush held the upper hand; if the president said a "no pain" deal was sufficient, congressional leaders could hardly convince the public otherwise.

But media access and the veto are more powerful as negative than positive weapons. In the spring of 1990, when Bush concluded that a real deficit-reduction deal was necessary, he tried to employ those weapons to force Democrats to propose taxes first and to agree to his capital gains tax cut. The concerted campaign by the White House and congressional Republicans to pressure the Democrats failed. Because the president needed action, he was eventually forced to capitulate and renege on the major promise of his campaign. The decision was clearly necessary to get an agreement, yet it eventually led to a reframing of the debate so as to disadvantage the president. Undoubtedly, strategic mistakes made the outcome worse than it had to be. Basically, however, the president's problem was that his bargaining position was weak.

The Costs of Divided Control

In the end, the president and Congress agreed on a deficit-reduction package of significant proportions. Unlike the budget deals of former years, the 1990 agreement contained a minimum of "smoke and mirrors." Although most experts believed its economic assumptions were too optimistic and it would not lead to a balanced budget by the projected date, they nevertheless gave it generally good reviews. Yet reaching even this partial solution was extraordinarily difficult and time-consuming. In the process, the president incurred heavy political costs. More serious, public confidence in government received another severe blow. Pollsters, politicians, and reporters discovered anger and disgust everywhere. A mid-October poll found 60 percent of those questioned disapproved of the way Bush and the congressional Democrats were handling the deficit. "It doesn't seem like anything is working anymore," a woman said. "Congress doesn't do its job and the president doesn't work with Congress."[39]

As we have seen, the fault is not one of personal frailties, ineptitude, and disreputable motives, as the media often suggest, but of structures, incentives, and conflicting policy goals. A budget is a statement of priorities, and when resources are tight, decisions about priorities are hard choices. These decisions cut to the heart of decision makers' policy and electoral concerns. One set of priorities will further a given decision maker's notions of what is good public policy or advantage the constituencies on whom he relies for reelection or both. Another may be devastating to his policy and electoral concerns.

When no crisis is looming, democracies find it difficult to make hard choices. By definition, hard choices are ones that hurt some significant element of the public and thus will be unpopular, at least with that segment. Governments that depend on popular support understandably shy away from such decisions for fear of losing electoral support. After all, we value democracy because it produces governments responsive to the wishes of the populace, and elections are the mechanism we rely on to assure responsiveness. In essence, it is by design that democratic governments find it difficult to make unpopular decisions.

Governmental structure and party and electoral systems also affect the likelihood that elected decision makers will be able to make and implement hard choices. Our system, in which control of the executive and Congress can be and often is split between the parties, makes initial agreement less likely and implementation more difficult. The Democratic and Republican parties do represent different policy thrusts and different constituencies; to get an agreement requires that at least some of the participants compromise their policy and electoral goals. Many decision makers have strong policy preferences; for some, compromising sufficiently to get agreement across the party divide on budget priorities can cross the line to selling out their principles. Abandoning groups to which a decision maker owes his election can be not only costly in reelection terms; it can also be interpreted as breaking the compact between representative and represented. Acting in such a way as to reduce one's party's future electoral prospects will have a negative effect on future policy.

United control of presidency and Congress does not guarantee that the hard choices get made, much less made in a way satisfactory to most citizens. After all, in the 1990 budget battles, President Bush and House Republicans could not agree, and whether they could have if Republicans had controlled the House is unclear. Within our system, House Republicans were free to make their own decisions, and a majority decided that both budget deals the president had agreed to were bad policy and bad politics.

If united control does not guarantee good decision making, it does allow voters to affix blame and take retribution. The party in control can be voted out of office. When control is divided, it is difficult for the public to hold anyone accountable. Voters are left angry, disgusted, and wondering why the people they elect always seem to be incompetent, inept, and ineffectual.

Notes

1. See George C. Edwards III, *At the Margins* (New Haven: Yale University Press, 1989), Paul Light, *The President's Agenda* (Baltimore: Johns Hopkins University Press, 1983); and the literature cited therein.

2. Barbara Sinclair, "Agenda Control and Policy Success: The Case of Ronald Reagan and the 97th House," *Legislative Studies Quarterly* 20 (August 1985): 291–314; Darrell West, *Congress and Economic Policy Making* (Pittsburgh: University of Pittsburgh Press, 1987).

3. James Sundquist, *The Decline and Resurgence of Congress* (Washington, D.C.: Brookings Institution, 1981).

4. David Rohde, "Variations in Partisanship in the House of Representatives: Southern Democrats, Realignment and Agenda Change," paper presented at the annual meeting of the American Political Science Association, 1988. See also *Congressional Quarterly Weekly Report*, 19 November 1988, 3334–37.

5. Barbara Sinclair, "Strong Party Leadership in a Weak Party Era—The Evolution of Party Leadership in the Modern House," in *Why Congress Changes*, ed. Ronald Peters and Allen Hertzke (Armonk, N.Y.: M.E. Sharpe, 1991).

6. See Allen Schick, ed., *Crisis in the Budget Process: Exercising Political Choice* (Washington, D.C.: American Enterprise Institute, 1986).

7. *Congressional Quarterly Weekly Report*, 21 January 1989, 143.

8. *Congressional Quarterly Weekly Report*, 14 January 1989, 63.

9. *Los Angeles Times*, 13 November 1988.

10. *Congressional Quarterly Weekly Report*, 11 February 1989, 280.

11. Ibid., 248.

12. *Congressional Quarterly Weekly Report*, 4 March 1989, 467.

13. *Congressional Quarterly Weekly Report*, 18 February 1989, 335.

14. *Congressional Quarterly Weekly Report*, 15 April 1989, 804.

15. Ibid.

16. *Los Angeles Times*, 8 November 1989.

17. *Congressional Quarterly Weekly Report*, 22 September 1990, 2991.

18. *Congressional Quarterly Weekly Report*, 20 October 1990, 3511.

19. *Congressional Quarterly Weekly Report*, 4 August 1990, 2517.

20. *Congressional Quarterly Weekly Report*, 18 February 1989, 334.

21. Ibid.

22. *Congressional Quarterly Weekly Report*, 3 February 1990, 291–95; 24 February 1990, 603–4.

23. *Congressional Quarterly Weekly Report*, 24 February 1990, 603.

24. *Congressional Quarterly Weekly Report*, 29 September 1990, 3140; 6 October 1990, 3240; 27 October 1990, 3630; 3 November 1990, 3709.

25. *Congressional Quarterly Weekly Report*, 3 February 1990, 299–302.

26. *Congressional Quarterly Weekly Report*, 5 May 1990, 1332.

27. *Congressional Quarterly Weekly Report*, 12 May 1990, 1457.

28. Ibid., 1458.

29. *Congressional Quarterly Weekly Report*, 19 May 1990, 1592.

30. *Congressional Quarterly Weekly Report*, 30 June 1990, 2094.

31. *Houston Post*, 29 June 1990.

32. *Congressional Quarterly Weekly Report*, 6 October 1990, 3184–91.

33. Ibid.

34. Ibid.

35. *USA Today*, 11 October 1990.

36. *Washington Post, National Weekly Edition*, 22–28 October 1990, 37.

37. *Congressional Quarterly Weekly Report*, 20 October 1990, 3476–84.

38. *Washington Post, National Weekly Edition*, 15–21 October 1990, 6.

39. *Washington Post, National Weekly Edition*, 22–28 October 1990, 37.

7

The White House and Presidency under the "Let's Deal" President

Colin Campbell, s.j.

When Americans go to the polls, they do not elect the president *and* his White House staff. Neither do they vote for a candidate *and* his cabinet secretaries. In the course of any administration, however, individual White House aides and cabinet secretaries become household names. Certainly, George Bush's chief of staff, John Sununu, has gained notoriety around the kitchen tables of a good many American homes. By virtue of his critical position as secretary of state, James A. Baker III probably has gained fame in more American households than has John Sununu.

Fewer people would know that Baker had held Sununu's job during Ronald Reagan's first term. This fact itself says a great deal. Baker achieved unparalleled success as chief of staff. Yet, except among Reagan conservatives who disdained his "pragmatism," Baker's knack for camouflaging his influence sharply limited the dinner conversation in which his name would come up.

Presidents differ in how they organize and use their White House staff and the cabinet. This chapter looks closely at George Bush's presidential style. Along the way, we find that Bush is not an easy person to assess in this regard. Elsewhere in this book, authors have tried to resolve an enigma in Bush's style. On the one hand, he has pursued the job with great energy and apparent enthusiasm; on the other, he seems to lack a game plan. These characteristics have led several authors to style Bush a reactive, active president.

This chapter presses the categorization a bit further. It accepts that Bush displays no grand vision, but it argues that he is strongly motivated by what he perceives to be his ability to walk into a crisis situation and make deals to solve problems. Before launching into this analysis, however, we should first consider some important issues associated with the role of the White House staff and cabinet secretaries in the modern presidency.

The Interplay of White House and Cabinet
in the Modern Presidency

Over the years, severe controversies have emerged about how the president should organize his White House staffs and utilize the cabinet. Regarding the former, many observers have registered alarm about the proliferation of White House offices and staff positions. With respect to the cabinet, commentators have been divided between those who believe that the cabinet has little significance as a collective decision-making body in the U.S. system and those who acknowledge this but argue that it should.

The issues of how the White House and cabinet function interact. The reliance of presidents on personal staff would have become less pronounced if the American executive branch operated in a more collective way. In all other advanced liberal democracies, chief executives must work closely with cabinet members to develop consensual positions that are "government" or "cabinet" decisions, not British Prime Minister Major's, German Chancellor Kohl's, or Canadian Prime Minister Mulroney's.

How the U.S. cabinet and its various councils operate highlights this point. Presidents will hear their cabinet secretaries out in formal meetings, yet they almost invariably reserve judgment until a later time. In parliamentary democracies, chief executives discern the consensus among cabinet members —normally without a vote—and immediately announce it to their cabinet "colleagues."[1] Their decisions, therefore, become actions and utterances in the name of and on behalf of the entire government (and their political party). Constitutional watchdogs in such cabinet systems would protest loudly if chief executives billed such decisions as their own. Indeed, such chief executives would be forfeiting one of their most valuable public relations assets, the claim of cabinet mandates as a defense against criticism of them personally.

The monocratic nature of the U.S. executive system leads to severe problems of overload for the president. It stands to reason, thus, that incumbents will seek to alleviate the pressure by relying on their staffs. The fact that government itself has become increasingly complex means as well that presidents' staffs have become more multifaceted. The two pressures—the sheer workload and the intricacy of problems—have fueled an almost relentless multiplication of White House offices and positions. In fact, John Hart employs the term the "Presidential Branch" to capture the degree to which the offices and staff available to the president have taken on lives of their own, quite distinct from the rest of the executive branch.[2] This historic trend has raised the specter of personalization and aggrandizement of the presidency.

Just about everyone would allow that presidents should have more assistance than prime ministers. Nevertheless, serious anxieties develop when presidents use their resources to override completely the input of departments and agencies. One would find it hard to appeal to the Constitution in an effort to warn presidents off this approach. After all, the president holds complete sway over the executive branch—unless Congress specifically orders departments and agencies to pursue certain policies and programs.

Yet presidents who ignore the counsel of those parts of the executive branch not housed either in the West Wing of the White House or the Old Executive Office Building do so at the peril of embracing bad policies and making bad decisions. The Tower Commission report on Ronald Reagan's handling of aides' plans to give arms to Iran and covert assistance to the *contras* drives this point home strongly:

> The President's management style is to put the principal responsibility of policy review and implementation on the shoulders of his advisors. Nevertheless, with such a complex, high-risk operation and so much at stake, the President should have ensured that the NSC system did not fail him. He did not force his policy to undergo the most critical review of which the NSC participants and the process were capable ... the most powerful features of the NSC system—providing comprehensive analysis, alternatives and follow-up—were not utilized.[3]

The tensions resulting from presidents' personalization of the executive branch and the relatively low salience of cabinet consultation have ebbed and flowed over time. In the late 1930s, the view emerged that the president needed a central bureaucratic apparatus to give greater direction to the executive branch. In 1937, the Brownlow Commission recommended creation of a professionally competent staff housed in an agency reporting directly to the president. In a partial response, Congress passed legislation establishing the Executive Office of the President (EOP).[4]

Presidents Roosevelt, Truman, Eisenhower, Kennedy, and Johnson all presided over increases in the size and complexity of the EOP. But they also called to varying degrees on their personal staffs in the White House Office (WHO) to handle more directly partisan activities and advice. These presidents thus modulated their reliance on professionally competent staff in EOP units such as the Bureau of the Budget (now the Office of Management and Budget) by consulting partisan appointees. The latter might indeed bring a high level of professional competence to their work; however, they usually owed their presence in the White House to skill at partisan electoral or executive politics and close personal association with the president or his inner circle of advisers or both.

The Kennedy administration saw the quickening of a process whereby recent presidents have manifested a preference for partisan—as against more detached and analytic—professional advice.[5] The ensuing thirty years have witnessed two developments: (1) The WHO has gradually eclipsed the EOP as the core presidential advisory resource; and (2) the ascendancy of partisan appointees in the EOP itself has severely constricted the ability of professionally competent permanent officials to proffer advice once-removed from purely partisan considerations. Nixon advanced this process the furthest, both by developing the WHO into a counterbureaucracy and supplanting the traditionally career-based leadership of EOP units (such as OMB) with partisan appointees.[6]

The political excesses of the Nixon administration focused attention on two flaws in the U.S. executive system, one associated with the organization of the White House Office and the other with the way in which the president relates to his cabinet secretaries. First, the Nixon tack of centralizing executive branch decision making led to overload in the White House. To get through the workload, Nixon began to rely excessively on his chief of staff, H.R. ("Bob") Haldeman, who in turn took an overly hierarchical approach to decision making.

Nixon's neuroses combined with Haldeman's imperiousness to breed unprecedented degrees of White House isolation, backstabbing, paralysis, and paranoia. The resulting liberties taken with the rule of law, especially in the Watergate break-in and its attempted cover-up, convinced most observers that the hierarchical White House with a strong chief of staff presented real dangers for continued democratic rule.

Nixon's two immediate successors—Ford and Carter—forswore the strong chief-of-staff model. Both, in fact, embraced the view that the White House should run according to a spokes-in-a-wheel approach. Here, several senior advisers enjoyed relatively autonomous control over separate domains. Each reported directly to the president without first resorting to the chief of staff. This model held sway from 1974 until 1984—the beginning of Ronald Reagan's second term. At that point, Donald Regan reintroduced many of the hierarchical features of the strong chief of staff. The results took a similarly disconcerting turn, although they fell short of the magnitude of abuses during the Nixon years. Regan resigned in the midst of the Iran-*contra* affair early in 1987. Ronald Reagan served out the rest of his presidency with two chiefs of staff—Howard H. Baker and Ken Duberstein. Both proved adept at giving firm direction without resorting to hierarchical control.

The dysfunctions of imposing overly tight discipline on the executive branch alerted observers to the second defect in the executive system that came to light during the Nixon years. With the inadequacies of the cabinet and its councils as consultative bodies, it becomes exceedingly difficult for administrations to instill a sense of teamwork among department and agency heads. Faced with this reality, Nixon in his second term and Reagan in his first attempted to impose a coherence from above. To this end, they centralized clearance of partisan appointments in the White House and closely monitored the activities of secretaries and key subcabinet officials.

The Nixon administration, especially after it gained its renewed mandate in 1972, abused its prerogatives so blatantly that many began to worry about the imperialization of the presidency. To counter these fears, Presidents Ford and Carter took pains to style their approaches to executive leadership as cabinet government. Indeed, Ronald Reagan, who used his cabinet quite heavily while governor of California, adopted similar language at the outset of his administration.

Presidential Character and Style

No discussion of how a president organizes and uses his White House staff and cabinet can prescind from a treatment of his character and management style. For instance, Bob Haldeman's hierarchical White House would not have achieved such notoriety had it not fed into Nixon's passion for control. Similarly, Donald Regan would not have arrogated to himself so much power had not Ronald Reagan slumped in the second term from a relatively detached to an alarmingly disengaged president. And only an incurable optimist like Reagan could place such immense trust in one adviser.

The prima facie evidence suggests that presidential character and style work strong effects on the organization and operation of presidential staff and the cabinet. Yet political science has striven with only modest success to find out how exactly the personal qualities of presidents link into organizational and operational issues surrounding administrations. Virtually everyone accepts the existence of a relationship; the exact functioning of the gearbox connecting one to the other has largely escaped rigorous empirical inquiry. Thus, to lay the groundwork for assessing the effects of George Bush's character and style on the way in which he has organized and operated his administration, we have first to examine what we mean by *character* and *style*.

In his treatment of presidential personalities and the management of the foreign policy process, Alexander George discusses at length the need to tailor the design and management of the national security process to each individual president:

> each president is likely to define his role in foreign policy making somewhat differently and to approach it with a different decision making and management style. Hence, too, he will have a different notion as to the kind of policy-

making system that he wishes to create around him, feels comfortable with, and can utilize.[7]

Presidential self-knowledge rests at the heart of this process, and it often proves imperfect. As George recounts, Richard Nixon tried at the start of his administration to encourage the kind of multiple advocacy that had worked so well under Roosevelt and Kennedy. But he soon abandoned the system in favor of "by far the most centralized and highly structured model yet employed by any president."[8] If Nixon had been able to acknowledge some of his deepest character flaws, he would have recognized that his embracing this highly formal model would simply exacerbate his tendency to seek excessive control.

In my own research, I have pointed up the degree to which Carter overburdened himself by not seeking structures in the White House and cabinet that would serve as checks for his passion to master every conceivable detail before making a decision.[9] Observers have told us that Ronald Reagan gave virtually no personal reflection to the swap between James A. Baker and Donald Regan that saw the latter become White House chief of staff.[10] Had he given some time to the question, he might well have seen that Regan would arrogate power in areas where Reagan, either because of his view of government or declining interest in his job, had left a vacuum.

The frequency with which presidents seem to lack adequate self-knowledge constitutes just one dimension of the issue of personality. More fundamentally, the issue takes us into the difficult task of defining the parameters of presidential character. A bitter debate broke out among political scientists in the 1970s in response to James David Barber's classification of presidents according to four personality types: active-positives, active-negatives, passive-positives and passive-negatives.[11] According to Barber, active presidents come across as "human cyclones" with boundless energy, while passive presidents evoke memories of Calvin Coolidge, who indulged himself in eleven hours of sleep each night plus a nap in the afternoon. Positive presidents find a great deal of fun in their job, while negative ones at best take grim satisfaction in tasks well done.

Most of Barber's problems with the rest of the political science community stem from his assertion that he has developed a predictive model of presidential performance. At best, his model simply helps us understand the psychological factors associated with presidential performance. We can detect some early-warning signals of potential behavior. We cannot with certainty say that a president with particular psychological traits will invariably behave in a specific fashion.

When we turn down the volume in the heated scholarly exchange, we find some common ground regarding presidential character. For instance, Richard Neustadt faults Barber for appearing to force presidents into the boxes of his paradigm without sufficient accommodation of differences and nuances.[12] But he does, in trying to diagnose what made the presidential experiences of Nixon and Johnson so unhappy, agree with Barber's assertion that both embraced the challenges of office with "relatively intense effort and relatively low emotional reward."[13] Neustadt maintains that both presidents' behavior betrayed deep personal insecurity:

> Back of their bad grace when things went wrong lay insecurity, or so it seems, a stressful inner turmoil that would go away only when things went right. Apparently both men were in the grip of human hungers they endeavored to appease by being President.[14]

Neustadt maintains that we should have seen the ways in which Johnson abused his Senate staff and Nixon let Bob Haldeman run his campaign staff as harbingers of how they would approach the presidency. Along the same lines, George attributes Nixon's proclivity for formalistic approaches to decision making as rooted in the fact that he had "developed a cognitive style that enabled him to cope with deeply rooted personal insecurities by adopting an extremely conscientious approach to decision making." Whereas we might quibble with Barber's labeling (i.e., the positive-negative dimension), it appears that just about everyone recognizes that presidents range from those with strong self-esteem to those who are, for some reason, insecure. Neustadt characterizes Roosevelt and Kennedy as among the former when he says both "approached the office as their natural habitat and drew security from being themselves."[15]

This leaves us with Barber's active-passive axis. At first blush, it appears that Barber has focused on a dimension that taps solely the degree to which the president has engaged himself in his job. But it becomes clear that, in Barber's mind, presidents who put activity together with a sense of efficaciousness maintain perspective—and their effectiveness—while those who do not lose both. The former type of president "shows an orientation toward productiveness as a value and an ability to use his styles flexibly, adaptively.... He sees himself as developing over time toward relatively well-defined personal goals—growing toward himself as he might yet be."[16]

There are two problems with this formulation. First, it seems to assume adaptability and growth during the entire length of office when, in fact, presidents, especially as the job begins to wear on them, often become less flexible and more turned in on themselves. In this regard, analysts should always ask questions about a president's resilience. For instance, what would have Kennedy looked like as president in January 1969 after completing two terms and weathering problems associated with Vietnam and civil rights similar to those that Johnson faced?

Second, we have to take care to delineate different kinds of activity. For instance, some presidents become cautious in their second term as they begin to think of how they will stand in the history books. But Reagan, prodded on by his wife, actually gave greater attention to one policy area when he began worrying about the legacy he would leave. Thus, we saw in his final years a number of overtures to the Soviets that contributed immensely to the end of the cold war. Activity is often in the eye of the beholder.

This chapter construes activity as a multifaceted dimension. Presidents like Roosevelt, Kennedy, and Johnson earn high ratings as actives because they sought to establish a *new order* either in domestic or international affairs. Thus, Roosevelt brought in the New Deal and then led the U.S. effort to stop fascism and militarism in Europe and Asia; Kennedy sought to focus American attention on the New Frontier and urged that Americans "ask not what your country can do for you but what you can do for your country"; Johnson advanced civil rights in this nation more than any other president and pressed the "war against poverty."

Jimmy Carter embraced no overarching objectives that called for the establishment of a new order. Carter's concerns focused much more on pragmatism. His activity was *executive*. The assumption that "there must be a better way" drove him to probe in exhaustive detail how the government worked and how it might become more efficient and effective.

Ronald Reagan, whom most would rate as a passive president, in fact proved to be a *being-there* active. He threw himself massively into the symbolic dimensions of the job. He took no real interest in the executive functions. Further, the new-order goals he presented—tax cuts, reduced spending, and increased defense expenditure—played into the minimalist view of the federal government's domestic responsibilities and the anxieties about America's decline as a world power that prevailed at the time. Nonetheless, Reagan so utilized and exploited the immense prerogatives of the head of state function—a sort of high priest of the national liturgy—that he turned Americans around. They began to feel as good about their country as Ronald Reagan did about himself.

This leaves us with the final type of active president. George Bush exemplifies the "*let's deal*" active. During the Gulf crisis, he ultimately rallied the nation with a promise of a new world order. However, events since the U.S.-led forces expelled Iraq from Kuwait have suggested that the president's vision was illusory at best. Additionally, Bush has still not defined to the nation any clear image of his domestic policy agenda. The president has demonstrated that he will not shy away from exercising his prerogatives as commander-in-chief. yet, Bush proves himself a finicky eater indeed when it comes to intractable domestic issues or, for that matter, the less palatable parts of the Gulf War aftermath. He is not, thus, an executive-active president. His difficulty with—and, at times, distaste for—communicating to the nation makes him somewhat less than a being-there active. Indeed, we can legitimately ask whether Bush would have reaped the rally effect he realized when the war commenced in the Persian Gulf had the Pentagon and the field commanders not provided such superlative film footage.

Bush thrives on crises and brushfires. His first reflex when a tricky problem arises is "let's deal." In search of a solution, Bush will immerse himself in direct contact with all the key players—often on the phone—until he has knocked heads together. When presented with a situation in which some persons are not prepared to deal, Bush will react indignantly, pointing all along to the impressive list of right-minded people who have become equally exasperated with the recalcitrant parties.

In linking presidential personality to how incumbents organize and operate their advisory system, we must look at their management style. Here we refer to the way in which they prefer to do business. In previous work, I have maintained that executive leaders' management styles fall into four categories.[17] *Priorities-and-planning* leaders seek an advisory system that will optimize choice and creativity. They will tend to expand White House and Executive Office of the President resources so that they can tap views alternative to those issuing from the various departments and agencies. But they will not stifle the competition of viewpoints.

Priorities-and-planning presidents will—minimally—give assignments and/or create units in ways that will optimize choice. They might as well foster competition between departments and agencies by establishing cabinet councils and task forces that will expose secretaries and their top aides to the purifying fires of face-to-face criticism.

Both Roosevelt and Kennedy were priorities-and-planning presidents. Nevertheless, neither took the approach so far as to establish regularized mechanisms for engaging cabinet secretaries in a collective process of canvassing alternatives. The style requires the president to think big and to enjoy enough self-esteem to enter into the give and take of an open advisory system. Thus, only new-order actives with a high degree of personal security need apply to be priorities-and-planning managers.

Broker-politics presidents seek the countervaillance provided by multiple points of view. But they tend much less than priorities-and-planning presidents to institutionalize—either through creating advisory positions or utilizing collective decision-making bodies—the process whereby they obtain alternative advice. As well, they shy away from "big picture" scenarios. They prefer instead to work from relatively modest game plans. They will tend to channel their energies more into resolving crises than into probing issues that do not cry out for immediate attention. "Let's deal" active presidents will find in broker politics a good fit between their personality and style. So will executive active presidents.

Administrative-politics presidents neither seek a multiplicity of views nor institutionalized countervaillance. They prefer to devolve as many issues as possible down to departments. Thus they see themselves as engaging in the process only when problems prove too difficult to resolve lower down. Jimmy Carter organized his White House and cabinet systems as if he were an administrative-politics president. But his passion for detail undercut the appropriateness of this approach. That is, a serious disjunction emerged between the frequency with which the president immersed himself in issues and the relatively meager institutional apparatus available to handle the resultant caseload. Normally, we would expect a being-there, active president to embrace administrative politics.

Finally, *survival-politics* presidents appear mostly to resort to this approach only when the other styles have failed. If they started out fostering countervaillance, they increasingly cut down on the number of advisers that they consult and their reliance on collective consultative bodies. If they seek to devolve decisions to departments, they will turn more and more to specific advisers or units in the White House or the Executive Office of the President. These will increasingly operate as a counterbureaucracy to departments and agencies. Nixon gradually slid into survival politics, even though he started in broker politics. Carter adopted survival politics in the summer of 1979 when concerns about the intractability of the American policy process and re-electability concentrated his mind on giving some direction to his administration.

The Bush Administration at First Glance

THE EARLY PROJECTIONS

Immediately after the 1988 election, analysts and commentators turned their attention to the approach that Bush would take to the presidency. The observations focused both on issues of character and style. For instance, James David Barber published a personality profile of Bush just before the inauguration (1989). He rated the president-elect as an active-positive. He pinned his assessment on Bush's skills as a negotiator, the fact—which came to light in the 1988 campaign—that his rhetoric is "coachable," and his tendency toward assuming "missions" during his career.

In fact, Barber's active-positive rating for Bush was one part analysis and one part preinaugural pep talk. This comes through in his rendering of the faults that he believed Bush would have to overcome. Bush, Barber noted, reveals little curiosity about issues and lets his homework slide, displays a prejudice in favor of the rich, and views the media and public opinion as things to be manipulated. Such caveats should prompt us to question the validity of Barber's rating of Bush, first by examining the degree to which the president comes out as "positive," and, second, in what sense we can consider him to be "active."

The phrase "goal seeking" does not leap to one's mind when thinking of George Bush. Even during the campaign for president (and subsequently, for that matter), he did not establish himself as a man of vision. If we mean by *positive* that a person must dream exciting dreams, engage others in realizing them, and relish the challenge of leadership, we find precious little in Bush's demeanor and rhetoric to suggest that these qualities constitute central dimensions of his character.

Except when responding to an offense from a person he disdains, Bush does come across as an amiable man. When he first assumed office, he derived special glee from warmly welcoming all comers to the White House. When he pledged to usher in a kinder, gentler America, however, he could not do this on the grounds that he presented himself as embodying such qualities more convincingly than did Reagan. He could only imply that there would be a better gearbox in his administration—a greater level of consistency between presidential character and concern for persons dependent on and subject to the policies that issue from the White House. In this respect, Bush is unfortunate. Ronald Reagan is a tough act to follow if your strong suit is amiability.

Analysts such as Barber, in my view, would have correctly conceded a "positive" rating to Bush if it were not for the 1988 campaign, which ended up as one of the ugliest in memory. Bush's victory came at a price that voters continue to pay. It failed to convey what he stood for—some sense of his "vision" for the nation. As one political scientist—Greg Markus of the University of Michigan—told the *Washington Post,* the Bush administration would start off with no mandate, bitter opposition from offended congressional Democrats, a polarized electorate, and "the shortest honeymoon in history."[18] In an article published shortly before the election, David Broder suggested that Bush's campaign was of a piece with some fundamental character flaws: a proneness "to let the end justify the means" and—as manifested in the pledge not to raise taxes and the selection of Dan Quayle as his running mate—a "readiness to sacrifice the future for temporary political advantage."[19]

Well aware that the campaign had tarnished his image, the "spin doctors" went to work in an attempt to show that it had not reflected the true George Bush. Just before the inauguration, a spate of articles appeared arguing, in the words of one reporter, that Bush had turned himself around from "pit bull" to "statesman far removed from the fray of the campaign."[20] As one Bush friend, Republican consultant Rich Bond, put it: "I think what you have in George Bush is a man who has been a very, very disciplined understudy in numerous contexts throughout his career. All that people are really seeing is the true Bush who was always there, but it was never his time. Now it's his time."[21]

To be sure, Bush's inauguration speech hit a conciliatory note, even if it fell short on the inspirational and visionary levels. Soon after the address, Democratic congressmen took umbrage at the cynicism of Bush's budget proposals—no commitments to defense cuts beyond the next fiscal year and a package of social policy "add ons" that could be paid for only with unacceptable cuts in existing programs. But Bush's calculated politicization of the budget hardly separated him from Reagan or, for that matter, other recent presidents.

The failed nomination of John Tower to be secretary of defense offered the most concrete suggestion that Bush might bring a notably negative streak to the office. Close friends, such as Treasury Secretary Nicholas F. Brady, cautioned Bush against making the nomination, and media and insider reactions to speculation that Tower would receive the nod appeared notably cool. Still, Bush pressed on.

Once committed, Bush doggedly stuck by Tower, even after it became clear that the Senate would not confirm him. Bush had allowed his loyalty to a highly questionable candidate to delay the gearing up of his administration for one of its most important tasks: getting control of the Pentagon. His obdurance conjured up memories of Jimmy Carter, a president more interested in proving points than getting on with the project of governance.

To grant that Bush is an active president does not resolve the issue of the nature of his activeness. As noted above, presidents can be "new-order," "executive," "being-there," and "let's deal" actives. Right after the election, the spin doctors got to work on projecting how Bush would pursue an active mode. Stories billing Bush as a hands-on manager—as opposed to Reagan's passive, detached approach—began to abound in the media. This would not have warranted our characterizing Bush as a new-order active; the absence of vision precluded that categorization. Nonetheless, the projections did resonate with an executive approach.

Analyses along these lines congealed in some commentators' minds when Bush—ignoring the counsel of James Baker, who urged the president-elect to adopt a Reagan-style triumvirate—chose John Sununu as his chief of staff. Observers considered Sununu, who while governor of New Hampshire had helped Bush capture the primary in that state, highly likely to operate in a hierarchical manner. In fact, some Republicans saw the choice of Sununu as a validation of Bush's decisiveness and toughness.[22] It suggested that the president would keep a watching brief on the entire compass of government activity.

DESIGN OF THE WHITE HOUSE STAFF

Only new-order active presidents will benefit from adopting a priorities-and-planning style, which complements their desire to optimize choice and creativity. Assumption of this style implies two things, given the size and complexity of the modern executive branch. One, the intense involvement of the president in a wide array of issues will draw a relatively high proportion of these into the White House. Two, the president will recognize the benefits of competition—sometimes feverish—between his aides as a stimulant to their and his imaginativeness. It seems, therefore, that a relatively fluid spokes-in-the-wheel approach to organizing the White House best suits a new-order active president.

Thus George Bush's selection of a strong chief-of-staff, hierarchical structure for his White House Office in preference to a spokes-in-a-wheel format did not in itself present difficulties. Even if Bush would fulfill the standards of hands-on management, it appeared he would oversee the executive branch selectively rather than comprehensively. Further, Bush's policy goals lacked definition and thematic coherence sufficient to engage an administration in a priorities-and-planning mode. At best, Bush would prove to be an executive-active president. But even his early performance suggested that he usually follows a "let's deal" mode. Either categorization might have tempted analysts to say that it did not matter, therefore, if Bush opted for a hierarchically structured White House Office. Before settling on this assessment, however, observers had to take a close look at the White House as organized under John Sununu.

The early press on Sununu was ambivalent. Even just before his appointment, some Bush aides questioned whether he had demonstrated an ability to delegate and to mediate between competing elements of the president-elect's coterie.[23] The decision of Robert M. Teeter, Bush's poll taker and political strategist during the primaries and the election, not to join the White House staff served as another caution signal. Although Teeter cited personal reasons, insiders believed that he did not relish the idea of working with Sununu in a triumvirate that might also have included Craig Fuller, Bush's vice-presidential chief of staff during the second Reagan term.[24] Negotiations with Teeter dragged on until early January 1989. When he gave his final no, several key Republicans voiced their concern that this left the White House with nobody with experience comparable to Teeter's in "conceptualizing and framing a national message" or overseeing the complex operations that presidential communications require.[25] As we later see, this sentiment has taken on prophetic significance.

Under Ronald Reagan, Donald Regan had downgraded the level at which many key White House posts were staffed and, in filling vacancies, betrayed a partiality for persons who owed their career advancement to his patronage.[26] Sununu demonstrated greater self-restraint in indulging the latter prerogative. Nevertheless, he carefully rationed the number of White House units headed by full-fledged assistants to the president. Indeed, the initial complement of thirteen officials at this rank fell nine short of the number for the Reagan administration.

We could interpret Sununu's parsimony as an attempt to trim the White House organizational chart, which always seems to be burgeoning. Nonetheless, most traditional functions still received some form of organizational incarnation. The Bush people clearly wanted to get the message out that they sought a low-profile White House. This view came through in a *Wall Street Journal* article that extolled the Bush approach.[27] With close friends such as James A. Baker and Nicholas Brady in his cabinet, Bush, who according to the *Wall Street Journal* would be an "activist," would rely less on his White House staff to work out difficulties in the administration than did Reagan. The latter, the article maintained, required a more senior, interventionist staff to prod him. Bush would look more for a White House that would simply flesh out his initiatives.

At the outset of the administration, Sununu ran a relatively systematized White House. He met with his senior staff each morning at 7:30. At 8:00, he joined the president in the Oval Office for briefing on national security by a Central Intelligence Agency official and a discussion of key issues with Brent Scowcroft, the assistant to the president for national security. Sununu then had a private session with the president to plan the day ahead. He again met with the president at 4:45 P.M. to debrief on how the day had gone. Late each Friday, the senior staff of the White House ran through the events of the week to review how effectively they had handled the issues that had come up over the week and to assess the state of play in matters that still required resolution.

Early reports suggested that Sununu preferred an informal management style. One observer noted that this corresponded with the way in which the president preferred to do business. Sununu liked to drop into people's offices for a chat and did not mind if staffers popped in to ask him questions. As one White House aide put it: "He's surprisingly conscious of the frustrations of this place and keeping as many people in the loop as possible. He's inclusive, anybody can drop into his office."[28]

Sununu himself went on record as relying on informal conversations rather than memoranda when aides sought approval for their actions. But the reader will discern more than a hint of the hierarchical in Sununu's characterization of his role: "I tell the staff, 'If you've got a problem, don't write a five-page memo. Come ask. And if I can't answer it ... I'll go in and ask him [Bush] and for the most part you'll get your answer within two hours.'"[29] Sununu went on to stress that he believed face-to-face exchanges would greatly assist the process whereby staff would start to pull together.

Even before being tested by time, some dangers presented themselves in Sununu's placing himself as the final judge of whether aides could proceed with what they proposed or Sununu should first consult with the president. To begin, aides with opposing viewpoints might become disenchanted if they found themselves consistently left out of decisions on matters that overlap with their responsibilities. That is, Sununu's pivotal role might have prevented some issues from receiving sufficient review from disparate segments of the White House. Second, Sununu might have been denying the president sufficient direct exposure to his aides and their exchanges on the merits of various initiatives. Countervaillance of this sort can leave the president with a clearer sense of his aides' abilities and the reasoning behind their deepest commitments.

SIGNS OF STRESS

Any administration, no matter how well organized and staffed, will begin to show signs of stress. Some of them will reach a magnitude whereby we have to ask whether they point to fundamental flaws that, if left uncorrected, could damage the president's performance and electoral viability. But the early months of the Bush administration seemed to present an instance in which things seemed to be going wrong fairly early.

It appeared that fluidity rather than hierarchy was prevailing in White House dynamics. This fact summoned up in some observers' minds images of the Carter White House. Bush, apparently, had involved himself in a fair amount of presidential minutia. This had prompted one Republican strategist to remark: "My sense is that Bush is in a way doing his own staff work. . . . He doesn't stay within carefully defined channels."[30]

If this became the established pattern of the Bush White House, John Sununu would find himself on the wrong side of a paradox. When things go wrong, people would tend to blame him even if he had not installed the hierarchical command structure whereby he had a hand in all the major actions and decisions emanating from the Oval Office. This would take the joy out of being a lightning-rod chief of staff. Strong chiefs of staff draw blame away from the president, but they also imbibe the heady wine of making things happen.

On two occasions early in the administration Sununu took the brunt of criticism leveled at major failures of the White House machinery. The first arose at the outset of the term. It involved the abortive attempt by Richard Darman, the budget director, and Nicholas Brady, the treasury secretary, to levy a tax on deposits in bank accounts. The public outcry over this proposal, which Darman and Brady packaged as necessary for the rescue of the increasingly shaky savings and loan companies, caused the administration to beat a hasty retreat. Bush could not afford to go back on his no-new-taxes pledge right after the inauguration.

In this instance, Sununu was quick to come out with a diagnosis. It called for greater consistency in the packaging and communication of administration goals to the public and Congress. As he opined to one reporter:

> Probably the most important thing we did not do well was that we could have more discipline in the packaging of the message.... One piece of self-correction is that when we provide consultation to the Hill, we need to be a little more effective in having the positive sides put out early, so that members of Congress who are friendly to us are encouraged to go out early and talk about it.[31]

One administration official made some pointed remarks about the lessons—concerning his own performance—that Sununu could have drawn from the savings and loan experience: "[He] still has a few things to learn about Washington. The first is that when you've got an idea floating that may not fly, you keep it out of the White House. That's why you have a Secretary of Treasury or head of OMB."[32]

The second major occasion in which Sununu drew a lot of fire occurred after Bush's first hundred days in office. To mark the event, Bush went on a four-day barnstorming trip that fell flat in that it attracted very little media attention. Considerable dissension arose in the White House over the failed trip. Sununu refused this time to accept blame. In fact, he shifted responsibility to aides for "grousing" to the media.

Nonetheless, Republican strategists outside the White House took the opportunity to note that the trip seemed to validate the concerns they had registered in January. They had asserted then that a White House without a senior political operative like Robert Teeter was not going to be able to enshrine and communicate a national message. One such Republican laid the blame at the feet of Sununu: "[He] thought he could do it himself, doesn't think it's that vital anyway, and now that it is not working, is saying it is working, and if it isn't, it's not my fault."[33]

Sununu did not respond immediately to such criticism. But Stephen Studdert, Bush's first special assistant for "activities and initiatives" and the White House person responsible for tending the president's image, left the administration in late summer 1989. His successor, Sig Rogich, a Las Vegas advertising executive who claims Frank Sinatra and Donald Trump as former clients, played an instrumental role in the development of Bush's negative commercials during the 1988 campaign.[34]

The Bush White House's handling of congressional relations suggested at the outset another area in which Sununu might have overestimated his ability to get by with low-profile staff. Sununu himself was escaping blame until discussions with Congress over the administration's proposal for a reduction in the capital gains tax rate began to break down during the summer of 1989. At one stage, Sununu had to make a special trip to Capitol Hill to soothe the Republican caucus.[35] A week before, he had offended the party's leadership by berating them about the need for greater loyalty to the president. Much of the exchange had centered on the wisdom of the administration's making its reform of the capital gains tax the centerpiece of its legislative program.

Sununu ran into a further spate of trouble in the fall when he began to proffer renderings of the president's wishes regarding basic pieces of legislation, including bills concerning Medicare catastrophic coverage, funding of abortions, and clean air, which contrasted sharply with what department and agency heads had requested from Congress. Ultimately, the capital gains reform, which had occasioned the summer row with the Republican leadership, met insuperable resistance in the Senate after passing through the House of Representatives. Generous assessments of the recurrent inconsistencies in the administration's legislative positions suggested that Sununu's frequent interventions had amounted to last-minute efforts to compensate for the inadequate staff work of an inexperienced congressional relations office.[36]

Later, in fall 1989, a strong secrecy motif emerged in evaluations of the administration. The way in which the Malta Summit between Bush and Mikhail Gorbachev and the Scowcroft/Eagleberger visit to China were arranged and sprung on Washington insiders and the nation alike aroused some fears about a lack of consultation in the administration. Certainly the national security process—the only cabinet-level collective apparatus mandated by law—performed in less than a stellar fashion in the first instance that tested the administration's skill at crisis management. This was its response to the October 1989 coup attempt against General Manuel Antonio Noriega of Panama.

Senior members of the administration made it known privately that its handling of the coup attempt had exposed serious flaws in Bush's dependence on informal contacts with those cabinet secretaries and aides whom he genuinely trusted. In fact, internal dissent led Sununu to attempt to cool criticism by launching an inquiry into how the existing machinery had performed during the crisis.[37]

The ensuing cacophony of administration voices ultimately tipped the externally equanimous president to anger and a strict order that aides must cease second-guessing the administration's handling of the coup attempt.[38] Just over a week later, one well-placed administration official persisted in venturing a condemnation of Bush's unstructured style:

> For 10 months, they've had this collegial, informal atmosphere.... They just continued as they had. They took in the facts as they needed them. They shut out the bureaucracy. The flow of information into them should have been more organized. There should have been a central collection point. There was never a point where someone said, "Let's call a meeting." That's not the kind of thing you do if it's just the boys. You just say, "Let's go in and talk."[39]

We might find ourselves tempted to conclude that Bush's indecisiveness during the coup attempt did not matter in the end. After all, the December 1989 invasion of Panama resulted in Noriega's overthrow and, after an interval, capture. And the administration reaped a huge windfall in presidential support from the invasion.

Yet Bush's handling of Panama suggested—just as did his dramatic switch from statesman to pit bull in the 1988 election—that he can turn very mean indeed when backed into a corner. Thus the magnitude of his action against Noriega indicated that we should keep a weather eye for occasions where Bush's impatience with a nettlesome problem in which the antagonist resists a deal leads him to vindictive overreaction. This might take us far in explaining why Bush became so determined to go to war against Iraq.

The behavior of C. Boyden Gray during the early months of the administration falsely suggested that Sununu might have to share the role of lightening-rod-designate. Gray, who as counsel to the president serves as the White House's chief lawyer, had stumbled into the midst of several administration crises. In fact, his approach seemed to nullify the original plan that Bush's White House would distinguish itself from Reagan's in the degree to which staffers assumed a low profile.

Gray is heir to a multimillion-dollar tobacco fortune. He worked for eight years in Bush's vice-presidential office. He has a passionate interest in substituting grain-alcohol fuel for gasoline. Observers have suggested that the

Bush-Gray relationship takes root in their mutual standing as patricians. As one colleague from the vice-presidential days has noted:

> I'm totally convinced it's class solidarity and nothing else. Boyden's background is amazingly similar to Bush's—they come from this narrow spectrum of American society. The president feels very comfortable around him, and it enables Boyden to understand better what goes on in the president's mind. I mean, how many rich WASPs are there anymore.[40]

The late Lee Atwater remarked, perhaps regretfully: "[Bush has] developed a confidence and trust level with Boyden that's not going to be shaken."[41]

On more than one occasion during the early months of the administration, Gray crossed the line between low- and high-profile staff to become a loose cannon. At the outset, Gray gave a private briefing to Republican senators on the Federal Bureau of Investigation's report on the original Bush nominee for defense secretary, John Tower.[42] This infuriated Sam Nunn, the chairman of the Senate Armed Services Committee, to the point where it proved impossible to win his assent to the Tower nomination.

Gray also ignored the advice of his deputy and retained the chairmanship of his family's communication company. Only after an uproar in the press did he resign the post and put his assets in a blind trust. Gray holds the key position in the administration for assuring that appointees adhere to conflict-of-interest legislation.

Bush's apparent indulgence of Gray suggested that the president would not be able to maintain discipline in his administration over the long haul. Indeed, Gray's behavior provoked some questioning of the administration's plan not to let White House aides compete for power with cabinet secretaries. Gray twice locked horns with no less a personage than James Baker.

On the first occasion, Gray—no doubt reeling from his own embarrassment over continued involvement in his family business—took Baker to task for holding shares in Chemical Bank. Gray maintained that since Chemical had some $4 billion in outstanding Third World loans, Baker's investment constituted a conflict of interest. One mutual friend of the president's and the secretary's offered that Baker, normally the picture of gentility, was "wild" with anger that Gray had implicitly questioned his integrity.

Not to be cowed, Gray seized the next opportunity to confront Baker. In late March 1989, Baker had successfully negotiated an agreement with the congressional leadership that would allow aid to the *contras* to expire after November of that year unless four congressional committees wrote letters approving continued support. Gray argued within the White House that this arrangement would infringe on presidential powers. After failing to arouse a similar response among his White House colleagues, Gray went public by giving an interview to the *New York Times*.[43] Baker shot back with the assertion that the policy did not violate presidential prerogatives and, furthermore, had won the approval of a higher White House official than Gray.[44]

The next day, the president and John Sununu had a private session with Gray in which they made it clear that he was not to go public in this way in the future. One White House official put the administration's frustration with Gray this way: "We carefully work out something with congressional support—a hell of an accomplishment, a very positive thing, in only the first two months—and what happens but we have somebody out of personal pique [raising questions]."[45]

Gray has kept a lower profile since this episode. Nevertheless, he has spearheaded some pro-business efforts at heading off administration compromises with Congress. For instance, he intervened strenuously in an attempt to protect corporations from stiff mandatory sentences when convicted of felonies. His actions resulted in the Justice Department's revoking a letter in support of stricter punishment. That prompted the deputy attorney general to resign his position in protest.[46] Gray also joined forces with John Sununu in opposing an administration compromise with Congress on the 1990 Civil Rights Act.[47]

As Reality Sinks In

THE LET'S DEAL (BUT-I'LL-GET-ANGRY-IF-IT-TAKES-TOO-LONG) PRESIDENT

I cannot expunge from my mind two images of Bush. The first is the president's hyperkineticism in August 1990 as he simultaneously built the allied coalition against the Iraqi invasion of Kuwait and relentlessly pursued his vacation in Kennebunkport, Maine. The second is the wobbly and painfully protracted retreat from the no-new-taxes pledge that he originally made during the 1988 New Hampshire primary.

The first month of the crisis in the Persian Gulf provided the nation with an unforgettable illustration of "let's deal" presidential style. It appeared at long last that something had actually gotten Bush's adrenaline flowing. Virtually every day, he ticked off yet another litany of world leaders with whom he had met or spoken on the phone. The contacts that he reported to the nation on 5 August in an impromptu news conference give the flavor:

> I've got to go in now. I'm getting another call from President [Turgot] Ozal of Turkey with whom I've been in previous conversation. Yesterday I talked to

him. I talked this morning to [Japanese] Prime Minister [Toshiki] Kaifu, and I applaud Japan's stance, crack down on the imports from Iraq. I just hung up there in Camp David, talking from, with [Canadian] Prime Minister [Brian] Mulroney. We're all in the same accord. He and [French] President [François] Mitterrand, with whom I've spoken, [West German] Chancellor [Helmut] Kohl, [British Prime Minister] Margaret Thatcher....[48]

The frenzied and overwhelmingly successful effort to galvanize world leaders against Saddam Hussein left no doubt that the president was acting decisively. George Bush can singlehandedly build international coalitions. Only his whirlwind rounds of "golf polo"—eighteen holes in an hour and forty-two minutes—rivaled the energy with which he pursued a diplomatic fix to the crisis.

His progress on the domestic side has proven less auspicious. For instance, Bush stirred a hornet's nest on 14 August when he claimed that the Democrats' delaying tactics on the budget had created an impasse as threatening to the nation as the Persian Gulf crisis.[49] With the logjam still unbroken in mid-October, Bush took the words out of many observers' mouths by styling himself as a foreign—as against domestic—policy president: "on the domestic side, here I am with Democratic majorities ... having to try to persuade them to do what I think is best. And it's complicated."[50]

In the next breath, Bush waxed on about how he reveled in the "complexities" of foreign policy:

I don't want to get stretched out on the couch too far in terms of analysis now—but, you know, when you get a problem with the complexities that one—that the Middle East has now, and the Gulf has now, I enjoy trying to keep this—put the coalition together and keep it together and work towards what I think is a proper end, seeing that this aggression doesn't succeed.

Bush's admission of a lack of stomach for the budget negotiations prompted a bitter attack from Edward J. Rollins, the former co-chairman of the National Congressional Committee: "There's no plan. They just wish this would go away so they could deal with something easy like Saddam Hussein. But with four weeks left until Election Day, they're eroding the Republican voting base."[51] Rollins then enraged Bush by sending a memo to Republican House candidates urging them to distance themselves from the president and positions advanced in Congress in support of cuts in Medicare or increases in taxes.[52]

In view of Bush's problems, some commentators began reading across from lessons learned in his handling of the Persian Gulf to his role in seeking a solution to the budget deficit, and vice versa. In August 1990, David S. Broder cautioned against too much applause for Bush's mastery in setting up the anti-Saddam coalition.[53] Broder wondered how long it will take —after the wave of patriotic support has subsided and the consequences of Bush's strategy have sunk in—for people to start asking why the United States allowed Saddam to invade Kuwait in the first place. He gave a high score to Bush as a "reactive president" and low marks for exercising his powers to avoid situations—domestic as much as foreign—that only brinkmanship will resolve:

> a president must be able to launch and sustain initiatives of his own, not just wait for others and then figure out how to react.
>
> Bush's reluctance or inability to do that shows vividly at home as well as abroad—particularly in the matter of the federal budget.... He reacted to the savings-and-loan crisis and the signs of a weakening economy by calling a budget summit three months ago and finally abandoning his unrealistic campaign pledge.

As frustrations took hold over Saddam's intractability and the uncertain utility of the embargo, Bush began to reveal to the entire world his deep anger about his adversary, whom he styled as worse than Hitler. When asked whether he had adopted inflammatory language, Bush once again put himself on the couch and disclosed the degree to which his revulsion for Saddam had taken charge of his thinking. As he put it, "I've had it [with the occupation of Kuwait]," and he added, "I don't think I'm overstating it. I know I'm not overstating the feelings I have about it." Shocked at the extent to which Bush had personalized the crisis, George F. Will quoted approvingly two administration officials who drew parallels between Bush's inability to identify and work patiently toward a strategic goal in regard both to the Persian Gulf and deficit crises:

> A "top official" tells The New York Times, "It's the budget mess all over again—flip-flops, a message out of control and nobody in charge." Another official says, "We seem to be zigzagging because sometimes it's less a matter of a game plan and more a matter of the president's moods."[54]

Thus, to many critics of his handling of the Persian Gulf crisis, Bush's reactive agility had exceeded his aptitude for defining and sustaining viable strategic objectives. Late into fall 1990, the president appeared to have mishandled the delicate task of bringing Congress along on a key policy. As R.W. Apple, Jr., noted:

the Administration had either failed to take key Democrats into its confidence—failed to assure them that this was brinkmanship, not a headlong rush into combat—or had failed utterly to convince them. Whatever the explanation, the partisan split was a major setback for the Administration, its first big stumble of the gulf crisis.[55]

THE TRANSMISSION FALLS OUT

Every administration must pay close attention to two relatively mechanical issues. First, how does the president interact with his White House staff to develop and implement successful policies? Second, how do the president and his advisers work together to assure that the rest of the executive branch functions in coherent and cohesive fashion? In both respects, the operation of the Bush administration has begun to show clear signs of faulty assembly and serious wear and tear. This applies both to the parts of the White House that focus on national security and those that manage the domestic policy process and the president's political affairs.

Foreign Policy. As we have seen, the administration did not in its first year conduct its foreign policy in a sufficiently collective manner. Even with respect to the dominant issue of the first year—how to react to reform in the Soviet Union—a massive four-month review achieved little but the exasperation of the president.[56] Ultimately, the ponderous nature of the process led Bush personally to redraft speeches on Soviet issues. His dramatic announcement of U.S. support for sharp reductions in conventional forces in the spring 1989 NATO summit lent an aura of decisiveness to a deeply divided administration.

In the aftermath of the failed Noriega coup attempt, it became clear that the administration had handled the crisis in an ad hoc manner, uninformed by an overarching strategy and unaided by a systematic consultative process. As noted, the president had failed even to convene a meeting of his national security advisers. He worked, instead, through a crazy quilt of phone calls and informal gatherings.

Constantly at the president's side stood Bush's national security adviser, Brent Scowcroft. Scowcroft had proven the neutral broker par excellence when he held the same position during the Ford administration. That is, he became custodian of the integrity of the national security consultative process. Under Bush, Scowcroft has spent so much time at the president's side that he finds little opportunity to manage hands-on the interagency decision processes.[57]

Bush's whirlwind operating style led to Scowcroft's dramatic change in approach. Scowcroft's availability to the president has provided the almost continual presence of one of the calmest minds ever to serve as national security adviser. Yet Bush's desire to have Scowcroft at his side

through much of the day does present the threat of disjointed management of interagency relations. Scowcroft finds it hard to keep up with the
paper generated by the national security process. He also must delegate to
subordinates coverage of important meetings that work on preparing issues
for presidential review and decision. The absorption of Scowcroft by the immediate preoccupations of the president has hampered considerably the dynamics of interagency coordination. This can expose the president to situations in which he reaches decisions without sufficiently canvassing alternate
views and potential dangers.

Over the past two years, numerous instances have emerged in which the
president has followed the counsel of a limited group of advisers without
bringing other legitimate players into deliberations. For instance, he did not
tell Secretary of Defense Richard Cheney or CIA Director William H. Webster about his invitation made in July 1989 to hold a summit with Gorbachev
in the fall.[58] Accounts suggest that the pique of the chairman of the Joint
Chiefs of Staff, General Colin Powell, at developments in Panama tipped the
scales toward an invasion that caught many insiders by surprise.[59]

Similarly, the announcement of Scowcroft's and Deputy Secretary of
State Lawrence S. Eagleberger's visit to Beijing in December 1989 led to characterizations of Bush's initiative as inconsistent with his stated policies
toward China.[60] Such criticism resulted ultimately in the administration's
embarrassing admission that the pair had secretly visited Beijing one month
after the massacre in Tienanmen Square.[61]

In the wake of these revelations during fall 1989, articles about Bush's
penchant for secrecy and distrust of open discussion—even within the administration—of key foreign policies began to supplant those purveying the
previous conventional wisdom.[62] This had breezily argued that Bush held
foreign policy so closely to his chest only because he preferred to serve as his
own secretary of state.[63] One Republican knowledgeable about both the
Reagan and Bush administrations suggested that the president's secrecy
amounted to an obsession that distorted other values:

> A lot of the way the White House operates is based on the leaks thing ... I
> think you know how obsessed George Bush is about leaks. What you don't
> know is the fullness of the obsession. It's right up there as one of his core
> values. You know, service, family, religion, leaks.[64]

A former Reagan official, who has worked closely with Bush, asserted that his
secretiveness stemmed from his impatience with the messiness of democratic
processes: "[The president] thinks our system—with an excess of Congress
and Press involvement—has made it impossible to do what is right."[65]

The administration's handling of the Persian Gulf crisis, whatever the acclaim it has received, has exposed two deficiencies in the president's approach to managing foreign policy. We discussed the first of these in the preceding section, namely the president's distaste for the difficult task of selling his response to the nation and to Congress. The second concerns the mechanics of managing the administration's handling of Saddam Hussein's original threats.

Americans expect little of the machinery for coordination of collective deliberations within the executive branch. Thus it stands to reason that observers normally avoid dwelling on the operation of the decision process in connection with the handling of an impending or actual crises. Few, for instance, have asked, regarding the Persian Gulf crisis, whether the administration responded adequately to the early signs of Saddam's designs on Kuwait.

We all know now of the soothing words that the U.S. ambassador to Iraq, April Glaspie, allegedly used with Saddam Hussein just days before the latter's invasion of Kuwait. An Iraqi transcript of this exchange depicted her as conveying the assurances of the administration that the president would not seek to impose trade sanctions on Iraq. According to the Iraqi rendering of the meeting, she added: "President Bush is an intelligent man. He is not going to declare an economic war against Iraq."[66] In Washington, both State Department spokesperson Margaret Tutwiler and Assistant Secretary for the Middle East John Kelly publicly stated that the United States saw no obligation to come to Kuwait's aid if it was attacked.[67] Glaspie waited until March 1991 to assert that the Iraqi transcript omitted her words of caution to Saddam. Observers ask why it took fully six months for her to assume this line of defense. Furthermore, the Tutwiler and Kelly statements still stand as the definitive U.S. position immediately before the invasion.

Glaspie (as portrayed in the Iraqi transcript), Tutwiler, and Kelly were all expressing the administration's public position. Their stance comported with administration efforts in the months leading up to the crisis to oppose congressional initiatives that would employ trade sanctions against Iraq. Commentators have subsequently uncovered evidence that the State Department had, in fact, launched an attempt to impose sanctions against Iraq. After a particularly bellicose outburst by Saddam in April 1990, James Baker endorsed a State Department proposal of trade restrictions; however, the measures became ensnarled in interagency review led by Robert Gates, the deputy national security adviser.[68]

The intractability of the process owed in part to Bush's tendency, noted above, to view Brent Scowcroft as an aide-de-camp rather than a ringmaster for the national security decision system. With Baker preoccupied with U.S.-Soviet relations, a more senior White House official than Gates would have to have led the process of knocking heads together to achieve a timely and coherent response to Saddam's threatening language. In addition, Bush's preference for informal consultations over structured review sessions exacerbated the problem.

That Baker can swing the president and interdepartment processes his way when he focuses on a problem has become a well-established part of the book on the Bush-Baker relationship.[69] Yet Baker never revisited the sanctions question long enough before Saddam's invasion to bring the matter up with the president.[70] With Gates as a weak cog and Baker absorbed by the Soviets, a timely handling of State's sanctions proposal became a remote prospect.

In the aftermath of the 1982 Argentine invasion of the Falkland Islands, it became clear that Margaret Thatcher and her cabinet had failed miserably in responding to the impending crisis. As a result, her foreign secretary and two of his ministers resigned immediately after the invasion. Further, the opposition forced the government to strike a committee of privy councilors to examine exhaustively what went wrong and whether the lessons learned might call for reforms of the national security process in the British cabinet.[71]

Nobody effectively pinned blame on the ultimate culprit—the prime minister's ad hoc and personalistic management style.[72] Yet Mrs. Thatcher's government did not go on blithely as if it had done all that it could to avoid the Argentine invasion. In the Persian Gulf crisis, in contrast, the Bush administration has almost totally escaped scrutiny for its handling of Saddam's increasingly aggressive threats. This speaks volumes about the low standards for the interagency coordination that prevail in the United States, notwithstanding the statutory base of the National Security Council and the pious platitudes in the Tower Commission report calling for its fuller engagement.

DOMESTIC POLICY

When George Bush became president, he appointed as assistant to the president for economic and domestic affairs Roger Porter, a professor in Harvard's Kennedy School of Government. Much like Scowcroft, Porter brought to the White House immense experience at providing neutral brokerage of interagency decision processes.[73] Porter and his staff in the Office of Policy Development, along with members of the White House Office of Cabinet Affairs, shoulder responsibility for the operation of the Economic Policy Council and the Domestic Policy Council. These two bodies, which absorbed the work of fully eight policy committees managed from the White House during the first term of the Reagan administration, consist of cabinet secretaries and prepare issues for presidential decision.

During Reagan's first term, a senior White House official noted that on a scale of 10, cabinet councils can do a good job of reconciling issues up to a level of 7 in difficulty. Beyond that, he observed, you "are really close to the guts of the administration, it becomes essential for the president's staff to mount an effort to get around the council process. That's when we really need to get deeply involved; ... beat the drum and figure out how to get it through the Hill."[74]

Under the Bush administration, the official would probably revise the line of demarcation at least a notch lower, to level-6 problems.[75] That is, the Bush White House more often bypasses the cabinet council system in resolving key issues. As well, it more often short-circuits the interagency process when it becomes clear that it will not yield what the prime shakers in the White House seek.

We all have become well acquainted with the roles of Chief of Staff John Sununu and Budget Director Richard Darman in negotiations with Congress. But both the hidden and not-so-hidden hands of this pair have become manifest in virtually every other contentious policy decision. Through his many interventions, Sununu has established himself as the staunch conservative conscience of the administration, in particular championing the cases of business interests. Darman's interventions follow less clear ideological lines, focusing on beating back proposals that would add to public spending.

Together, Sununu and Darman have pretty much eclipsed the role of Treasury Secretary Nicholas F. Brady during administration negotiations with Congress over the deficit. For Sununu, this constituted no small feat. Rarely do chiefs of staff take such a direct role in detailed budget negotiations. And Brady, supposedly, enjoys unparalled personal access to the president—which he apparently did not fully tap.[76] A true patrician, he perhaps eschewed the pit bull approach of his two economic policy colleagues. Whatever, the Economic Policy Council failed to serve as a context for administration deliberations on its proposals for handling the deficit. And this would fit the Reagan administration as well.

The frequency of significant interventions on the part of John Sununu in lower-level issues suggests his lack of patience with interagency consultative process. By way of example, Sununu in October 1989, on behalf of conservative Bush supporters, got the president to squelch provisions that would have extended federal funding for abortions to the victims of rape and incest.[77] In February 1990, Sununu played an instrumental role in weakening an agreement between the Environmental Protection Agency (EPA) and the Army Corps of Engineers concerning the enforcing of federal rules against filling wetlands. Sununu had responded to strenuous representations from developers, local governments, and oil companies.[78] In May 1990, Sununu weighed in for the veto of an act passed by Congress that would protect the rehiring rights and medical benefits of those taking leaves of absence from work in order to care for ill children or parents.[79] He had publicly promised business lobbies that Bush would veto the legislation. In December 1990, Sununu locked horns with Nicholas F. Brady in an unsuccessful attempt to head off the reappointment of Comptroller of the Currency Robert L. Clarke. Responding to intense lobbying from large contributors to the Republican party, Sununu had pressed the view that Clarke had forced banks to tighten their lending standards excessively.

Darman has shared Sununu's skepticism of environmentalism, especially if it threatens economic growth. For instance, the pair reversed in May 1990 an EPA-State Department accord whereby the United States would support a plan presented by European governments to help developing countries reduce chlorofluorocarbons released into the air.[80] Ostensibly, they balked at the $25 million price tag for U.S. participation in the program.

Sununu and EPA Director William K. Reilly have been playing cat and mouse with one another to the point of making a mockery of the Domestic Policy Council's (DPC) deliberations. In May, Sununu got the better of Reilly with a sleight of hand. In a DPC meeting, a united front consisting of Reilly, the White House science adviser D. Allan Bromley, and representatives from the departments of State and Energy pressed for Bush to make a speech on global warming in which the administration would acknowledge for the first time the seriousness of the difficulty.[81] Sununu appeared to acquiesce; however, he later used his access to the final drafts of the speech to shift the administration's emphasis back to the uncertainties of scientific projections of global warming.

Sununu, an engineer, has taken the need to debunk global warming theories so seriously that he developed stripped-down versions of complex climate models. Some skeptical observers have wondered whether he believes his intellect to be so superior that it can unravel mysteries that lesser scientists probe with supercomputers.[82]

Sometimes Reilly has gotten the better of Sununu.[83] In October 1990, Sununu made a last-ditch attempt to gut part of the Clean Air Act. He attempted to have the EPA issue a letter endorsing an interagency task force's report that would suggest that midwestern utilities would be required to make greater cuts in emissions than anticipated by the act. Representative Michael G. Oxley (R-Ohio) argued that the EPA letter would carry much more clout with conferees than would the task force report. Sensing the Sununu plot, Reilly retreated to his weekend home where he stayed out of touch until the coast was clear. A frustrated White House could not extract the requisite letter from EPA in the absence of its director.

POLITICAL AFFAIRS

It has become an old saw that Bush uses John Sununu in a "good cop/bad cop act" whereby the latter communicates in brusque terms—unbecoming a president—what the former actually believes. Sununu, in fact, asserted that he deliberately modulates his outbursts to achieve a specific effect:

> I guarantee you that contrary to the legend, any strong statements on my part are both [sic] controlled, deliberate and designed to achieve an effect. There is no random outburst. It all is designed for a purpose. And I think the efficiency of the result is underscored by what we've been able to achieve.[84]

Mr. Sununu lacks perspective, unless he was speaking tongue-in-cheek. He overrates both his ability to control his temper and the accomplishments of the administration. Rather than advance the interests of the president, Mr. Sununu now serves as a major encumbrance to the administration's achieving its objectives, which, by the way, it has yet to clearly define. A "good cop/bad cop act" requires that the president's and the chief of staff's message and moods remain synchronized. The mounting evidence suggests that they have not—with serious consequences for the administration's relations with Congress and ability to define and communicate its message.

The first serious doubts about John Sununu's performance emerged in the summer and fall of 1989. They centered on his vigorous attempts to rally Republican support around the president's proposal for a cut in the capital gains tax (discussed earlier in this chapter). But at that point a consensus developed that Sununu was conveying in unambiguous terms the president's core commitment. One *New York Times* account quoted a Republican strategist as saying: "Capital gains permeates everything. George Bush wants to win at all costs, even if it so ruptures the atmosphere that meaningful deficit reduction becomes doubtful."[85]

Even an in-depth assessment in the *Washington Post* at the beginning of 1990 pulled up short of putting a fine point on criticisms of Sununu.[86] The story argued that Bush essentially serves as his own chief of staff, preferring to handle details himself. Thus, he requires a hard-nosed operator, rather than a statesman. The article, in fact, gave the impression that Sununu ran a somewhat ad hoc White House. On the one hand, he placed himself as the funnel through which issues must pass to reach the president. But he himself eschewed a structured way of handling White House business—avoiding meetings with fixed schedules and groups with formal names. He did not delegate well.

As for control of his temper, the *Post* account noted that Sununu restricted the number of times that he hung up on the chairman of the House

Republican Policy Committee, Representative Mickey Edwards (Okla.), to three. Sununu's only reprisal for Senator Pete Wilson after the two had a row on the phone was to refuse to approve a visit by Bush to California to help Wilson's campaign for governor.

Sununu shoulders a burden far beyond that of any chief of staff in several administrations. James Baker, when chief of staff during Ronald Reagan's first term, enjoyed the support of first-rate congressional relations, communication, and political affairs colleagues. The Bush team has proven singularly thin in all three fields. Bush's legislative liaison, Frederick D. McClure, has worked in the shadow of Sununu and Richard Darman. The president's aversion to spin-doctoring has left the task of meshing daily media relations with the administration's central thematic messages pretty much untended. Finally, the lengthy illness of the late Lee Atwater, until November 1990 the Republican National Committee chairman, left a vacuum in the management of Bush's political affairs.

Sununu has encountered special difficulty compensating for the loss of Atwater. Bush had initially devolved much of the White House's responsibility for political affairs to the Republican National Committee. At the time, this made good sense. Atwater had proven his skills as a political operative in the 1988 campaign. Atwater's illness placed the White House in the awkward situation of having to reappropriate responsibility for political affairs while remaining respectful of the incapacitated chairman of the Republican National Committee.

That Sununu lacked the requisite finesse to handle congressional relations, communication, and political affairs himself became apparent during the 1990 budget negotiations. Throughout the process, Sununu—along with Richard Darman—took heavy fire from participants for his bumptious behavior toward senators and congressmen, whether Democrats or Republicans.[87]

One Sununu misstep irreversibly damaged the entire tone of the negotiations at a very critical time. This took place on 9 May, the day after the president had agreed to enter into emergency talks on the budget with "no preconditions." An outcry arose immediately among Republicans fearful that "no preconditions" meant the president had abandoned his no-new-taxes pledge.

When contacted by the *Washington Post* on a flight with Mrs. Bush, Sununu carelessly allowed himself to be quoted as "a senior White House official traveling with ... First Lady Barbara Bush and White House Chief of Staff John H. Sununu."[88] He then proceeded to fuel the suspicions of Democrats who feared that the "no preconditions" pledge might constitute a trap forcing them to come forward with proposals for new taxes that the administration would then bat down:

We're allowing them to bring their good arguments for taxes to the table.... They were not persuasive last time, and they are likely not to be persuasive again.... It is their prerogative to put them on the table, and it's our prerogative to say no. And I emphasize the no.

Without identifying their source, White House Press Secretary Marlin Fitzwater strongly disavowed Sununu's remarks.[89] Still, Bush's credibility had suffered serious damage. With the administration's strategy revealed so baldly, the Democrats simply refused during the rest of the negotiations to make a move unless the president stepped out in tandem. Observers immediately noted that a damaging gaffe of this nature demonstrated the extent to which the administration missed Atwater and the pitfalls of Sununu trying to fill the breach.[90]

In late fall, after the budget debacle had played itself out, the White House busied itself trying to pick up the pieces. In what appeared initially as a stroke of genius, Sununu talked Bush's drug czar, William J. Bennett, into taking over the chairmanship of the Republican National Committee. But this effort to soothe the feelings of conservative Republicans upset about the budget became unstuck. Assumption of the chairmanship would require Bennett to forfeit speaker's fees, and he required a large outside income to meet his financial obligations.

At the same time, administration officials began to tear into one another over the State of the Union address. In the previous several months, a group of administration conservatives had been generating ideas for the revitalization of the administration's mandate. The group, including Housing and Urban Development Secretary Jack Kemp, House minority whip Newt Gingrich, and James P. Pinkerton, a thirty-two-year-old deputy assistant to the president for policy planning, borrowed the term "new paradigm" from Thomas S. Kuhn to capture what the administration sought.

As readers probably have concluded on their own, the administration would be conceding a chronic incapacity to define its domestic objectives if it used such an obscure term as a rallying call. Richard Darman said as much in a blistering attack in a speech given before the Council for Excellence in Government titled "Neo-Neo-ism."[91] This did not stop the administration from striking a task force under Jack Kemp to prepare proposals for inclusion in the State of the Union address. Using the more congenial term "empowerment," the group probed the prospect of reducing the role of government in individual's lives through a voucher scheme to enforce parents' choice in selecting schools, tax credits for child care, tenant ownership of public housing, tax-free savings accounts for health care, and providing tax incentives to businesses located in "urban enterprise zones."[92]

Very little of its work saw the light of day either in the State of the Union address or subsequently.

Conclusion

This chapter has assessed the relationship between Bush's presidential style and the way in which he has organized and utilized his White House staff and the cabinet. It began by stressing the extent to which modern presidents have employed the White House and the Executive Office of the President (EOP) to compensate for inherent weaknesses in the American cabinet system. Initially, presidents attempted to build up the "neutral competence" of their advisory system, especially through the expansion of the Bureau of the Budget and other EOP units. At least since Kennedy, however, they have eschewed this approach in preference for direct White House intervention in departmental and administration decisions.

This approach presents several dangers. Presidents can become captured by the strongest personality in their White House. Bob Haldeman had this effect on Nixon, as did Donald Regan on Reagan. Second, the president and the White House can absorb so much into the "Iron Gate"—micromanagement of issues, handling congressional relations, modulating the administration's messages, and managing political operations—that they begin to collapse under the weight of too much work. Carter and his White House suffered chronically from this difficulty.

Third, the administration can become so absorbed with retention of its approval ratings that it stops looking after the long-range interests of the United States. The systematic discounting of the advice of career civil servants and the reflex to accuse dissenting cabinet secretaries of having "gone native" serve as the principal symptoms of this condition. The Reagan administration displayed this syndrome to an unparalleled degree. We need only point to the still unresolved deficit issue and its many consequences for economic, social, and foreign policy to highlight the dysfunctions of White Houses governed by polls.

The chapter began by accepting that Bush presents himself in mysterious and paradoxical ways. But it did argue that the seeming contradiction of his style—reactive, active—makes greater sense if we consider the degree to which he views himself as a deal maker par excellence. Bush clings to the timeless American saying "If it ain't broke, don't fix it." But when things do break down, Bush wants to walk onto the shop floor and knock heads together toward a quick solution. The longer the down time, the more impatient he becomes.

We would not have expected Bush, as a "let's deal" president, to spend a great deal of energy setting up a White House organized to provide him with countervailing voices or a cabinet system that attempted to scan the radar screen for departmental policies on a possible collision course with one another six or twelve months in the future. But Bush, strangely for a Washington insider, seemed not to take the rudimentary precautions necessary to avoid the three dysfunctions of an interventionist White House listed above.

To begin, Bush risked becoming captive of a strong personality by appointing John Sununu chief of staff without taking on board one or two equally strong individuals. This analysis might be jumping the gun, but it now counts three disastrous strong chiefs of staff—Haldeman, Regan, and Sununu. When will presidents learn?

Second, the Bush administration started out wanting to give lower profile to congressional relations, communication, and political affairs. The further we get into the first term, the more the White House finds it must micromanage these sectors. Nevertheless, it has done virtually nothing organizationally to shift gears. This greatly exacerbates Sununu's position as he deals simultaneously with serious overload and a sizable backlash to his authority.

Finally, Bush's hyperkineticism, along with his bloated support in public opinion polls, prevented the administration from making hard decisions in a timely way. Thus we have the Panama invasion to compensate for inaction in the face of the Noriega coup attempt and the immense expenditure of military power and contortion of foreign policy priorities to compensate for the failure to anticipate and prevent the Iraqi invasion of Kuwait. On the domestic side, we have the damaging retreat from the no-new-taxes pledge and an increasing number of embarrassing intra-administration squabbles brought on by the White House second-guessing departmental and inter-agency agreements.

Notes

1. Peter Hennessy, *Cabinet* (Oxford: Basil Blackwell, 1986).

2. John Hart, *The Presidential Branch* (New York: Pergamon, 1987).

3. President's Special Review Board (Tower Commission), *Report* (New York: Bantam Books, 1987), 79–80.

4. Larry Berman, *The Office of Management and Budget and the Presidency, 1921–79* (Princeton: Princeton University Press, 1979), 10–15; and Hart, *Presidential Branch*, 24–36.

5. Richard E. Neustadt, *Presidential Power: The Politics of Leadership* (New York: Wiley, 1960), 51–52.

6. James P. Pfiffner, "OMB: Professionalism, Politicization, and the Presidency," in *Executive Leadership in Anglo-American Systems,* ed. Colin Campbell, S.J., and Margaret Jane Wyszormirski (Pittsburgh: University of Pittsburgh Press, 1991); Richard P. Nathan, *The Administrative Presidency* (New York: Wiley, 1983).

7. Alexander George, *Presidential Decisionmaking in Foreign Policy: The Effective Use of Information and Advice* (Boulder, Colo.: Westview, 1980), 146.

8. Ibid., 155.

9. Colin Campbell, S.J., *Managing the Presidency: Carter, Reagan, and the Search for Executive Harmony* (Pittsburgh: University of Pittsburgh Press, 1986), 60–63, 83–84.

10. Bob Schieffer and Gary Paul Gates, *The Acting President: Ronald Reagan and the Supporting Players Who Helped Him Create the Illusion That Held America Spellbound* (New York: Dutton, 1989), 193–95.

11. James David Barber, *The Presidential Character: Predicting Performance in the White House* (Englewood Cliffs, N.J.: Prentice-Hall, 1972); Alexander George, "Assessing Presidential Character," *World Politics* 26 (January 1974): 234–82; James H. Qualls, "Barber's Typological Analysis of Political Leaders," *American Political Science Review* 71 (March 1977): 182–211; James David Barber, "Comment: Qualls's Nonsensical Analysis of Nonexistent Works," *American Political Science Review* 71 (March 1977): 212–25.

12. Richard E. Neustadt, *Presidential Power and the Modern Presidents: The Politics of Leadership from Roosevelt to Reagan* (New York: Free Press, 1990), 206–7.

13. Ibid., 206. Neustadt cites Barber, *Presidential Character,* 12.

14. Ibid.

15. Neustadt, *Presidential Power and the Modern Presidents,* 207.

16. Barber, *Presidential Character,* 12.

17. Colin Campbell, *Governments under Stress: Political Executives and Key Bureaucrats in Washington, London, and Ottawa* (Toronto: University of Toronto Press, 1983); and Campbell, *Managing the Presidency.*

18. Paul Taylor and David S. Broder, "Perfecting a Negative Campaign: Bush Aides Started Early and Made It an Art Form," *International Herald Tribune,* 29–30 October 1988.

19. David Broder, "Bush: Competence Plus Disturbing Signals," *International Herald Tribune,* 2 November 1988.

20. David Hoffman, "Bush's Metamorphosis: From Loyal Subordinate to Self-Assured Leader," *Washington Post,* 20 January 1989.

21. Ibid.

22. R.W. Apple, Jr., "Bush Making It Clear That He Will Be a Hands-On President," *International Herald Tribune,* 21 November 1988.

23. Joe Pichirallo, "Governor Is Expected to Be Bush's Chief of Staff," *International Herald Tribune,* 17 November 1988.

24. David Hoffman, "Why Sununu? Aides Say Bush Felt He Needed a Battle-Ready Politician," *International Herald Tribune,* 19–20 November 1988.

25. Ann Devroy, "Teeter, Citing Family Concerns, Says No to White House Post," *Washington Post*, 10 January 1989.

26. Campbell, *Managing the Presidency*, 110.

27. Gerard F. Seib, "Bush, in Assembling Staff of His Administration, Takes the Experienced but Not the Power-Hungry," *Wall Street Journal*, 17 January 1989.

28. Bernard Weinraub, "Sununu, the Chief of Staff Is Learning the Ropes the Hard Way," *New York Times*, 6 February 1989.

29. David Broder, "Will This Easy Style Work?" *Washington Post*, 1 February 1989.

30. Gerald M. Boyd, "The Bush Style of Management: After Reagan, It's Back to Details," *New York Times*, 19 March 1989.

31. Maureen Dowd, "Bush's Week: A Few 'Ripples' but No Bursting Bubbles at Champaign Time," *New York Times*, 29 January 1989.

32. Weinraub, "Sununu, the Chief of Staff Is Learning the Ropes the Hard Way."

33. Ann Devroy and David Hoffman, "Sununu Rebukes Aides for 'Grousing' to Media," *Washington Post*, 2 May 1989.

34. Maureen Dowd, "An Image Polisher Leaves Nevada Neon to Sharpen a 'Beige' White House," *New York Times*, 3 October 1989.

35. Ann Devroy and Gwen Ifill, "All's Not Quiet on the Sununu Front," *Washington Post*, 3 August 1989; and R.W. Apple, Jr., "Emotions in Check, Intellect Not, Sununu Wins Reluctant Respect in Capital," *New York Times*, 13 September 1989.

36. Andrew Rosenthal, "Bush's Ties to Congress Show Strain," *New York Times*, 16 October 1989.

37. Bernard Weinraub, "White House Studying Handling of Panama Crisis," *New York Times*, 6 October 1989.

38. Ann Devroy, "Bush to Aides: Stop Second-Guessing, President Angered by Recriminations over U.S. Response to Rebellion," *Washington Post*, 11 October 1989.

39. David Hoffman, "On Panama, Bush Characteristically Cautious: Scowcroft, Shunning Role of Crisis Manager, Maintained Informality," *Washington Post*, 15 October 1989.

40. Phil McCombs, "The Distant Drum of C. Boyden Gray," *Washington Post*, 31 March 1989.

41. Ibid.

42. Andrew Rosenthal, "On the Road to the Vote on Tower: A Series of White House Missteps," *New York Times*, 26 February 1989.

43. Robert Pear, "Pact Challenged by Bush Counsel," *New York Times*, 26 March 1989.

44. Ann Devroy, "Baker Denies Contra Accord Saps Presidential Authority," *Washington Post*, 27 March 1989.

45. David Hoffman, "Sununu Rebukes Counsel," *Washington Post*, 28 March 1989.

46. Michael Isikoff, "No. 2 Aide at Justice Quits Post," *Washington Post*, 12 May 1990; David Johnson, "Justice Aide Quits amid Tensions over Thornburgh's Stewardship," *New York Times*, 12 May 1990.

47. "Administration Renews Threat to Veto Civil Rights Act," *Washington Post*, 13 October 1990.

48. "Transcript of Bush's Impromptu News Conference," *Washington Post*, 6 August 1990.

49. Maureen Dowd, "Bush Warns of Budget Impasse, Comparing Crisis to That of Persian Gulf," *New York Times*, 15 August 1990.

50. "Excerpts from the Bush News Conference on the Budget and the Mideast," *New York Times*, 10 October 1990.

51. R.W. Apple, Jr., "Bush Shifts Stand on Tax Rise Again; Congress Baffled," *New York Times*, 11 October 1990.

52. Ann Devroy, "Candidates Spurn Bush's Embrace," *Washington Post*, 24 October 1990; Dan Balz, "Bush Seeks Firing of Party Official," *Washington Post*, 26 October 1990.

53. David S. Broder, "Reactive President," *Washington Post*, 19 August 1990.

54. George F. Will, "Still a Line in the Sand: Did You Ever See a Policy Go This Way and That?" *Washington Post*, 7 November 1990.

55. R.W. Apple, Jr., "Notes from the Brink: Hostage Decision and U.S. Doubts May Give Iraq a New Edge," *New York Times*, 9 December 1990.

56. David Hoffman, "Four-Month Policy Review Produced Little," *Washington Post*, 26 May 1989.

57. David Hoffman, "On Panama, Bush Characteristically Cautious: Scowcroft Shunning Role of Crisis Manager, Maintained Informality," *Washington Post*, 15 October 1989.

58. David Hoffman, "Zip My Lips: Bush's Secret Conduct of U.S. Policy," *Washington Post*, 1 January 1990.

59. Bob Woodward, "The Conversion of General Powell," *Washington Post*, 21 December 1989.

60. Andrew Rosenthal, "Bush Gamble in China Trip," *New York Times*, 13 December 1990.

61. Ann Devroy and David Hoffman, "White House Reveals Earlier China Mission," *Washington Post*, 19 December 1989.

62. Ann Devroy and David Hoffman, "Summit Disclosure Investigated," *Washington Post*, 4 November 1990; and Hoffman, "Zip My Lips"; Maureen Dowd, "Bush Takes the Chance to Play Hide and Seek," *New York Times*, 1 February 1990.

63. Don Oberdorfer, "Baker's Evolution at State," *Washington Post*, 16 November 1989; Rosenthal, "Bush Gamble in China Trip."

64. Devroy and Hoffman, "Summit Disclosure Investigated."

65. Hoffman, "Zip My Lips."

66. Jim Hoagland, "Transcript Shows Muted U.S. Response to Threat by Saddam," *Washington Post*, 13 September 1990.

67. Jim Hoagland, "... And the Tale of a Transcript," *Washington Post,* 19 September 1990.

68. Robert S. Greenberg, "Policy Snafu: How the Baker Plan for Early Sanctions against Iraq Failed," *Wall Street Journal,* 1 October 1990; David Hoffman, "U.S. Policy Wavered on Saddam," *Washington Post,* 1 October 1990.

69. Maureen Dowd and Thomas L. Friedman, "The Fabulous Bush and Baker Boys," *New York Times Magazine,* 6 May 1990; Oberdorfer, "Baker's Evolution at State."

70. David Hoffman, "Gulf Crisis Tests Baker as Diplomat, Politician," *Washington Post,* 2 November 1990.

71. Great Britain, Committee of Privy Councellors, Franks Report, *Falkland Islands Review* (London: Her Majesty's Stationery Office, 1983).

72. Colin Campbell, Harvey Feigenbaum, Ronald Linden, and Helmut Norpoth, *Politics and Government in Europe Today* (San Diego, Calif.: Harcourt Brace Jovanovich), 152–55.

73. Campbell, *Managing the Presidency,* 144.

74. Ibid.

75. Maureen Dowd, "Bush's Adviser on Domestic Policy: The Perfect Man to Process Details," *New York Times,* 29 March 1990; Spencer Rich, "Domestic Forum Can Sway a President," *Washington Post,* 15 August 1990.

76. David E. Rosenbloom, "The Treasury's Mr. Diffident," *New York Times,* 19 November 1989.

77. David Hoffman, "Bush Makes Rare Bow to GOP's Conservatives," *Washington Post,* 18 October 1990.

78. David Hoffman, "Bush Struggles for 'Balance' Between Two Sharp Edges," *Washington Post,* 20 April 1990.

79. David S. Broder, "If Ever There Was a Motherhood Issue," *Washington Post,* 13 May 1990; John M. Berry, "Sununu Said to Want Comptroller General Replaced," *Washington Post,* 7 December 1990.

80. Michael Weisskopf, "U.S. Intends to Oppose Ozone Plan," *Washington Post,* 9 May 1990.

81. Michael Weisskopf, "Shift on Warming Sought," *Washington Post,* 3 February 1990.

82. Jessica Matthews, "The Greenhouse Hold Out," *Washington Post,* 9 November 1990.

83. Michael Weisskopf, "With Pen, Bush to Seal Administration Split on Clean Air Act," *Washington Post,* 15 November 1990.

84. Ann Devroy, "Citing Year of Triumph, Sununu Defends Actions," *Washington Post,* 12 December 1990.

85. Andrew Rosenthal, "Bush's Ties to Congress Show Strain," *New York Times,* 16 October 1990.

86. David Hoffman and Ann Devroy, "Chief of Staff Sununu: Bush's Fiery Enforcer," *Washington Post,* 10 January 1990.

87. David E. Rosenbaum, "Bush Hearing Many Voices in Talks on Cutting

Deficit," *New York Times*, 24 May 1990; Rowland Evans and Robert Novak, "Friction in GOP," *Washington Post*, 20 August 1990; Dan Balz and Ann Devroy, "Tiring of Hardball, Hill Ready to Bench Sununu," *Washington Post*, 9 October 1990; Maureen Dowd, "Bush's Woes Stir GOP Grumblings over Sununu," *New York Times*, 29 October 1990.

88. Ann Devroy and John E. Yang, "White House Shores Up No-Tax Stand," *Washington Post*, 10 May 1990.

89. David Hoffman and John E. Yang, "Bush Repeats 'No Preconditions' for Deficit Talks; Sununu Remarks Disavowed," *Washington Post*, 11 May 1990.

90. Andrew Rosenthal, "In Tax Debate, Clear Signs of Broader Role for Sununu," *New York Times*, 11 May 1990.

91. Steven Mutson and Dan Balz, "OMB Head Asks Restraint on 'Neo-Neo-Ism' of Ideas," *Washington Post*, 17 November 1990.

92. The several accounts of the struggle in the administration over the "new paradigm" include: David Gergen and Kenneth T. Walsh, "The Bush Presidency: Running on Empty," *Washington Post*, 11 November 1990; Gwen Ifill and Ann Devroy, "GOP Wrestles with Vision of New Domestic Order," *Washington Post*, 1 December 1990; E.J. Dionne, Jr., "The Idea Man with a Vision Thing," *Washington Post*, 5 December 1990.

8

The President and the Executive Branch

Joel D. Aberbach

While some tension in the relationship between the president and the executive branch is a common feature of the federal government, a product of differences in needs and time horizons, tensions were heightened in the recent presidencies of Richard Nixon, Ronald Reagan, and, to a lesser extent, Jimmy Carter.[1] Nixon launched an assault on the career bureaucracy with his "responsiveness program,"[2] Carter's "campaign to build public support for the Civil Service Reform Act of 1978 ... emphasized poor performance and the need to be able to fire civil servants more easily,"[3] and Reagan attacked government and its career employees with unusual vigor. The Volcker Commission, for example, quotes President Reagan's remark that "when you are up to your eyeball in alligators, it's sometimes hard to remember that you came here to drain the swamp."[4] Reagan also worked hard to cut back the domestic programs of the federal government, programs he regularly disparaged.

The first two years of the Bush administration have probably led to an easier relationship between the president and the executive branch. Few of the worst elements that marked the situation in previous administrations are present. In fact, Bush has been careful to treat the role and mission of career civil servants with respect, he has appointed cabinet officials who are not hostile to the statutory goals of their agencies, and he has allowed these officials much greater leeway than his predecessor did in selecting their subordinates. Career executives, not surprisingly, are likely to be comfortable with presidents who respect government and its personnel and do not push them to do things to which they object (or better, encourage what they like). Bush, basically, has been on the right side of both criteria, especially when compared to his immediate predecessor. His relations with the career bureaucracy have, therefore, been relatively smooth, reinforced by the moderate nature of his appointees.

My plan of analysis is straightforward. First I present background information and data on executive branch politics and on the executive branch situation Bush inherited. Next I look at Bush's attitude toward government service and at his political philosophy and program as they affect his relations with the executive branch. I then turn to the nature of the administration's appointees and appointments process, and examine some of its actions in the domestic agencies with the aim both of understanding the administration's goals better and of seeing the impact of the president's appointees and appointments process on policy. I close with a brief consideration of future prospects. Throughout, there is an emphasis on the role of top civil servants. The data I bring to bear, as well as my substantive analysis, are focused on domestic agencies and domestic policies, the areas I know best.

Background

President Bush succeeded the most virulently antigovernment president in modern American history. With the exception of the defense and security sectors, Ronald Reagan mounted a broad effort to undermine much of the government. He attacked government and its civil service employees in rhetoric that the National Commission on the Public Service (the Volcker Commission) described delicately as "sometimes extreme."[5]

While the Reagan administration was indeed extreme in its rhetoric and actions, it was not the first administration to have difficulties in its relationship with the "permanent government." The transition from one administration to another is a particularly rocky time for all, a time when uncertainty and tension rise within the American federal bureaucracy.

> New program priorities and emphases and the introduction of new personnel create some inevitable difficulties of adjustment under the best of circumstances. Politically appointed executives with typically short career spans and often limited experience in bureaucratic politics must learn to come to grips with the complexities of their jobs. With astonishing quickness they must come to know whom they can trust among their career subordinates; who among them will be cooperative and loyal and who will not.[6]

In a now immortal simile, a high-level Agriculture Department official in the Eisenhower administration indicated that new political executives and career executives "go around sniffing each other like dogs."[7] Generally, however, the initial pattern of suspicion dissipates over time as the president, his appointees, and top career executives form and re-form alliances on specific issues. Flexibility and open-mindedness are useful traits for those who must navigate their way through the fragmented centers of power in American government.

The initial approach of the Nixon administration to the executive branch was quite traditional. Nixon selected a cabinet "to represent major interests in the inner councils of government."[8] He even allowed his cabinet officials to select the subcabinet appointees who served with them in the departments.[9] As his first term progressed, however, Nixon grew more and more disillusioned with the federal executive—both with his own appointees and with the body of career executives he had suspected from the start. He was particularly concerned about signs of accommodation between the two, a phenomenon his aide John Erlichman described in a picturesque image: "We only see them [top appointees] at the annual White House Christmas party; they go off and marry the natives."[10]

Over the course of his first term, Nixon enlarged the White House staff and expanded its power. His aim was to run the government from within the White House. When this proved ineffective, he moved to take more direct charge of the departments. Immediately following his reelection in 1972, Nixon asked for the resignation of all presidential appointees. His purpose was to appoint "loyalists" to key positions, especially at the subcabinet level. Dom Bonafede summarizes the significance of these personnel moves in a statement valid for the modern presidency: "For the first time, a U.S. president was intent on using his appointment power on a grand scale to exercise control over the federal bureaucracy."[11]

The Watergate scandal kept Nixon from fully carrying out his experiment in control, but his efforts were not forgotten. In fact, E. Pendleton James, who was in charge of Ronald Reagan's preinaugural talent search and then became assistant to the president for personnel, had worked under Fred Malek, Nixon's personnel chief.[12] Malek was the author of the infamous "Malek Manual," a guide to political appointees, which emphasized a telling message: "You cannot achieve management, policy or program control unless you have established political control."[13] The Nixon experience, then, was more than just a historical aberration. It was a school for many who followed; its lessons were assimilated and applied with telling effect in the Reagan period.

Nixon wrote openly about his failings in the appointments process in his first administration and his plans for the second:

> I regretted that during the first term we had done a very poor job in the basic business of every new administration of either party: We had failed to fill all the key posts in the departments with people who were loyal to the President and his programs. Without this kind of leadership in the appointive positions,

there is no way for a President to make a major impact on the bureaucracy. . . .
I was determined that I would not fail in this area again, and on the morning
after my re-election I called for the resignation of every non-career employee in
the executive branch.[14]

Malek was even more pointed about the problems Nixon political appointees might have with top civil servants in his 1972 "Manual":

Because of the rape of the career civil service by the Kennedy and Johnson administrations . . . this administration has been left a legacy of finding disloyalty
and obstruction at high levels while those incumbents rest comfortably on career civil service status. Political disloyalty and in simpatico relationships with
the administration, unfortunately, are not grounds for the removal or suspen-
sion of an employee. Career employees . . . can only be dismissed or otherwise
punished for direct disobedience of lawful orders, actions which are tanta-
mount to the commission of a crime, and well documented and provable incompetence.[15]

Malek then went on to describe techniques designed to "skirt around the adverse action proceedings" required to proceed against civil servants in a legal
manner. All were designed "to remove undesirable employees from their positions."[16]

Clearly, the atmosphere in the Nixon administration by the second term
was more than tense; it was downright confrontational. But Watergate intervened, and the administration slowly retreated into a defensive posture to be
followed by the healing interlude of the Ford presidency.

Next came President Carter. As noted, the Volcker Commission criticized Carter, along with President Reagan, for "running campaigns that not
only strongly criticized Washington but also attacked the people who work
for the government."[17] The atmospherics of the administration, therefore,
were not overly favorable for relations with the bureaucracy.

Moreover, while it is unlikely that Carter meant any harm by the bill,
the Civil Service Reform Act (CSRA) of 1978, one of the major legislative
achievements of his administration, provided his successor, Ronald Reagan,
with new tools for achieving control over the senior civil service. In fact, some
of the actions that the "Malek Manual" had advised Nixon's administrators
to take by stealth could now be done openly. For example, a member of the
Senior Executive Service (SES), the new elite corps established by the CSRA,
can now be reassigned easily within his or her agency, even to positions outside the member's geographic "commuting area." Most important, under the
law, administrations can now designate 10 percent of SES positions for

noncareer people—up to 25 percent in any single agency—and fill them with appointees of their choice. Effectively employed, this gives administrations the leverage to affect policy ("responsiveness") that Nixon and his inner circle could only dream of achieving by the convoluted plotting that helped drive them from office.

When Ronald Reagan came to the presidency, then, a change-oriented incumbent who had the will now had means beyond those available to Nixon to influence the executive branch. Further, Reagan had the example of Nixon's experience to learn from—the techniques used and the pitfalls. And he entered office on the heels of a predecessor who had also played the Washington outsider and had attacked government (although with nowhere near Reagan's vitriol) and in a period of widespread public reaction to big government. (This was, after all, the era of Proposition 13 in California and deregulation at both federal and state levels.)

The Reagan administration had a coherent strategy for dealing with the executive branch from the beginning. As Richard Nathan noted in his book, *The Administrative Presidency,* written about two years into Reagan's first term: "The essence of the Reagan approach to management is the appointment of loyal and determined policy officials. This, of course, is not a new idea; the difference is that the Reagan administration has in substantial measure carried it out."[18]

Reagan's appointments process was designed and implemented by Edwin Meese and E. Pendleton James. According to Nathan, they started planning six months before the 1980 presidential campaign even got under way.[19] They had very firm ideas about what they wanted.

A major aim was to select people ideologically in tune with the incoming Reagan administration—a comparatively easy task for the recruiters, since Reagan was unusually clear about his goals. Unlike Nixon, for example, whose conservatism was inconsistent in the early years of his tenure and who chose a set of notables representing diverse viewpoints as his initial appointees, Reagan knew from the beginning what he wanted and that he wanted to appoint people who would above all else be dedicated to carrying out his administration's agenda. Howell Raines described the Reagan appointments strategy in the *New York Times* in 1981 as "a revolution of attitudes involving the appointment of officials who in previous administrations might have been ruled out by concern over possible lack of qualifications or conflict of interest or open hostility to the mission of the agencies they now lead."[20]

The appointees, then, not only had to agree with Reagan's policies, but policy agreement was in most cases the sine qua non of appointment, especially to posts below cabinet level. Whereas in past administrations, notables who had good relations with established interest groups or good connections with key people on congressional committees were likely to get the jobs, in the Reagan administration political ideology was the key. And "to assure and maintain the ideological purity of the cabinet and subcabinet, the Reagan White House ... relied on training or indoctrination activities to an unusually high degree. During the transition, cabinet members learned about their departments from conservative task forces rather than from personnel within their agencies." [21]

Appointments to subcabinet positions were controlled by the White House. Members of the cabinet were consulted if on board already and ultimately gave their assent, but unlike the early Nixon and Carter administrations, cabinet members did not have the selection of subcabinet members turned over to them. As James Pfiffner notes:

> The Reagan White House resolved that it would not make the mistakes of earlier presidents and lose control of its personnel appointments. In order to keep tight control, they insisted on a narrow definition of loyalty to the president and had cabinet members agree to accept White House selection of their subordinates.... This rigorous ideological screening ensured that appointees would put loyalty to the president and his policies above the tugs of Congress, interest groups, and the bureaucracy.[22]

In addition to a coherent policy for appointees, the Reagan administration used the available personnel process to great advantage. Reagan's appointees took "advantage of opportunities to transfer and remove career officials in domestic agencies felt to be unsympathetic to the administration's objectives," they used reductions in force (RIFs) to push senior civil servants they did not trust into routine positions, and they used the power to appoint noncareer SES officials aggressively.[23]

Finally, the administration took advantage of the circumstances of Reagan's electoral victory to push its programs vigorously. While the Reagan victory of 1980 was by no means overwhelming, it was much more definitive than Nixon's 1968 win. (Reagan received a majority in a three-man race, while Nixon received less than 44 percent.) Reagan also brought a Republican Senate in with him, leading Washingtonians to view his election as a sign of significant change in the underlying political compass of the country. The fact that his campaign and reputation were so clear in their conservative, some might even say radical conservative, definition also impressed the Washington establishment that his election had deep significance. With these factors as background, Reagan struck quickly to change the government. In his first year in office, he managed a surprisingly successful attack on discretionary domestic spending (mainly through the 1981 Reconciliation) and he was able to limit federal revenue potential significantly through the so-called Economic Recovery Tax Act (ERTA) of 1981.[24] By his success in these endeavors, he put domestic agencies on the defensive and turned the agenda of American politics into one focused on deficit reduction, rather than program development and improvement. The question preoccupying the bureaucracy and congressional leaders throughout most of Reagan's eight years in office, especially in nondefense areas, was the question Reagan wanted on the agenda: "What ought we *not* do?"

The Executive Branch Bush Inherited

Before discussing Bush and the executive branch, it is helpful to look briefly at the nature of the executive branch, particularly the bureaucracy, Bush inherited. For, as noted, Bush came into office on the heels of an administration with a firm and well-developed strategy for influencing both the composition and the behavior of executive branch personnel.

To accomplish this goal, I use some data comparing the Reagan bureaucracy with the Nixon bureaucracy. Bert Rockman and I conducted extensive interviews in 1970 with senior federal executives from a wide array of domestic agencies in metropolitan Washington, D.C. The sample was divided between upper-level political appointees (below the rank of undersecretary) and senior (then called "supergrade") career civil servants. Each supergrade civil servant had to be the top career official within a particular administrative hierarchy (and had to report directly to a politically appointed official) to be included in the sampling universe.

We did a follow-up study in 1986–87, once again interviewing political appointees and senior career civil servants based in Washington, D.C.–area domestic agencies. The career civil servants were drawn mainly from the Senior Executive Service (SES) created by the Civil Service Reform Act of 1978. Since the act allows greater flexibility than was previously the case in moving SES executives around, a result of the provision that SES status inheres in the person rather than in the position, we interviewed two sets of senior civil servants in the follow-up. The first group occupied the top rung in their administrative units and reported directly to a politically appointed official and therefore represented the closest parallel to the senior civil servants interviewed in 1970 (I call them "Civil Servants I" in this chapter). The second group is also composed of SES career officials but was drawn randomly from a list that excluded the top career officials in each administrative hierarchy (I call them "Civil Servants II" in the text). All executives in the analysis presented in the next few pages have line (program) responsibilities.

Note in table 8.1 the effectiveness of the Reagan recruitment effort to appoint executives who were close to the President in partisan and ideological terms. Whereas only 66 percent of Nixon's early appointees were Republicans (remember that Nixon aimed first for a traditional mix of appointees), 93 percent of Reagan's appointees were Republicans. More impressive still is the remarkable increase in the conservatism of his appointees compared to Nixon's.

TABLE 8.1

PARTISAN ORIENTATION AND IDEOLOGY OF TOP
FEDERAL EXECUTIVES, 1970 AND 1986–87

	1970		1986–87		
	Political appointees	Civil servants	Political appointees	Civil servants I	Civil servants II
Percentage Republican	66 (57)	17 (58)	93 (54)	40 (48)	24 (37)
Percentage opposing an active role of government in the economy, including those opposing "with reservations"	19 (53)	13 (62)	72 (54)	47 (49)	28 (40)

Note: Number of cases in parentheses.

On the civil service side, whereas only 17 percent of the top civil servants in the sample interviewed under Nixon in 1970 were Republicans, that number was up to 40 percent in 1986–87 under Reagan for the Civil Servants I group. It was up, although only modestly, to 24 percent for the Civil Servants II group. The same kind of change is apparent in the measure of conservatism used in the table: the percentage opposing an active role of government in the economy. Only 13 percent of Nixon's civil servants opposed an active role for government, but that figure stood at 47 percent (more than three times as great) for the Civil Servants I group in 1986–87 and at 28 percent for the Civil Servants II group.

The probable causes of these changes among the top civil servants are discussed in detail elsewhere,[25] but a few are particularly useful for understanding the relations of the Bush administration and the bureaucracy. First, the elite (both administrative and political) intimately involved with public policy has been affected by alterations in the intellectual climate. The shift from a concern with equity in the 1960s and early 1970s to efficiency in the 1980s influenced the thinking and probably even the party affiliations of at least some civil servants. As one of our respondents put it in 1986: "In the 1960s, the Democrats espoused ideas that moved and inspired the country. Now it's the Republicans who are doing that while the Democrats drift about."[26] Some of the shift in party and ideology one sees in the data are almost certainly linked to the shift in ideas in the general intellectual climate.

Nevertheless, the differences between the Civil Servants I and Civil Servants II groups in the 1986–87 data clearly demand an explanation beyond a change in the intellectual climate. The Civil Servants I group was significantly more Republican and conservatively oriented than the Civil Servants II group. The most likely explanation is that this was accomplished through effective use of provisions of the Civil Service Reform Act of 1978 allowing political executives to move members of the SES about. Civil Servants I, for example, were half again as likely as Civil Servants II to have served in an agency other than their present one (36 percent versus 23 percent); and our data show very clearly that "the Reagan administration was able to sort out SES career personnel in the social service agencies [previously dominated by liberal Democratic civil servants] very well, putting Republicans at the very top and placing the SES Democrats in those agencies in slightly lower [i.e., Civil Servants II] positions."[27]

It is also important to note the difference between the views of Reagan's appointees and the views of careerists, including careerists in the more sympathetic career Civil Servants I group—a clash that was, if anything, even more marked than the clash between Nixon's more moderate early political appointees and his more liberal civil servants. Other than the fact that it is still easier for an administration (especially one in control of the Senate, as Reagan's was during its first six years) to work its will at the political level than at the career level, even after the SES reform, there are factors that limit the impact any single administration is likely to have on the civil service. People drawn to a career in American government are likely to be sympathetic to arguments in favor of governmental solutions to society's problems, even when they are skeptical about government's capabilities. This both limits movement toward the conservative end of the spectrum and probably makes closet moderates out of many career administrators who adopt conservative positions. And career bureaucrats are generally more cautious and skeptical than the persons a zealous administration is likely to appoint to administrative positions. It would probably have been difficult for the administration to find enough career SESers whose views it agreed with for top positions, even if it had been so motivated.

The bottom line is that Reagan left Bush a bureaucracy that was at least somewhat more Republican and noticeably more conservative than had probably been the case in recent history. He also left him a bureaucracy that, whatever the changes, was still far more moderate than the political appointees he had chosen to lead his administration. And he left a record that indicated how to structure the appointments process to find and place committed conservatives in appointive positions and how to use the new civil service law to influence the positioning of key top civil servants.

In addition to this, Reagan left Bush a bureaucracy that had been subjected to "jigsaw puzzle management," a method of utilizing top career managers "to carry out programs while keeping them in the dark as to the overall strategy being pursued."[28] Their job was to carry out instructions, not to play a prominent role in suggesting or shaping policy.

Data from our study suggest the Reagan administration's effectiveness in this regard. Tables 8.2 and 8.3 (pages 230 and 231) show changes in patterns of perceived influence and contacts reported by top officials.

Clearly, Reagan administration civil servants believed that they had suffered a sizable loss in influence over policy (table 8.2). Almost half of the top civil servants interviewed in 1970 reported that they had "a great deal of influence." In 1986–87 this percentage had dropped below 20 for both our samples of civil servants. Where senior civil servants once believed that their group was in a class with members of Congress and department secretaries in influencing policy, by 1986–87 they viewed themselves as the least influential of the government authorities.

Table 8.3 indicates the Reagan administration's success in decreasing the access of civil servants to others in the policy process. When compared to the sample of supergrade civil servants interviewed in 1970, SES career executives in the Civil Servants I category in 1986–87 reported fewer contacts with most other actors, particularly members of Congress, interest-group representatives, and the public. The one increase in the level of contacts reported is with the White House—a finding consistent with the notion of increased White House control.

Political appointees also reported increased levels of contact with the White House in 1986–87.

Unlike senior civil servants, however, they also reported increased contacts with the public and with members of Congress, and their level of contact with interest group representatives was just about the same in both surveys. In effect, while they, like civil servants, were noticeably more oriented in 1986–87 than in 1970 to the White House and somewhat less to other executive branch officials (including their own department heads), unlike civil servants they maintained or increased their external contacts. Overall, the pattern for politi-

TABLE 8.2

INFLUENCE OVER POLICY ATTRIBUTED TO VARIOUS ACTORS BY TOP FEDERAL EXECUTIVES, 1970 AND 1986–87

Influence attributed to	1970				1986–87					
	Political appointees		Civil servants		Political appointees		Civil servants I		Civil servants II	
	Pct[a]	Num[b]	Pct	Num	Pct	Num	Pct	Num	Pct	Num
Senior Civil Service	35%	34	46%	46	21%	52	16%	40	18%	39
Department secretaries (agency heads)	65	56	43	60	65	52	40	50	62	39
Members of Congress	63	57	51	57	33	52	36	50	49	39
Party leaders (in Congress)	22	46	19	37	25	52	46	48	42	38
Interest groups (general)	26	57	33	60	19	52	14	50	13	39

a. Pct = percent reporting "a great deal of influence"
b. Num = number of cases

TABLE 8.3

CONTACTS REPORTED BY TOP FEDERAL EXECUTIVES, 1970 AND 1986–87

| | 1970 | | | | 1986–87 | | | | | |
| | Political appointees | | Civil servants | | Political appointees | | Civil servants I | | Civil servants II | |
Contacts with	Pct[a]	Num[b]	Pct	Num	Pct	Num	Pct	Num	Pct	Num
White House	25%	53	5%	64	41%	54	20%	50	3%	40
Own department head (Sec'y of department)	61	54	31	61	48	54	22	50	5	39
Other department heads	19	48	18	57	6	54	2	49	3	39
Officials at your level in other departments	57	53	42	65	43	54	30	50	36	39
Members of Congress	42	52	43	65	48	54	20	50	21	39
Political party leaders	8	53	0	63	6	54	0	50	0	39
Interest group representatives	69	52	69	65	67	54	46	50	39	39
Public	55	51	55	62	67	54	41	49	44	39

a. Pct = percent reporting "weekly or more contact"
b. Num = number of cases

cal executives is compatible with an executive selection process designed to find political appointees below the secretarial level who would owe more than before to their departmental leadership, and who would be more significantly drawn into the White House orbit.[29]

Reagan, then, left Bush a top career bureaucracy that was, at least on a stalwart indicator like the role government ought to play in the economy, more moderate to conservative in its orientations than the liberal bureaucracy Nixon faced.[30] Reagan's political appointees were, however, generally much more conservative than the civil servants his administration worked with, so there was a significant clash in the views of the two, much as there had been in the Nixon administration. The top career bureaucracy under Reagan had also apparently lost much of its self-perceived influence and had fewer contacts than before with other significant actors in the policy process save the White House. This was a bureaucracy likely to appreciate as president someone with more moderate political views than Reagan's, someone more willing to give it a role in the policy process, someone who respected rather than "bashed" it. Given many of its experiences under Reagan, it was likely to be grateful initially for small positive changes.

Bush and the Executive Branch

People all over the executive branch must have been heartened by some of George Bush's early speeches and actions. During the election campaign itself, Bush issued a statement about the federal service. It was reproduced in its entirety in the *Bureaucrat,* a journal aimed at civil servants. The *Bureaucrat's* editors introduced Bush's statement with the following comment: "This unusually explicit set of proposals gives hope to the bureaucracy."[31]

Bush said: "My experience ... has given me a very high regard for the overall competence of career civil servants and for the vital role they have in our democratic form of government." He went on to say that "despite our determination to cut the size and costs of government, we recognize that the nation needs a highly skilled and dedicated civil service to perform those governmental services that we, as a people, decide we want." He promised that his "appointees will work closely with career civil servants to provide the teamwork needed to implement my policies, and to manage more effectively necessary programs across the government."[32]

Bush's words went even further after his inauguration. On 26 January 1989 in Constitution Hall, he addressed the Senior Executive Service, the first group he spoke to as president outside the White House. He told them:

You are one of the most important groups I will ever speak to.... Our principles are clear. That government service is a noble calling and a public trust. I
learned that from my parents at an early age, and that, I suspect is where many
of you learned it as well.... I want to make sure that public service is valued
and respected because I want to encourage America's young people to pursue
careers in government. There is nothing more fulfilling than to serve your
country and fellow citizens and to do it well. That's what our system of self-
government depends on. And I have not known a finer group of people than
those I have worked with in government.[33]

Bush's messages to the bureaucracy contain numerous clues about his
political philosophy, particularly as it affects his likely relations with the executive branch and his views on the role of political appointees and the career
bureaucracy in the policy process. In the balance of this section I look at the
nature of Bush's political philosophy, what is sometimes called (in Bush's
case) "the vision thing," at the nature of the appointments process in the
Bush administration and the nature of the appointees themselves, and at the
nature of decision making in the Bush administration. Comparisons to previous administrations, particularly the Reagan administration, are at or near
the surface at all times.

BUSH'S POLITICAL PHILOSOPHY AND PROGRAM

It is clear from Bush's statements that he values and respects the role of civil
servants. They are in service to the nation, one of the higher callings in his
scheme of things. This is a familiar view for a traditional conservative. It is
only jarring in contrast to his predecessor, Ronald Reagan, a radical conservative who had little use for those serving the nation in a nonmilitary or non-
security capacity, and to Richard Nixon, who apparently valued personal
power almost exclusively.

Nelson Polsby recently gave an excellent characterization of Bush's
brand of conservatism:

Bush is a genuine conservative, an American tory. There are known characteristics of that breed: They care about the society and the government that is
handed to them; they want to keep the boat afloat. Bush is a professional in
public service, which means he has respect for other professionals. Conventional wisdom means something to him. He pays attention to people who are
supposed to be experts. These are qualities he does not share with his predecessor.[34]

Bush's concern with competence and professionalism in administration and his seemingly genuine, although somewhat passive, concern about society are reflected in what he has looked for in his appointees.

> Bush, by and large, has filled his administration with practical men and women who are generally conservative but not obsessively so, who tend to be—as he is—civil, cautious and conciliatory. They like to face problems and solve them, using a few shared values—prudence, marketplace wisdom, compassion in word if not in need—as their guide.... He has hired few crusaders.... If previous administrations' decision makers had something they wanted to do, Bush's prefer simply to do something.[35]

It is hardly surprising that Bush and his key appointees have not engaged in "bureaucrat bashing." Indeed, they have much in common with stereotypical bureaucrats—pragmatism, lack of an overall vision ("the vision thing"), and an "affection for governing."[36]

Erwin Hargrove described Bush as "ideally suited—and positioned—to be an effective President of Consolidation ... a centrist Republican who desires to manage government well after Ronald Reagan's anti-government and anti-communist activism."[37] "Presidents of Consolidation," to use Hargrove's label, not only respect good civil servants, they need them for their institutional memory and their knowledge, and they are willing to use their skills. It is almost inconceivable to imagine Ronald Reagan's feisty director of the Office of Personnel Management (Donald Devine) issuing this statement, made to the Senior Executives Association by Constance Newman, Bush's director of OPM: "We can't run a good government if we are not working together through a mutual relationship of trust ... it must be made clear that you have the background and the experience needed to help guide political appointees."[38] Mr. Reagan's civil servants, in contrast, were there to be guided, not to guide.

While the Bush administration apparently cares about society and government and values public service and civil servants—characteristics sure to enhance its relationship with the civil service, especially when compared to the approval of its predecessor—it is possible that its fuzzy vision and its lack of money for program improvements or new initiatives may create some difficulties down the road once the glow of improved relations dims a bit. An example of domestic policy planning during the first two years of the Bush administration will help clarify the administration's situation in this regard.

The example is the administration's review of the nation's antipoverty efforts. Soon after the inauguration, the administration convened an interagency group to consider alternatives. The group reportedly came up with a dozen broad alternatives, but a higher-ranking group, the President's Domestic Policy Council, decided that the options were too expensive or would stir too much political controversy. The council, a cabinet-level advisory body, concluded that the Administration should simply try to make current programs work better.

A White House official summarized the upshot this way: "Keep playing with the same toys. But let's paint them a little shinier."

Another administration official, acknowledging that Mr. Bush had promised "a kinder, gentler nation" in the 1988 campaign, insisted that the President was not reneging on his promise.

"We have decided to abjure a glitzy, splashy, high-profile announcement of new programs and a grand new strategy," the official said. "We concluded there were no obvious things we should be doing that we weren't doing that would work."[39]

This is an almost classic example of the Bush administration at work in the domestic area. It wanted to consider ways to deal with one of society's pressing problems and went about searching for alternatives in a systematic, if uninspired, way. In the end it decided that it lacked the money to do much, and had the typical Tory skepticism that anything new would work well anyway. As an administration official said: "The members of the Domestic Policy Council wanted to do something about poverty, but we realized that we didn't have any cash. We wanted to adopt a set of principles, but couldn't figure out how to convert our enthusiasm to anything concrete."[40]

The administration's final decision to "keep playing with the same toys. But let's paint them a little shinier" likely had some appeal to many of its top civil servants. After all, the administration did not denounce the government's current poverty programs or the idea of using government to deal with at least some of society's problems (as its predecessor did), it did look to expert opinion, and it did indicate that it would consider minor modifications in existing programs—a task it would likely entrust mainly to top civil servants. Yet one suspects that the Bush administration's failure to provide political leadership and the frustration its bureaucracy will face in trying to combat a massive problem without additional money or new programs will eventually frustrate even its moderate top civil servants in this area, and perhaps its political appointees as well.

NATURE OF BUSH'S APPOINTEES AND APPOINTMENTS PROCESS

Both George Bush's appointees and the appointments process he used differed in important ways from Ronald Reagan's. He looked for experienced, mainstream, pragmatic people, not ideologues.

As Burt Solomon, the White House correspondent for the *National Journal,* said in an article in 1989:

> Bush put in place a cabinet and a White House staff that foretell a style of governance—a conscientious, relentlessly mainstream Republican administration filled with pragmatists who prize public niceness. Bush promised fresh faces but hired old friends.... Packed with skilled, centrist Washingtonians, Bush's cabinet "could have been put together by the National Academy of Public Administration," Brookings Institution senior fellow Stephen Hess said. "These are people who won't make silly mistakes, people who are interested in governance."[41]

The Reagan administration centralized decisions on subcabinet appointments in the White House, but the Bush administration "decided to give significant leeway to cabinet secretaries to choose, in consultation with the Office of Presidential Personnel, their own management teams at the subcabinet level.... Mutual accommodation was the rule."[42]

In short, Bush's administration, while outwardly maintaining the personnel office mechanism of the Reagan administration, returned to a more traditional mold of making appointments. Cabinet members were primarily establishment types with reputations as pragmatists, and subcabinet members were, for the most part, chosen by cabinet appointees. According to Charles (Chase) Untermeyer, director of presidential personnel under Bush, the new president "wanted to make clear this was a new administration, not Ronald Reagan's third term, but George Bush's first."[43]

The results of the Bush administration's efforts to define itself as "new," rather than merely a continuation of the Reagan administration, can be inferred from statistics on its appointments. The goal was to keep no more than 20 percent of Reagan's appointees in the government in any capacity. And according to a *Los Angeles Times* story written in July 1990, "of the Reagan administration's political appointees who were in office when the 40th President left Washington on January 20, 1989, approximately 22 percent were retained in some capacity."[44] When one considers that some of the Reagan administration people retained by the Bush administration were people Bush originally helped place, it is clear that the goal of a "new administration" was largely reached.

As far as I know, there have been no systematic studies yet of the views of Bush's appointees, but press reports stress their moderation. In an article by Jack W. Germond and Jules Witcover, for example, tellingly entitled "Reaganites Worry about Fading of Reaganism," the authors wrote of reactions to those whose appointments had been announced just before Bush's inauguration:

> Although President-elect Bush's cabinet appointments may have been deni-grated by many as being unimaginative, they have been greeted with a sense of relief by those Republicans who have accommodated themselves to the Reagan Revolution rather than truly embracing it. They see in the appointments ... that for all his pledged fealty to Reagan during his eight years as Vice President, Bush is really a closet moderate.[45]

And Burt Solomon wrote a month later of the subcabinet appointments: "As with his cabinet and White House staff, Bush's subcabinet selections foretell an earnest, pragmatic, intelligent, not overly imaginative administration."[46] One would expect the effects of these appointments to show in the policy leadership given by Bush administration appointees.

NATURE OF BUSH'S DOMESTIC POLICY
A look at some of the still sketchy material available on domestic policy in the Bush administration suggests the impact of Bush's appointees, and therefore of Bush's appointments strategy, on policy. The list of possible examples is long and, of course, not always consistent, but a few cases should give a flavor of what the Bush administration, through its appointees, has tried to do.

The Occupational Health and Safety Administration (OSHA) of the Labor Department was a prime target of the Reagan administration. Reagan appointed administrators who were hostile to OSHA's primary goal, government efforts to promote worker safety and health, and cut its budget severely. Under George Bush's first labor secretary, Elizabeth Dole, however, there were definite signs of what the *National Journal* described as "OSHA's Turn-about."[47] Dole made workplace safety a priority, announced fines against corporations violating health and safety rules, and worked to increase the agency's budget.

Perhaps most telling, Gerald F. Scannell, the person the Bush administration appointed as labor's assistant secretary with responsibility for OSHA, had "served at OSHA in several capacities in the 1970s, including director of the office of standards, where he wrote regulations that continue to govern the workplace."[48] Few doubt his dedication to OSHA's mission. Even such critics of OSHA as Joseph A. Kenney of the National Safe Workplace Institute noted that the morale of OSHA's staff "is 100 times better than it was under [Scannell's Reagan-appointed predecessor] because there seems to be a sense of redirection."[49]

Not surprisingly, the *National Journal* still reported criticisms of OSHA, focusing on the Office of Management and Budget's disapproval of proposed OSHA rules. Critics were concerned that OSHA would have to "take on" OMB or OMB would continue its practice of disapproving or forcing the withdrawal of the health and safety rules OSHA must issue to carry out its legislative mandate. Secretary Dole reported that she had discussed the matter with the OMB director (Richard Darman) and expected to have a cooperative relationship between OSHA and OMB in the future.[50] Future research will show whether the efforts by OSHA's Bush-appointed administrators to improve the agency's performance (OSHA received its first enforcement budget increase in a decade under Bush) will run up against the desires of Bush's OMB personnel to hold down costs to industry.

Possible OMB-agency clashes also worried those encouraged by the performance of one of the early stars of Bush's cabinet, Transportation Secretary Samuel K. Skinner. Skinner has been "blasted" by conservative critics for "pursuing what they call an 'industrial policy'—a concept that they had hoped was buried during the Reagan administration."[51] Skinner advocated a national transportation policy and set his staff to work drawing one up. He had the Department of Transportation examine a leveraged buyout of Northwest Airlines to determine whether it was a sound financial move, required the auto industry to improve vehicle fuel efficiency, and generally talked about the country's need to make large investments in its transportation infrastructure. As Representative James Oberstar (D-Minn.), on the House Public Works and Transportation Committee, said of Skinner: "I see Skinner as a guy with a real sense of public service. He's a free enterpriser, but he wants to referee free enterprise."[52]

A typical concern about Skinner's future was expressed by Representative Bud Shuster (R-Pa.), who is the ranking minority member on the House Surface Transportation Subcommittee and served as Bush's chief transportation adviser during the 1988 election campaign: "Frankly, if I had to express a concern, it is that Sam Skinner is so bright and so capable and so energetic and the transportation needs of our country are so clear, that if he gets his hands tied by OMB or the White House, he could become a very unhappy man."[53] Skinner's ultimate success may remain in doubt, but there is no doubt that he has energized his department.

Another area where the Bush administration's appointees have moved to reinvigorate government's role is antitrust. The man appointed assistant attorney general for antitrust at the Justice Department, James F. Rill, for example, was described as

the consummate insider, a lawyer with 30 years of practice who is not associated with the free-marketers of the Chicago school of economics, who fared so well under President Reagan. "I expect Rill will be more of a centrist, more pragmatic," [Robert] Pitofsky [a former FTC commissioner and now at Georgetown University Law Center] predicted. The recipient of upbeat press coverage so far, Rill has promised more aggressive enforcement.[54]

Not only has the Justice Department become more active in the anti-trust area, but the Federal Trade Commission (FTC) was recently described as "slowly emerging from the laissez-faire attitude of the Reagan administration, [and] starting to use its antitrust muscles and renew its interest in cases that affect the public's pocketbook."[55] Tellingly, Janet Steiger, the Bush FTC chair, "described herself much as others do, not as an ideologue but as a bureaucrat who can be expected to take a middle course. 'I want this to be a judicious enforcement agency that is interested in the public's health and welfare,' she said."[56]

Steiger reportedly has boosted staff morale, made public pronouncements that have pleased advocates of antitrust enforcement, and made some staff appointments from the ranks of long-time agency personnel. A problem she faces, one common to all areas discussed in this section, is that "even the most aggressive enforcement posture [should she want to pursue it] would be limited by budget constraints."[57]

In sum, in the domestic areas I have looked at, and in many others, the Bush administration's appointees have moved, usually cautiously, though sometimes more aggressively, to undo the Reagan administration's efforts to conform agency activities to the tenets of "Reaganism." Agencies are described as "reemerging," no longer "asleep," undergoing a "turnabout," or scraping off the "rust" of the Reagan years. This does not usually go with new policy ideas or adventurous administration—the Transportation and Housing Departments may be exceptions here—but an administration of moderates is generally letting the bureaucracy enforce the law and carry out programs within the constraints imposed by limited resources and the still aggressive micromanagement of OMB. The goal is rarely to do more, but it is to do the conventional and, if possible, to do it better.

Overview and Prospects

George Bush inherited an executive branch battered by the Reagan administration, an administration that had firm ideas about the proper role of government in most domestic matters (small) and the proper role of the career administrators in decision making (also small). Given what he wished to achieve, Reagan pursued an effective strategy in his relations with the bureaucracy. His appointed officials were carefully screened to ensure, to the maximum extent possible, that they agreed with his goals. His top career officials were generally kept from a central role in decision making and apparently maneuvered into positions (utilizing the tools available through the Civil Service Reform Act of 1978) the administration thought best for them. Reagan's early tax reform also served to limit government revenues, effectively putting the administration's key question, What should we *not* do? in a central place on the agenda.

Reagan and his advisers had a firm grasp on their goals, as well as a keen grasp of power politics. Reagan needed loyal appointees with consonant values, and he succeeded in placing them in the executive branch. He did not shy away from conflict when necessary, because he intended to make changes. His career civil servants, while more conservative than those the Nixon administration faced, were still quite moderate in comparison to his appointees. Their diminished role, however, mitigated this fact.

The first two years of the Bush administration indicate a very different sort of President. Bush seems to be an American Tory, looking for harmony, social and otherwise. His ideological views remain unclear; perhaps he has no clear vision of American society beyond one that holds firm to traditional values. He does not seem to be opposed to a state role in any fundamental way, but he is skeptical of it. He clearly does care about institutions of the state, including the bureaucracy. He values the advice of experienced, skeptical people, and respects the views of experts.

While Bush must operate in an environment shaped by the scarce resources currently available to government, it is doubtful that he minds much. He probably would not like the politics a budget surplus would induce, for in that event he might have to decide what to do beyond resurrecting and improving some of the traditional programs of government brought low by the Reagan administration.

For the moment, my guess is that the career bureaucracy, particularly in the domestic agencies, finds Bush a welcome relief. He is not their opponent symbolically, and he has usually named as their chiefs men and women who are not opposed to the basic missions their agencies were created to carry out.

As a top career executive with long service in the executive branch said of the change from the Reagan to the Bush administration: "It is very satisfying to be in a working environment where the secretary of the department and his top leadership all want to accomplish something, as opposed to dismantling or to standing pat."[58] At the same roundtable discussion with top federal executives that produced the preceding remark, a Reagan appointee made the following revealing comment: "I refused to come back into the Bush administration . . . because I didn't see any commitment for my services.

I was willing to leave my career, but there was no political activism for me in this administration."[59]

For now at least, there is probably an excellent match between the "do a little" Bush administration and the bureaucracy with a relatively moderate cast that it inherited. Working to put the government in order and even to accomplish small things must be far more satisfying to most civil servants than the negative approach of the Reagan administration. Civil servants have probably regained some of their role in the decision-making process, and it would be shocking if they did not savor the administration's respect for expertise and its open approach to most problems.

The lingering question is how stable this condition is. An administration that values professionalism and respects career civil servants probably does not select those in our Civil Servants I category (the highest civil servant in a hierarchy) with the same attention to their politics as does an administration that has a clear policy agenda. Therefore, the very top civil service positions may now be held by more liberal personnel than those our surveys revealed in 1986–87. In addition, the bloom of good relations between the administration and its top civil servants may fade if government programs to deal with growing domestic problems are seen as woefully underfunded by an administration that lacks an agenda beyond doing one's best with what is available. Civil servants with more freedom to act may work, if they have not done so already, to refurbish their somewhat faded contacts with congressional Democrats and push their own ideas more actively and effectively in the political process.

Nevertheless, compared to their experience from 1981 to 1989, the last two years must look awfully good to most in the executive branch. If the bloom fades, it is likely to fade slowly. A moderate presidential administration and a relatively moderate bureaucracy, when and if they clash, are likely to do so in a very genteel manner.

Notes

1. Ford, in the peculiar post-Watergate situation he faced, vetoed bills freely and initiated a program of deregulation, but was generally nonconfrontational in his relationship with the bureaucracy.

2. See U.S. Senate, Select Committee on Presidential Campaign Activities, Executive Session Hearings, *Watergate and Related Activities: Use of Incumbency—Responsiveness Program,* 93rd Cong., 2nd sess. 1973, books 18 and 19. Hereinafter cited as Watergate Hearings.

Nixon, it should be noted, was also disillusioned with his political appointees. See Richard P. Nathan, *The Administrative Presidency* (New York: Wiley, 1983).

3. National Commission on the Public Service (Volcker Commission), *Leadership for America: Rebuilding the Public Service* (Lexington, Mass.: Heath, 1989), xxiii. Hereinafter cited as Volcker Commission Report.

4. Ibid., 63.

5. Ibid.

6. Joel D. Aberbach and Bert A. Rockman, "Clashing Beliefs within the Executive Branch: The Nixon Administration Bureaucracy," *American Political Science Review,* no. 70 (June 1976): 456–68.

7. David T. Stanley, *Changing Administrations* (Washington: Brookings Institution, 1965), 87.

8. Nathan, *Administrative Presidency,* 30.

9. Dom Bonafede, "The White House Personnel Office from Roosevelt to Reagan," in *The In-and-Outers,* ed. G. Calvin Mackenzie (Baltimore: Johns Hopkins University Press, 1987), 41.

10. Quoted in Nathan, *Administrative Presidency,* 30.

11. Bonafede, "White House Personnel Office from Roosevelt to Reagan," 40.

12. Ibid., 40, 48.

13. Watergate Hearings, book 19, 8907.

14. Richard M. Nixon, *RN: The Memoirs of Richard Nixon* (New York: Grosset and Dunlap, 1978), 768.

15. Watergate Hearings, book 19, 9006.

16. Ibid.

17. Volcker Commission Report, 63.

18. Nathan, *Administrative Presidency,* 74.

19. Ibid.

20. Howell Raines, "Reagan Reversing Many U.S. Policies," *New York Times,* 3 July 1981, as quoted in Nathan, *Administrative Presidency,* 75.

21. Nathan, *Administrative Presidency,* 75.

22. James P. Pfiffner, "Nine Enemies and One Ingrate: Political Appointments during Presidential Transitions," in MacKenzie, *In-and-Outers,* 60–76.

23. Nathan, *Administrative Presidency,* 77.

24. Paul E. Peterson and Mark Rom, "Lower Taxes, More Spending, and Budget Deficits," in *The Reagan Legacy,* ed. Charles O. Jones (Chatham, N.J.: Chatham House, 1988), 220.

25. Joel D. Aberbach and Bert A. Rockman, with Robert Copeland, "From Nixon's *Problem* to Reagan's *Achievement*—The Federal Executive Reexamined," in *Looking Back on the Reagan Presidency,* ed. Larry Berman (Baltimore: Johns Hopkins University Press, 1990), 175–94.

26. Ibid., 191.

27. Ibid., 182.

28. Peter M. Benda and Charles H. Levine, "Reagan and the Bureaucracy: The Bequest, the Promise, and the Legacy," in Jones, *Reagan Legacy,* 102–42.

29. Joel D. Aberbach, "Volcker and Bush: A First Appraisal" (paper presented to the Conference on Career Public Service, IPSA Research Committee on the Structure and Organization of Government, Dalhousie University, Halifax, Nova Scotia, 5–7 October 1990).

30. Seventy-six percent of the Civil Servants I group in the Reagan administration was on the center (29 percent) or conservative (47 percent) side of this issue, and even 55 percent of the more liberal Civil Servants II group took either the center (27.5 percent) or conservative (27.5 percent) position. The comparable figure for Nixon administration career supergrades was 47 percent, 25 percent in the center and 22 percent on the right. Perhaps the most significant indicator of the overall shift to a more centrist or conservative position in the civil service samples is the fact that in 1986–87 only 2 percent of the Civil Servants I group strongly favored an active government role in the economy, as did 10 percent of the Civil Servants II group. The comparable figure for career supergrades in 1970 was 32 percent.

31. "Buckslip," *Bureaucrat,* Winter 1988–89, 7.

32. George H. Bush, "On the Federal Service," *Bureaucrat,* Winter 1988–89, 7.

33. George H. Bush, "To Some of America's Finest," *Bureaucrat,* Spring 1989, 3.

34. "IGS Panel Assesses Bush Administration," *Public Affairs Report,* September 1990, 5.

35. Burt Solomon, "A Gathering of Friends," *National Journal,* 10 June 1989, 1402.

36. Burt Solomon, "Vulnerable to Events," *National Journal,* 6 January 1990, 8, 10.

37. Erwin C. Hargrove, "The President Who Can't Lead Unless He Hears the Roar of the Crowd," *Los Angeles Times,* 21 October 1990, M1.

38. Constance B. Newman, "Challenges of Public Service," *Bureaucrat,* Fall 1989, 16.

39. Robert Pear, "Administration Rejects Proposal for New Anti-Poverty Program," *New York Times,* 16 July 1990, A1.

40. Ibid., A10.

41. Burt Solomon, "Bush Promised Fresh Faces... But He's Hiring Old Friends," *National Journal,* 21 January 1989, 142.

42. James P. Pfiffner, "Establishing the Bush Presidency," *Public Administration Review,* January/February 1990: 68–69.

43. James Gerstenzang, "Bush's 'Gatekeeper' Starting Over," *Los Angeles Times,* 10 July 1990, A5.

44. Ibid.

45. Jack W. Germond and Jules Witcover, "Reaganites Worry about Fading of Reaganism," *National Journal,* 7 January 1989, 35.

46. Burt Solomon, "Culling Lists and Throwing Bones... and Slowly, a Sub Cabinet Forms," *National Journal,* 11 February 1989, 354.

47. Kirk Victor, "OSHA's Turnabout," *National Journal,* 25 November 1989, 2889–92.

48. Ibid., 2890.

49. Ibid.

50. Ibid., 2891–92.

51. Kirk Victor, "Skinner's Takeoff," *National Journal,* 10 February 1990, 329.

52. Ibid., 332.

53. Ibid., 330.

54. W. John Moore, "Rusty Trust-Busters," *National Journal,* 30 September 1989, 2403.

55. Barry Meier, "FTC Re-Emerges as a Watchdog on Prices," *New York Times,* 28 January 1991, A1.

56. Ibid., A14.

57. W. John Moore, "Stoking the FTC," *National Journal,* 19 May 1990, 1218.

58. Transcript of the Brookings Institution Roundtable convened by Joel D. Aberbach and Bert A. Rockman, "Project on the Changing Federal Executive," 13 December 1990, 18.

59. Ibid., 111.

9

Good Government and the Politics
of High Exposure

ANTHONY KING
AND
GILES ALSTON

On the walls of the Sala della Pace in the Palazzo Pubblico, the old City Hall of Siena, are painted two murals by Lorenzetti. Painted in the fourteenth century, the murals depict on one wall Good Government and its effects and on the other Bad Government and its effects.

Good Government is symbolized by the magisterial figure of a king: white-bearded, calm, grave. Beside the king are portrayed the six civic virtues: justice, temperance, magnanimity, prudence, fortitude, and peace. The effects of Good Government are shown to include handsome public buildings (with Siena's cathedral in the background); comfortable private homes; citizens dancing in the streets; and well-tended wheat fields, olive groves, and vineyards. The whole scene bustles with human activity, activity made possible by the presence of Security, a winged figure that floats in the sky, invisible to travelers on the road below but vigilant to safeguard their interests.

On the opposite wall of the Sala della Pace is painted Bad Government. A malevolent figure with fanglike teeth and horns, Bad Government is clad in chain mail, holds a sword, and sits enthroned among cruelty, perfidy, fraud, anger, discord, and war. Avarice, tyranny, and vainglory hover above, while justice, in chains, cowers below. The effects of Bad Government are everywhere to be seen. Once-proud palaces stand in ruins. Violence, murder, and rape are rife. A desolate countryside is dominated not by Security but by Terror, and a sinister band of armed men moves on horseback and foot toward a victim or victims unknown.

From the point of view of the political scientist, two features of Lorenzetti's murals stand out. The first is the distinction that Lorenzetti makes in a rough kind of way between causes and effects, between Good Government itself and the effects of Good Government. In other words, the artist distinguishes between what political scientists call *political process* and *political sub-*

stance. The second point is related and is more important. Not only does Lorenzetti distinguish between political process and political substance, between Good and Bad Government and their effects; he at the same time assumes, or appears to assume, that one kind of Government, whether Good or Bad, is invariably associated with one kind of outcome: Good Government with well-tended fields and plentiful harvests, Bad Government with civil disorder and physical desolation.

But a moment's reflection suggests that the real world is a good deal more complicated than that. The government of a country may be good in the sense that the country has a fine constitution, outstanding leaders, and honest and competent public officials; yet this good government may not produce, in Lorenzetti's terms, the "effects of Good Government." The best endeavors of the best of governments may be nullified by factors beyond its control or influence—by crop failure, disease, foreign invasion, a sudden fall in worldwide demand for its products, the presence in its population of lawless or alienated minorities. Countries in Subsaharan Africa, such as Chad, Mali, and Mauritania, could have the best governments in the world, yet they would still probably suffer from most of what Lorenzetti calls the "effects of Bad Government." Similarly, bad governments may sometimes produce, or at least be associated with, good results. Governments that we in Western liberal democracies would regard as bad are often surprisingly popular with their own people.

This possibility, of a disjunction between the quality of a nation's political institutions and political personnel on the one hand and the quality of its economic and social life on the other, suggests the need, in assessing the performance of any country, to "factor out" the effects of government, both good and bad, from the effects of other factors and agencies (e.g., drought, world commodity prices, "criminal elements") that are, or may be, beyond government's control and even beyond its capacity to influence. Anyone in a position of governmental authority is liable to distinguish in his or her mind between factors that are firmly under the government's control (the design of the country's army uniforms, to take a trivial example) through factors that the government may possibly be able to influence to some extent (such as the country's rate of economic growth) to factors that are essentially beyond its control (such as foreign demand for the products the country exports).

It behooves political scientists, and ordinary citizens, to make the same distinction. Whether a specific government or administration is adjudged to have "succeeded" or "failed" in any task it has set itself, or might have set itself, should be determined not only in the light of the government or administration's actions but also in the light of what it was intrinsically possible for the government or administration to do. The fact that there will always be arguments about what is or is not possible for a government to do—about how far the potential reach of government actually extends—should not be allowed to detract from this central truth. If government is, as Bismarck claimed, the art of the possible, then practitioners of government should be judged in terms of what is actually possible or at least what is deemed to be possible. Any other course is not justifiable either morally or intellectually.

This point perhaps needs to be addressed especially to readers in the United States. Americans have usually enjoyed Good Government, at least at the federal level—they certainly take pride in the American Constitution —and have usually enjoyed "the effects" of Good Government (high incomes, big cars, comfortable homes, social mobility). And, perfectly naturally, they tend to equate in their minds Good Government and the effects of Good Government: "America the free" equals "America the well-off." The equation may be apt; it probably is true that American political institutions have contributed, perhaps substantially, to American prosperity. But, as we have indicated, the connection is not automatic and should not be taken for granted; the connection between the two needs to be demonstrated empirically. Americans also tend to have high expectations of government, to see it as a device for "solving problems." It may be that American government, or any other government, does not in fact always have the capacity to solve problems—and it may be unrealistic to imagine that it has. The reach of any government, as the Soviet Union has recently been demonstrating, may exceed its grasp. Some problems may just have to be lived with.

It is against this background that we proceed, as observers from outside the United States, to assess the first two years of the Bush administration in terms of its capacity or incapacity to deal with three of America's major problems: the federal budget deficit, drugs, and what is often referred to as "the underclass." We have selected these problems partly because they are ones that attract our attention as outsiders, but principally because two of them are also high on the Bush administration's own agenda.

The Federal Budget Deficit

The American federal budget, like the budget of many other countries, has been in deficit more or less continuously since World War II. Since the end of that war, the U.S. federal government has run a surplus only in 1956, 1957, 1960, and 1969.[1] Moreover, the long-term trend has been for federal budget deficits to increase both in absolute dollar terms and as a percentage of gross national product (GNP). These deficits did not begin to cause serious alarm, however, until the 1980s. Under the Reagan administration, the deficit for the first time topped $200 billion in absolute terms and 6 percent of GNP.

There were no mysteries about the proximate causes of Reagan-era deficits. On the one hand, President Reagan, backed by public opinion, persuaded Congress to cut taxes. On the other, Congress, also backed by public opinion, refused to accede to repeated presidential requests to cut government spending by amounts that would enable the soaring deficits to be contained, let alone substantially reduced or eliminated.

The most striking single political fact about the deficits was that almost everyone—presidents, congressmen, senators, newscasters, newspaper editors, bankers, economists, the great mass of ordinary voters—agreed that they constituted "a problem." They offended long-established canons of American public morality.[2] They led to high interest rates. They were alleged to squeeze out private investment. They made America's economy dependent on heavy foreign borrowing. They exacerbated America's chronic and seemingly intractable trade imbalances. They threatened to bequeath a heavy burden of debt to future generations of Americans. "Something," everyone agreed, "should be done."

One rather strange thing was in fact done. In 1985 Congress passed, and President Reagan signed, what became known as the Gramm-Rudman-Hollings Act. Gramm-Rudman-Hollings provided that the federal budget deficit should be reduced to zero by 1993 and established a set of deficit-cutting targets to be reached in each of the intervening years. If the targets were not reached, deep cuts in defense and domestic programs would automatically take place.

From the point of view of politicians, the act had two distinct advantages. (In the absence of these advantages it would not have been passed.) The first was that it looked like the taking of action on the deficit, but at the same time in reality it postponed the taking of action. Those who voted for it, and signed it, were made to feel good and look good; but, just as the budget deficits themselves were alleged to bequeath heavy debt burdens to future generations of citizens, so the effect of Gramm-Rudman-Hollings was to bequeath heavy political burdens to future generations of politicians.

The act's second advantage was that it had, and was meant to have, an air of inevitability about it. If X, then Y. The politicians created for themselves a *deus ex machina* or, as the economists like to say, "an exogenous variable." The idea was that when, if ever, the time came when Gramm-Rudman-Hollings had to be implemented, the politicians doing the implementing would be able to claim that in raising taxes, cutting federal spending, or both, they were not really doing what they wanted to do: They were merely doing what Gramm-Rudman-Hollings mandated them to do. There is safety in numbers; there is also safety in an act of Congress. Or at least that was the idea.

Between 1985 and early 1990, a period spanning the Reagan and Bush presidencies, nothing much happened. Whenever it looked even remotely likely that the provisions of Gramm-Rudman-Hollings would have to be invoked, the president and Congress made sure that they would not be. The president and Congress "cooked the books" (as the Americans say) or "fiddled the figures" (as the British say). Meanwhile, the deficits were anyway tending to decline for reasons that had little to do with either presidential or congressional action. (And, at the same time, many voters and some politicians were coming to regard them as somewhat less important than they had once thought; after all, the budget deficits remained high, but America prospered, so why worry?)

Why was nothing effective done about the budget deficit throughout the 1980s, even though almost everyone in the United States regarded it as a major, if not *the* major, social, economic and even moral problem that faced the nation? A nation faces a problem. Its citizens are almost unanimous in agreeing that the alleged problem is indeed a problem. Yet little or nothing is done to solve it. Why not?

The answer to that question throws considerable light on the problems of achieving Good Government not only in the United States but in other democratic countries.

Part of the answer becomes apparent if we start by considering, not federal budget deficits in the United States as such, but a similar problem that faces governments, or should face them, in a large number of democracies. In many democratic countries, including the United States, the tax system has been designed so as to encourage home ownership. Those who borrow money to purchase their homes receive tax relief on their interest payments. Such people are in effect subsidized by the government—that is, by other taxpayers—to increase their personal stock of capital wealth. They are assisted in acquiring a capital asset, which may be a very substantial one.

The arguments against such fiscal arrangements are very powerful. Tax subsidies to home buyers are grossly inequitable because they treat in a different way different people who are identically placed except that one happens to be buying his or her home on a loan or mortgage, while the other is not. Why should someone who is renting a home (and therefore not acquiring a capital asset) subsidize the person living next door, possibly in an identical house, who happens to be buying his or her home (and to be increasing thereby his or her personal wealth)? Economists are worried about this inequity. They are also worried about the considerable economic distortions that such arrangements give rise to. They encourage borrowing rather than saving. They encourage borrowing for one kind of purchase, rather than others. They artificially increase the demand for homes, thereby forcing up home prices and diverting scarce economic resources into the home-building industry. They likewise tend artificially to restrict the supply of rental housing, since government subsidies are not usually paid to rent payers (certainly not to all rent payers).

To these arguments there is no cogent reply; and the voices of economists, and the occasional lone politician, are heard from time to time urging the abolition of such subsidies. Yet in no country with such tax arrangements has there ever been a serious attempt, let alone a successful one, to remove this glaring moral and fiscal anomaly. Why not?

The answer is obvious—and is well captured by the old American saying "Everybody's business is nobody's business." The repeal of home-purchase subsidies, even if partially offset by tax reductions in other fields, would have an immediate, palpable, adverse effect on millions of people, rich and poor alike, who were doing nothing more wicked than buying their own home and who would almost certainly have come to regard their home-purchase tax break as a normal, reasonable, legitimate part of "the natural order of things." They would lose; they would know they had lost; and they would almost certainly punish the politicians they blamed for their loss. Against that, the undoubted benefits accruing from withdrawing home-purchase subsidies would be spread thinly and widely; they would, to a considerable extent, be random in their impact; and they would be likely to make themselves felt only in the medium and long term. Almost everyone would win, but most would win only in the long term, and few would notice that they had won. There would certainly not be many votes to be won (except perhaps from older economics professors whose homes were already paid for). On the contrary, this particular fiscal adjustment, however desirable in itself, would undoubtedly be a vote loser, probably on a large scale. Small wonder that no such adjustment is made—or is ever likely to be made.

This simple argument can obviously be generalized to the American budget deficit. Any proposal for reducing the deficit necessarily involves higher taxes or cuts in federal spending or both. These are painful remedies, and the pain is felt, usually quickly, sometimes immediately, by identifiable individuals. By contrast, the benefits that politicians and economists claim will follow from deficit-reducing measures are, like cuts in tax relief on home loans, almost certain to be both long term and widely diffused. It follows that no one should be surprised that little deficit cutting went on during the 1980s. The surprise should be that, in the end, a serious attempt was made in 1990.

The problem just described—"everybody's business is nobody's business"—is common to liberal democracies. There is, however, an additional problem that is to a large extent peculiar to the United States. It might be summarized as the problem arising out of "the politics of high exposure."

The politics of most liberal democracies is dominated in the 1990s by "career politicians," that is, by men and women who see politics as their primary vocation, who spend most of their waking hours in political activity, and who have as their main, sometimes their sole, ambition in life the acquisition of political office. Career politicians not only want to be elected to office; they desperately want not to be unelected. Office is their ultimate aim, loss of office their ultimate deprivation. Defeat in an election frequently means not just the loss of one job but the end of a whole career. It is something that, if at all possible, should be avoided.[3]

American politicians are no more (and no less) anxious about reelection than elected officials in other countries. What distinguishes American politicians is their extraordinarily high level of exposure to the vicissitudes of electoral politics and, specifically, to the almost continuous possibility of electoral defeat. American politicians, more than other politicians, are practically always running—and they are practically always running scared. Given the situation in which they find themselves, it is perfectly rational for them to do so.

To appreciate the contrast between the United States and other countries, consider, for example, the position of the average British member of Parliament (who, being average, is a man and whom we will therefore call "he"). Once elected, the average British MP knows that he will probably not have to seek reelection for another four or five years. To secure renomination by his party all he has to do is maintain a reasonably good working relationship with a few dozen (or, at most, a few hundred) local party leaders. The issue of raising money scarcely arises, since British election campaigns are mainly fought at the national level and very strict limits are placed on campaign spending in local districts. The purchase of advertising time for political purposes on British radio and television is not permitted. Above all, the average British MP knows that his chances of reelection depend almost entirely, not on anything that he personally may do or fail to do, but on the national fortunes of the political party he happens to belong to. British voting is overwhelmingly party voting; voters respond to the record of the national government and the policies of the national opposition and hardly at all to the actions and preferences of individual MPs. There are thus no electoral incentives for the average MP to defy his party's leadership on votes in the House of Commons. On the contrary, most MPs believe that a party seen by voters to be divided is likely to suffer electorally as a consequence. The motto is "We had better hang together because, if we don't, we will all of us hang separately."

As must be evident, these political forces, when taken in combination, have the effect of greatly reducing the average MP's personal political exposure. The need to run for reelection surfaces only rarely. Renomination is seldom a problem. There is no need to worry too much about local party activists and their views. Money is not a problem, and there is therefore no need to worry about fund-raisers, potential campaign contributors, or political action committees. The only thing the average MP really has to worry about is his party's performance in the eyes of the national electorate—and that is not usually something that he can do a great deal about (except sometimes behind the scenes). The only British MP who suffers maximum political exposure is the MP in a swing district in the months immediately before a national election; and such an MP is exposed, if he is, because his party is exposed. Yet again, the emphasis is on party unity, on hanging together.

One result is that British governments are often able to take very tough, very unpopular decisions, especially in the first two or three years of their five-year terms. Clement Attlee, the postwar Labour prime minister, used to recommend that all incoming administrations should "get the worst over" as early in their term of office as possible. This is when prime ministers and governments are at their least exposed. Predictably, prime ministers and governments usually pay increasing attention to the views of the electorate—and are increasingly likely to adapt their policies accordingly—as the next election approaches. If, however, a prime minister and government decide for whatever reasons not to bow to electoral pressure and to persist in pursuing an unpopular line of policy, they can almost invariably still count, for the reasons just given, on the united support of their party supporters in the House of Commons. British voters therefore cannot be confident of being spared pain, even in the run-up to a national election. While the United States was running large budget deficits in the 1980s, Britain in not dissimilar circumstances was repaying a large portion of its national debt and, in some years, even running budget surpluses.[4]

The contrast between the position of the average British MP and the average elected official in the United States could hardly be starker. The contrast has nothing to do with British MPs' or governments' moral superiority; the British editorial writer who, writing about the 1990 budget crisis in the United States, headlined his article "Cowardice on the Hill" had missed the point.[5] The contrast has to do, instead, with American politicians' far higher degree of political exposure. In Great Britain political exposure is concentrated principally on a few national party leaders and is concentrated in time; in the United States it is widely diffused among the nation's political elites and is almost continuous in time.

The facts as they relate to the United States are well known. Every member of the House of Representatives has to run for reelection every two years. Every third member of the Senate has to do the same. The renominations of all of them may be contested in primary elections. They all have to build up enormous campaign war chests, both to finance election campaigns and to deter serious challengers from entering races against them. All of them, in order to amass these war chests, have to pay heed—some would say court—to wealthy individuals and innumerable special-interest groups. They also have to pay court to the media, especially the local media. On top of all this, American politicians, especially members of Congress, cannot shelter under the umbrella of party. Party cohesion in Congress, while not nonexistent, is at much lower levels than in the legislatures of most other democracies. More to the point, American politicians believe—and in this they are largely right—that American voters are only partly influenced by considerations of party. American voters also vote on the strength of the individual congressman's or senator's record, on what he has said and done in Congress and on what he has or has not done for the people in his state or district.

For the British MP, there is safety in numbers (or, at least, if there is a risk to one of them, there is a risk to all). American politicians, by contrast, know that it is perfectly possible for them to be picked off one by one. Not only are the stakes high (after all, they are career politicians), but they are on their own. The fact that most congressmen and senators are reelected if they choose to run for reelection is neither here nor there. If they succeed in being reelected, it is because they live in constant fear of not being reelected and adjust their behavior—very nearly all of it—accordingly.

In short, if there were an "international index of political exposure" (and such an index could, in principle, be constructed), elected officials in the United States would probably turn out to be more exposed more of the time than elected officials in any other liberal democratic country. This is one of the most important single characteristics of the American political system as it functions in the late twentieth century.

Confronted with a problem like the federal budget deficit, the American system is therefore now saddled with both the "everybody's business is nobody's business" problem and the "politics of high exposure" problem. Some way around both problems has to be found if anything is to be done.

One possible way around both problems immediately suggests itself. An attempt should be made to take the issue, whatever the issue, "out of politics." In other words, all the politicians involved should agree, first, that the issue is of such overriding importance to the nation as a whole that it must be solved at almost any cost; second, that therefore the politicians involved must be prepared to sink all their ideological and other differences in the interests of finding a solution (almost any solution); and, third, that having found a solution they must stick together—must provide political cover for each other—in presenting it to what will inevitably, given the kinds of circumstances we have been describing, be a disgruntled and probably hostile electorate. The idea, of course, is that universally shared blame is less likely than other kinds of blame to be taken out on individual elected officials. There is—or, more precisely, there may be—the aforementioned safety in numbers.[6]

The tactic in question has elsewhere been called "the collusion of elites."[7] It was used successfully to pass the 1986 tax reform in the United States and, three years earlier, to enact another urgently needed reform, that of the U.S. social security system. Paul Light in *Artful Work* has described how the measure to reform the social security system was painfully pieced together by the Gang of Nine, an inner group of congressional and executive representatives who met secretly for weeks and who finally "built a compromise, wrapped it in a bipartisan flag, and rammed it through Congress."[8]

This tactic, as everyone knows, was attempted by President Bush and congressional leaders in 1990. Bush and his budget director, Richard Darman, concluded early in the spring of 1990 that the books could no longer be cooked, the figures no longer fiddled. The forecast deficits for fiscal 1991 were running at $120–160 billion, compared with the Gramm-Rudman-Hollings target of $64 billion. Tax revenues were turning out to be substantially less than forecast, and the necessity of dealing with the aftermath of the savings-and-loan fiasco was one of a number of factors tending to push up federal spending at the same time. Against the background of upward pressure on interest rates worldwide, Bush and Darman were especially worried that an extra-large U.S. budget deficit would force up interest rates to unacceptable levels in the United States. High interest rates coupled with a severe credit shortage could tip the economy into recession.[9]

The president knew that Congress would have to be actively involved in the working out of any measures to deal with the deficit. He also knew that, if such measures were both to be agreed on and to be effective, everyone engaged in the process would, if at all possible, have to provide political cover for everyone else engaged in the process. No one should be overexposed (or, ideally, exposed at all). Accordingly, on 5 May 1990, he proposed that budget meetings should be held between the administration and congressional leaders without preconditions on either side. Bush's suggestion that the meetings be held without preconditions hinted at a willingness to drop the "no new taxes" pledge that he had made somewhat disingenuously (under conditions of maximum political exposure) during the 1988 election campaign; and on 26 June, with the president under pressure from Democrats in Congress, his election pledge was duly, and publicly, abandoned. The circumstances were significant. No one was to be allowed to break ranks. The Democratic leaders insisted that Bush take personal responsibility for abandoning the pledge; they negotiated the actual form of words with him and Darman at the White House; and they insisted that the president issue his statement before they left the building. In return, they kept their promise not to gloat and "gravely commended the President's statesmanship."[10] But many Republicans outside the inner circle were aghast, and lower-ranking Democrats felt no need to conceal their rejoicing at the president's discomfiture.

The budget meetings proposed by the president began in the spring, and in a wide variety of forms and an equally wide variety of venues they continued until well into the fall. Sometimes a smallish group of negotiators met under President Bush's chairmanship in the White House. Sometimes a larger group met on Capitol Hill under the chairmanship of Representative Richard Gephardt, the House majority leader. In early September the negotiations were moved to the more neutral (and more austere) setting of Andrews Air Force Base, a little distance from Washington. In late September they were moved back to the Capitol. The numbers of negotiators tended to decrease through time. By the end of September five congressional leaders and three top administration officials—dubbed, inevitably, the Gang of Eight—were meeting almost around the clock in a private dining room on Capitol Hill or else in a conference room belonging to House Speaker Thomas Foley.

The aims of the exercise were clear. The elites in Congress and the administration, and in both political parties, were to meet to agree on a solution to a pressing national problem. They were to meet in private so that everyone would be in a position to speak freely. And they were to assume joint responsibility for whatever agreement they reached, first, so that the chances would be maximized of the agreement's being accepted by Congress and, second, so that the chances would be minimized of either side's blaming the other for what had happened. Everyone—and no one—was to be responsible for the tax increases; everyone—and no one—was to be responsible for the cuts in domestic programs. The two sides, as someone put it, were to jump together, locked in fond embrace, off the political cliff.

But although the aims of the exercise were clear, so were the difficulties. One, obvious from the beginning, concerned the size of the negotiating group. The ideal group would be small. Only if it were small could mutual trust and a sense of group cohesion begin to develop. A smallish group would also have the effect of reducing the complexity of the negotiating process. But, against that, the smaller the group, the more likely it would be that those excluded from the group would resent their exclusion and would not feel bound to honor whatever decisions the group came to.[11] Another problem concerned leaks. The group would function best, and would be most likely to arrive at mutually acceptable outcomes, if there were no leaks of its deliberations; at the same time, it was obviously in the interest of every individual member of the group to leak, both to protect his own personal position and to bring pressure to bear on the group's other members. Not surprisingly, there was never any sustained agreement during the spring, summer, and fall of 1990 on what the size and composition of the negotiating group ought to be; and, right from the beginning, leaks abounded. Newt Gingrich, although the House minority Whip, never showed any disposition to play the collusion-of-elites game. On the contrary, it clearly gave him much pleasure to be seen not playing it.[12]

These "structural" difficulties, which would have beset any comparable set of negotiations, were compounded by the brute facts of American politics as they existed in 1990. There were ideological differences. Liberal Democrats in Congress conscientiously believed that the deficit should be reduced by means of higher taxes, mainly on the rich; conservative Republicans, by contrast, equally conscientiously believed that the deficit should be reduced by means of deep cuts in federal spending, mainly on domestic welfare programs. The president himself seemed almost fixated on the idea of reducing the capital gains tax. These genuine ideological and policy differences were further compounded by purely partisan considerations. In an election year (almost every year is an election year in the United States) Democrats and Republicans alike had a vested interest in trying to blame the other for the pain that any serious attempt to reduce the deficit would inevitably inflict on voters.

Nevertheless, despite the structural difficulties and despite the fact that both the ideological differences and the partisan considerations were reflected in the makeup of the final negotiating group, a deal was ultimately struck. The negotiators were acutely conscious that, partisan politics apart, circumstances were conspiring against the United States. The Persian Gulf crisis, beginning in August, was forcing up world oil prices and interest rates. A U.S. recession seemed more and more probable. Estimates of the size of the fiscal 1990 deficit had soared from $120–160 billion earlier in the year to more than $290 billion. And the specter of Gramm-Rudman-Hollings, with its indiscriminate cuts in federal spending, was looming larger and larger. On 30 September the weary negotiators met with President Bush at the White House to announce a package of measures that, if accepted, would cut $40 billion from the revised deficit in the first year and $500 billion over the next five years to 1995. The package was tough. It included, on the one hand, reductions in federal contributions to Medicare (to placate the conservative Republicans) and, on the other, increased sales taxes on luxury items such as yachts and private airplanes (to placate the Democrats). Excise taxes on gasoline, alcoholic beverages, and cigarettes were also to be sharply increased. President Bush pronounced the package "balanced" and "fair," adding: "In my view it is what the United States needs at this point in our history."[13] Two days later, the president went on television to commend the deal to the American people.

But neither Bush nor the Gang of Eight had reckoned—perhaps there was no practical way in which they could have reckoned—with the seemingly inexorable logic of high-exposure politics. On 2 October 1990, the midterm congressional elections were little more than a month away. In all, 405 members of the House and 32 members of the Senate were running for reelection in those elections. It was in the interests of none of the 437 to vote for the package that Bush and the Gang of Eight had put together. It was in the interests of all of them not to vote for it. They would vote for it only if they broadly sympathized with the purposes it was trying to serve and the way in which it was trying to serve them and they believed that there would be near-unanimity in Congress in favor of the proposals, thereby providing them with some reasonable measure of cover in the coming elections. A necessary condition of the deal's being accepted was that the members of both parties in Congress should believe that a majority of the members of the other party would vote for it. All that had to happen for the deal to collapse was for some significant number of congressmen, possibly only a minority, to announce that they were going to vote against it. At that point, their political cover having been blown, large numbers of other congressmen, certainly by now a majority, would be bound to join them in their opposition. They would not want to be left exposed.

This was precisely what happened during the next few days. Alan Greenspan, the chairman of the Federal Reserve Board, spoke in favor of the proposals. So did three former Republican presidents, Nixon, Ford and Reagan. The Senate minority leader, Robert Dole, quoted Tom Paine ("These are the times that try men's souls"). Congressmen were urged to "rise above party" and to "put the country first." But Republicans resented the fact that the president had reneged on his no-new-taxes pledge and had later abandoned his drive for a cut in the capital gains tax; many Republicans reckoned that, having won their seats as tax cutters, they might lose them as voters for tax increases. On the other side of the aisle, Democrats objected to those parts of the Bush-Gang of Eight package that were fiscally regressive, that cut Medicare, and that appeared to offer new tax breaks to the very rich; many of them began to wonder whether, even in an off year with a Republican in the White House, their seats would be safe if they voted the wrong way. Conservative Republicans, led by Newt Gingrich, began the flight from the deal; but, the flight having begun, they were soon joined by fellow Republicans and an increasing number of Democrats. On 5 October the House of Representatives, in spite of intensive White House lobbying, turned down the package by 254 votes to 179. The aim had been to secure a bipartisan majority for the deal. In the event, majorities in both parties voted against it. The deal—in its way a bold attempt to grapple with the kind of problem that democracies least like to face—was dead.

In this instance, there proved to be life after death. President Bush kept up the pressure on Congress by refusing to sign a temporary measure that would have enabled the federal government to continue to operate despite the absence of a budget. One by one, the Statue of Liberty, the Washington Monument, the Smithsonian museums, and even the National Zoo were shut until further notice. Tourists locked out of the zoo went and sat in the public galleries of Congress instead—and claimed they could hardly tell the difference. Meanwhile, teams of negotiators from the administration and Congress were busy working out a revised version of the deal, and this revised version was eventually passed by narrow majorities shortly before the end of October. The new deal omitted some of the original deal's cuts in Medicare, reduced income tax on many of those with middle incomes, and substantially increased taxes on the rich. Not surprisingly, Democrats in both the House and the Senate were keener on the deal than Republicans (majorities of whom refused to vote for it). The president, in his own words, "gagged" at some of the bill's provisions, but he signed it all the same.

The effects on the public reputations of most of those involved were devastating. President Bush's approval ratings fell by between 10 and 19 points in a month; more than half of those interviewed expressed dissatisfaction with his handling of the economy; and large majorities blamed Congress for the protracted stalemate. Worse, in mid October no fewer than 79 percent of Americans told the *Washington Post*-ABC News poll that the nation was "pretty seriously off on the wrong track." [14] In the midterm elections on 6 November, most congressmen and senators who were running for reelection kept their seats (many of them had taken the precaution of voting against both of the budget deals), but the turnout of voters was the lowest since 1944.

In the concluding section of this chapter we look again at some of the wider implications of the efforts (and nonefforts) to cut the federal budget deficits. Suffice it to say here that they can hardly be thought to have represented Good Government in either the procedural or the substantive sense (at least if one assumes that large budget deficits are not a good thing). If Lorenzetti had been painting his murals in 1990, he would probably have depicted the citizens of Siena making rude gestures in the direction of their political masters.

The Underclass and the Drug Problem

The federal budget deficit, as we have seen, finally rose to the top of the political agenda in 1990. It did so not because politicians wanted it there—they most emphatically did not—but because both the president and the leaders of Congress had concluded that to delay dealing with it any longer would be practically impossible, given the existence of Gramm-Rudman-Hollings, and might have calamitous consequences for the American economy.

We turn now to two quite different issues, ones frequently linked in the public mind in the United States: the problem of America's "underclass" and the problem of drugs. And here the foreign observer is immediately puzzled. Both problems would, on the face of it, appear to be worthy of being addressed by politicians. The existence of America's underclass, especially as it manifests itself in the downtown areas of America's big cities, appears to be inconsistent with all that America claims to be and to stand for. It juxtaposes America the Beautiful and America the Ugly; in a land built on hope, the presence of the underclass in itself seems the ultimate in mass despair. Lorenzetti would have had no trouble depicting the underclass, and he would have known on which wall of the Sala della Pace it should appear. Yet the problem of the underclass was not on either President Bush's agenda or Congress's in 1989–90. By contrast, the problem of illegal drugs was high on the agenda of both. What accounts for this difference in treatment, especially since many in America believed then, and believe now, that the problem of the underclass and the problem of drugs are inextricably linked?

Those who study America from outside are not surprised by the fact that America has a problem with drugs and an underclass. Instead, they are surprised by the very different degrees of government action that each has provoked. The first question to ask, therefore, is this: By what means do issues actually make it onto the political agenda? We need to account for the discrepancy between the saliency given to the drug issue by politicians and their comparative neglect of the underclass.

From the time of the New Deal and the subsequent growth of the modern presidency, Americans have become used to looking to the White House to take the lead in tackling pressing issues of the day. While nominally responsible for formulating as well as enacting legislation, Congress during the last half-century has usually been content to consider and debate draft legislation that has originated in the executive branch. It is the administration that is now expected to toss the first ball of the policy-making process into Congress's court. But how does the White House decide which issues to pick up, concentrate on, and bring to the attention of Congress? This question has been addressed by, among others, Nelson Polsby and John Kingdon.[15] Relevant factors clearly include the state of expert opinion on an issue (is there a

coherent policy option available somewhere that the White House can develop?); the president's own background (had he concentrated on a particular
policy area before being elected, or had he at least campaigned on it?); and
the general lie of the legislative landscape (is Congress friendly or hostile?
Can the president claim an electoral mandate?). Factors such as these can
play a part in creating what Kingdon calls a "policy window," or an opportunity for action on a particular issue.

Of course, the combination of factors will change with different issues,
as Barbara Kellerman found when she looked at some issues that recent presidents have chosen to bring to Congress. Kellerman's account of the genesis
of Lyndon Johnson's War on Poverty and Ronald Reagan's plan to cut federal spending suggest two possible ways in which issues might reach the political agenda.[16] Johnson saw that the shocked national response to President
Kennedy's assassination might give him the opportunity to push forward
some draft plans recently drawn up within the executive branch on ways to
fight poverty. At the end of 1963, the extent of poverty in America was not
visible at any point on the national political agenda, but by the following
spring it was the number-one item.

Johnson used every means open to him as president to stress the problem of poverty: addressing Congress, appealing to influential individuals, appearing on television, and, perhaps most effectively, by traveling to afflicted
areas such as the Appalachians, the media in tow, to demonstrate to the nation the full extent of the poverty problem. But at the same time as he demonstrated the problem's existence, Johnson also offered the nation a solution
to it: the proposed Economic Opportunity Act, which included a wide range
of measures and would cost $1 billion in its first year alone. This was an au-
dacious attempt to extend federal government intervention into this area of
social welfare; but, helped by the force of his own personality, his intimate
knowledge of Congress, and his talent for maximizing any political opportunity, Johnson saw to it that an act was ready for his signature by the end of
August 1964—less than nine months after he first attempted to put poverty
on the agenda.

A generation later, in 1981, Ronald Reagan found himself in a situation
that was the opposite of Johnson's. Reagan as president did not have to strive
to push his central concern to the political forefront. He had fought a strong
campaign on a simply articulated platform, one with which he had long been
identified, and his election victory ensured that the campaign's central
plank—the desirability of tax cuts together with budget cuts—would dominate the national agenda. Like Johnson, Reagan then moved with great speed
to make the most of his opportunity.

Between these two fairly extreme examples, of course, lie others; but what has stood out clearly in recent years has been the central role played by the White House in forcing certain issues onto the national political agenda. Why, then, has the executive branch not chosen since the 1960s to present the problem of the underclass to the political system as one deserving concerted action?

Part of the answer lies in the lack of agreement among experts about what exactly the underclass is. As a term, "underclass" is now in such widespread use that laypeople tend to use it without being clear what exactly it is supposed to describe. Those whose job it is to study the causes and effects of poverty have never in fact been happy with it. Some see the term as an overinclusive labeling of several distinct groups. Others see it as too value laden, implying that a section of the population is somehow outside, or beneath, the bounds of "proper" society.[17] The experts' opinions on how large that section actually is vary with how it is defined; and estimates range from 500,000 to no fewer than 8 million people.[18] Nevertheless, the experts do agree on the existence of an identifiable group that remains stranded at the foot of the socioeconomic ladder for reasons that lie largely outside its members' individual control. But the exact nature of these reasons is also a subject for debate. Part of the problem is related to the urban geography of the inner cities, such as poor transport and educational services. In sociological terms, there seems to be a tendency for those in the underclass to develop forms of social behavior that deviate from prevailing norms and create a distinct and (to the majority) "alien" subculture. Such behavior can in turn exacerbate the problems of social exclusion that follow from a prolonged period of poverty, such as difficulty in holding employment. But separating cause and effect, and assessing the relative importance of these and other factors, is proving far from easy.[19]

Academic experts, in addition, are divided over the part that the Great Society measures undertaken in the mid 1960s may have played in producing the current situation. Some see the Washington-led assistance programs of that period as having been largely on the right track until they were derailed by the political and economic consequences of the Vietnam war. In recent years, others have argued that, by providing a wide range of government "handouts," the federal government inadvertently encouraged recipients to take self-destructive decisions, with a guaranteed entry into job-training schemes lessening the consequences of dropping out of school and financial aid to single mothers actually encouraging teenage pregnancies.[20] Such a debate over something as fundamental as the merits of the Great Society program, which was after all the federal government's last major attempt at a comprehensive welfare policy, shows just how far the experts are from a consensus on how best to proceed.

In other words, no firm agreement exists among the experts about what the underclass is and why it exists, nor is there any consensus about how the government might act even to alleviate the problem, let alone "solve" it. As a result, one of the links in the process by which an issue makes it onto the political agenda is missing. While there is widespread evidence of the existence of an underclass, no clear policy options are being offered up to the White House or other politicians by the community of experts who study it. In the absence of a viable solution that can be debated, and preferably implemented, there is little to encourage the political system to focus its concern and attention on the issue.

The absence of agreement among experts might not matter so much, however, if there were other forces in the system encouraging politicians to take an interest in the plight of the underclass—or at any rate forces not discouraging them from doing so. But the opposite is the case.

The first point to be made is that there are virtually no practical incentives for politicians to put the underclass on the political agenda at the national level. Because much of the underclass is heavily concentrated in big-city ghettoes, few individual congressmen actually represent districts where the problems of the underclass are dominant. On a wider level, the underclass is part of a much larger group, comprising roughly one-third of adult Americans, who never or almost never vote in elections. The result is that politicians believe, probably rightly, that they have little to gain electorally from championing the underclass's cause. On the contrary, it would be the more articulate and electorally active groups who would have to pay for any alleviating measures that were taken. On a still wider level, the demographic shift that has taken place in the last two decades, with people moving from the industrial centers of the north and east toward the south and west, has had a political as well as an economic impact on those left behind. Falling population figures have meant the reapportionment of seats away from older urban areas at both state and national levels, further weakening these areas' potential for influencing policy making.

Thus, the structural incentives of the system—principally the electoral links between politicians and their electorates—in no way encourage the top levels of government to seek to grapple with the problem of the underclass. Instead, in recent years there has been a factor positively discouraging politicians from doing so: the budget deficit. Given the sheer scale of the underclass problem, any attempted solution would inevitably make heavy demands on government resources just at a time when any additional federal expenditure needs special justification. The early Bush years were clearly not the time to rock the economic boat by taking on board additional federal commitments—unless, of course, there had been strong indications of enthusiastic support from the country at large.

But there were no such indications. Why not? Why were politicians right not to sense a strong popular desire that they act to deal with the suffering, despair, and social exclusion that are apparently the lot of those who are trapped in the underclass? After all, one might suppose that human suffering is one of the hardest things for a liberal society to bear; despair is at odds with traditional American optimism and faith in progress; and social exclusion has always been regarded in theory and, more recently, in practice as profoundly un-American. Might there not be some "moral imperative" in the political environment that would encourage the political system, despite the cost-benefit calculations of individual politicians, at least to place the problem of the underclass on the political agenda? In fact, it would seem that there is not.

If we take as a guide to the values and beliefs that underpin American politics Samuel Huntington's analysis of the "American Creed," we find that these values are open to more than one interpretation.[21] The beliefs in liberty, equality, democracy, individualism, and the Constitution are accompanied by beliefs in minimal government, in equality of opportunity rather than of condition, and in the duty as well as the right of the individual to stand on his or her own two feet.[22]

This last point is important because it suggests that in America a person needs to meet at least minimal standards of personal behavior in order to be seen as deserving of external assistance.[23] And here we find a link with the popular view of the problem of the underclass that has been prevalent in the United States for the past fifteen years. During that time, "the popular view of the underclass became one of people with serious character flaws entrenched by a welfare subculture and who have only themselves to blame for their social position in society."[24] In this way, the image of the group itself as contributing substantially to the perpetuation of its own position at the foot of the socioeconomic ladder has done much to prevent the development of any widespread sense among most Americans that the underclass deserves large-scale help and relief. Although opinion surveys suggest that the American public has few objections in principle to the government using its resources to help the poor, most Americans also seem to expect recipients to make obvious and concurrent efforts to help themselves.[25] Far from being inconsistent with all that America stands for, a government that is reluctant to approach a problem of this kind in an interventionist manner can appeal to a strongly held set of values and beliefs that actively discourages such a role. Government should be good, but not *too* good—certainly not to the point of helping those who will not help themselves.

Here, then, are several possible explanations of why the problem of the underclass did not feature on the political agenda during the Bush administration's first years. Which factor or factors are the most crucial? Certainly, in the absence of any apparent consensus in the academic community about how best to tackle the problem, it is less likely that the political community will choose to focus on it. But even if clear solutions had been formulated and were being advocated, would any leading actor in national politics have attempted to put the issue on the political agenda? Given what we have said so far, it seems unlikely. The president, who might have been expected to lead, had not previously been identified with the issue, had not campaigned on it during the 1988 campaign, and has yet to show any sign of believing that the American people are willing to be led in a major attempt to tackle the underclass problem. Equally, for the majority of congressmen, there was little incentive to acknowledge a new requirement for government spending just as moves to reduce spending were approaching crisis point. The budget deficit in itself made any large-scale relief effort in the early 1990s unlikely. When coupled with the lack of public pressure for action, or even any public acknowledgment of the need for action, the underclass's absence from the political agenda is hardly surprising.

What does all this tell us about the goodness or otherwise of the American system of government? The underclass still exists, visible to any who care to walk—or, more prudently, drive—through any number of tired and blighted urban areas. Does the underclass's existence mean that America suffers from Bad Government? Or, more modestly, how can a society that values Good Government allow the underclass's continued plight to go undebated at the highest political level?

The answer appears to be linked to the "politics of high exposure" referred to earlier. In a system where those engaged in national politics, particularly in the House of Representatives, are highly dependent for their survival on constituency approval of their individual legislative actions, the interests of a poor and isolated minority are unlikely, in general, to be catered to. They may be catered to, of course, if securing their interests is relatively costless. In the case of civil rights legislation in the 1960s, the economic costs of moving against racial discrimination were comparatively slight, and so were the political costs everywhere except in the South. The result was that, even if many politicians derived little direct benefit from the passing of civil rights legislation, they also paid little or no political price.

A minority may also be catered to if it can mobilize sympathy and support among the majority, perhaps by appealing to a widely shared sense of what is right or fair. Under these circumstances, the majority may in its turn provide incentives for those in Washington to act, as with the 1935 Social Security Act and other New Deal legislation. In addition, if the minority has something with which to bargain, and the organization necessary to be able to bargain with it, then the minority may succeed in bringing its own pressure to bear on central government. The underclass in the early 1990s, however, does not meet any of these requirements. Meaningful help would be exceedingly costly, both economically and politically; the underclass's image is such that it does not arouse much sympathy; and the underclass has nothing with which to engage in political bargaining.

The problem of drug abuse stands in sharp contrast. It was already a central concern both in the White House and in Congress by the time President Bush took office. During the 1980s, the federal government had almost quadrupled the funds available for antidrug measures—from $1 billion in 1981 to just under $4 billion in 1988—and such phrases as "zero tolerance of drugs" and "just say no" were staples of political rhetoric. By mid 1988, with the election campaign in full swing, opinion polls were indicating that the public saw drugs as the most important problem facing the country, placing it well above both the state of the economy and the budget deficit.[26] Clearly the issue would be high on the agenda of the new administration. But what was it about the drug problem that caused it to attract so much political attention? Why was it treated so differently from the problem of the underclass?

One answer cannot be that there is an academic consensus, or a consensus of experts, on the drug problem. While there are undoubtedly some disagreements among academic experts as to the structural factors underlying the plight of the underclass, there is no agreement at all among those studying the drug problem, or, more precisely, those who study the problem agree that there is almost nothing they can say with any certainty about addiction—whether to narcotics or to alcohol—and that more research is needed. The view is widespread that until the relationship between the physiological, psychological, and sociological factors in the addiction process is better understood, those working to prevent drug abuse will be fighting an uphill battle. Understanding the causes of the drug problem is probably less advanced than understanding the underclass problem.

The position is slightly different when it comes to the question of how best to limit access to drugs. Work in this area has highlighted a number of policies that could prove effective. Interdiction—the prevention of drugs from actually entering the country—combined with strict enforcement of domestic antidrug laws may, within limits, restrict supply; freely available treatment for current addicts and antidrug campaigns aimed at the young may, again within limits, help lower demand. As a result, politicians have been offered a range of policy options that might help to reduce both supply and demand.[27] Each requires money, and research has yet to prove that any one of them is markedly more effective than the others. But when it comes to combating drugs, the academic community has at least given those in government the choice of several different areas in which to invest any funds they decide to provide.

But the provision of such options, important though it is, does not guarantee an issue a place on the political agenda, nor does it automatically mean that politicians will choose to devote limited resources to an area, however well thought out the planning. Thus, the differing states of the academic debates on the underclass and the issue of drug abuse cannot account for the different reaction of the political system to the two problems. A far more important explanation lies in the extent to which the general public sees one problem as more pressing than the other. While the prevailing orthodoxy in the 1980s may have stressed less government spending and regulation, and thus have worked against the prospects of the underclass appearing on the national agenda, the general public and politicians seemed happy to make an exception in the case of illegal drugs.

A number of factors combined during the 1980s to raise the profile of illegal drugs. One was the role played by the needles of intravenous drug users in spreading the newly discovered AIDS virus. Another was the increasingly fashionable use of cocaine among young professionals. But perhaps most important was the arrival of crack, a cheap and dirty form of cocaine that proved highly addictive. The so-called crack epidemic strengthened the perceived link between drug abuse and urban violence, suggesting forcefully that the drug user was no longer simply a danger to himself and an inconvenience to others, but an actual threat to American society.

The widespread media coverage of these issues, particularly crack, ranged from the learned to the lurid, but it helped create, by the mid 1980s, a feeling that drugs now posed a three-tiered threat to the American people. On the individual level, widespread and easy access to drugs, especially for the young, raised the prospect that a friend or family member might be directly confronted with the temptation to try them. More broadly, the fear existed, heightened by the debate over random drug testing, that those to whom one regularly entrusted one's safety and well-being, be they bus drivers, air traffic controllers, doctors, might be working even though their competence was impaired by illegal drug use. Finally, there was the sense that society itself was in danger of being swamped by a rising tide of drug-related crime. From negligence in the workplace by casual users, through street muggings by addicts, to internecine turf wars among dealers, drugs seemed a root cause of the appreciable increase in crime and violence.[28] Previously associated with university campuses and then with inner-city ghettoes, drugs and their consequences now seemed to be affecting large sections of society—and therefore, of the electorate.

All the same, beyond the idea that drugs were now a threat, this widespread concern was only vaguely articulated and carried with it few precise demands for action. Why did it nevertheless meet with such a ready response from the federal government? Part of the answer is that the federal government already had a long tradition of engaging in the paternalistic protection of its citizens from potentially corrupting substances. While Prohibition is obviously the most famous, or notorious, example of this tendency, Washington has been involved in circumscribing the importation of debilitating narcotics since fears about the coming of opium from China in the 1880s. Following its attempts to shield Americans from the misuses of alcohol, Congress tried to stem the arrival of Latin American marijuana in the 1930s and Asian heroin after both World War II and the Vietnam war. The curtailment of a citizen's access to narcotics appears to be one of the few government restrictions on individual freedom that Americans not only tolerate but enthusiastically approve of; where government action against poverty might find only limited support from deep-seated American values, government action against drugs seems to face no such ambivalence.

The actual prevention of the importation of narcotics across America's borders is clearly a matter for the federal government and as such is a direct concern of Congress. Moreover, if the government's antidrug role is more broadly interpreted, then virtually every congressional committee can feel itself linked to a "war on drugs," allowing nearly every member of Congress to claim some degree of credit for taking part in the fight. Opportunities to join in the antidrug crusade are now available to congressmen concerned with the armed services, foreign affairs, health, education, transport, banking and science, as well as the judiciary. The central point, however, remains the essential illegality of drugs, which legitimates congressional activity in this area in a way that the merely moral concern over poverty cannot match. While it may choose to alleviate suffering, Congress has a positive duty to concern itself with the law and its enforcement, and this is how it has seen its role in the war on drugs.

Having in 1984 taken steps to deter international drug traffickers in the Comprehensive Crime Control Act, in 1986 Congress passed the Anti-Drug Abuse Act, which attempted to limit the supply of drugs available to Americans by allocating an additional $1.7 billion to be used mainly to increase interdiction. Two years later, Congress passed a second Anti-Drug Abuse Act, which authorized an extra $2 billion for antidrug activity, with a portion of it earmarked this time for drug education and treatment programs. Beyond the fact that both were widely supported at a time when concern about the budget deficit was already high, two things are striking about this sequence of measures. One is that very little in the way of evaluation seems to have been done between 1986 and 1988 that might have allowed anyone to gauge the relative effectiveness of different antidrug activities, the result being that no one could really judge how best to allocate extra resources. The other is that the Anti-Drug Abuse Acts were passed by Congress in late October of an election year, just before congressmen returned to their districts for the last round of campaigning. Taken together, these two facts suggest that congressmen's principal concern was not so much to forge a successful, cost-effective antidrug strategy as to forge a successful, cost-effective reelection strategy. Many experts viewed the politicians as throwing money and effort indiscriminately in every conceivable direction; the politicians viewed themselves as being in tune with the nation.

The dovetailing of political action with public concern reached its height in September 1989, when President Bush unveiled his new antidrug strategy at the start of the new school year. Scheduling his television address for mid-morning so that children could watch in class, he promised a new strategy to coordinate antidrug efforts and outlined plans for more prisons, treatment centers, and Coast Guard resources. More interesting than the speech itself, however, was the careful preparatory work by his staff that preceded it. During August, always a slow month for news, the White House had informed the television networks that a major presidential address on drugs was imminent.[29] As a result, for the three weeks preceding the broadcast, the nightly news programs highlighted drug-related stories, talk shows discussed drug abuse, and prime-time current affairs specials examined various aspects of the drug problem. The consequence of this publicity blitz was that, even before the president spoke, Americans were reminded of their own concern about the issue, with one Harris poll indicating that 87 percent believed the drug problem to be "very serious." Government and public were united in a shared concern and a communal call for action. In fact, the Bush plan differed little from that of his predecessor, with its heavy emphasis on interdiction and law enforcement; but immediately following its unveiling, a *New York Times/CBS News* poll showed that a staggering 64 percent of the public now viewed drugs as the most important single problem facing the country.[30]

Although that figure soon fell, the public continued to see drugs as the country's major problem well into 1990. Media attention to the issue during this period was prevented from declining by a series of spectacular news stories. Interest in the deadly Medellin drug cartel, which was defying the Colombian government while supplying the American cocaine market, was surpassed only by that in Panamanian President Manuel Noriega, whose transformation from staunch regional ally to international drug trafficker was a swift precursor to the American invasion that removed him. Before excitement about the invasion had died down, the mayor of Washington, D.C.,

Marion Barry, had been arrested for possessing crack. But even so, as 1990 progressed, concern about the budget deficit and the economy began to rise, while concern about drugs declined. By mid August, a year after the storm of media and presidential attention, the start of the Persian Gulf crisis had pushed drugs back to fourth place in the ranking of national concerns. On the anniversary of his antidrug speech, President Bush stated that curbing the use of illegal drugs continued to be the nation's top priority, even though the nation's attention might currently be diverted elsewhere. But, as one *New York Times* writer observed:

> In recent politics there always seems to be another subject to preoccupy the public. Who ever talks about the Berlin Wall or Tiananmen Square any more? Getting the public's attention, particularly on a subject that the polls show is already gnawing at people, is no real trick for a President, even a President who lacks a knack for the bully pulpit part of his job. The trick is holding that attention.[31]

If the trick is holding the public's attention, we might ask what happens when that attention slips, as it appears to have done in the case of illegal drugs. Will a fall in public interest be followed by a lessening of political action?

For politicians operating in an environment that leaves them highly exposed to the public's response, combating drug abuse has proved irresistible. It is an issue with few partisan overtones, it attracts much media coverage, and it offers ample opportunities for action or at least activity. At a time when most new spending has been limited by the size of the federal budget deficit, widespread support for a war on drugs has allowed both Congress and the White House to produce new and expensive antidrug policies. These have mostly involved increasing funds to law enforcement agencies, and the money spent has yielded statistics that testify to its effectiveness: more drugs seized, more arrests made, more drug pushers behind bars. In the words of the old saying, activity is the politician's substitute for achievement, and the present policies have succeeded admirably in conveying to a clearly worried electorate the idea that their representatives are indeed actively waging a war against drugs.

Perhaps, given the nature of the drug problem, that is the best that can be hoped for. But it is striking that those who are studying the problems of drug selling, drug addiction, and drug-related crime are saying that if the politicians really wanted to tackle the issue they would be using many more of the available resources to sponsor research into the underlying causes of the problem as opposed to merely combating its symptoms. As James Q. Wilson has said,

I have watched several "wars on drugs" declared over the last three decades. The wars typically begin with the statement that the time for studies is past and the time for action has come. "We know what to do; let's get on with it."

In fact, we do not know what to do in any comprehensive way, and the need for research is never more urgent than at the beginning of a "war." That is because every past war [on drugs] has led, after brief gains, to final defeat.[32]

This may be the real cost of the politics of high exposure. While there is no reason to doubt the sincerity of politicians' desire to tackle the drug issue, their response seems to have more to do with the public's concern about the drug problem than with the problem itself. Experts question whether the government actually has a comprehensive antidrug strategy, but the government takes care to be seen as "acting." The element of charade, of sharp practice, is unmistakable.

President Bush and High-Exposure Politics

We have suggested that elected officials in the United States are particularly vulnerable to the problems associated with high-exposure politics. These problems circumscribe the freedom of action of members of Congress, career politicians whose overriding objective in most cases is to secure their own reelection. To be reelected, they must face an electorate that holds them individually accountable for the way they have cast their votes in Washington and that has grown accustomed to expect low tax bills and high benefits. As a result, Congress finds it increasingly difficult to make hard choices—and politics is, at bottom, about making hard choices.

What of the president in this context? He in a sense is doubly exposed, especially during his first term. Every first-term president is, from the moment of his inauguration, a candidate for reelection for a second term. And in his candidacy he is largely on his own, with little support from a party organization and with relatively little in the way of party identification among voters that he can fall back on. He is also on his own in the sense that, in the American system, it is not a "government" or an "administration" or a "coalition" that is on trial; it is him, personally. A first-term president is liable to consider everything he does in the light of whether it will, or will not, enhance his chances of reelection (and, even if he is not thinking in these terms, everyone else will assume that he is). In addition, the president is crucially, if indirectly, affected by the high political exposure of members of Congress. *Their* exposure determines in large part whether he will be able to achieve *his* ends, including the ultimate end of reelection. George Bush was—and behaved as though he felt he was—highly exposed at least until the end of the

Gulf War, not least because he began his administration without a number of the advantages that his predecessor had enjoyed.

Winning the 1988 presidential election brought Bush to an office whose standing in relation to the other branches of government, and with the public at large, had been greatly improved during the previous eight years. The trend of disappointment and disillusionment that had marked the general feeling about the presidency in the 1970s had been arrested and reversed by Ronald Reagan during the 1980s. Despite some hiccoughs toward the end, high personal regard for Reagan had helped restore respect for the office both across the country and on Capitol Hill. But along with a strengthened presidency, part of the legacy handed on by the departing Reagan and his team was a tendency in the White House to regard relations with Congress in adversarial terms; Congress was largely viewed as an obstacle to be got around rather than as a partner in government. To help in overcoming congressional opposition to his policies, Reagan was able to use his prestige with the American public to influence the actions of those he dealt with "inside the Beltway." But he often went further and appealed directly to the American people to show their support for his policies by lobbying their representatives on his behalf.[33] In competition with Congress, this strategy of "going public," appealing to the country over the heads of its elected representatives, made the best possible use of the president's own gifts—but, if only for that reason, it offered little by way of a model for his successor.

Indeed, George Bush's arrival in the Oval Office strongly suggested the need for a different approach to presidential relations with Congress. In the first place, despite winning forty states and some 54 percent of the popular vote, he could not claim, as did Reagan, to have been swept into office with a mandate for change. On the contrary, Bush had fought a campaign based on a promise of no precipitous shifts in policy. Second, Bush had not projected a strong ideological message during the campaign, both because he had trouble formulating "the vision thing" and because he lacked Reagan's ability to imbue his messages with urgent sincerity. Finally, Reagan's advantage of entering office with a Republican-controlled Senate was also denied. Facing a strongly Democratic Congress without a distinct agenda and without Reagan's persuasive skills, conciliation rather than conflict must have looked to the incoming Bush team—shorn of some of the Reagan team's more ideological members—as the most promising way of approaching the legislature.

This also fitted with Bush's own personality and inclination. Despite an impressive career in public service, the most notable positions he had held prior to the presidency were ones that called on qualities other than combativeness. As Republican party chairman in the difficult years of the early 1970s, loyalty—first to President Nixon, but ultimately to his party

—was Bush's defining characteristic. His terms as ambassador to the United Nations, and then to China, required tact and diplomacy, as did his brief period as CIA director, when his main task was to reestablish the agency's working relationship with Congress after the damaging investigations of the mid 1970s. And, unlike some other vice-presidents, perhaps most notably Nixon under Eisenhower, Bush had maintained a low political profile while in that office. Experience as well as temperament, therefore, inclined Bush to be more a diplomat than a crusader, a man who viewed consensus as desirable rather than dishonorable. His aim, typically, was compromise rather than ideological conversion. One result has been his tendency to make domestic policy by means of wide-ranging consultation, with the attainment of less-than-ideal agreements seen as preferable to coming away from the negotiating table with clean, but empty, hands. Bush's nature is to search for, and then try to build on, common ground.

This was certainly the message that came across in his Inaugural Address, which included several phrases lauding the desirability of dialogue and communication and calling specifically for cooperation between the White House and Congress.

> We need compromise; we've had dissension. We need harmony: we've had a chorus of discordant voices.... To my friends—and yes, I do mean friends—in the loyal opposition—and yes, I do mean loyal—I put out my hand. I'm putting out my hand to you, Mr. Speaker. I'm putting out my hand to you, Mr. Majority Leader. For this is the thing: this is the age of the offered hand.[34]

The message was not lost on members of Congress, who also detected a desire on the electorate's part to see cooperation in government. Many in Congress felt Bush's pragmatic style to be a welcome change from that of the previous administration. During the early period of Bush's presidency, negotiation between the White House and Capitol Hill produced progress and substantial agreement on clean air legislation, aid to the Nicaraguan *contras,* and the bailing out of stricken savings-and-loan associations. Such was the cooperative spirit that was now abroad that, reviewing his first six months in office, a *Time* cover story dubbed Bush "Mr. Consensus," concluding that "after eight years of the Reagan revolution, Bush's modest pragmatism seems more welcome than unwavering single-mindedness."[35]

When it came to dealing with the budget deficit for the first time in 1989, however, the depth of the new pragmatic understanding between the president and Congress was never really put to the test. Bush's budget director, Richard Darman, was able to use a combination of unexpectedly high

tax receipts and highly optimistic forecasts about the size of the deficit to produce a deficit-reduction package that avoided triggering the automatic spending cuts of Gramm-Rudman-Hollings. In addition, while avoiding the need
for any new taxes, he was able to provide Democrats with some increased
spending in areas such as education and social programs. Darman negotiated
support for his proposals to avoid spending cuts with a group of senior Democrats, and they in turn pushed the resulting agreement through Congress.
Already, however, some dissent was apparent in both parties at what looked
like a growing tendency of White House officials and congressional leaders to
negotiate package deals in private and then present them to the rest of Congress for approval more or less on a "take it or leave it" basis. Complaints that
the settling of issues by agreement outside the House and Senate chambers
was usurping the ability of the rank and file to legislate mingled with resentment that increased bipartisanship at the top of the party hierarchies was
blurring the fundamental distinctions between what Republicans and Democrats stood for.[36] But the more general reaction was one of satisfaction that
some measure of agreement had at last been reached.

In 1990, as we have seen, the budget negotiations proceeded in a similar
way, and Bush, to his credit, was prepared to take substantial political risks to
secure an agreement. Part way through the year, he outraged many Republicans, and both startled and dismayed many voters, by reneging on the "no
new taxes" pledge that many thought had won him the 1988 election. Then
in September and October, on the eve of the congressional elections, he first
agreed to an unexpectedly tough package of deficit-reducing measures, including increased gasoline and cigarette taxes, and then publicly identified
himself with the package in a series of press statements and in a television address to the nation. Bush was a first-term president who desperately wanted
to be reelected and whose personal popularity ratings at the time were by no
means secure; and he himself disapproved of some of the elements in the
compromise package. Yet, convinced that the deficit crisis had somehow to
be overcome in the national interest, he was more than ready to put his head
above the parapet. He had, in a phrase he was later to use in another context,
"gone that extra mile." It was now up to members of Congress to do their
part.

In fact, of course, they did not do so, and the White House was deeply
disappointed. Bush's investment in the budget package had been great. He
had even made an offer, just before the crucial vote, that would have allowed
congressmen to blame him personally for the financial hardships that would
result from its measures. Richard Darman responded to the original plan's
demise with a barbed reflection: "How is that with 350 unopposed [members
of the House], they have so much trouble looking at the general interest?"[37]

But Darman knew perfectly well that it was precisely a studious ignoring of the general interest over many years in favor of the local interests likely to secure their reelection that had led to, if not 350, then certainly a great many, incumbents being without serious opposition. It was just this fear of the general interest that had led to the unorthodox way in which the package had been put together. As a British journalist based in Washington noted:

> The procedure of drafting through a secret cabal—open disagreements secretly arrived at, you might say—is obviously undesirable, and has been denounced; but it was imposed by the general reluctance of almost any politician . . . to speak words of discomfort in public.[38]

The phrase "reluctance to speak words of discomfort" gets to the heart of the matter, not merely in connection with the budget deficit but in connection with the underclass, drugs, and a variety of other domestic matters. The budget deficit was eventually tackled, but late in the day and in a manner that left all participants dissatisfied. The underclass in the late 1980s and early 1990s remained politically sidelined. The way in which the drug problem was tackled was an almost classic instance of highly exposed politicians claiming to solve a problem that they could not solve—and, moreover, attempting to solve it in a manner calculated to impress the media and the voters, but not anyone who actually knew anything about the subject.

Against that background, Bush's own performance, both before his election and during his first two years in office, was at best creditable and at worst forgivably (or at least understandably) self-interested. On the credit side, he ran considerable risks with his popularity over the budget deficit, and he stood firm against Saddam Hussein over the latter's invasion of Kuwait, even though to begin with it was by no means clear whether either the Congress or the American people would stand behind him. On the debit side were his manipulation of the drug issue, his ignoring of the underclass (though in this case he may genuinely have felt that there was nothing much the federal government could do), and, above all, the original making of his "no new taxes" pledge.

Peggy Noonan has described in *What I Saw at the Revolution* how that pledge came to be made in the form that it was. She was the author of Bush's acceptance speech at the 1988 Republican National Convention, at which the pledge was made. She recalls in her book that she coupled the phrase "Read my lips" with the phrase "No new taxes" because, as she thought at the time, "It's definite. It's not subject to misinterpretation. It means, I mean this."[39] But did he mean it? The uncharitable would say that he was lying, and knew that he was lying: that, fearing that his Democratic opponent, Michael

Dukakis, would beat him in November, he cynically made a pledge that he did not intend to keep or else knew he would be unable to keep. The more charitable would say either that he was being very naive economically or, more plausibly, that, like most politicians since the beginning of time, he simply hoped that something would turn up: that he would never have to go back on his pledge because the budget deficits would, somehow or other, just go away. We incline toward charity, but, whatever the explanation, the episode is a striking illustration of the expedients to which highly exposed politicians can be driven.[40]

The issue of timing in the context of high exposure is, of course, crucial, and it highlights an important difference between the Congress and the presidency. Members of the House of Representatives are the most highly exposed politicians in Washington (and therefore in the world?) by virtue of having to run for reelection every two years. For House members, there is no such thing as a good time for risking unpopularity. Individual members of the Senate are differently placed, having to stand for reelection only every six years; but the Senate as an institution is by no means insulated from the politics of high exposure because at all times fully one-third of its members are up for reelection—and know they are up for reelection—sometime within the next two years.

The president's position is somewhat paradoxical. On the one hand, a first-term president has four years ahead of him at the time of his inauguration; on the other, a second-term president, one who has succeeded in securing reelection, cannot be reelected again and therefore becomes at a stroke the *least* politically exposed senior politician in the American system. In this sense, a first-term president and a second-term president can almost be said to occupy two different offices.

More than a member of the House, although less than an individual senator, a first-time president knows that he has a "window of opportunity," lasting perhaps for two years, during which he can, without imminent fear of not being reelected, seek to bring about major changes of policy and changes in the policy agenda. Ronald Reagan famously took advantage of this window of opportunity in 1981 to cut federal spending and federal taxes by unprecedented, and irreversible, amounts. He took risks, and they paid off. George Bush, by contrast, not being an ideologue and not really having an agenda of his own, was relatively passive during his first two years in office, especially on the domestic front. Despite his earlier rhetoric, he did not in his first year attempt in any serious way to tackle the budget deficit; he tackled it only when he felt forced to do so in his second year. In 1991 and 1992 it seems probable that Bush, with the 1992 presidential election looming ever larger before him, will, if anything, be even more concerned with compromise and consensus building than during his first two years. Increasingly high exposure and his own instincts will point in the same direction.

It will be interesting, however, to see how he behaves if he is reelected. The instincts will remain, but the high exposure will not. Whatever he does, he personally will have nothing to lose, except his reputation in the eyes of history and the American people. So far, there have been only two full second-term presidents during the period since presidents were limited to two terms by the Twenty-Second Amendment. One was Dwight D. Eisenhower (1953–61); the other was Ronald Reagan (1981–89). Neither, as it happens, sought to take advantage of his political invulnerability to educate the American people into new ways of thinking about America or America's place in the world. Eisenhower felt no need to; Reagan probably felt that he already had. Bush seems likely to conform to the same pattern. He is not a man who goes looking for controversy; he shows no signs of wanting to lead the American people in any direction in which they do not already want to go. But any second-term president could—and Bush might—use the opportunity provided by being no longer politically exposed to adopt a more visionary role, to seek to be remembered as someone who had deliberately "gone out ahead."

Conclusions

In the meantime, the conclusions we are driven to are somewhat gloomier than we would like. America in the early years of the Bush administration appears, at least to two Europeans, to be exhibiting a number of "the effects of Bad Government." The consequences of the chronic federal budget deficits are as yet fairly abstract and lie (if they lie anywhere) more in the future than in the present; but the plight of the underclass and the problems associated with illegal drugs are both concrete and immediate. Taken together, they cause large parts of America's big cities (and some American rural areas too) to resemble the poorer countries of the Third World more than they resemble either Western Europe or the more prosperous parts of the United States. The only significant difference between most cities in the Third World and many cities in the United States is that the latter are more dangerous and violent. An Arab recently described New York as "a kind of violent Cairo."

The problem of the federal budget deficits was identified as being a problem long before it was put effectively on the political agenda. When it finally arrived at the top of the agenda in 1990, it was dealt with in a way that few of those who participated in the policy-making process, let alone the majority of the American people, thought was satisfactory. And the deficit problem has by no means been solved; it has merely been rendered temporarily less acute. In the case of the underclass, most politicians and most ordinary citizens have tacitly agreed to pass by on the other side; the underclass has not gotten onto the political agenda and does not look like it will be doing so. In the case of illegal drugs, the problem is on the agenda but is being dealt with in a manner that owes more to Good Politics (and Good Campaigning) than to Good Government. (Often the two are the same, but they are evidently not in this case.)

The problem of the budget deficits, the problem of the underclass, and the problem of illegal drugs differ widely. President Bush and most members of Congress are concerned about deficits and drugs, but not much about the underclass. America's political culture predisposes people in the United States to be concerned about the budget deficits and illegal drugs, but with regard to the underclass it leads at best to a degree of ambivalence, at worst to positive hostility. The intellectual standing of the three issues also differs. Americans believe they know what causes budget deficits and what could be done (in principle at least) to reduce them. They are less confident about both causes and potential cures when they contemplate the underclass. In the case of illegal drugs, they seem determined to act, if only for the sake of action, despite the absence of anything approaching an expert consensus on the genesis and dynamics of the presenting problem.

But we believe that an important factor underlying the way in which government in America has dealt, or not dealt, with all three problems is the phenomenon we have been labeling in this chapter "the politics of high exposure." As we said earlier, American politicians are unique in the democratic world in the extent to which they are exposed to the vicissitudes of electoral politics. They are always running, and usually they are running scared (even if, in the end, the great majority of them—precisely because they have run, and run scared—do succeed in winning reelection). Far more than politicians in other democratic countries, American politicians are forced to concern themselves on a daily, almost hourly, basis with primary elections, general elections, constituency service, fund-raising, local interest groups, national interest groups, and the mass media. The incentive system of American politics rewards attentiveness to the minutiae of state and district concerns, and punishes, or threatens to punish, any degree, however slight, of inattentiveness. The European politician is clad in the armor of party; the American politician goes naked and alone onto the field of battle.

One consequence is that, although America's politicians are personally as honest and courageous as any other country's, they have little alternative but to be politically risk averse. They do what the people (or at least *their* people) want them to do; they do not do what the people (*their* people) do not want them to do; they seek to appear to be acting even when they know or suspect that their action is misdirected; and they are frequently tempted to address themselves to the public's concerns about problems instead of to the problems themselves. The politics of high exposure is conducive to the taking of short-run views rather than long-run views; it is not conducive to the taking of tough decisions, especially decisions that seem likely to impose costs on constituents. The politics of high exposure tends to create a disjunction between the governmentally—and nationally—desirable and the politically feasible. To repeat: American politicians are not more cowardly or craven than their opposite numbers in other countries. Quite possibly they are less so. But the American system, as it now operates, forces them to be attentive to public opinion—or, more precisely, to electorally relevant public opinion—to an extent that is virtually unknown elsewhere.

We believe that we have seen some of the results of high-exposure politics in connection with each of the three problems discussed in this chapter. Decisions on the budget deficit were at first postponed, then fudged, because politicians feared the electoral consequences of increased taxes and reductions in federal spending. The underclass was meanwhile largely ignored because efforts to relieve its plight would cost money and lose more votes than they won. The drug problem, in contrast, was tackled by the president and Congress, but in a way that clearly owed more to the desire to impress the voters than the desire to reduce drug usage and addiction. Perhaps drug use and addiction cannot be substantially reduced by actions of the federal government. In that event, a great deal of money was wasted at a time of alleged budget stringency.

In short, we believe that some of "the effects of Bad Government" that are apparent in the United States in the 1990s are traceable in part to a defect in the American political system as it now operates—in other words are traceable to "Bad Government" itself, or at least to an element of Bad Government. Concerned American citizens, if they think we are right, might like to give some thought in the coming years as to how the politics of high exposure might be reduced. It will not be easy, given the U.S. Constitution and the unique emphasis that Americans place on democracy at the expense of other political values; but an attempt to give America's political leaders somewhat greater room for policy maneuver, to enable them to tackle, effectively, some of the nation's most serious problems, would appear nevertheless to be worth making. Too much of what can be seen in America today—poverty, violence, despair—is much too close for comfort to what Lorenzetti painted on the walls of the Sala della Pace six hundred years ago.

Notes

1. David Rapp, "Is Anyone Really Trying to Balance the Budget?" *Congressional Quarterly Weekly Report*, 26 November 1988, 3379–87.

2. On the balanced budget as a kind of American icon, see James D. Savage, *Balanced Budgets and American Politics* (Ithaca, N.Y.: Cornell University Press, 1988).

3. On the concept of the career politician, see Anthony King, "The Rise of the Career Politician in Britain—and Its Consequences," *British Journal of Political Science* 11 (July 1981): 249–85.

4. This is not to suggest that the British economy was better managed during this period than the American. A case could be made that neither was very well managed. The point being made is simply that the British political system (combined in the 1980s with the personality of Margaret Thatcher) made it possible for the incumbent government to pursue a particular line of policy, even though the line of policy was unpopular (and its economic consequences even more so).

5. The headline was used on the main editorial in *The Times* (London), 8 October 1990. Many American writers also referred to senators' and congressmen's cowardice and urged them to be more "courageous." Perhaps some members of Congress did lack courage, but to ask a member of Congress to vote for a measure that will almost certainly lead to his defeat in a forthcoming election is rather like asking an air force pilot to lead a *kamikaze* attack. The pilot can undoubtedly be accused of lack of courage for refusing the request, but most observers would think it was the request that was unreasonable, not the refusal.

6. They could all be punished by the voters, of course, but the idea is that if the majority for the proposed solution is overwhelming the voters will be more likely to accept the solution as a national necessity than they would be if the politicians were divided among themselves. Agreement between the parties is obviously especially important. If the parties are agreed, controversy over the solution cannot take the familiar form of party vs. party but would have to take the unfamiliar (and bizarre) form of incumbents of all parties vs. nonincumbents of all parties. However unpopular the solution, it seems unlikely that voters under these circumstances would be ready both to ignore all the familiar partisan cues and to ignore all incumbents' past services and stands on other issues.

7. See the discussion in Anthony King, "The American Polity in the 1990s," in *The New American Political System*, rev. ed., ed. Anthony King (Washington, D.C.: AEI Press, 1990), 301–3.

8. Paul Light, *Artful Work: The Politics of Social Security Reform* (New York: Random House, 1985), 232.

9. The case for action was set out in detail in "Let the Dealing Begin" in *The Economist* (London), 12 May 1990, 41–42.

10. *Time*, 9 July 1990, 26.

11. There were numerous complaints during the summer and fall of 1990 from the "excluded." A Republican not involved in the negotiations asked his colleagues: "Are we in charge as we were sent here to be, or have we become a house of political eunuchs?" A Democrat said: "Even if we weren't happy with what was going on,

we'd be a lot more comfortable if we knew what was going on." Both are quoted in *Congressional Quarterly Weekly Report,* 29 September 1990, 3094.

12. At the end of one week, when the Republican leaders in both the House and the Senate had backed away from President Bush's insistence that the budget package contain cuts in the capital gains tax, Gingrich declared: "There are going to be days [when] we're not singing off the same sheet of music." Ibid., 3096.

13. Quoted in *International Herald Tribune,* 1 October 1990.

14. Quoted in *The Independent* (London), 17 October 1990.

15. See Nelson W. Polsby, *Political Innovation in America: The Politics of Policy Initiation* (New Haven: Yale University Press, 1984); and John W. Kingdon, *Agendas, Alternatives and Public Policies* (Boston: Little, Brown, 1984).

16. Barbara Kellerman, *The Political Presidency: The Practice of Leadership* (New York: Oxford University Press, 1984), 89–124, 221–53. See also Charles O. Jones, "Ronald Reagan and the U.S. Congress: Visible-Hand Politics," in *The Reagan Legacy: Promise and Performance,* ed. Charles O. Jones (Chatham, N.J.: Chatham House, 1988).

17. Widespread use and awareness of the term in the 1980s is often linked to Ken Auletta's *The Underclass* (New York: Random House, 1982), which sought to portray the human aspects of the problem.

18. Theodore J. Marmor, Jerry L. Mashaw, and Philip L. Harvey, *America's Misunderstood Welfare State: Persistent Myths, Enduring Realities* (New York: Basic Books, 1990), 114–16.

19. For an overview of current thinking, see William Julius Wilson, "The Underclass: Issues, Perspectives, and Public Policy," *Annals of the American Academy of Political and Social Science* 501 (January 1989): 182–92. (This issue of the *Annals* is devoted to "The Ghetto Underclass.") For Wilson's own ideas, see his *The Truly Disadvantaged: The Inner City, the Underclass, and Public Policy* (Chicago: University of Chicago Press, 1987). Another useful example of recent work in this area is *The Urban Underclass,* ed. Christopher Jencks and Paul Peterson (Washington, D.C.: Brookings Institution, 1991).

20. For this view, see Charles Murray, *Losing Ground: American Social Policy, 1950–1980* (New York: Basic Books, 1984).

21. Samuel P. Huntington, *American Politics: The Promise of Disharmony* (Cambridge: Harvard University Press, 1981), 1–60.

22. For a helpful discussion of this point, see Hugh Heclo, "The Political Foundations of Antipoverty Policy," in *Fighting Poverty: What Works and What Doesn't,* ed. Sheldon H. Danziger and Daniel H. Weinberg (Cambridge: Harvard University Press, 1986), 312–40.

23. Michael B. Katz, *The Undeserving Poor: From the War on Poverty to the War on Welfare* (New York: Pantheon, 1989): 1–35.

24. Wilson, "The Underclass," 183.

25. Heclo, "Political Foundations of Antipoverty Policy," 326–32.

26. See "Experts Skeptical of Congress' Anti-Drug Effort," *Congressional Quarterly Weekly Report,* 25 June 1988, 1711–14.

27. For a recent discussion of the relative effectiveness of these options, see Michael Tonry and James Q. Wilson, eds., *Drugs and Crime,* vol. 13, *Crime and Justice: A Review of Research* (Chicago: University of Chicago Press, 1990).

28. A *Wall Street Journal*/NBC News poll taken in March 1989 found 94 percent agreeing with the view that the nation's crime rate had risen because of illegal drug use.

29. Michael Oreskes, "Drug War Underlines Fickleness of Public," *New York Times,* 6 September 1990, A22.

30. A fortnight later, that figure had fallen to 54 percent, but drugs still remained far ahead of the second-ranked problem, which was the economy. "The Public's Shifting Priorities," *New York Times,* 6 September 1990, A22.

31. Oreskes, "Drug War Underlines Fickleness of Public."

32. James Q. Wilson, "Drugs and Crime," in Tonry and Wilson, *Drugs and Crime,* 543.

33. Reagan's tone on such occasions is well caught by a line in his television address of March 1983, soliciting support for increased defense spending: "The choice is up to the men and women you have elected to the Congress and that means the choice is up to you." *Congressional Quarterly Weekly Report,* 6 March 1983, 629.

34. *New York Times,* 21 January 1989, 10.

35. Michael Duffy, "Mr. Consensus," *Time,* 21 August 1989, 16–22.

36. Chuck Alston, "Rules of Political Navigation Altered by Bush Centrism," *Congressional Quarterly Weekly Report,* 6 May 1989, 1017–19.

37. Michael Duffy, "Man in the Muddle," *Time,* 15 October 1990, 29.

38. Anthony Harris, "Ironic Triumph of the U.S. Constitution," *Financial Times,* 8 October 1990.

39. Peggy Noonan, *What I Saw at the Revolution* (New York: Random House, 1990), 307.

40. Chancellor Kohl's highly optimistic forecast of the low economic costs of reunification made just before the first all-German elections in 1990 is a European example of the same phenomenon. Kohl, like Bush, promised not to raise taxes and subsequently did raise them. Kohl paid a heavy political price.

10

Conclusion

Colin Campbell, s.j.
and
Bert A. Rockman

Nearly thirty years ago, James MacGregor Burns offered a blunt diagnosis of what ailed political leadership in the United States.[1] In *The Deadlock of Democracy*, he argued that the incapacity of the federal government resulted from the separation of powers. This had created four national parties: presidential and congressional, Democrat and Republican. We should keep in mind that Burns was writing in the midst of an eight-year period of "united government" from 1961 to 1969 during which Democrats held both the presidency and the majorities in the House of Representatives and the Senate.

Burns's analysis resonated with an earlier critique of leadership in the federal government. In a 1950 statement, the Committee on Political Parties of the American Political Science Association presented a manifesto calling for a more responsible two-party system.[2] Such a system would require the parties to set out programmatic goals with greater clarity and maintain sufficient cohesion to deliver on these commitments. The effect would be to increase the accountability of the political leadership.

The British parliamentary system operated as the model for the APSA committee's assessment. Since the Great Depression, a significant school of liberal American political scientists has believed the United States responded too ponderously in setting up the welfare state. The great strides taken by Britain immediately after the war in installing social programs made the U.K. system appear to be exceptionally responsive to the requirements of modern governance. Many also believed that Britain conducted its war effort more effectively than did the United States.[3]

We should not imply that political science reached an unshakable consensus on the desirability of responsible party government. Indeed, dissenting voices abounded. Robert Dahl, arguably the dominant figure in political science through the 1960s, wrote several important works designed to remind Americans of the "pluralistic" nature of their brand of democracy.[4] This pluralism facilitated the checks and balances that derive from the separation of powers. Charles Lindblom, in addition, registered doubts that elected politicians in a pluralistic democracy could achieve more than incremental decisions.[5] That is, comprehensive rationality would exceed the capacity of leaders within such a system to agree about their central ends.

There emerged as well in this period a public-choice tradition. Such theorists as James Buchanan, Gordon Tullock, and William Niskanen argued that the United States should have less government, not more.[6] Public choice considered both the responsible two-party and the incrementalist models as missing the point. Given greater knowledge about their options, voters and their representatives will make only those choices that correspond to the highest-ranked selections on their preference schedules. They emphasized the notion of accountability in the form of a principal (the citizen) and an agent (the elected representative). Because party organizational control would distort rather than enhance that relationship, they believed that this might violate the tenets of democratic accountability by short-circuiting the direct responsibility of individual incumbents to their electors. In any event, the public-choice consensus is that given the incentives operating on politicians, they would have little to gain and much to lose by tying their electoral fates exclusively to their party.

The diversity of views existing in the 1950s, 1960s, and 1970s on the appropriateness of responsible two-party government in the United States links directly to a central theme that has run through the present volume. Several authors—most notably Bert A. Rockman, Charles O. Jones, Paul Quirk, and Anthony King and Giles Alston—dwell on the fact that the United States has undergone a prolonged period of divided government in which one party has not controlled the presidency and *both* houses of Congress since the end of the Carter administration in 1981. And that interval saw divisions between Carter and Congress reach the point where even Burns's four-party thesis could not capture the degree of fragmentation prevailing in Washington. Thus, none of our contributors have taken as their model responsible two-party leadership. Automatically, this lowers the bar. None of us expects from Bush the high-jump performance of a Roosevelt or a Johnson—much less a Churchill or an Attlee.

In view of the prospect of yet more divided government, many authors in this volume report a good fit between George Bush's style and the art of the possible under such circumstances. Rockman notes that the times call for "syndicating responsibility"; Jones observes that we can understand Bush's continued support only if we recognize that "diffused responsibility" has supplanted party responsibility as the order of the day; Quirk draws on his own theory of cooperative resolution of policy conflicts to assert that Bush must employ "flexible rigidity."[7] And in this environment, Aberbach contrasts Bush's respect for a browbeaten Washington executive establishment, particularly the senior civil service, with the Bush administration's more ideologically inspired and less respectful predecessor.

Larry Berman and Bruce W. Jentleson found two sides to Bush: the "politician" and the "presidentialist." When operative, the former "nonconfrontational, nonideological, pragmatic" Bush works effectively within the context of divided government. The other Bush—as shown by his handling of China after Tiananmen Square, the FS-X deal with Japan, or controlling the spread of chemical weapons—has seemed to pursue the guardianship of executive prerogatives at the expense of consistent policy principles. Barbara Sinclair pointed out that both Bush's and Congress's paucity of political resources at the outset of the administration forced each to work cooperatively, and King and Alston argued that the "collusion of elites" constitutes the best way around divided government.

Jones weaves together observers' caveats against misunderstanding Bush's low-key style, and, in doing so, includes an observation made by an astute student of presidential transitions, James P. Pfiffner,[8] that George Bush, unlike his predecessor, started off seeking to consolidate rather than push for radical change and tried to find a harmonious new balance rather than confrontation between the president and Congress. In their own ways, other contributors to this volume view the times as calling for cooperative leadership. Most authors see a strong correspondence between Bush's style and the requirements of cooperative leadership. A smaller group, including Colin Campbell, finds Bush's style not especially suited for cooperative leadership or, as Berman and Jentleson suggest, is less convinced that Bush's muted leadership style is appropriate to grappling with the underlying problems affecting America's capacity to play an effective international role or to deal successfully with major social problems (see King and Alston; Aberbach).

The weakness of Bush's mandate proves worrisome throughout this volume. Quirk alerts us to potential difficulty when he dwells on the need for presidents to maintain flexibility about means and rigidity about ends. Presumably, presidents can cling more ferociously to the latter because they have effectively enshrined them in the election. Thus, Ronald Reagan pressed his triad of core commitments—reduce taxes, cut domestic spending, and increase defense expenditures—with the early support of a sufficient minority of Democrats. Congress can move toward cooperative behavior when a presidential election seems to have registered a dramatic shift in public opinion—when, in other words, there seems to have been the proverbial "mandate."

The mandate is not merely a matter of size. It is a matter, especially, of clarity of goals. Just how weak, then, was Bush's mandate? And what effect has this had on his performance?

Rockman, Jones, George C. Edwards III, and Sinclair all dwelt at length on the implications of Bush's mandate for his performance. Rockman styles the mandate as consisting of a permit from the electorate to continue Ronald Reagan's policies, but in a more tempered way. In discussing Bush's problems with the 1990 round of budget negotiations, Rockman likens Bush to Jimmy Carter. He argues that lack of a core constituency makes leadership difficult when times get tough. Jones asserts that the election results told us more about what people did not want than what they did want. They sought neither a liberal nor someone who would expand government. This, Jones adds, made the broadening of its public approval a vital task for the administration, especially if Congress was to consider Bush "worthy" of cooperative leadership.

Sinclair adds to these assessments a word of caution about Congress. Because Democrats feel the need to rehabilitate their image for effective governance, they also have allowed their leadership to take greater initiative in exerting legislative authority. Edwards grants Bush's mandate faint praise, allowing that voters' support of Bush failed to leave the impression, especially with Congress, that the 1988 election had proven a point. Yet, this has not hobbled Bush for three reasons. First, people like and trust him. Second, especially during his first year, no burning problems emerged whose salience focused people's attention on Bush's performance. Third, even if some problems had achieved salience, the public and the press might have chalked these up as holdovers from the Reagan years.

As we move to a consideration of Bush's performance, we begin to see ways in which our authors have adapted some more clearly divergent views. A great deal of the discussion centers on whether and how personality and style relate to actual performance. Here Rockman presents a fairly agnostic view. He notes that good leadership is often in the eye of the beholder. For instance, two prominent presidency scholars, Richard Neustadt and Fred Greenstein, employ dramatically different criteria for presidential leadership. Neustadt focuses on the incumbent's success at "goal maximization" and holds up Franklin D. Roosevelt and John F. Kennedy as paragons. Greenstein stresses instead a president's ability to promote "public harmony and government legitimacy" and views Dwight D. Eisenhower as an exemplar of this form of leadership.

In this regard, Berman and Jentleson express concern that Bush might have excessively narrowed the circle of aides within the foreign policy field, making the appearance of administration harmony in foreign policy illusory. That is, Berman and Jentleson register concern that a small inner circle runs the risk of shutting "expertise and information out of the decision-making process."

Edwards reminds us that voters, not analysts, make the ultimate decisions about presidential performance. They do not always make the connection between neglected or mismanaged issues and the president's personality and style. Sinclair offers the most emphatic caveat against judgments about a president's personal performance, arguing that commentaries dwelling on alleged personality flaws (such as "playing politics" or "lack of backbone") are themselves flawed. They ignore the role of circumstances in sharply constraining the art of the possible for a president. A president's retreat to apparently opportunistic or pragmatic politics can be an optimal strategy under certain circumstances. Echoing Edwards, she asserts that electoral success serves as a valid test of leadership performance in a democratic society.

Although Sinclair observes that Bush made strategic mistakes during the 1990 budget negotiations, and faults both Richard Darman and John Sununu for bargaining styles that helped undermine congressional trust of the president's intentions in resolving the deficit problem, she emphasizes as crucial the bargaining context of Bush in relation to Congress. Thus it seems fair to say that the modal chapter in this volume focuses chiefly on the task of understanding the Bush administration in a wider context than merely judging the president's personal performance in accordance with Neustadtian (or other nonsituationally driven) tenets of presidential performance.

Rockman characterizes Bush as a president for good times. Along with Aberbach, Rockman believes that circumstances calling for little presidential intervention are those that suit Bush well. The 1990 budget crisis and the situation in the Persian Gulf, Rockman notes, presented situations in which doing "nothing well would not suffice"—the implication being that the summer of 1990 might serve as a watershed in the Bush presidency. Aberbach also sees potential problems looming ahead for Bush if the present set of lowered policy expectations should fade. What would happen, Aberbach wonders, "if government programs to deal with growing domestic problems are seen as woefully underfunded by an administration that lacks an agenda beyond doing one's best with what is available."

Rockman views Bush as a consummate insider who has proven much more adept at cutting deals with other leaders than at sensing the wider implications of his policies. Similarly, Jones identifies Bush's style as a restrained, "be prepared" approach to leadership whereby he "awaits events and then acts to resolve a sure thing." Jones acknowledges that while Bush might have slipped up in not responding adequately to Iraq's designs on Kuwait, the president's swift response to the invasion illustrates well the effectiveness of his "actively reactive strategy."

Although several chapters offer criticism of Bush's personal performance (see especially Quirk, Berman and Jentleson, Campbell, and King and Alston), all see his administration operating in a context of severe constraint. Quirk diagnoses Bush's situation as requiring cooperative leadership; Berman and Jentleson underscore the benefits of Bush's usual knack for crisis management and diplomacy; Campbell accepts that the times appear to call for "broker politics" and that Bush's "let's deal" approach might be appropriate in these conditions; King and Alston, similarly, acknowledge placing a premium on the "collusion of elites" under the dual burden of divided government *and* "the politics of high exposure." These chapters, nonetheless, cite Bush for failures in executing his chosen leadership style.

Quirk attributes to Bush a high aptitude for cooperative leadership. But he views him as failing to narrow his legislative agenda to a manageable and understandable set of goals, for too often settling on the lowest common denominator when trying to achieve a deal, and for too frequently reversing the requirements of flexible rigidity by becoming rigid about means and flexible about goals.

Berman and Jentleson present a mixed picture of Bush's leadership. But this picture contains some telling criticisms, including a concern that Bush has failed to pay sufficient attention to the U.S. "domestic core," which, Berman and Jentleson argue, has become the sine qua non of continued power in a period of rapid global transition. Thus, in assessing Bush's performance in a number of foreign policy cases, Berman and Jentleson convey a portrait of a president who excels in the resolution of crises, but who can be inattentive to the long-term consequences of some of his deals, a leader who is maladroit at adaptation and innovation, and one who (as they maintain was true with the Iraqi invasion of Kuwait) fails to concentrate as much on averting crises as on solving them.

Campbell's chapter expresses concerns about Bush's aptitude for cooperative leadership, citing the tone of his 1988 election campaign, his reluctance to abandon the Tower nomination, and his vindictive pursuit of Noriega in the wake of the failed coup attempt. These incidents suggest that the president's behavior sometimes reflects a counterproductive personalization of domestic and international political struggles. Campbell argues further that Bush's choice of John Sununu as chief of staff and a consequent neglect of the details of White House and cabinet organization exacerbate the difficulty of achieving cooperative leadership.

King and Alston caution that procedure and the quality of government are not unrelated. The problems they cite are regarded as endemic to the United States and are likely to affect American political leadership generically. High-exposure politics leads to risk aversion. Risk aversion, in turn, leads to an inability to deal with serious problems that extract political costs. Collusion of elites might help. But in their view, Bush's tendency for risk aversion has overtaken his propensity for collusion in tackling hard problems of government. They wonder whether a less exposed second term might lead Bush to exploit opportunities for risk-taking, but their skepticism that he will do so is strong.

In the end, leadership is defined in terms of the confluence of systems, situations, and personal style.[9] There is little doubt that the American system makes the task of leadership complicated, especially if it is to flow more or less strictly from the presidency. Given the complexities of the American political system, the task of presidential leadership can be made more or less complicated by the political situation the president faces. A president with maximum objectives in Bush's political situation likely would find himself in great difficulty. So, from the standpoint of what seems to be politically commodious, Bush's style of leadership, the situation in which he is operating, and, of course, the omnipresent system all seem to be largely consistent with one another.

As we have tried to point out, such consistency is neither inherently good or bad. Between the editors, Rockman believes that Bush is engaging merely in the art of the possible, whereas Campbell is convinced that Bush's approach is impossibly unartful. No doubt analysts of the presidency and this president will quarrel about other matters as well. Some would say that Bush's minimalist designs simply avoid the need to provide leadership. In one view, for example, he has missed the opportunity to strengthen his party's commitment to principles and bolster its identity. From another standpoint, he may have missed opportunities to be a trustee for the nation, guiding it toward meeting long-term needs at the cost of short-run popularity. Yet the image of Jimmy Carter, leaving the field of political battle on his shield, has a sobering effect on would-be trustees convinced of the righteousness of their ways and the small-mindedness of others with whom the system demands they deal. In the end, of course, we tend to evaluate presidents by our goals, rather than theirs.

The "reactive-active" style of George Bush makes him a moving target. We all knew what Ronald Reagan wanted: less, except for the military. But we do not fully know what George Bush wants. The answer, aside from re-election, may be to manage what comes before him. We differ in our views as to how well he has done this, and we may differ in our views as to whether or not this style of leadership is in the public interest. We do know that, by luck or design, Bush's minimalism coincides with a high degree of presidential approval, but is not clear whether that approval is fungible currency because it is not clear that Bush has any purposes on which he wants to spend it. Perhaps, years from now, we will see a "hidden hand" interpretation of Bush's presidency. But, equally well, we may simply see amiable aimlessness. We do know that Bush's style is to deal with what is before him, not what lies ahead of him. How comfortable we are with that may rest on how confident each of us in turn feels about what is likely to lie ahead. For the first time since Eisenhower, and perhaps the brief interregnum under Ford, we are getting to see a truly conservative presidency—one with limited ambitions and an agenda to match.

The editors of this volume agree about much of what they see and disagree about both its relative importance and its consequences. This may say as much about our own conceptions of leadership and of what it is possible to do in the American system as it does of Bush. It also may reveal differences in our views as to what each of us thinks Bush has and has not achieved, and what the system and Bush's political situation allow him to achieve. In foreign policy, Desert Storm has been a major achievement for Bush; its aftermath more ambiguous. Arguably, there have been other achievements. In domestic policy, it is clear that Bush has not yet left bold footprints. Possibly he never will. Would that mean he is deficient in his leadership or successful? Bush-watching, we can be sure, promises to evoke strong opinions about a man who seems to have few of his own.

Notes

1. James MacGregor Burns, *The Deadlock of Democracy: Four-Party Politics in America* (Englewood Cliffs, N.J.: Prentice-Hall, 1963).

2. American Political Science Association, Committee on Political Parties, *Toward a More Responsible Two-Party System* (New York: Rinehart, 1950).

3. Anna Kasten Nelson, "National Security I: Inventing a Process (1945–1960)," *The Illusion of Presidential Government*, ed. Hugh Heclo and Lester M. Salamon (Boulder, Colo.: Westview, 1981), 231.

4. See, for instance, Robert A. Dahl, *A Preface to Democratic Theory* (Chicago: University of Chicago Press, 1966); and Robert A. Dahl, *Polyarchy: Participation and Opposition* (New Haven: Yale University Press, 1971).

5. Charles E. Lindblom, *The Intelligence of Democracy: Decision-Making through Mutual Adjustment* (New York: Free Press, 1965).

6. James M. Buchanan and Gordon Tullock, *The Calculus of Consent: Logical Foundations of Constitutional Democracy* (Ann Arbor: University of Michigan Press, 1962); and William A. Niskanen, *Bureaucracy and Representative Government* (New York: Aldine Atherton, 1971).

7. Quirk derives this term from Dean Pruitt, *Negotiation Behavior* (New York: Academic Press, 1982).

8. James P. Pfiffner, "Establishing the Bush Presidency," *Public Administration Review*, January/February 1990, 70, as cited by Charles O. Jones.

9. This formulation derives from Bert A. Rockman, "The American Presidency in Comparative Perspective: Systems, Situations, and Leaders," in *The Presidency and the Political System*, 3rd ed., ed. Michael Nelson (Washington, D.C.: CQ Press, 1990), 57–82.

Index

297

ABOUT THE AUTHORS

JOEL D. ABERBACH is professor of political science and director of the Center for American Politics and Public Policy at the University of California, Los Angeles. His most recent publication is *Keeping a Watchful Eye: The Politics of Congressional Oversight.*

GILES ALSTON is a lecturer in the Department of Government at the University of Essex. He recently received his doctorate from Oxford University, where he specialized in American space policy.

LARRY BERMAN is professor of political science at the University of California, Davis. He is the editor of *Looking Back on the Reagan Presidency.*

COLIN CAMPBELL, S.J., is University Professor in the Martin Chair at Georgetown University, where he heads the Graduate Public Policy Program. His books include *Governments under Stress* and *Managing the Presidency,* which won the American Political Science Association's Neustadt Prize for the best book on the presidency.

GEORGE C. EDWARDS III is Distinguished Professor of Political Science and the director of the Center for Presidential Studies at Texas A&M University. He is the author of *Presidential Approval.*

BRUCE W. JENTLESON is director of the Washington Center for the University of California, Davis, and associate professor of political science. He is co-editor, with Larry Berman, of *Foreign Military Intervention: The Dynamics of Protracted Conflict.*

CHARLES O. JONES is the Hawkins Professor of Political Science at the University of Wisconsin-Madison. His is the author of *The Trusteeship Presidency: Jimmy Carter and the U.S. Congress* and the editor of *The Reagan Legacy.*

ANTHONY KING is a professor of government at the University of Essex. He is the editor of *The American Political System.*

PAUL J. QUIRK is associate professor in the Department of Political Science and the Institute of Government and Public Affairs at the University of Illinois at Urbana-Champaign. He is the co-author of *The Politics of Deregulation,* with Martha Derthick.

BERT A. ROCKMAN is a senior fellow in the Governmental Studies Program at the Brookings Institution and professor of political science and research professor, University Center for International Studies at the University of Pittsburgh.

BARBARA SINCLAIR is professor of political science at the University of California, Riverside. She is the author of *The Transformation of the U.S. Senate,* which won the American Political Science Association's Fenno Prize in 1990.